De Stijl:

The Formative Years

The MIT Press
Cambridge, Massachusetts
London, England

De Stijl: The Formative Years

1917–1922

translated by Charlotte I. Loeb and Arthur L. Loeb

Carel Blotkamp

Hans Esser

Sjarel Ex

Nicolette Gast

Cees Hilhorst

Els Hoek

Marijke Küper

Eveline Vermeulen

Second Printing, 1990

This translation of *De Beginjaren van De Stijl 1917–1922* is published by arrangement with Uitgeverij Reflex, Utrecht, The Netherlands, and was made possible by a grant from the Nederlandse Organisatie voor Zuiver-Wetenschappelijk Onderzoek.

Major funding for the original publication was provided by the Netherlands Ministry of Culture, Recreation, and Social Work, the Prince Bernhard Fund, and F. van Lanschot, Bankiers n.v.

This book was set in Gill Sans by Achorn Graphic Services, Inc., and printed and bound by Halliday Lithograph in the United States of America.

Library of Congress Cataloging-in-Publication Data

De Beginjaren van De Stijl, 1917–1922. English.
De Stijl, the formative years.

Translation of: De Beginjaren van De Stijl, 1917–1922.
Includes bibliographies and index.
1. Stijl. 2. Art, Modern—20th century—Netherlands. 2. Art, Modern—20th century—Netherlands. 3. Artists—Netherlands—Biography. I. Blotkamp, Carel. II. Title. III. Title: De Stijl.
N6948.5.S8B4413 1986 709'.2'2 [B] 86-7279
ISBN 0-262-02247-8 (hardcover)
0-262-52149-0 (paperback)

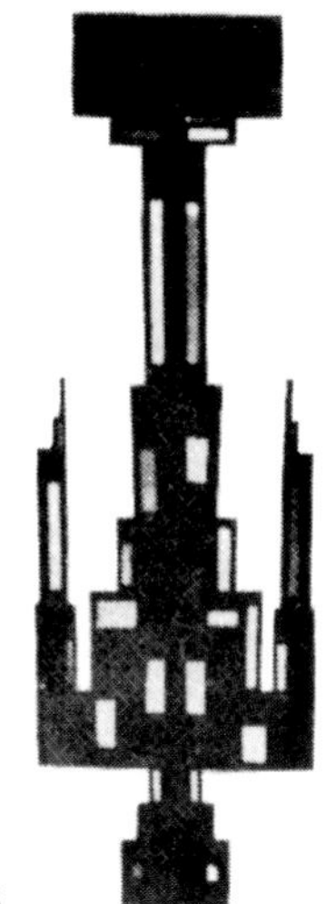

Contents

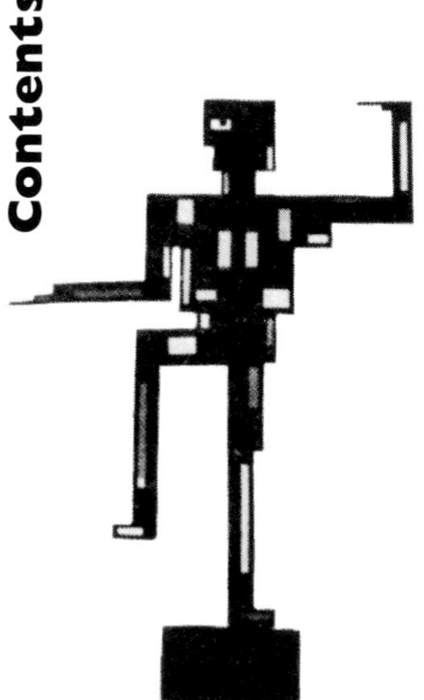

Acknowledgments

This book is the work of a group of graduate students in art history at the Rijksuniversiteit in Utrecht. The historical research into the origin of De Stijl and the first five years of its existence was started in January 1980 and concluded in the spring of 1982.

During the preparation of this book we received assistance from a large number of persons and institutions. We would like to mention first the Rijksdienst Beeldende Kunst in The Hague, in which Theo van Doesburg's extensive estate was deposited in 1981. Van Doesburg's correspondence with the various contributors to the periodical *De stijl* was the most important source for our research. In addition, the estate contains a wealth of visual material. We were able to study letters, photographs, and drawings at other places as well: the Nederlands Documentatiecentrum voor de Bouwkunst in Amsterdam, which houses the archives of van 't Hoff, Oud, Wils, and Rietveld (in part); the collection of the Fondation Custodia in Paris, which includes letters written by van Doesburg, Mondrian, and Oud; and the Rijksbureau voor Kunsthistorische Documentatie in the Hague. The libraries and photographic archives of the Stedelijk Museum in Amsterdam, the Van Abbemuseum in Eindhoven, the Gemeentemuseum in The Hague, the Museum Kröller-Müller in Otterlo, the Kunsthistorisch Instituut in Utrecht, the Rijksdienst voor de Monumentenzorg in Zeist, and the municipal archives, registers of inhabitants, and municipal building and housing authorities of The Hague, Katwijk, Rotterdam, Utrecht, Voorburg, and Zeist gave us their fullest cooperation. We extend our special thanks to the following persons at these institutions: A. van den Berk, P. Couvée, G. Imanse, M. Kentie, A. van der Jagt, E. van Straaten, K. ter Wal, T. Wiersma, W. de Wit, and D. van Woerkom. Very special thanks go to J. M. Joosten of the Stedelijk Museum in Amsterdam for his generosity in making his time and his great knowledge of De Stijl available to us again and again.

In addition, countless private persons have been helpful to us, among them several relatives, friends, and acquaintances of the artists who were involved with De Stijl during its early years. Of those who gave us information, showed us work in their possession, and furnished us with visual material, we mention G. Baines, S. A. C. Begeer, W. L. Berssenbrugge, F. Bless, J. Boyens, K. Broos, F. van Burkom, B. Colenbrander, M. H. Cornips, L. Couwenbergh, P. ten Doesschate-Chu, E. Eskes-Rietveld, W. de Graaf, G. van de Groenekan, P. van de Ham, M. van der Heijden, C. J. Hoogenboom, B. Huszár, J. Huszár, J. C. Huszár-van der Steen, H. K. Jap A Joe, G. Jonker, H. H. Kamerlingh Onnes, J. A. Klaarhamer, E. van Leckwijk, J. Leering, K. S. Levisson, H. de Lorm, O. Mácel, T. Mercuur, A. Moes, B. Mulder, A. van Niekerk, G. J. Numan, B. H. Nijland, G. Oorthuys, F. F. Oostingh, J. M. A. Oud-Dinaux, G. Persoons, I. van Peski, H. Salomonson, P. Sanders, N. Schonk-van der Leck, T. Schröder-Schräder, M. Seuphor, P. de Smalen, P. Smeets, A. and J. P. Smid, P. Smit, L. Tas, N. Tummers, F. Vanhemelrijck, H. Verburg, B. de Vries, G. Wils-van der Veen, N. Zwart-Cleyndert, and some who wish to remain anonymous.

Editor's note

In this edition, titles of works, books, and periodicals are set in italic type and without the traditional capitalization. Thus, the title of the periodical is always given as *De stijl.* De Stijl (in Roman type, and with capitalization) signifies the group of artists connected with the periodical.

In some places, the Dutch word *beeldende*—literally, *visual*—has been translated as *plastic* because *Nieuwe Beelding* is conventionally translated as *Neo-Plasticism.*

The term De Stijl is usually associated with paintings showing only horizontal and vertical lines and planes of red, yellow, and blue, with buildings resembling colored blocks, and with artists so puritanical and dogmatic that they considered a diagonal line a mortal sin. This stereotyped image came into being mainly because of Piet Mondrian's work and personality. However, it does not hold even for Mondrian, let alone for the other artists who were involved with De Stijl.

In general reviews of twentieth-century art, and also in the literature pertaining to De Stijl, it is almost invariably remarked that De Stijl was the name of a periodical, not of a group. Nevertheless, the regular contributors are often pictured as a cohesive body. That too is a cliché. De Stijl was not such an artists' collective; at least, it was not like the other avant-garde movements of the first half of this century. The painters of Die Brücke in Dresden often worked together in one studio, or outdoors in summertime, and the dadaists in Zurich and Berlin and the surrealists in Paris had their cabarets and literary cafés where they met daily and planned new campaigns against the bourgeoisie; however, such strong personal ties were not present within De Stijl.

During the years when *De stijl* was published, there was not one single exhibition in which all the collaborators participated. As far as is known, there was never a meeting where more than three or four of the men involved were present simultaneously—not even in the beginning, when there was sufficient reason to discuss their collaboration and the principles they would manifest collectively. By Dutch standards the artists lived rather far apart. At the time of the founding of De Stijl, Mondrian and Bart van der Leck worked in Laren, Theo van Doesburg and J. J. P. Oud in Leiden, Antony Kok in Tilburg, Vilmos Huszár and Jan Wils in Voorburg, and Robert van 't Hoff in Huis ter Heide; Georges Vantongerloo and Gerrit Rietveld, who joined in 1918 and 1919, worked in The Hague and Utrecht, respectively. They kept in touch mainly by mail, and mainly through van Doesburg, who, as the sole editor, bore the responsibility for the journal. Often it took years for contributors to meet in person, and in some cases no personal encounter ever occurred. They knew of one another's work and ideas mainly from *De stijl.* Perhaps that was a good thing; there is reason to assume that the differences among them would have come to light much earlier and more sharply had they been in closer contact, and that this could have resulted in the premature demise of the journal.

Thus, the existing image of De Stijl as a collective, with a clear-cut artistic program stricter than that of any other avant-garde movement in the twentieth century, needs some correction. This book aims to provide that correction. We pay attention to each artist separately more than is usually done in the literature about De Stijl. We examine their backgrounds and their early works, compare the characters of their outputs and their ideas, and consider their individual motives for disengaging themselves from De Stijl. Yet we do not mean to represent De Stijl as a mere association of convenience, a private undertaking of Theo van Doesburg, who chanced to involve a number of important artists for shorter or longer periods with his venture. Undoubtedly there existed a common ground; otherwise the journal would never have come into being. Apparently van Doesburg's initiative was a response to the need of a number of artists, working in different fields, to manifest themselves outside the existing journals and associations.

Within the context of artistic life in the Netherlands during the First World War, the founding of De Stijl is of particular importance. On the one hand, unlike other groups that resigned themselves to isolation, the artists of De Stijl tried to break through their isolation and to seek international contacts such as had existed during the years 1910–1914, when there had been a lively exchange between the Netherlands and the centers of the French, the German, and the Italian avant-garde. The announcement of the forthcoming periodical *De stijl,* in the summer of 1917, listed a number of impressive contributors, including Picasso and Archipenko. Their contributions did not amount to much, but the intention to make this an international publication was there right from the beginning. On the other hand, it can never be emphasized enough that De Stijl was deeply rooted in the cultural and social traditions of the Netherlands. The artists involved in the group shared the ideal of a spiritualized, world-changing abstract art with many other Dutch artists, although they differed in their opinions of how this ideal should be expressed. The theories unfolded in *De stijl* contain many elements that can be understood only in relation to the ideas that were current in certain artistic circles in the Netherlands at the end of the nineteenth century and the beginning of the twentieth. This holds true, for instance, of the esoteric notions that permeate the theories of some of the De Stijl artists. It also applies to the notion of the unity of visual art and architecture, which relates to older ideas about monumental art (or "community art," as it was sometimes called). It is significant that, in addition to Picasso and Archipenko, the architect H. P. Berlage and the painter Jan Toorop—two esteemed culture-bearers of the previous generation—were on *De stijl*'s original list of contributors. (They did not actually contribute, however.)

In its first years, *De stijl* had only a few regular contributors: van Doesburg, Huszár, Kok, van der Leck, Mondrian, Oud, and Wils.

Carel Blotkamp

Shortly afterward, van 't Hoff and Vantongerloo joined, followed by Rietveld. Although there were frequent resignations because of artistic or personal differences, the group created an outward impression of strong unanimity. Almost all the members signed the first manifesto of De Stijl, which was published in four languages in November 1918 and which begins with these well-known lines: "There is an old and a new consciousness of time. The old is connected with the individual. The new is connected with the universal." With utter self-confidence they summoned "all who believe in the reformation of art and culture" to follow their good example and move toward a radical purification of the arts, in the process of which impediments such as "traditions, dogmas, and the domination of the individual" would be eliminated.

The charter members of De Stijl agreed on this rather broad formulation. In their periodical they explained how they aimed to bring about the purification of the different fields of the arts, such as painting, sculpture, and architecture (and, later, literature and music), by searching for the most fundamental elements of each separate field of art and then uniting these elements in a well-balanced relationship. In this respect, they were engaged in polemics against some of the other artists who claimed to represent a new art-consciousness. To give themselves a clear profile, they removed themselves from certain art forms with which some of them had been closely allied. Van Doesburg agitated against expressionist tendencies in visual art; Oud contested the architecture of the Amsterdam School. They even lashed out at artists who were rather close to De Stijl, such as the painter Peter Alma and the architect Huib Hoste. After the war, the profile of De Stijl as a radical movement was enhanced with redoubled energy, and on an international scale. The post-cubist development in Paris and the Bauhaus in Germany were then viewed particularly critically.

At first, *De stijl* preached to a small congregation. Before the periodical was published, an edition of 1,000 copies had been under consideration; the actual printing was probably quite a bit smaller. In the early years the number of subscriptions varied between 100 and 200, and it did not increase much in the later years. Most of the subscribers were friends and acquaintances of the artists who published in the journal. But despite the modest size of its circle of readers, *De stijl* caused a sensation with its immediate statement of principles, and it elicited many critical reactions in the press. In November 1917, J. P. Mieras tore into the theories proclaimed in *De stijl* in the architectural journal *Bouwkundig weekblad,* wondering "Are the painters who act as spokesmen still painting nowadays?" In 1919, van Doesburg's onetime friend and supporter Erich Wichman vented particularly venomous criticism in an article titled "Camouflage, Monsieur Theo van Doesburg et son Style," which appeared in the French-language journal *La revue du feu.* Wichman referred to "an artistic movement, or rather an artistic non-movement, which is particularly curious from a national viewpoint, because this immobile movement, this ferocious negation of Life itself, this rigid, sterile art, this patient dilettantism, crystallized and frozen in small colored squares and orthodox straight lines, hanging mournfully in the void, is nowhere else imaginable than in the Low Countries, those Very Low Countries." Some years later, when De Stijl started to penetrate other countries, it often ran into foul weather there as well. The German critic Paul Westheim, for instance, wrote the following in 1923 in *Das kunstblatt,* on the occasion of a Bauhaus exhibition: "The people of De Stijl are having a protest exhibition in Jena: they claim to have the only true squares." Around the same time, the Belgian dadaist Paul Joostens expressed his view on the art of Mondrian, van Doesburg, and their ilk in a witty drawing that paraphrased a Flemish altarpiece (figure 1). These are but a few of the many sarcastic or hostile comments on their work and ideas which the artists of De Stijl received. Although there were also positive reactions and expressions of support inside and outside the Netherlands, supporters of de Stijl were still in the minority. The criticism contributed to the formation of a united front among the artists against the outsiders, which in turn suggested a greater unity of opinion than actually existed among them.

De stijl was published with some regularity from 1917 to 1928, and in 1932 a final issue appeared in commemoration of the recently deceased van Doesburg. According to its title, this book deals only with the early period: the years from 1917 to 1922. There are two reasons for this limitation. The first one is practical: The amount of material was found to be very extensive. A detailed treatment of the whole De Stijl period would require much more space. But, more important, internal evidence demonstrates that De Stijl experienced a discontinuity around 1922. Several of the artists had already withdrawn, mostly after difficulties with van Doesburg. This happened in turn with van der Leck, Wils, van 't Hoff, Vantongerloo, and (temporarily) Huszár. In 1922, however, there was a split in the inner circle of De Stijl, between van Doesburg and Oud. In the same year, the differences between van Doesburg and Mondrian that were to lead to Mondrian's resignation surfaced for the first time. Therefore, a basic distinction can be made between De Stijl in the period before 1922, when Mondrian, van Doesburg, and Oud were the dominant personalities, and the period after 1922, when van Doesburg alone filled that

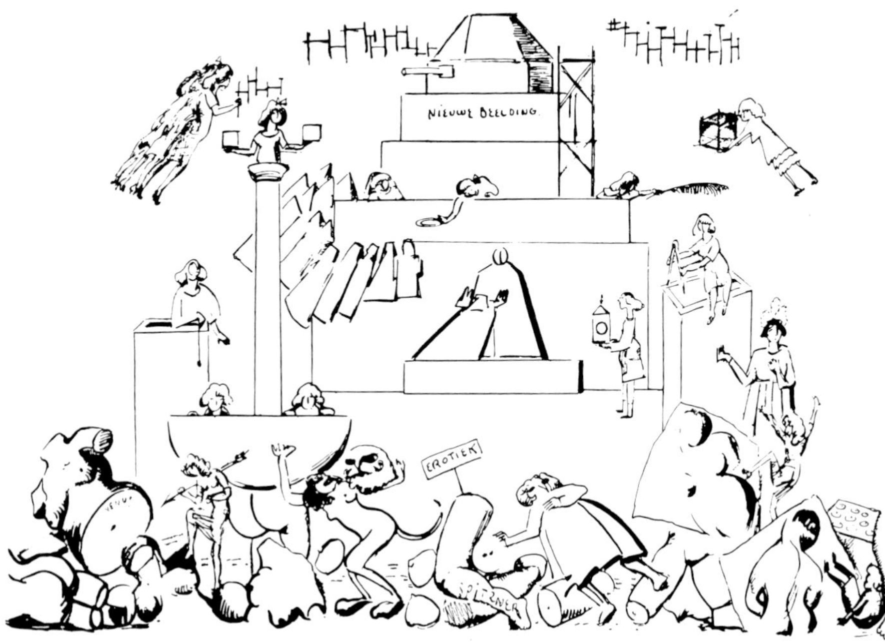

1 Paul Joostens, *Nieuwe Beelding—al wat benen heeft is onzedelijk* [*Neo-Plasticism—everything that has legs is immoral*], ca. 1922. 30.8 × 41.3 cm. Private collection.

role. Until 1922 the periodical was mainly filled with contributions from Dutch painters and architects; thereafter it had a more international circle of contributors. In the second phase it was less orthodox and somewhat less cohesive.

The changes were, no doubt, related to the somewhat nomadic existence van Doesburg led from 1921 on. They were also related to developments in his thinking. From the beginning to the end, van Doesburg was the sole editor of *De stijl.* In the light of his personality it is understandable that the journal strongly reflects his oscillating sympathies and dislikes.

The theme of the relationships between van Doesburg and the other contributors in *De stijl*'s first phase runs like a red thread through the subsequent monographic chapters, the sequence of which was determined by the date (insofar as can be determined) when each of the artists first came into contact with van Doesburg. Each of the chapters goes deeply into the implications of the relationship and how it was severed.

A chapter is devoted to each of nine artists: four painters (van Doesburg, Huszár, van der Leck, Mondrian), four architects (van 't Hoff, Oud, Rietveld, Wils), and one sculptor-painter (Vantongerloo).

Perhaps the reader will look for a chapter on one other man who was among the founders of *De stijl* and who signed some of the manifestos: the poet Antony Kok. But Kok was an outsider to the periodical, which was originally meant solely for the visual arts. That he was permitted to publish a few short articles and "think-extracts" in the first volumes, and that his name appeared under some of the manifestos, was probably mainly a gesture by van Doesburg, who did not want to exclude his old comrade. Kok hardly made any creative contribution to *De stijl,* however, and his essays are of only marginal importance. His regular appearance in this book results from his having been an important partner in the conversations and the correspondence of van Doesburg, and also those of some of the other artists.

There would have been more reason to devote a chapter to Gino Severini, an Italian painter who lived in Paris. The first two volumes of *De stijl* featured a series of articles by this artist, in French. (These articles had been published earlier in the periodical *Mercure de France.*) During the war years, Severini was the only person outside the Netherlands with whom the De Stijl artists had regular and fruitful contact. He did not sign any of the manifestos, but on the occasion of De Stijl's tenth anniversary, in 1927, he was mentioned on the list of "collaborators in principle" for the years 1917–1919. Severini certainly was important as a contact in Paris and as an author, but he stood, literally and figuratively, too far apart from the other artists to be properly considered as part of De Stijl. For this reason we refrained from discussing him separately.

The various chapters, which cover each artist's contributions to the De Stijl movement, begin with a discussion of the artist's education and his development in the period prior to De Stijl. A number of important topics will recur steadily. In the case of a painter, these will be the relationship between the abstract work of art and the visible reality, the use of color (whether or not it was strictly limited to pure primary colors), the use of form (whether or not rectangular and orthogonal), the merging of the figure and the ground of a painting into absolute flatness, and the question of equilibrium in the composition. In the field of architecture, diverse topics will recur, such as the influence of Frank Lloyd Wright, the difference between designs executed and those not executed, and the relation between beauty and function. Finally, each chapter will go into the collaboration between painters and architects, one of the most crucial aspects of De Stijl. These were topics about which the opinions of the artists sometimes diverged far more than is usually believed.

As was stated above, the existing literature on De Stijl has most often emphasized the collectivism of the movement. This literature tends to be general rather than specific. We prefer to emphasize the specific and the individual. This means that we will pay a relatively large amount of attention to dating and to the determination of mutual influences. The question how a certain principle of design or a certain idea of an artist was assimilated by his colleagues is not just academic, even in the case of a basically anti-individualistic art such as that of De Stijl.

The artists' development, in their work as well as in their thinking, is described on the basis of data of diverse kinds and origins. In the first place, their work has been studied, either on the basis of extant originals or on the basis of reproductions. In addition, catalogs, exhibition reviews, and texts written by the artists have been analyzed. Everyone who is familiar with their writings—those published in *De stijl* and those published elsewhere—knows how problematical and obscure they sometimes are. Perhaps I may cite in this context a statement about a contemporary and a countryman of the De Stijl artists, the famous mathematician L. E. J. Brouwer, made by E. T. Bell in his book *Men of mathematics:* "The primary revelations of the creed are veiled in Dutch language. German and English expositions are available but it is said by converts with expert knowledge in both the languages and the mathematics that only those who can think in Dutch can grasp the finer shades of meaning." That sounds much too optimistic, for even we Dutch authors sometimes have not the slightest idea, after half a century, of the meanings of certain statements made by these elated men. Their letters, which are much less formal and philosophical in their language, can sometimes clarify a great deal, not only about facts but also about opinions. We have made extensive use of these letters. A particularly rich source was Theo van Doesburg's estate, which after his widow's death was willed to the Dutch government and which recently has been made fully available for research. Numerous letters found elsewhere, for example in the collections of the Fondation Custodia in Paris and the Nederlands Documentatiecentrum voor de Bouwkunst in Amsterdam, were also consulted. Some important letters proved to be inaccessible (such as those in Vantongerloo's estate, which is in Max Bill's hands); others have been lost (for example, Mondrian destroyed the letters written to him). Although blank spots remain, we hope that this book may contribute to the creation of a more variegated image of De Stijl in its important early period.

Theo van Doesburg, *Compositie IV*, 1917. (See also figure 14, page 17.)

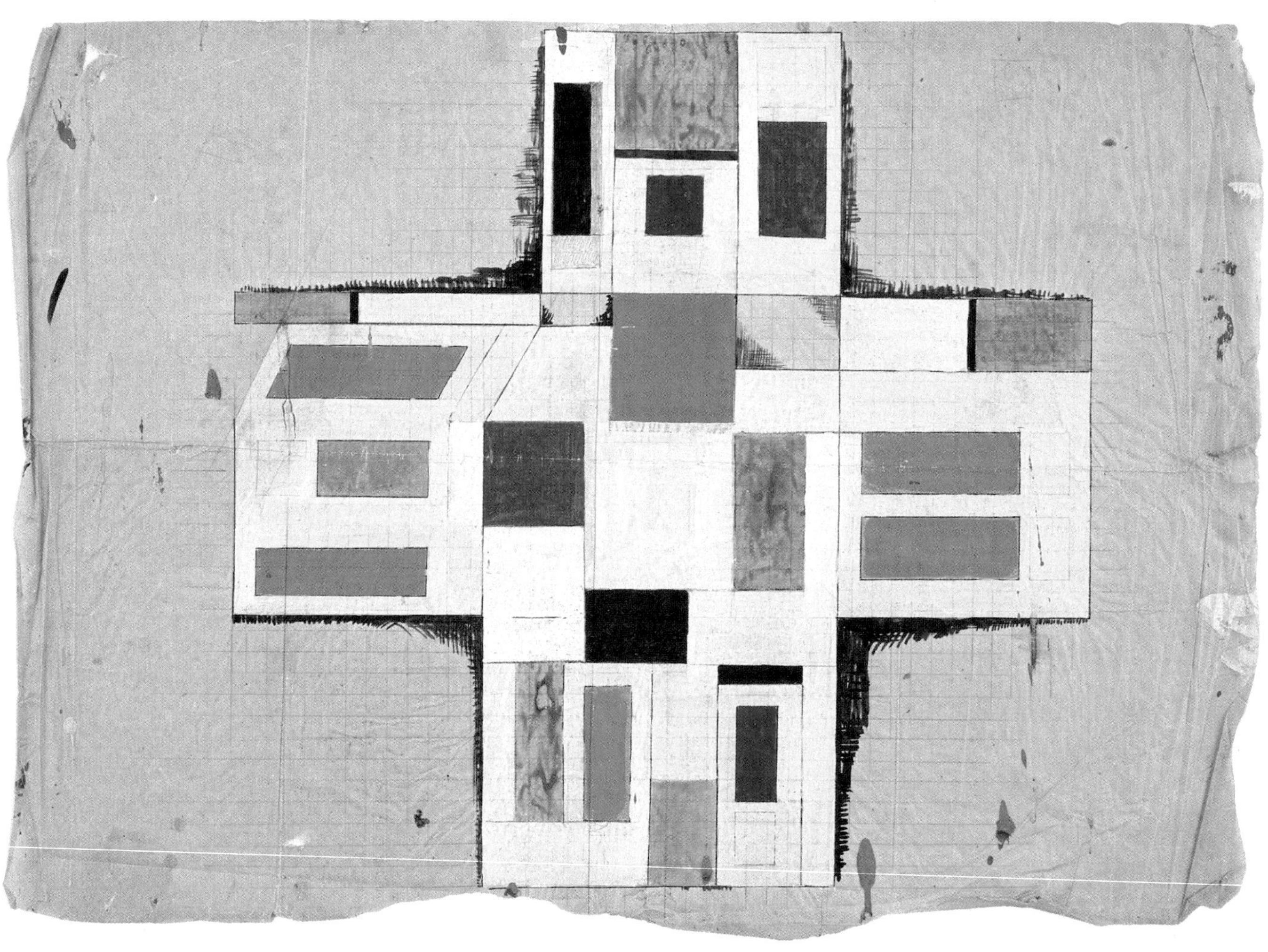

Theo van Doesburg, design of color application for room in de Ligt house, Katwijk, 1919. (See also figure 29, page 33.)

Theo van Doesburg, retouched photograph of room in de Ligt house, Katwijk. (See also figure 30, page 34.)

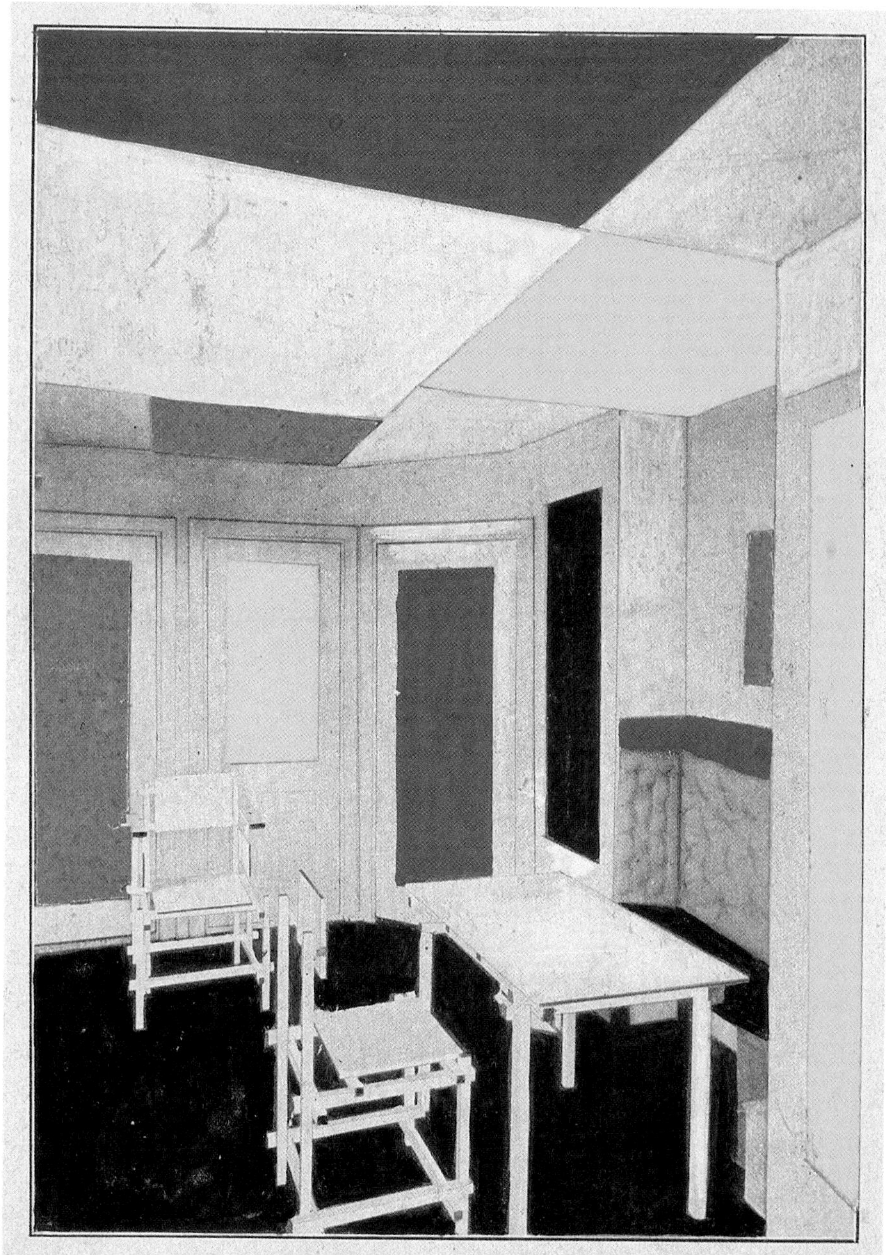

THEO VAN DOESBURG. PROEVE VAN KLEURENCOMPOSITIE IN INTÉRIEUR (1919). MEUBELEN VAN G. RIETVELD. BIJLAGE XIV VAN „DE STIJL" 3E JAARGANG No. 12.

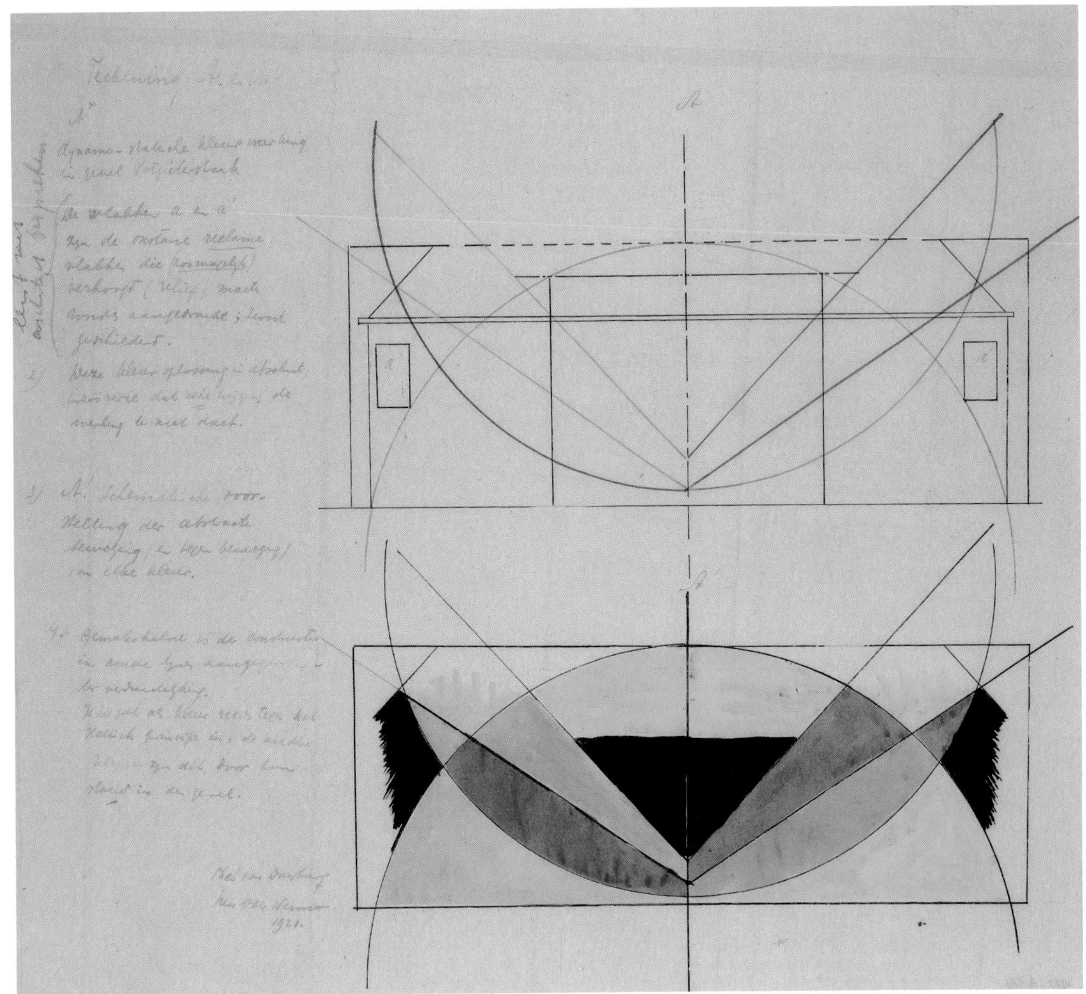

Theo van Doesburg, design for color application for housing block on Potgieterstraat, Rotterdam, 1921. (See also figure 31, page 35.)

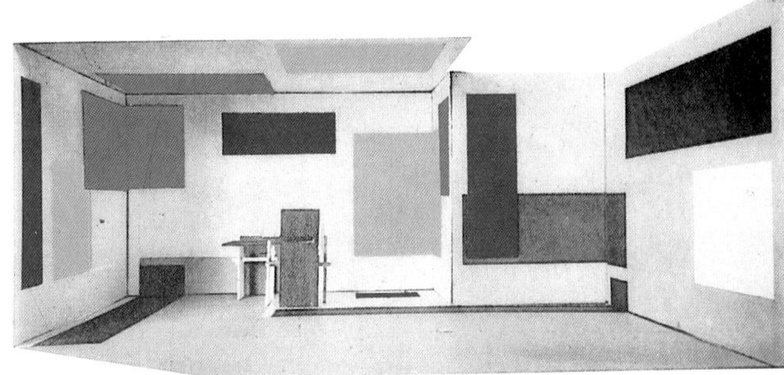

Gerrit Rietveld and Vilmos Huszár, maquette of spatial color composition for exhibition space, 1923. (See also figures 101 and 261, pages 112 and 274.)

Bart van der Leck, *Compositie 1918, no. 1*. (See also figure 155, page 170.)

Bart van der Leck, *Design-interior,* 1918. (See also figure 165, page 176.)

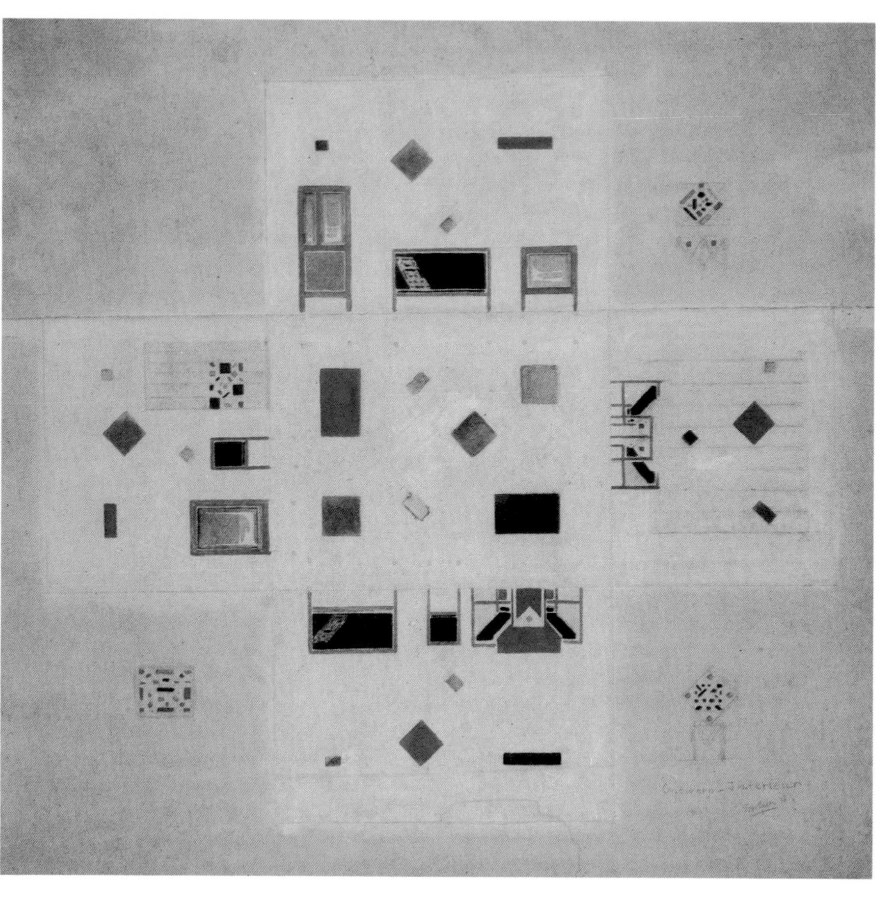

Georges Vantongerloo, *Triptiek,* 1921. (See also figure 242, page 255.)

De Stijl:

The Formative Years

2 Theo van Doesburg and Helena Milius, Leiden, 1917. On the easel is *De kaartspelers* [*The card players*], as yet unfinished. This painting (oil on canvas, 120 × 149.5 cm) is now in the collection of the Rijksdienst Beeldende Kunst, in The Hague.

Theo van Doesburg

Carel Blotkamp

More than fifty years after his death, we still do not have a clear image of Theo van Doesburg.[1] This chapter cannot fully correct that. His estate, which recently came into the possession of the government of the Netherlands, is a rich source of material, and with these resources we will gradually be able to separate truth from fiction. The extant correspondence, for instance, clarifies a great deal about van Doesburg's complex relationships with other artists, and it also elucidates the creation of his visual works, which are often dated incorrectly. But it is doubtful that we will ever succeed in creating a complete image of the man. He is as difficult to grasp now as he was during his lifetime, when he occasionally operated under pseudonyms as the poet I. K. Bonset and as the philosopher Aldo Camini. Perhaps we should even consider the name Theo van Doesburg, which he used as a painter, author, and theoretician, to be a pseudonym; this was not the name given him at birth, but one he adopted when he was a young man. These name changes were due in part to an inner need for mystification in his contacts with other people, but also in part to a tendency that was directly related to van Doesburg's creativity: his desire to express the different facets of his personality in very different ways.

From all his creations and writings, and from what else is known about him, van Doesburg emerges as an extraordinarily impulsive figure. He could immediately fly into enthusiasm for something or somebody, and he exerted himself beyond all limits to express these feelings. But his enthusiasm could just as suddenly turn into deep disappointment, rejection, and furious criticism as the result of an incident that someone else would have considered insignificant. All his undertakings took a turbulent course because of this characteristic, and De Stijl was no exception. Van Doesburg is always named as the motive force of the movement, and this is undoubtedly true, but he did move in two opposite directions. He brought kindred spirits together, but he also drove them apart again.

The same impulsiveness that manifested itself in van Doesburg's behavior can be seen in his work. He crossed the boundaries between art forms effortlessly, occupying himself—at one time intensively, at other times to a much lesser extent—with painting, applied art, architecture, typography, literature, music, and film. In all these fields he was active as a theoretician, and in most of them as a practicing artist as well. These various activities were strongly determined by what he saw and read and by what emerged from his discussions with others. He absorbed like a sponge whatever appealed to him. In this he was selective to a certain extent, but the background of his selections is often hard to determine. Also, it is often not clear how he incorporated new impulses into his established opinions.

Van Doesburg must have been aware of his capricious artistic personality. As he grew older he came to see this less as a weakness and more as an asset, and to a certain extent this was justified. At first he needed "Bonset" and "Camini" as mouthpieces to vent opinions that were difficult to match with the statements of others in *De stijl.* In the last years of his life, however, he openly proclaimed that for him dynamism and constant change were precisely the essentials of modern artistry. In his autobiographically colored introduction to the tenth-anniversary issue of *De stijl* we find this typical passage: "No fulfillment of culture or oneself without destruction, of oneself (in the first place) and of one's view of life (in the second)."[2] This was van Doesburg's definitive creed.

Beginnings as painter, author, and critic

"Sergeant Küpper" is the name that sometimes appears on postcards mailed by Theo van Doesburg during his military service. He was born on August 30, 1883, in Utrecht, as Christiaan Emil Marie Küpper. At an early age he adopted the name of Theodorus Doesburg, the man his mother had married a few years after he was born, who was probably his natural father.

The young Theo van Doesburg had artistic aspirations in diverse directions. He loved acting, and seems to have studied for a short while at an acting school in Amsterdam. He wrote poetry and prose and busied himself with drawing and painting. Apart from studying with a certain Arie Grootens, he was self-taught as a painter—on principle, out of aversion for the academy, if we can believe the biographical data he sent to the critic Albert Plasschaert in 1912. (In this material van Doesburg also mentions having exhibited 46 works in 1908 at a show held by the Haagsche Kunstkring [Hague Artists' Circle].) He earned a living for himself and for Agnita Feis, whom he married in 1910, by teaching drawing in Amsterdam.

In 1912 van Doesburg came into the limelight as an author and critic. In that year he became a contributor to *Eenheid,* a weekly that was aimed at Theosophists, Freemasons, Rosicrucians, Spiritualists, vegetarians, and teetotalers. In long articles under the pretentious title "Proeve tot nieuwe kunstkritiek" ["Specimens of new art criticism"] he expostulated on how art should be judged not on its external beauty but on its ability to express pure, deep feelings.

If this sounds familiar, it is because of the strong emphasis that was later put on the spiritual value of art in *De stijl.* In 1912, however, van Doesburg's taste was still very conventional.[3] His first series of articles was occasioned by the International Exhibition of Art Works of Living Masters, held in the Stedelijk Museum in Amsterdam in the summer of that same year. (Van Doesburg himself was represented there by a painting entitled *Manskop* [*Man's head*].) That which he considered as good, real art in his review consisted of—as far as can be determined—rather bland paintings in a generally traditional exhibition. At the time, there were occurring in the Netherlands sensational manifestations of French cubism, Italian futurism, and German expressionism—avant-garde movements with which the Dutch artists Mondrian, Sluyters, Gestel, and Schelfhout were connected. Van Doesburg paid little attention to this work, although the artists were of his own generation. When he did pay attention, he had nothing favorable to say about it; he criticized these art forms as pathological, bestial, and materialistic.

That van Doesburg gradually revised his negative judgment in the following years can be explained mainly in terms of the influence of Apollinaire and, particularly, Kandinsky. Through his reading of articles and books such as *Über das geistige in der kunst* and *Rückblicke,* van Doesburg came to see that Kandinsky's extreme abstraction originated with his aspiration toward spiritualization, an aim that van Doesburg also had conceived as the essence of art. In an article that appeared in *Eenheid* on December 6, 1913, he elaborated on this, answering negatively the question "Can painting do without the object?" He did not believe that an abstract composition of shapes and colors could convey a deep meaning, as natural objects could. Nonetheless, he showed more understanding and appreciation than before.

The work van Doesburg himself was producing at this time, as far as it is known, did not indicate his convictions clearly. In the spring of 1914 he participated in an exhibition for the first time in two years, sending three paintings to the Salon des Indépendants in Paris. One of the three was *Petite paysanne hollandaise* [*Little Dutch farmgirl*] (figure 3). Because of the subject and the heavy, somewhat clumsy handling of the paint, this painting was more in line with the tradition of Amsterdam impressionism than with the new trends. The other Dutch participants in the Paris exhibition, among them Jacoba van Heemskerck, Piet Mondrian, Adya van Rees, and Erich Wichman, showed daring cubist experiments and abstractions.

It seems justified to conclude that until the First World War—say, until his thirtieth year—van Doesburg occupied only a marginal position in the Dutch art world. As a painter he had not yet shown anything worthwhile, and as a writer on art in rather obscure periodicals he appeared to be more interested in aesthetic

3 Van Doesburg, *Petite paysanne hollandaise* [*Little Dutch farmgirl*], 1913. Oil on canvas, 34.7 × 54.5 cm. Rijksdienst Beeldende Kunst, The Hague.

and art-theoretical questions than in the actual practice of the arts at the moment. He was not a critic in the strict sense. Between 1912 and 1914 he wrote only four or five articles dealing directly with exhibitions of contemporary art. As far as we know, he had hardly any contacts with other visual artists, and he was not a member of any of the Amsterdam art associations (e.g., the Moderne Kunstkring [Circle of Modern Art], De Onafhankelijken [The Independents], or the more established St. Lucas group). He hardly participated in exhibitions. Perhaps his literary ambitions were still stronger than his ambitions in the field of visual art; in *Eenheid* he published a number of fairytales and a play entitled *Opstanding* [*Resurrection*] in addition to his articles on art.[4]

Association with the avant-garde

At the outbreak of the war, in the summer of 1914, van Doesburg was again called up for military service. At first he was stationed at the Belgian border near Tilburg; later, from around September 1915, he was in Utrecht. He was not released from the service until February 1916. It was during this period that he met (in Tilburg) Helena Milius, who would become his second wife in a few years. He also met such kindred spirits as the railroad official Antony Kok, who was also a music connoisseur and a poet, and the shoemaker-philosopher Evert Rinsema, with whom he had long conversations about culture and the human condition. Throughout his life van Doesburg kept up friendly relations with these two; reading the extant correspondence is one of the best ways to become acquainted with his personality and work.[5]

It was during this period of relative isolation that van Doesburg began to associate with what can be called the Dutch avant-garde. Because of the lack of precise information, one can only speculate about the cause of his change in position. He probably had plenty of time for reading, and the discussions with his friends may have had a clarifying effect. It is also possible that while on furlough in Amsterdam he came into contact with visual artists who were involved in the newest trends. The first indication of radical change in his own work can be seen in *Blozend meisje met ranonkels* [*Blushing girl with ranunculi*] (figure 4), which probably was painted in June or July 1914.[6] This is a remarkable half-figurative, half-abstract work; eyes, red cheeks, and a mouth stylized into a semicircular arc seem to float in an open space, which is bordered in the corners by something like stage wings. The distribution of shapes and blots is slightly reminiscent of Kandinsky's work, toward which van Doesburg had only a short time earlier been antagonistic.

In his writings, van Doesburg clearly manifested his changed viewpoint and taste for the first time in a review of the spring exhibition of De Onafhankelijken in Amsterdam, which was published in *Eenheid* on June 19, 1915, and in which he set himself up as a champion of such "true moderns" as Else Berg, Louis Saalborn, and Erich Wichman.

This sort of sudden enthusiasm was apparently so normal in van Doesburg's personality structure that it needed no further motivation or explanation. Even more remarkable, he acted toward his new friends as if his new artistic viewpoints had been formed years earlier. For example, he devoted a long paragraph in a letter to Antony Kok, dated June 7, 1915, to the representation of music through shape (which he thought more important to this end than color), and he included a small drawing entitled *Straatmuziek II* [*Street music II*]—which, he claimed, dated from 1912—as an example. This date seems improbably early; it must be a misrepresentation. *Straatmuziek II* and the similar *Straatmuziek I* were probably brand new and directly inspired by the "sound drawings" that Louis Saalborn and Laurens van Kuik had exhibited recently at the aforementioned exhibition of De Onafhankelijken.[7]

In 1914–15 a new period began in van Doesburg's public life. True, he continued to write for *Eenheid* for years, and he certainly did not disengage himself from that ethical and spiritual atmosphere, but his outlook broadened considerably and his self-confidence was renewed. He made many contacts, acquired friends and foes, wrote extensively, lectured, and tried to start societies and periodicals—in short, the van Doesburg we know began to emerge.

A circumstance that made it easier for van Doesburg to play his new role was his transfer to Utrecht, where he spent the second half of his military service. There he met, among others, a Dr. G. ten Doesschate, an eye specialist connected with the military hospital, who was interested in art. A painter himself, ten Doesschate published, aside from papers on eye diseases, writings on diverse subjects concerning visual perception. Van Doesburg often visited ten Doesschate's home, and painted a portrait of his young son. Through his acquaintance with this doctor, van Doesburg gained access to the art-loving upper classes of Utrecht, and this afforded him the opportunity to give several lectures at the end of 1915 and the beginning of 1916. In one of these, "The development of modern painting" (subsequently published in installments in *Eenheid*), van Doesburg tried to put a solid historical foundation under the new art he had begun to promote. He pictured the whole of Western art, from Giotto to the present moment, as a continuous development in which the depiction of natural reality had gradually given way to the representation of spiritual reality.

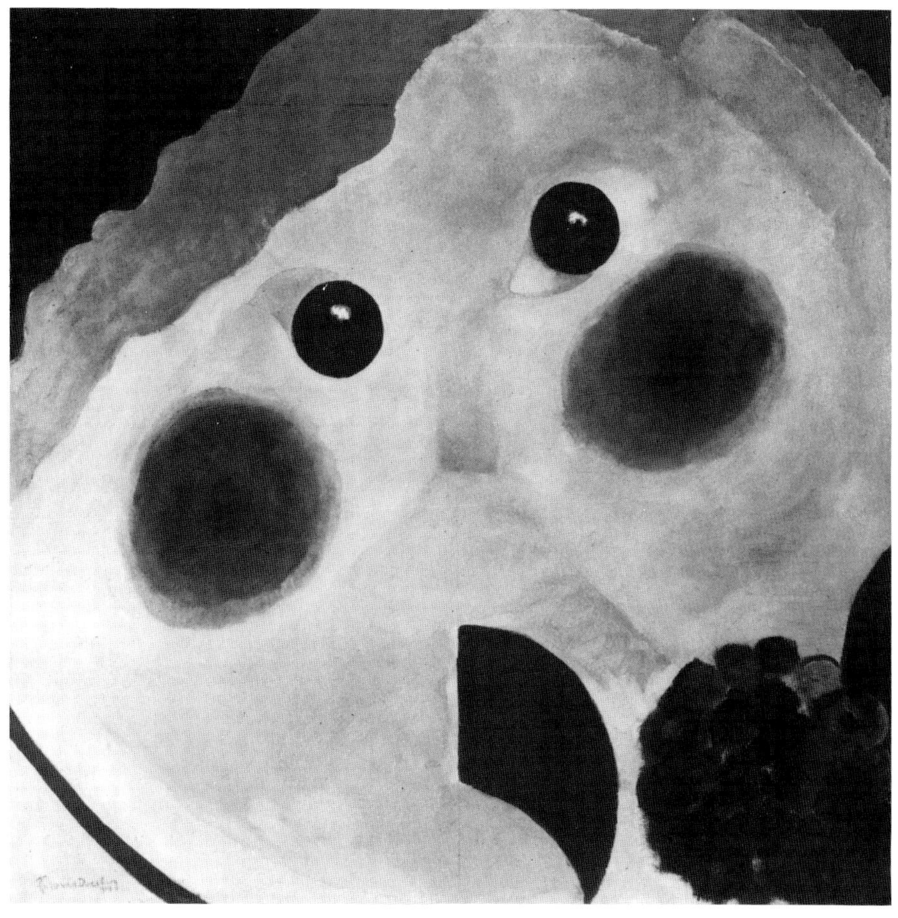

4

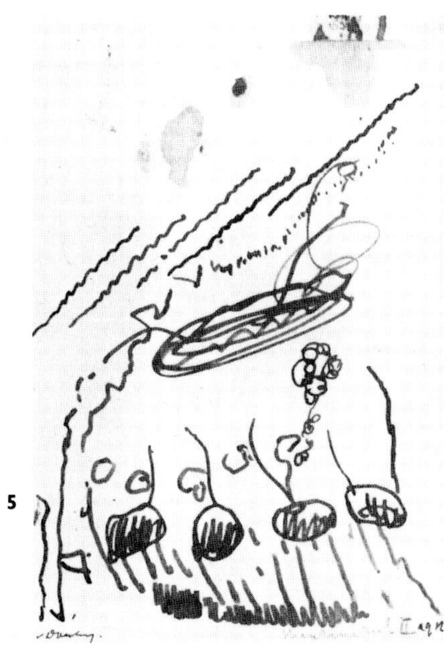

5

4 **Van Doesburg, *Blozend meisje met ranonkels* [*Blushing girl with ranunculi*], 1914. Oil on canvas, 79 × 79 cm. Yale University Art Gallery, New Haven.**

5 **Van Doesburg, *Straatmuziek II* [*Street music II*], 1915. Ink on paper, 15.3 × 10.2 cm. Rijksdienst Beeldende Kunst, The Hague.**

As mentioned above, he had already strongly emphasized the spiritual value of art, but now he apparently became convinced that this value could best manifest itself in abstract works of art, in which the frame of mind or the emotion of the artist could express itself directly in shape and color without an intermediate recognizable image. According to van Doesburg, this meant the dawn of a new era in visual art. In this context, he called Kandinsky a messiah who heralded "the artwork of the Future, the abstract, chaste, pure painting." In the Netherlands, he said, the new awareness of art was manifesting itself in the works of Mondrian, Huszár, Wichman, and de Winter.[8]

It was not without reason that van Doesburg mentioned these four artists; in 1915 and the following years they played an important part in his life, albeit at different moments and in different ways. His contacts with Erich Wichman were particularly influential on the new orientation of his artistic ideas.[9] Perhaps van Doesburg had become acquainted with Wichman through De Onafhankelijken; maybe also via their mutual friend ten Doesschate. In any case, van Doesburg had known Wichman since the summer of 1915. The latter had for years devoted himself enthusiastically and ably to the new art—for instance, in a polemic in the pamphlet series *Pro en contra* against C. L. Dake, a conservative professor at the Amsterdam Academy. He was, moreover, very versatile, being a critic, an author of ironic poems and prose, a painter, a graphic artist, and a craft designer.

Van Doesburg had many conversations with Wichman, who divided his time between Amsterdam and Utrecht, and he communicated some of the details of these from time to time in letters to his friend Antony Kok. In 1915, van Doesburg and Wichman developed serious plans for a periodical. They looked for sponsors and a publisher, and they consulted with the classicist G. Brinkgreve (who was to become co-editor) about the philosophical basis of the journal. This was not to be the sort of journal that *De stijl* eventually became; the idea was to publish a general cultural periodical that would position itself against the more conservative journals such as *De kunst.* The German magazine *Der sturm* served as an example.

Van Doesburg was in need of a forum of his own, not only for his art-theoretical writings but also for his literature. He had difficulty airing the latter in the existing journals, as is apparent in a letter to Kok dated October 26, 1915: "Of course, I urgently need a periodical of my own! I am dying to dash my poems against their obtuse brains." The poems he wrote in this period, often on subjects from military life (e.g., "Kazernekamer" ["Barracks Room"], "De looppas" ["Double time"], and "Ruiter" ["Horseman"]), consisted of short, clipped sentences with much onomatopoeia and rhyming of vowels—stylistic means also used by Kok. In 1915, both van Doesburg and Kok conducted modest experiments with phonetic poems, in which the meaning of the word is completely subordinated to the sound.[10] As the correspondence reveals, they oriented themselves toward the German expressionist poetry of August Stramm and the work of the Italian futurist Marinetti.

Wichman was a good conversational partner for van Doesburg and an ally in developing plans for periodicals and exhibitions; however, there must have been from the beginning an essential difference in outlook between the two artists. Wichman had a rather nihilistic attitude; he treated every aspiration toward a higher goal in art or life with cool irony or biting sarcasm. Van Doesburg, on the other hand, capricious though he could be, always devoted himself with an almost religious fanaticism to whatever he considered the right cause at a given moment. Therefore, Wichman could hardly become his model as an artist. This role was reserved for Piet Mondrian and Janus de Winter. Van Doesburg met both these men in the autumn of 1915, and for a considerable time he oscillated between their widely disparate views.

Encounters with Mondrian and de Winter

Van Doesburg must have seen Piet Mondrian's work earlier at exhibitions, but he first wrote about it when a number of new works were exhibited by the Hollandsche Kunstenaarskring in Amsterdam in October 1915. He was enthusiastic—particularly about Mondrian's most recent painting *Compositie X* (figure 40 in this volume), which gave him a "purely spiritual" feeling. He characterized the work as follows in *Eenheid*: "The impression it makes is one of tranquility; the immobility of the soul."[11] Van Doesburg also expressed his admiration in a letter to Mondrian. The reply pleased him, and so the foundation was laid for a long-standing exchange of thoughts and collaboration. On October 26 van Doesburg wrote to Kok about Mondrian's first reaction: "I did perceive correctly the spiritual element in Mondrian's work. The fact that he writes after my review is proof of this." He also reported having dedicated a poem, "Kathedraal I," to Mondrian.

Thus van Doesburg found in his own country an abstract, spiritualized art that could stand comparison with that of Kandinsky. Still, it was quite a while before he, as an artist, was willing and able to follow that example in practice as well as in theory. An accurate reconstruction of the sequence of van Doesburg's works from late 1915 through 1916 shows that he had not yet grasped the radical abstraction that Mondrian practiced; not until 1917 did he succeed

6 Van Doesburg, *Wanhoop* [*Despair*], 1915. Black chalk on paper, 16 × 11.5 cm. Rijksdienst Beeldende Kunst, The Hague.

in this, and at first he had much difficulty accepting Mondrian's renunciation of the individual element. Van Doesburg still placed much value on the expressive faculties of abstract art, on the possibility of expressing personal feelings exclusively through shape and color. This may explain why he, although admiring Mondrian, felt more attracted for a while to Janus de Winter.[12]

Van Doesburg met this painter from Utrecht, probably in October 1915, through Erich Wichman. He described the first encounter amusingly in his booklet *De schilder de Winter en zijn werk* [*The painter de Winter and his work*], which he wrote and published in the summer of 1916. Once when he visited Wichman's studio he saw a curious small painting in purple and yellow; it bore the handsome title *De zuivere rede* [*Pure reason*], derived from the neo-Hegelian philosopher Bolland, who was then very popular among artists. His curiosity aroused by the stories about the maker of the painting, van Doesburg accompanied Wichman to visit de Winter. He was impressed by the man and his work. This work originated as in a frenzy, a half-conscious condition. Using abstract shapes, but also flowers, imaginary scenery, and strange animal figures, de Winter expressed emotions and psychic conditions which he claimed to observe in people around him not with his eyes but "when he concentrated his psychic attention on someone." He grounded himself more or less on the Theosophical theory that every human being is surrounded by an aura containing shapes and colors that characterize him.

Soon a strong tie developed between van Doesburg and de Winter. The latter had been living and working in great isolation, and had been appreciated only by Dr. ten Doesschate; he had even considered giving up painting. Van Doesburg, however, encouraged him to continue, and took with his usual energy to the task of promoting him. In December 1915 he had a call for financial support published in *Eenheid,* and he did his best to find opportunities for exhibitions. How highly van Doesburg valued de Winter at that moment is evident from his poem "De priesterkunstenaar" ["The priest-artist"], which appeared in *Eenheid* on January 22, 1916. The last lines of this poem, dedicated "to my friend A. de Winter," read: "The Artist, the priest who / pictures the will of the world in / shapes, / colors, / words, / sounds, / the Priest, to whom / we owe the new life."

As a soldier, van Doesburg had more opportunity for writing than for painting; however, the visual work he did in this period also demonstrates how deeply he had been impressed. Among the relatively few works known from 1915 (mainly pastels and drawings in sketchbooks) are a remarkable number of self-portraits, with a wide range of expressions. Apparently van Doesburg had a great need for psychic self-analysis in this turbulent period, during which he was carrying on a love affair with the much younger Helena Milius. He also expressed this in lyric prose, some of which appeared in 1915 and 1916 in *Eenheid.* His *Wanhoop* [*Despair*], a more or less abstract drawing in a sketchbook from 1915 (figure 6), may refer to the problems this affair caused in his marriage. (Agnita Feis, van Doesburg's wife, also aired her emotions freely, in literary and visual form; the latter was probably new for her. On October 8, 1915, van Doesburg reported to Kok that he had seen a few drawings of Agnita's with such titles as *Hatred, Passion,* and *Fright,* and he generously added: "I am convinced that it is highly original work." A few months later Feis exhibited drawings of this kind in an exhibition of De Onafhankelijken.[13]) It is not my intention to go deeply into van Doesburg's amorous adventures, but to show how strongly he still believed in the expression of individual feelings in this period. *Heroïsche beweging* [*Heroic movement*], which he painted in the beginning of 1916, can be interpreted as an autobiographical expression, an evocation through line and color of the feeling of self-assertion he had developed. The painting seems completely abstract, but it apparently originated from a drawing in a sketchbook from late 1915 that bears the inscription "Studie voor mouvement heroique" and shows a figure with protruding chest and raised fists. (See figures 7 and 8.) This painting does have some characteristics of its own, but the pastels van Doesburg made around the same time lean very heavily toward de Winter's work.

In the first months of 1916, van Doesburg continued his promotion of de Winter with unabated zeal. On Sunday, February 6, 1916, he visited Mondrian for the first time in the artists' colony at Laren, where he also met the composer van Domselaer, the philosopher Schoenmaekers, and the painter Alma. The next day he reported the meeting in a very interesting letter to Kok: "I had

7

8

also brought a few works by de Winter. They found the work very beautiful but not very spiritual. They got the impression of a transformation of nature. Dr. Schoenmaekers thought it simply representation of astral visions. On the whole I got the impression that van Domselaer and Mondrian are totally under the spell of Dr. Schoenmaekers's ideas. The latter has just published a book about 'Plastic Mathematics.' Sch. stands on a mathematical basis. He considers mathematics as the sole pure thing; the only pure standard for our feelings. Therefore a work of art must, according to him, always be based on a mathematical foundation. Mondrian implements this by taking the two purest forms for the expression of his emotions, i.e., the horizontal and the vertical line." Van Doesburg added as good news that Schoenmaekers and Mondrian knew his articles in *Eenheid* and *De avondpost* and were willing to contribute to a new periodical.

Not yet strongly affected by Mondrian's and Schoenmaekers's criticism of de Winter, which accompanied their appreciation, van Doesburg continued to promote the latter's work. In March 1916 he founded the association De Anderen [The Others], together with Erich Wichman and Louis Saalborn. In May they held their first exhibition at the d'Audretsch gallery in The Hague. Four days before the opening, de Winter withdrew his contribution. In a letter of May 4 to Helena Milius, who did a lot of the organizational work for De Anderen, he wrote that his decision was partly inspired by "the development of Theo's most recent work."

Van Doesburg experienced this withdrawal as some kind of betrayal, and suddenly he did not find de Winter's work so good any more; it was "too passionate to be spiritual in a plastic sense," he wrote to Kok on May 18. In a letter written ten days later he explained what had happened. De Winter had been more or less snatched away by Henri Borel and Frederik van Eeden, who, as famous authors, had greater authority and who had been able to arrange a large one-man show for de Winter in the Stedelijk Museum in Amsterdam. "Of course I was filled with indignation," van Doesburg wrote, "because the whole affair [the exhibition of De Anderen] really had been set up for him." A short while afterward, the quarrel abated somewhat, and van Doesburg published the aforementioned booklet about de Winter, which was dated July 27, 1916. After that, the split became definite, and the two artists had only scornful words for each other. For instance, de Winter wrote to Kok, who viewed the whole affair from a distance, that van Doesburg was "a spiritually thoroughly uncouth person and a childish upstart."[14]

7 Van Doesburg, study for *Heroïsche beweging* [*Heroic movement*], 1915. Pencil on paper, 16 × 11.5 cm. Rijksdienst Beeldende Kunst, The Hague.

8 Van Doesburg, *Heroïsche beweging* [*Heroic movement*], 1916. Oil on canvas, 120 × 80 cm. Rijksdienst Beeldende Kunst, The Hague.

9 Van Doesburg, *Stilleven III* [*Still life III*], 1916. Oil on canvas, 82 × 67.5 cm. Private collection.

9

Encounters with Huszár and Oud

De Winter's influence on van Doesburg was short-lived but intense. Perhaps it was Schoenmaekers's and Mondrian's criticism that caused him to waver; in any case, van Doesburg's work began to show a greater distance from de Winter.

After his demobilization in February, van Doesburg had more time for painting again. In the spring he painted, in fairly rapid succession, three still lifes that differ rather strongly from his previous work. They are constructed from geometrical forms, mainly circles and triangles. A more striking departure from his former practice is that these forms are placed within a regular grid—a subdivision of the picture plane into rectangles (numbers I and II) or triangles (number III, figure 9).[15] It is said of these paintings that they demonstrate a turning of van Doesburg's interests toward Cézanne and cubism. In a general way this is correct; nevertheless, one looks in vain for readily comparable works by those French artists—the only painter who comes relatively close is Delaunay. Nor do van Doesburg's still lifes have any connection with the paintings of Mondrian, the most important link between French cubism and Dutch art. Mondrian's rigid restriction to horizontals and verticals is at odds with van Doesburg's exuberant use of circles. However, there is no reason to assume that van Doesburg was very original in this series of still lifes; these paintings were probably influenced directly by Vilmos Huszár. Van Doesburg must have met this Hungarian-born artist during the preparations for the exhibition of De Anderen, and the fact that he called him "a force of the first order" in a letter to Kok (dated May 18, 1916) proves that he regarded him highly.

We can get an impression of Huszár's work from that time only through a single reproduction of *Schilderij (geel)* [*Painting (yellow)*], which must date from the first months of 1916. It was, together with some other works, exhibited in May at the De Anderen show, where van Doesburg showed his *Heroïsche beweging* and the three aforementioned still lifes. Van Doesburg either bought *Schilderij (geel)* or, more probably, traded his own *Stilleven I* for it.[16] From the reproduction (figure 66) it cannot be discerned whether *Schilderij (geel)* had a starting point in visual reality. The picture plane is filled with symmetrically arranged circles and angular planes that overlap one another but yet remain visible, as if they are somewhat transparent. These same characteristics can be recognized in van Doesburg's still lifes. However, in Huszár's work the shapes near the border disappear in darkness, and the basic geometric structure is hard to recognize. Van Doesburg greatly emphasized individual shapes and strongly brought out the grid.

After the exhibition of De Anderen, in June and July of 1916, van Doesburg executed a painting with a tree motif and a fourth still life; stylistically these were linked to the paintings mentioned earlier. However, in letters to Kok he also mentioned works of a different nature: pastels with titles such as *Heimwee* [*Nostalgia*] and *Het worden* [*The becoming*].[17] This may be an indication that van Doesburg's distance from de Winter was smaller than might be expected from the still lifes. The fact that van Doesburg began to use a more or less cubist formal language does not mean that his starting points had become rational and objective. From his correspondence and publications it is clear that he still valued the expression of personal feelings and experiences highly. For instance, on July 2, 1916, he wrote to Kok about *Stilleven IV,* on which he was working: "The still life, for instance, is only an excuse, for what I am painting is my state of mind, my *états d'ame.*" And two weeks later a somewhat excited letter followed, of which the following passage is typical: "Through our last day—I mean in the medieval museum and the Saint Bavo church—I have found my task: the crystal atmosphere. I have a positive plan for creation and what I shall create now will top everything. I don't talk to anyone about it. Only to you. I have perceived your psyche as an internally glowing and sparkling crystal." He wanted to express that psyche in a painting, apparently also a still life, and he asked whether Kok could lend him crystal objects to this end.

Under the surface of van Doesburg's cubist paintings was an exaltation that strikes us as expressionist. At the same time, they represent a turning point. From these paintings, there followed a clear development toward his work of the De Stijl years. The still lifes of 1916 have a high degree of visual clarity, and this quality, mastered with difficulty, is even more evident in the later paintings.

In 1916 van Doesburg got to know not only Mondrian and Huszár but also some others who later would become actively involved with De Stijl, including Oud, Wils, and van der Leck. His connection with Mondrian was at first rather loose. Now and then they corresponded, and van Doesburg visited a few times in Laren. It was probably on one of these occasions that he met Bart van der Leck, with whom he started a correspondence in December 1916. For the time being, van Doesburg's association with Huszár was much more intensive.

In the middle of the year 1916, van Doesburg came into contact with J. J. P. Oud. Oud took the initiative. On May 30 he wrote in a letter that he had heard from a mutual acquaintance, the painter Kamerlingh Onnes (Sr. or Jr.), that van Doesburg planned to start an association of modern painters in Leiden. He pleaded for the inclusion of architects in this venture, because the development of modern painting clearly led toward architecture. A meeting took place, probably the next day; May 31, 1916, was designated as the founding date of the Leidsche Kunstclub De Sphinx [Leiden Art Club The Sphinx], with Oud as president and van Doesburg as vice-secretary.

In this period van Doesburg already spent much of his time in Leiden, where Helena Milius had moved; however, since his demobilization in February 1916 and his split with Agnita Feis he had really lived in Haarlem with his mother and his sister Amalia. This shared accomodation did not make van Doesburg very happy, but it inspired his "Expressionistisch-literaire komposities."[18] In Haarlem he also seems to have founded an art association named Thans [Now], the activities of which are no longer known.

The second half of 1916 was a dismal time for van Doesburg. He could not paint much for lack of a studio, his plans for exhibitions and periodicals did not fare well, and his writings were only partly published. Under those circumstances, the association with Oud was a blessing; not only did it cause van Doesburg to become more interested in the problems of collaboration between architects and visual artists, it also resulted in commissions from Oud, which somewhat alleviated van Doesburg's financial needs.

The first commission was very modest. Van Doesburg was asked to design a small stained-glass window, containing the municipal coat of arms, for the house of the mayor of Broek in Waterland, which Oud was building. This window was to be placed in a door.[19] He told Kok about this in a letter dated August 4, 1916, adding laconically that he still had to master the technique. In the same letter he mentioned a visit to "my Hungarian friend, the painter Huszár," and it seems likely that he learned something from Huszár's experience in stained glass. The result (figure 72), which was ready around the end of the year, is—certainly in the border of the coat of arms—strongly reminiscent of Huszár's 1916 window *Zonnebloemen* [*Sunflowers*], and still more reminiscent of *Schilderij (geel),* shown in figure 66. The more or less symmetrical combination of circle fragments, rectangles, and angular planes in van Doesburg's window is in some places almost a copy of Huszár's painting. (The four small windows over the door are much more strictly subdivided and much more abstract, although a bird motif can be recognized. Those windows were, however, designed in April 1917, according to van Doesburg's correspondence with Kok.) Huszár's example, therefore, was important not only for van Doesburg's painting but also for his first works in stained glass.

An event that had important consequences for both Huszár and van Doesburg was their confrontation with van der Leck's most recent work. Van der Leck had written to van Doesburg in December 1916 and asked him to have a look at these works at the home of his patroness, Mrs. Kröller-Müller, in The Hague. Van Doesburg and Huszár went on a day between Christmas and New Year's Eve, and they were deeply impressed—most of all by the *Mijntriptiek* [*Mine triptych*], shown below as figure 148. On New Year's Eve, van Doesburg sent an enthusiastic letter to van der Leck announcing that he would write a book about his work. "The triptych in particular," he wrote, "struck me with its qualities of universal life, solved in harmony with the pure means of painting."[20]

In his paintings from the second half of 1916, van der Leck stripped a figurative representation until all he had left was separate blocks and stripes of color on a white or a black background. That Huszár adopted this technique almost immediately after the visit is apparent from his *Compositie II* (the so-called *Skaters*), shown below as figure 74. Van Doesburg had more difficulty in mastering such a radical abstraction, no matter how much he admired it. Until May of 1917 he continued to build solid compositions from round or pointed shapes, in a more or less cubist way. *De kaartspelers,* his most elaborate painting of this type, was created in the spring of 1917—quite some time after he first saw van der Leck's work. In this painting, the three sitting figures and the one standing figure have certainly been geometrized; however, they are intact, not spread out in separate blocks over the background as in van der Leck's work (and also in Huszár's most recent paintings).

Van Doesburg did allow himself one liberty in this period: He had no qualms about painting figures upside down. In the beginning of 1917 he made two small stained-glass windows (see *Dans I* in figure 10), probably without commission, in which he treated the same motif of female Indian dancers that he had used in November 1916 for a painted diptych. Both of the windows feature a dancer in "normal" position and an identical second figure rotated 180

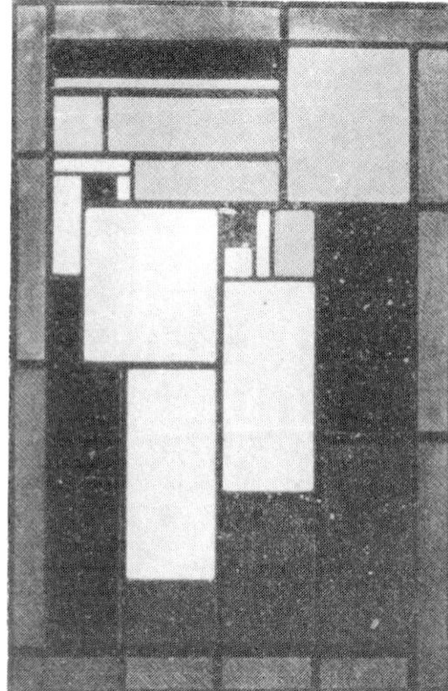

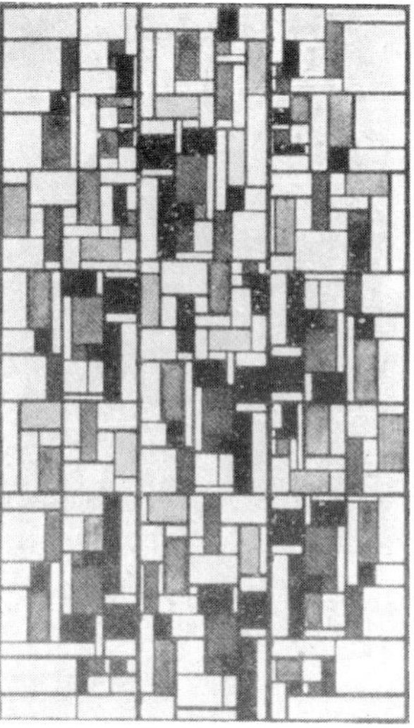

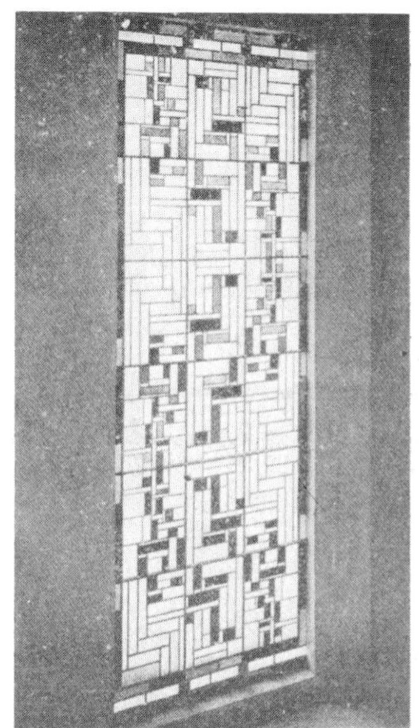

10 Van Doesburg, stained-glass windows, 1917. *Bouwkundig weekblad* 39, no. 35 (1918), pp. 201–202. Upper left: *Motief "Vrouwekop."* Upper right: *Compositie V,* 1918. Middle left: *Dans I.* Middle right: *Compositie II,* 1917. Lower right: *Compositie III,* 1917.

degrees. This treatment seems to subdue the value of the subject somewhat, but it has a particular formal importance. Van Doesburg later made frequent use of rotations, mirror images, and other methods of obtaining variations within a set pattern. The small windows with dancing figures, the first examples of this, were immediately followed by the windows with bird motifs over the door of the mayor's dwelling in Broek in Waterland (figure 72).

Compositions in stained glass with rectangular planes

The windows mentioned so far still show combinations of round and rectangular shapes, as do the paintings that can be dated with certainty to the spring of 1917, such as *De kaartspelers.* Van Doesburg's first work executed exclusively in rectangular planes dates from April and May of 1917. This is the time when van Doesburg had just moved from Haarlem to Leiden. He had found an adequate studio at no. 3 Korte Galgewater, and was living with Helena Milius, whom he married on May 31. On April 22 he wrote to Kok that the view from his studio was so magnificent that he could make the most beautiful compositions from his window. In this same letter he mentioned that he had not yet completed the rectangular motif that Kok had seen already; he was still enlarging it. It is not certain which work in progress van Doesburg was referring to (perhaps it was the window for Villa Allegonda, which will be discussed), but it is possible to date almost exactly another early work with a "rectangular motif": the small window *Vrouwekop* [*Woman's head*], shown in figure 10. On May 7, van Doesburg wrote jubilantly to Kok: "I have designed a portrait of Helena in stained glass! It completely beats the Middle Ages to pieces! I was still trembling for hours afterwards, and even now when I look at the sketch, tears well up in my eyes. It is the most beautiful thing that has ever been done in stained glass." Van Doesburg's enthusiasm is understandable in this respect: He had accomplished for the first time a well-balanced composition of horizontally and vertically oriented rectangular planes, a composition of the type that would become so characteristic of De Stijl. However, he still had adhered closely to the visual starting point that had inspired him; the line pattern gives an abstract impression, but it really is a stylized representation of a woman's head in profile. The eye, the ear, the mouth, and the hair are, with some effort, recognizable. The colors of the glass (white for the face, blue for the eye and the hair, green for the dress, black for the background) facilitate the identification of the subject still more. Van Doesburg wanted to give Kok the impression that he had created something marvelous and new, but one is certainly justified in questioning its originality somewhat when one compares it with *Meisje* [*Girl*] and *Familieraam* [*Family window*], two stained-glass windows designed by Huszár some months earlier (figures 68 and 69). Other windows made by van Doesburg during 1917 also manifest a certain dependence on his Hungarian friend. These show, better than his paintings, the swift changes in van Doesburg's work during this period.

The first window is another commission obtained through Oud.[21] Together with the painter Menso Kamerlingh Onnes, Oud had been working since the fall of 1916 on a drastic renovation of Villa Allegonda in Katwijk, and he succeeded in involving several visual artists in the work. Harm Kamerlingh Onnes, the young son of Menso, designed a ceramic nameplate, and van Doesburg designed a stained-glass window, known as *Compositie II* (figure 10). Van Doesburg was probably alluding to this window when he first spoke about a "rectangular motif" on April 22 in a letter to Kok. On May 9 he reported that the design was finished: "Finished the large window, 2.25 × 75. I had stretched it on the wall in black and white in three parts above each other; only white planes (I had not yet put in the colors), separated by black lines. When I surveyed the whole, I (and Lena too) got an indescribably beautiful impression. . . . Monday I put in the colors, but felt that the sacredness of the black and white drawing had got lost." This passage is interesting not only because it shows what van Doesburg had also repeatedly said in his articles, namely that he attributed a special spiritual value to compositions in black and white, but also because it clarifies the process of his designing. Apparently, while drawing he plodded along until he obtained a satisfactory composition; only then did he put in separate color planes.

Though *Vrouwekop* has a recognizable motif, it is harder to recognize one in *Compositie II,* which was created at almost the same time. The window does contain many repetitions in its eighteen compartments; actually there are only three different compartments, which are grouped differently every time. The upper third of the window is identical with the bottom third, while the middle part is a mirror image of the other two. Moreover, there is a rotation within the parts. But what exactly is mirrored and what is rotated is not clear at first sight.

In the summer of 1918, Oud wrote an article about van Doesburg's work in stained glass in which he says about the Allegonda window that "the motif has been decomposed and transformed and also assimilated into the space, the white light, in such a way that the aesthetic idea on which the work is grounded, the 'rhythmical rising of the surf' is represented only by relationship. . . ."[22] One might get the impression from this that van Doesburg had taken the surf as his visual starting point—something that would be quite appropriate for a villa at the seashore, although an unusual choice of subject for him. However, Oud makes a distinction between the motif, which he does not mention any further, and the aesthetic idea. The motif, therefore, does not have anything to do with the sea or the surf; indeed, on closer observation it appears to be a sitting figure in profile, a motif which van Doesburg had been using more frequently as a basis for his compositions and of which several drawings (e.g., figure 12) are extant.

There is a comparable abstraction in a subsequent window, *Compositie III* (figure 10), which was made in five identical copies for a teacher's dwelling next to a school in St. Antoniuspolder. (The school and the house were designed by Jan Wils.) Oud says in the aforementioned article that these windows represent the fundamental visual idea of figure skating, and that one can discern a concentric and an eccentric movement in them. "Figure skating" is meant literally; van Doesburg used the motif of a small skating figure. Rotated in all possible directions, it appears four times turned to the inside and four times turned to the outside. Thematically this is a case of a direct derivation from Huszár, who had represented skaters in the aforementioned painting.

Recognizing motifs in almost abstract images seems an insipid game, yet it makes sense to seek the artist's starting point. This gives insight into his manner of abstraction and into his views about it. The artists who were to figure in De Stijl appear to have differed substantially in this respect.

Van Doesburg's manner of abstraction, at first, was closely related to that of Huszár and to that of their exemplar, van der Leck. In *Compositie III* the feet, legs, thighs, torsos, arms, and heads of the skaters are represented by small rectangular color planes in different positions and of different sizes, separated by white glass. The sizes of these color planes conform to human proportions. Connecting the planes by a loose contour once more produces a drawing of a skater. In point of fact this is also true of van der Leck. The studies for his paintings of this period show that he started with a flat representation of a figure, a silhouette, parts of which he then covered with white paint; what was left in the finished work was a conglomeration of small color planes on a white ground.

With Mondrian the situation was quite different. Through his long schooling in French cubism he had acquired a way of abstraction in which the object and the surrounding space were completely integrated. In this respect it is notable that, insofar as the motifs of his post-1914 paintings are identifiable, he had a certain

11

12

11 Van Doesburg, *Compositie II*, 1917 (detail). *Bouwkundig weekblad* 39, no. 35 (1918), p. 201. Dimensions and whereabouts unknown.

12 Van Doesburg, *Zittend naakt* [*Seated nude*], 1917. Van Doesburg, *Grundbegriffe der neuen gestaltenden kunst* (Munich, 1925). Dimensions and whereabouts unknown.

preference for the shapelessness, the diffuseness, that was inherent in the sea or the starry sky.

Van Doesburg, Huszár, and van der Leck had a simple, clear method of abstraction, and, with all their higher pretensions, they clearly had a need for concrete subjects: humans, animals, objects. Still, there were certain differences among the three. For instance, van Doesburg and Huszár often chose motifs involving a lot of motion, such as skaters and dancers; these do not occur in such a pronounced way in van der Leck's work. Van Doesburg, however, distinguished himself from the others mainly through preference for motifs to which he had personal ties; for example, the view from the window of his Leiden studio, or its interior with or without a figure (usually Helena Milius). He even made portraits of Helena Milius, and self-portraits, into abstract compositions. His estate contains four studies for a double portrait (probably not executed), on which he must have been working around the time of their marriage in May 1917. (See figure 13.) This striking need to represent his own world, however disguised, appears to be a remnant from the period when the expression of personal feelings had been central to his work; that period was not yet far behind him.

Thus, van Doesburg followed Huszár and van der Leck only partially in his choice of subjects. His manner of abstraction did strongly resemble theirs, however, at least in his work from the first half of 1917; afterwards, this changed. In an interesting letter to Kok, dated July 14, 1917, van Doesburg expresses dissatisfaction with his method: "There is still in my work a considerable shortcoming, which I fortunately realize myself. Once I have found a motif, I keep it too much together in the elaboration. In music, particularly by Bach, the motif is constantly elaborated upon in different ways. I would like to achieve that also, now with a new Dance Motif. I feel the dance to be the most dynamic expression of life and therefore the most important subject for pure visual art." It is not certain exactly which work in progress van Doesburg is talking about here—there are many works with dance motifs. More important is his comparison with music.[23] A musical motif is of course not the same as a visual motif, such as a dancing figure; the quote is a bit confusing in this respect. It is clear, however, that he took Bach as his example because Bach manipulated his musical motifs in all sorts of ways. In an analogous manner, van Doesburg began to apply the principles of repetition, mirror image, and rotation to his visual motifs. He had already done this to an extent in the windows with dancing figures, in *Compositie II,* and in *Compositie III,* but there he had still left the figures intact. In May 1917 he got a commission from Jan Wils for a series of three windows in the stairwell of the de Lange villa in Alkmaar, and in this design (*Compositie IV,* figure 14) he proceeded differently than in the past. He did not start abstracting from a nature study; he took two of the three compartments from *Compositie II,* changed the square format somewhat, multiplied them, and varied them by the aforementioned principles of mirror image and rotation. The original motif, the sitting figure, became completely dispersed.

Still more complicated is van Doesburg's next window, *Compositie V* (figure 10). This he divided vertically into three elongated rectangles, each of which he subdivided into several smaller compartments which are repeated elsewhere in the window in various ways (sometimes as a mirror image, at other times rotated or in different proportions). No definite system is evident, and yet the whole thing gives an impression of having been very carefully arranged. In this window van Doesburg came quite a bit closer to his Bach-like ideal. Little is known about the origination of *Compositie V.* The extant sketch is dated 1918, but this date is absent on early photographs; it must have been added later. To me it seems probable that van Doesburg designed the window in 1917, shortly after *Compositie IV.*[24]

The works reviewed here show that van Doesburg achieved a high level of abstraction in a period of only a few months. One could say that he caught up with Huszár, van der Leck, and Mondrian in the summer of 1917. Although he adopted many elements from them, he also developed qualities of his own, particularly in the implementation of the already often-mentioned principles of arranging, i.e., repetition, mirror image, and rotation.

It is striking that this swift development came about almost entirely in the production of stained-glass windows. In the first half of 1917 this activity was van Doesburg's first priority. He barely got around to painting, as is apparent from his correspondence. After *De kaartspelers* was completed, in the spring, no new paintings (at any rate, none in a definitive form) followed until early autumn. Financial considerations may have played a role in this; the windows were mostly made on commission. However, there could also have been artistic reasons for this apparent preference for windows. In stained glass, pronounced, rigid lines and bright colors are basic; the technique itself forces the artist, as it were, to a certain abstraction. It is possible to go into details and shade the colors by painting and burning the glass, but van Doesburg had consciously refrained from that since his very first commission. His insight into the special visual possibilities of the technique is also apparent in the way he used the heavy supporting irons which are necessary for the construction of a window. Even in his first larger window, *Compositie II* for the Villa Allegonda, the support irons

13

13 Van Doesburg, *Omhelzing* [*Embrace*], 1917. Ink on paper, 19 × 12.2 cm. Rijksdienst Beeldende Kunst, The Hague.

14 Van Doesburg, *Compositie IV*, 1917. Stained glass, 286.5 × 56.6 cm (each of three). Rijksdienst Beeldende Kunst, The Hague. (Color plate on page xiii.)

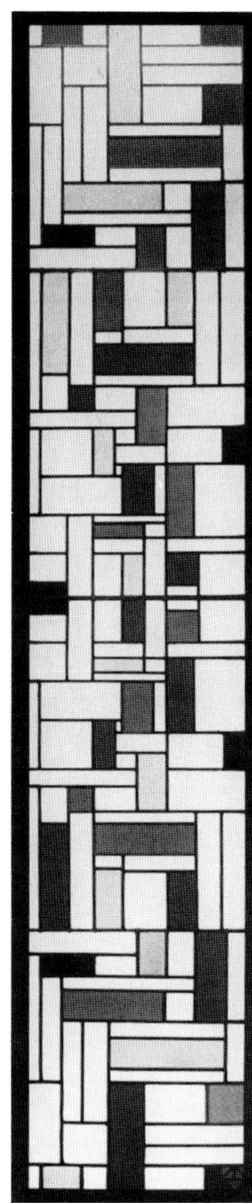

14

have a clear function as axes for mirroring the motif. In the more complex window *Compositie V* he (as Oud rightly wrote) "made them completely into an integral part of his image, a part that also has an aesthetic function and works together with the rhythm of the image."[25]

These stained-glass windows were van Doesburg's first contribution to Neo-Plasticism, the art form that he, together with a group of kindred spirits, would soon promote in *De stijl.*

The founding of *De stijl*

The first half of 1917 was important for van Doesburg not only because it was a time of rapid and energetic development in his visual work. On an organizational level, too, he unfolded initiatives that would have far-reaching results. He had quickly abandoned the organizations he had helped to found during the previous year. He had already detached himself from De Anderen at the end of 1916. He still took part in some of the Sphinx Club's cultural evenings, reading poetry by himself, Kok, and Feis, and he exhibited some paintings in the club's first exhibition in January 1917, but a few months later he quit. This club was probably too motley and too parochial for his taste. Instead of taking part in the activities of such societies, he plunged with renewed energy into the founding of a periodical of his own.

By May 19, 1917, van Doesburg could report to Antony Kok that the preparations had reached a critical stage. Mondrian and van der Leck, "the most important forces," were willing to contribute, and van Doesburg had reached an agreement with the publisher C. Harms Tiepen in Delft. The periodical would be named *De stijl* and would be printed in an edition of 1,000 copies. It was to get a square format (this did not actually happen), and it was to be illustrated with woodcuts, autotypes, and blocks. For the time being, there was one restriction: "It is meant only for visual and applied arts. If it fares well I will extend it enormously: music, literature, etc."

Two months later van Doesburg could correspond on *De stijl* stationery, and in August several announcements of the new periodical appeared in the press, with an impressive list of contributors. In view of the development of van Doesburg's theory and his art, it is understandable that he was much more selective in the choice of his collaborators than he had been in his organizational activities. Of the people with whom he had made plans some years before, only his old friends Kok and Wichman were left. Next to those were the names of H. P. Berlage, Jan Toorop, Mondrian, van der Leck, Archipenko, Picasso, Gino Severini, Huszár, Oud, Frits van Hengelaar, Dop Bles, and Wils. Mondrian's influence on the choice of the Parisians and of van Hengelaar and Bles, who belonged to his circle of acquaintances, is unmistakable. It seems that Toorop and Berlage were brought in mainly because of their prestige in the Netherlands. Their actual contributions did not amount to anything at all, and such was also the case with several of the other artists mentioned. As the list indicates, *De stijl* was to be filled primarily with the work of visual artists and architects. Some of them, such as van Doesburg and Oud, had a great deal of experience in publishing; others, such as Huszár and Mondrian, had never published anything.

In the editorial preface to the first issue, which appeared in October 1917, van Doesburg wrote that in this time the artist should engage in educating the public, partly because the art critics had failed to do so: "The truly modern—i.e., conscious—artist has a double vocation. First: to create pure visual art; second: to make the public receptive to the beauty of this pure visual art." It is of course questionable whether this goal was reached. Certainly *De stijl,* because of its fundamental orientation, elicited many reactions. Immediately after the appearance of the first issue van Doesburg wrote to Kok that Berlage and others had disengaged themselves. Berlage may have been hurt by van der Leck's article "The place of modern painting in architecture," in which architects were exhorted to rigorous self-restriction and the application of color to architecture was claimed to be the province of painters. After the second issue, Mondrian reported in a letter of December 12 to van Doesburg: "I perceive (van der Leck has also already noticed it in some people) that they are withdrawing a little from me now that I state matters bluntly. They went along with me to some extent, but now that they read what it is all about, now they don't want to have anything to do with it. This rather pleases me, because half-heartedness does not amount to anything anyway."

Visual art and architecture

One important subject that was raised in *De stijl* from the beginning was the relation between visual art and architecture. This is no wonder; nearly as many architects as visual artists contributed to the periodical. Although the impression was given to the outside world that the contributors agreed on this point, there were nevertheless rather profound differences of opinion between those in Laren (Mondrian, van der Leck) and those in Leiden/Voorburg (van Doesburg, Huszár, Oud, Wils).

In the first two issues of *De stijl,* van der Leck wrote two articles wherein he defined the relation between painting and architecture in very fundamental terms: Architecture was constructive and "plastic-natural," while modern painting aimed to destroy the plastic-natural. If painting were to be correctly applied to a building, the solid mass and the material character of the building would, visually, be destroyed. Van der Leck, who had already had some experience in collaborating with architects (particularly with Berlage), was rather skeptical about their willingness to let the painters play such a destructive part. Mondrian shared this skepticism. They did see possibilities for the collaboration of visual art and architecture in the future, but first architecture should jolly well undergo a purification similar to that which painting (*their* painting) had experienced. Van Doesburg and Huszár, on the other hand, seized every opportunity to collaborate with architects.

Van Doesburg's artistic contributions to the mayor's residence in Broek in Waterland and to the Villa Allegonda in Katwijk had been modest; the stained-glass windows were isolated works and thus rather traditional examples of the integration of visual art in architecture. However, van Doesburg had farther-reaching ideas. As he had repeatedly expressed in articles, he dreamed of a "monumental-collaborative art . . . wherein the different spiritual means of expression (architecture, sculpture, painting, music, and the Word) in harmony—that is, each individual one gaining by collaboration with another one—shall come to the realization of unity."[26] Through the collaboration between artists of different disciplines a living environment could be created that, through the various senses, would work beneficially on the minds of those who found themselves in it.

In the course of 1917, various opportunities for the realization of some part of that high ideal presented themselves to van Doesburg. The first involved a collaboration with Jan Wils. Van Doesburg had been commissioned to design three stained-glass windows for a villa by Wils in Alkmaar (the aforementioned *Compositie IV*). He had started work on them in May, and in the beginning of September the windows were already in place. So far this was a fairly traditional commission, although the work was certainly not traditional in appearance. On September 9 van Doesburg described in a letter to Kok his color scheme for the complete interior, and even the exterior, of the house. The commission had thus become much more extensive. Van Doesburg spoke of "das kolorierte Haus," a term he probably knew from *Der sturm* or some other German source.[27] The following passages indicate clearly how he visualized this colored architecture and what he planned to do: "To give you an idea of my viewpoint I tell you that I have started from the notion that all planes should be freed by means of a contrasting light color. For instance the door panels a deep blue, freed by means of white. This causes a sparkling of colors. . . ." He names the color schemes he has designed for the various rooms: "The study is the most magnificent: the bookcase green, black, and white. The wall covering is billiard cloth! Everything freed by means of white. The mantelpiece of green stone with red tiles on the sides. In the middle a glass mosaic designed by me.[28] The doors: black panels freed by means of white." He claims to have considered the "need" of those who use each room: ". . . thus for instance a girl's room: bright yellow, purple, and green. A guest room for children: yellow and blue. . . . The attic and adjoining servants' quarters white and blue. The kitchen ditto white and blue. The attic corridor and staircase yellow, black, and white. I have solved the cellars, including the wine racks and the fruit containers. . . ." In the letter he also says that he wonders whether everything will be executed as he has indicated. This seems to have been done—perhaps not in all the far corners of the house, but certainly in the most important rooms. A photograph of the hall (figure 15) gives an impression of the way in which the colors have been applied. The description sounds more exciting than what the photograph shows. The colors have been faithfully fitted into the architectural details of doors, paneling, cornices, and moldings. The "freeing by means of white" that is mentioned time and again only means that, for instance, a colored door is separated from the surrounding wall by a white edge.

The house in Alkmaar certainly must have made a colorful, even gaudy impression, but van Doesburg still was rather submissive to the architecture. He was already less so in a second collaborative project begun in 1917: the vacation home De Vonk [The Spark] in Noordwijk.[29] It is likely that here, just as with Wils's villa in Alkmaar, van Doesburg was first offered a small commission, and his share was extended later on. First he made three compositions for the glazed-brick work of the facade (figure 117). In the beginning of 1918 he designed tile floors for the hallway and for the corridor on the second floor, and finally he also designated the colors of the woodwork, including the fence and the shutters (figure 115).

There was a great to-do about the execution of the work at De Vonk, as is apparent from the correspondence between van Doesburg and Oud, and this continued into 1919. There were constant clashes about questions of domain, because the commission for the stained-glass windows in the stairwell and for the color schemes of the rooms had been given to another artist (Harm Kamerlingh Onnes). Van Doesburg complained repeatedly about the strange transitions the interior showed in places where his work was affected by that of Kamerlingh Onnes. He was particularly unhappy about the bad lighting in the hall, where he felt that the dark stained-glass windows completely destroyed the radiant effect of his tile floor.

15

16

The floor of De Vonk was apparently van Doesburg's great pride, and justly so. Many buildings from this period have tile floors with beautiful, regular patterns of blocks and borders in bright contrasting colors, but van Doesburg's creation for De Vonk has special qualities. Using commercially available white, yellow, and black square tiles, he designed a pattern that seems chaotic at first sight. Edges are repeatedly interrupted; tiles of a certain color appear sometimes singly and at other times grouped into bars or angular shapes, which are dispersed over the available space in such a manner that no one color is predominant anywhere. Gradually one recognizes in this puzzle of interlocking pieces the arranging hand of the artist. Van Doesburg has, just as in the stained-glass window *Compositie V,* ingeniously combined different principles of repetition. Some parts have simply been repeated, others mirrored or rotated. Because these portions have not been clearly partitioned but have been fitted into a continuing pattern, it is rather difficult to discern them in the drawing (figure 16); if one stands on the floor, one recognizes the arrangement in some places (for instance in the vestibule) but in other places not at all. Van Doesburg seems to have aimed to give the spectator an experience that would change as he moved through the building. In an explanatory article that appeared in *De stijl* in November 1918 he wrote: "One can say that the floor is the most enclosed surface in the house and it therefore requires from an aesthetic viewpoint an, as it were, gravity-defying effect by flat color and open space relationships. This has been consistently carried through here from the entrance through the entire lower and upper hall and corridors. . . . The development and elaboration of this entire composition—constructive-destructive—can only be seen . . . on the spot itself. . . ." A short while later he would emphasize the dynamic factor much more heavily in his considerations.

Studies and paintings, 1917–1920

In 1917, van Doesburg's windows and interiors were more confident and more constant in quality than his paintings. Apparently he found in the technical restraints and possibilities of working with stained glass and glazed tiles something he did not find in painting. Working on paper and canvas required immediate decisions about all kinds of problems. Nothing was certain; everything could be tried.

There is in van Doesburg's estate a study of a woman in an interior, executed in gouache (*Lena in interieur,* figure 17). The representation is a bit stylized, for example in the still life on the table and particularly in the woman's head, in which details such as the eyes and the mouth have been omitted. Space is suggested in a fairly traditional manner by light and shadow. Because of these characteristics one would be inclined to date this work before *Dansfiguren* (late 1916), which is constructed from flat, geometric forms, and *De kaartspelers* (spring of 1917). However, other clues lead to the conclusion that it was created after April 1917, when van Doesburg found dwelling and studio space in Leiden: Photographs show that the mantelpiece behind the sitting female figure corresponds to the one in the Leiden studio.[30]

Lena in interieur can be related to the ink drawing (figure 18) that was presented at a 1979 exhibition as "*Man at coffee table*, 1916."[31] That title and that date cannot be correct, since what I have said about the gouache also applies to this drawing: It represents a woman in an interior, and it must be dated after April 1917. The only formal relation between the two works is the occurrence of diagonal lines, which are very modest in the gouache but very pronounced in the drawing. Otherwise there is a vast difference. In the drawing, the figure and its surroundings are broken up into a large number of pointed shapes, with a gradual transition from light to dark as if they protruded from the white background of the paper. We are still reminded somewhat of van Doesburg's 1916 still lifes and of French or Italian examples (perhaps by Severini or Juan Gris). The drawing is out of keeping with the work that is usually dated 1917, but other extant studies from that year show the same cubo-futurist characteristics.

Starting from the motif "woman in interior," van Doesburg created in a sketchlike design a third work (figure 19) which is again completely different from the other two. It is almost entirely composed of rectangular planes (an oblique truncation occurs in only two places) filled in with primary colors and white, gray, and black, separated from each other by heavy, dark lines.[32] This study is closely related to van Doesburg's stained-glass windows of 1917, for which it may have been a design.

On stylistic grounds one would be inclined to date these three works far apart. Of course it would be difficult to prove that van Doesburg made them in quick succession; however, the fact that they must have originated after April 1917 does indicate that he continued to use his old and new methods side by side without qualms, at least in the design phase. In his sketches and studies he tried everything. This manner of design by no means always resulted in a definitive opus. Apparently it did not in the case of this "woman in interior" motif. However, it did in a number of other cases. Of *Compositie XIII* from 1918 (a still life motif) and *Compositie in dissonanten* from 1918 (another motif of a woman in an interior), the final phase as well as a number of preparatory phases are extant or are known from photographs which van Doesburg

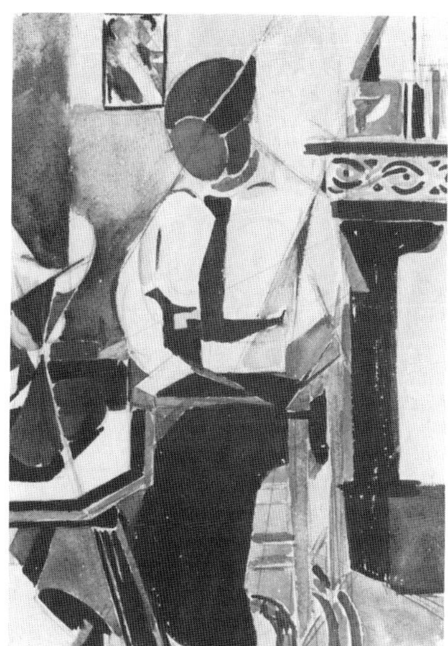

17

18

15 Van Doesburg, ground-floor hall and banister of villa by Wils, Alkmaar, 1917. J. Leliman, *Het stadswoonhuis in Nederland* (The Hague, 1924), p. 82.

16 Van Doesburg, design for tile floor of De Vonk, 1918. Gouache on paper, 98 × 74 cm. Rijksdienst Beeldende Kunst, The Hague.

17 Van Doesburg, *Lena in interieur*, 1917. Pencil and gouache on paper, 27 × 19.4 cm. Rijksdienst Beeldende Kunst, The Hague.

18 Van Doesburg, *Lena in interieur*, 1917. Ink on paper, 33.5 × 22 cm. Private collection.

19

himself published and explained in 1919 in an attempt to make the public understand how his incomprehensible block paintings came into being. When one looks at the preliminary phases of *Compositie in dissonanten* (figure 20), the development is clear enough but the progress is not as smooth as van Doesburg wants to make one believe. In particular, phase 3, with its radiating oblique lines, contains elements that seem to point in different directions than those of the final painting. One can still discern in this series, although perhaps to a lesser degree, the same penchant for experimentation that is evident in the three 1917 studies discussed above.

If one takes into account only the finished paintings (the consecutively numbered compositions and a few paintings with individual titles) and leaves the many sketches out of consideration, the development of van Doesburg's free works still seems very capricious. It can be said of Mondrian, Huszár, and Vantongerloo, and to a lesser extent of van der Leck, that they were working in rather experimental ways during the years 1917–1920. Van Doesburg, however, definitely carries off the palm. It seems as if he wanted to tackle a new problem with every painting, or to focus on an old problem in a new way. There are plenty of indications that he was highly sensitive to impulses of different kinds and origins. It is clear in a number of cases that his experiences in monumental art, particularly stained glass, enriched his free painting. Much more frequently, however, he seems to have been reacting to extraneous impulses. As in the years before De Stijl, he flew quickly into enthusiasms for whatever came up in the work of kindred artists and then just as quickly directed his attention to something else. He did not copy slavishly. He often proposed a much more radical solution to a certain problem. He was definitely original in the elaboration, but it was often based on what others had passed on to him.

After creating mostly stained-glass windows in the first half of 1917, van Doesburg devoted more time to painting in the second half of the year. Two paintings with separate blocks and bars in primary colors and white on a black ground, *Compositie VI* and *Compositie VII,* were probably done in late spring or early summer. In these paintings he followed from a distance the example of van der Leck's work (particularly the *Mijntriptiek,* in which black had been used for the ground in the side panels) and Huszár's (e.g., *Compositie II,* or "The skaters"). Van Doesburg's more robust paintings, however, give a more abstract impression, even though they have figurative starting points (in *Compositie VI* a digging man, in *Compositie VII* the three graces).[34]

20

19 Van Doesburg, *Lena in interieur*, 1917. Gouache on paper, 30 × 20 cm. Rijksdienst Beeldende Kunst, The Hague.

20 Lower right: Van Doesburg, *Compositie in dissonanten*, 1919. Oil on canvas, 63.5 × 58.5 cm. Oeffentliche Kunstsammlung, Basel. The other five panels show studies, the dimensions and whereabouts of which are unknown. Published in *De Hollandsche revue* 24, no. 8 (1919), pp. 470–476.

21

The painting *Compositie IX* (figure 21), also known under the title *Abstracte doorbeelding van de kaartspelers* [*Abstract decomposition of the card players*], has a very different character. Yet it must have originated shortly after the aforementioned compositions. On September 9, 1917, van Doesburg wrote to Kok that he had started on a new solution of his card players. "That should become enormously strong and exciting," he wrote. "When you come here you can see the already complete sketch." In December he reported to his friend that the painting was finished. In the final result we cannot recognize much more of the motif than the hands of the card-playing figures, indicated by groupings of small white bars in the center of the composition.

While the paintings with black grounds contain simple compositions of separate color blocks, the relation between the shapes themselves and between figure and ground in *Compositie IX* is very complex. In most places the planes have been put next to each other; in some places they overlap. A large part of the composition seems to have a black ground, but in the upper right part black planes are put on a white ground. This painting was van Doesburg's contribution to the debate about the figure-ground problem which several of the De Stijl artists were carrying on in 1917–18 (not only verbally and in writing, but also by means of the brush). The question was how the flatness of a painting could be maintained, notwithstanding the fact that to the eye colors and lines tend to interact spatially.

This problem had become acute in 1916, when Mondrian, like van der Leck, had started to put color planes and short line segments against a plain white ground. In May 1917, Mondrian exhibited in Amsterdam two small paintings, *Compositie in kleur* [*Composition in color*] *A* and *Compositie in kleur B,* in which he had partially superimposed small ochre, pink, and blue planes, with now one and now another color on top. Huszár probably painted his *Hamer en zaag* (figure 82) and *Stad* (figure 83) after seeing these paintings of Mondrian's; Huszár's works, however, show a much more rigorously carried through intertwining of figures and ground—the hierarchic relations that usually occur within a painting were, for the most part, absent.

Van Doesburg's large and ambitious painting of the card players is mainly oriented toward Huszár's example, but there are important differences. Huszár used only rectangles, and several colors; van Doesburg used only white, black, gray, and, in a few places, blue, but he included many complex forms. This *Compositie* creates a rather chaotic impression; it is nearly impossible for the viewer to get a grip on it.

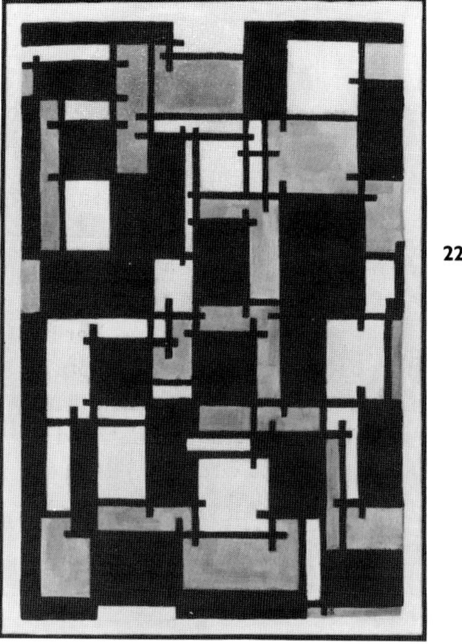

22

21 **Van Doesburg, *Compositie IX,* 1917. Oil on canvas, 116 × 106 cm. Gemeentemuseum, The Hague.**

22 **Van Doesburg, *Compositie X,* 1918. Oil on canvas, 64 × 43 cm. Private collection.**

Van Doesburg approached the figure-ground problem from another angle in a subsequent painting, *Compositie X* (figure 22), which was begun in early 1918. In this painting there is really no longer a question of a ground; white, black, and gray planes are more or less evenly distributed, without a dominant "color," within a pattern of rigid black lines. It is a miracle of clarity when compared with *Compositie IX.*

Compositie XI (figure 23) must also date from the first half of 1918. When van Doesburg showed it in September–October 1918 at an exhibition of De Branding [The Surf] in The Hague, together with *De kaartspelers* and *Compositie IX,* he called it in a letter to Kok "my last red-blue-yellow composition."[35] *Compositie XI* is again very different from the earlier paintings. Red, yellow, and blue rectangles appear on a solid white ground without any linear border or mutual connection. Van der Leck had been painting similar distributions of the primary-colored planes on a white ground since the end of 1916. Huszár and Mondrian followed suit for a short time in 1917, but neither of them found this a satisfactory way to achieve the desired equalization of figure and ground. Not only was van Doesburg's presentation of the same solution in 1918 late; it also appears to have been a step back.

The great differences between paintings made in a period of only about half a year can be seen as a sign that van Doesburg did not know exactly what he wanted. However, it is also possible to offer a more positive conclusion: Apparently van Doesburg had a less puristic, more adventurous attitude than his painter colleagues in De Stijl. Perhaps he was, in the end, not as interested as they in achieving absolute flatness in a painting, or in obtaining a perfect equilibrium between the pictorial elements, or whichever other high ideal was being promoted in the magazine. He did profess these ideals in his theoretical texts, but between the lines one can discern time and again small digressions from the norm. The same can be said of his paintings. It seems as if, while copying from others, he was delivering a rather pesky commentary. There is an anarchist undercurrent in van Doesburg's ways, maybe not quite conscious in the beginning but becoming more conscious and stronger through the years. This strain can be seen in some paintings he did a while after *Composities IX, X,* and *XI.*

In the spring of 1919 van Doesburg finished *Compositie in grijs* [*Composition in gray*], a painting that had originally been named *Ragtime.*[36] Guided by this title and by an extant study, one can recognize, with some difficulty, a dancing couple. The line pattern in this painting relates to the paintings with irregular grids done by Mondrian in the beginning of 1918 (e.g., figure 48), but there are obvious differences. Some lines do not continue to the edge of the

23

23 Van Doesburg, *Compositie XI,* 1918. Oil on canvas, 56.5 × 101.5 cm. Solomon R. Guggenheim Museum, New York.

24 Van Doesburg, *Compositie in grijs* [*Composition in gray*], 1919. Oil on canvas, 95 × 58.5 cm. Peggy Guggenheim Foundation, Venice.

24

painting. Still more striking, the planes are not filled in evenly, as Mondrian's are; they show for the most part a shading from light to dark gray, as if they were gleaming metal plates placed in a slanting or convex position and catching the light capriciously. A similar suggestion is often evoked in the work of Léger, a painter the De Stijl artists admired. The result is that the painting does not in the least make a flat impression; rather, it creates a certain spatial illusion.

In the summer of 1920 van Doesburg finished *Peinture pure,* also known as *Décomposition* (figure 25). This painting still shows some shading from gray to white in the lower left corner, but the rest of it is divided into even, touching planes in red, yellow, blue, white, gray, black, green, and purple. Like Huszár, van Doesburg sometimes used other than primary colors. Also like Huszár, he sometimes left out the grid of lines separating the colors, so that there was strong interaction between color planes. This effect differs from that achieved in Mondrian's paintings of the time, where the lines isolate the color planes and chain them to the flat surface.

The three paintings that make up *Compositie XVIII* (figure 26) were created shortly before *Peinture pure.* A letter to Evert Rinsema reveals that van Doesburg started to work on this composition in April 1920—immediately after returning from Paris, where he had seen Mondrian's most recent work.[37] The choice of colors (white, gray, black, blue, and orange) and the absence of lines between the planes are typical liberties à la van Doesburg, but it is unusual that the composition is made up of three separate canvases. According to the drawing shown here as figure 27, the center of the composition is situated in open space between the three canvases. Van Doesburg appears to have informed Mondrian of this discovery, for the latter criticizes it in a letter of June 12: "Remember that . . . the center should not be moved, but elimiated, removed. . . . When you only put the center outside the canvas, it still remains one canvas: your canvas then becomes only a piece of a larger canvas, doesn't it?" Mondrian's objection was that the paintings were in this way reduced to arbitrary fragments of an imaginary larger unity. He also could not agree with van Doesburg's starting point, the idea of a composition having a center, even if that center were situated outside the image. According to Mondrian, Neo-Plasticism had radically broken with the traditional viewpoint that every painting should have a center (or vanishing point). In any case, Mondrian himself was intent on eliminating this. The discussion had no consequences, perhaps because van Doesburg gave up this approach after only a few experiments.[38] As was so often the case, he did not explore its possibilities much further.

25

26

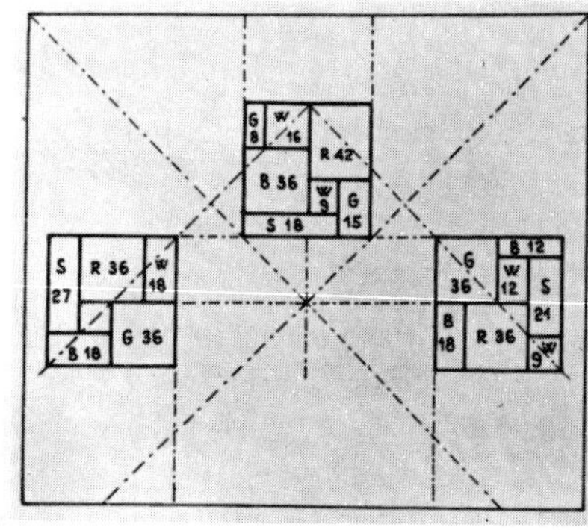

27

25 Van Doesburg, *Peinture pure,* 1920. Oil on canvas, 130 × 80.5 cm. Musée National d'Art Moderne, Centre Pompidou, Paris.

26 Van Doesburg, *Compositie XVIII,* 1920. Oil on canvas, 35 × 35 cm (each of three). Rijksdienst Beeldende Kunst, The Hague.

27 Van Doesburg, schema for *Compositie XVIII,* 1920. Published in S. Polano, *Theo van Doesburg, Scritti di arte e di architettura* (Rome, 1979). Dimensions and whereabouts unknown.

The examples mentioned above demonstrate that in 1919 and 1920 van Doesburg rather willfully took a stand different from Mondrian's. During this time their interests and viewpoints grew gradually apart. Van Doesburg seems to have realized this better than Mondrian, who had a nearly unbounded trust in their collaboration and who dismissed anything that hinted at a difference of opinion as an unimportant detail. ("The two of us must constitute the entire movement, that I clearly see," wrote Mondrian in his letter of June 12, 1920.) Van Doesburg did not intend to push their differences to the extreme, but privately he questioned unanimity, and in his work he followed an increasingly independent direction. In his paintings this can be discerned from the way in which he tested the formal means provided by Mondrian for their suitability for other applications—for example, by breaking through the flatness of the painting (*Compositie in grijs*) or the harmony of primary colors (*Compositie in dissonanten* and *Peinture pure*), and by putting the equilibrium between the compositional elements under pressure (*Compositie XVIII*).

The incipient contrast between Mondrian's static view of the world and van Doesburg's dynamic one would get stronger in the following years, culminating in a split between the two men. Mondrian's starting point was the eternal, the unvarying. In his heart there was no room for a confusing multitude of fleeting phenomena; he wanted to depict a timeless metaphysical ideal of peace and harmony. Van Doesburg, on the other hand, became more and more convinced that art should express a dynamic concept of reality. He found support for this viewpoint in the new scientific theories about space and time. These ideas could be expressed only to a small extent in his paintings, and that could be one reason why he stopped painting in 1921.

Before taking up his brushes again in late 1923, van Doesburg spent his time and energy on literary subjects and philosophical essays, which he wrote under the pen names I. K. Bonset and Aldo Camini, and on projects in collaboration with architects. In these fields he was able to shape his dynamic concept of reality.

The dynamic principle

As difficult as it is to trace the development of van Doesburg's thinking in general, it is even harder to trace his thinking about time and space, in which science and mysticism were almost inextricably entwined. The notion of a fourth dimension is a key concept here.[39]

Theories about the existence of other dimensions in addition to the three that are treated in Euclidean mathematics were very popular at the turn of the century, particularly in occult circles. It was widely held that our sensorially perceptible, three-dimensional world was only a projection of a world in four dimensions, which was in turn only a projection of a world in five dimensions, and so on. Van Doesburg must have been acquainted with this way of thinking; since 1912 he had been contributing to the magazine *Eenheid,* which often lent its columns to such speculations.

Van Doesburg saw quite early how the idea of the fourth dimension was linked with the visual arts. Probably as early as 1913 he read *Les peintres cubistes* by Apollinaire,[40] who remarked rather casually and superficially that the cubists worked from an intuitive sense of a fourth dimension, which was defined as "space itself, the dimension of infinity." Van Doesburg did not adopt this prosaic viewpoint, which is not surprising in the light of the spiritual nature of his ideas at that time. Some years later, however, we can discern in him a rapidly increasing interest in the fourth dimension. This interest may have been stimulated by his mingling with artists of the Rotterdam group De Branding; in 1916 Johan Tielens, whom van Doesburg knew well from De Anderen, described the concept extensively and elatedly in the periodical *Holland express.*[41] The subject was brought up within De Stijl by Gino Severini, who acted as a kind of intermediary in passing on views prevalent in the Parisian avant-garde. In the February 1918 issue of *De stijl* Severini devoted considerable attention to the fourth dimension, and in the next month's issue he continued the topic, quoting the French mathematician Henri Poincaré. Severini was trying to establish a scientific basis for the works of the cubists and the futurists, an absolute and exact representation of time and space with more or less geometric forms.[42]

Van Doesburg, who probably had Severini's texts in his home in late 1917, found in them a point of contact with what De Stijl advocated. The vagueness of the notion of the fourth dimension promoted by Tielens and company got at least a semblance of exactitude from Severini, with which Van Doesburg could better identify at that moment. In December 1917 he wrote about this for the first time to Mondrian. Mondrian knew of the fourth dimension in the occult sense, as a kind of clairvoyance, but could find no use for it in the creation of concrete art works; therefore, he was not very useful to van Doesburg as a partner in conversation about such things.

On the other hand, Georges Vantongerloo, whom van Doesburg probably met in the winter of 1917–18, shared (or adopted) van Doesburg's recently acquired interest in the link between art and science. It is perhaps better to put the word *science* between quotation marks, for in their readings van Doesburg and Vantongerloo did not make a sharp distinction between science and mysticism. For instance, in 1918 they both showed great interest in the pseudo-mathematics of M. H. J. Schoenmaekers.[43] As was mentioned above, van Doesburg had already met this philosopher when he had first visited Mondrian in Laren, in February 1916. When the plans for *De stijl* took definite form in 1917, Schoenmaekers was asked to contribute to the new periodical; however, the invitation was withdrawn before anything came of it. Both the invitation and the withdrawal happened at the suggestion of Mondrian. Van Doesburg probably had read little, if anything at all, by Schoenmaekers. Curiously, he began to study Schoenmaekers's most important books in 1918, at a moment when the split between Schoenmaekers and De Stijl was already definite. Van Doesburg wrote to Antony Kok on June 22, 1918, that he had read *Het nieuwe wereldbeeld* [*The new image of the world*] and was generally in agreement with it, although he disagreed on many points: "I also find many ideas still vague, dreamy, fantastic. For instance those about the art symbols seem far-fetched. One of the best things seems to me his conception of time and space, and his visual representation thereof. Some ideas which he expresses therein I have had exactly, even concerning the fourth dim.: movement." In the same letter he also mentions an important article by J. Ubink, "De vierde afmeting" ["The fourth dimension"], which had appeared in May 1918 in *De nieuwe gids.* On September 22, 1918, van Doesburg wrote that he now had read Schoenmaekers's *Beeldende wiskunde* [*Plastic mathematics*], a book by Poincaré in a German translation entitled *Neue mechanik,* and a book by E. Cohn entitled *Physikalisches über raum und zeit*; he also strongly advised Kok to read "the Relativity theory of Professor Lorentz."[44]

The first evidence of van Doesburg's newly acquired scientific knowledge occurs in his explanation of the interior of De Vonk in the November 1918 issue of *De stijl,* where he talks about an "as it were, gravity-defying effect by flat color and open space relationships." Whether or not he thought in such terms at the moment of design, in retrospect he represented the visual characteristics of the tile floor in terms of a kind of relativity of gravity. This was probably due to his acquaintance with general relativity, in which gravity plays a central part. Van Doesburg's art-theoretical writings of 1918 and the following years also contain other notions of scientific origin. These are often shrouded in a mystical haze, yet it is clear that he aimed to reconcile his art with the new scientific views of reality.

That van Doesburg's vision differed considerably from that of Mondrian became apparent to him when they met in June 1919 in Leiden, shortly before Mondrian moved to Paris. In a letter to Oud, van Doesburg reported on his long conversations with Mondrian during the visit: Mondrian was much more dogmatic than van Doesburg expected; he absolutely did not know what to do with the fourth dimension, and assumed that in the arts a final point had almost been reached. Van Doesburg could not accept such a static situation. He thought, on the contrary, that everything was in "mouvement perpetuel," as he wrote to Oud. It does not seem a coincidence that van Doesburg, after his confrontation with Mondrian, started to publish pseudonymous writings in *De stijl,* first as I. K. Bonset (as of May 1920) and later as Aldo Camini (as of July 1921). The creation of the dadaist poet and author Bonset was intended to mystify Mondrian (Kok and Oud know practically from the beginning that van Doesburg was behind the pseudonym), and as Bonset he could express himself in *De stijl* in a way which Mondrian, notwithstanding his general respect for dadaism, would probably not have accepted from van Doesburg.

Van Doesburg's newly developed vision of reality was reflected in poems as well as in critical prose. In May and July of 1920 two Bonset poems appeared in *De stijl* under the title "X-beelden" [X-images]. The title itself is a reference to scientific language. *X* in mathematical equations stands for the unknown quantity or is used as the first coordinate; it is, however, more probable that van Doesburg had x rays in mind. In the poems themselves he evoked a dynamic world in a way that reminds one of futurism. This was done by various means. On the one hand he still used language in a fairly descriptive way, as when he expressed the simultaneous experiences he had when looking out the window of his Leiden studio: "I am permeated by the room, through which the streetcar glides along / I am wearing a cap / organ sounds / from the outside through myself / are falling and breaking behind me."[45] On the other hand, as figure 28 shows, he also used separate words, letters, and numbers, often with strong typographic stress, in a sort of scientific formula: "0^n / − space and / − time / past present future / the behindhereandyonder / the pell mell of nothingness and being."

Everything remains vague enough (or, if one wishes, poetic), but it is clear that van Doesburg was trying in these poems to digest the new scientific insights into space and time that were furnished by the theory of relativity—a theory that also, according to van Doesburg, had brought about revolutionary changes in the human self-image. In one of his more philosophical moods, van Doesburg/Bonset wrote: "Every conquered spatial dimension serves at one time and for a while as a life-axis. As soon as this axis is worn out, a new spatial dimension is discovered, and all truths, facts of life, and representations of reality determined by a previous life-axis plunge inexorably into the abyss of nonexistent being."[46]

X-Beelden.

DOOR I. K. BONSET.

hé hé hé
hebt gij 't lichaamlijk ervaren
hebt gij 't **lichaamlijk** ervaren
hebt gij 't li **CHAAM** lijk er **VA** ren

O^{n}

— ruimte en
— tijd
verleden heden toekomst
het achterhierenginds
het doorelkaâr van 't niet en de verschijning

kleine verfrommelde almanak
die men ondersteboven leest

MIJN KLOK STAAT STIL

ZIG - ZAG

uitgekauwd sigaretteeindje op't
WITTE SERVET

vochtig bruin
ontbinding
GEEST
346 **VRACHT AU TO MO BIEL**

DWARS

trillend onvruchtbaar middelpunt

caricatuur der zwaarte
uomo electrico

rose en grauw en diep wijnrood

de scherven van de kosmos vind ik in m'n thee

Aanteekening: O^n: te lezen nul^n; — ruimte en — tijd: te lezen min ruimte en min tijd.

28 Van Doesburg, "X-beelden" ["X-images"], 1919 or 1920. *De stijl* 3, no. 9 (1920), p. 77.

Van Doesburg's problem was how best to express the dynamic view of life that he had developed since about 1917–18 in visual art. At first, he chose moving figures, such as dancers, as motifs for his paintings. Later he tried to give the relation between the abstract visual elements itself a dynamic accent, for instance by introducing spatial effects and dissonant color combinations. In the end, however, he must have felt restricted by the fact that space and movement in a painting are by definition illusory. As mentioned above, it was probably this realization that prompted him to stop painting (temporarily) and to direct his attention to other activities, particularly in architecture.

It is understandable that van Doesburg believed strongly in architecture, for time-space problems are, in point of fact, more directly applicable in architecture than in painting. A painting can be taken in at a glance, but the spatial effect of a building is experienced properly only over time. In his first architectural endeavors van Doesburg gave this matter little consideration; however, his studies of scientific and pseudo-scientific literature brought about a change in attitude. Gradually he came to realize the possibility of conveying a time-and-space experience to the spectator through the integration of painting and architecture. This intention was already somewhat perceptible in the interior of De Vonk.

In the autumn of 1918 van Doesburg became friendly with Bart de Ligt, a former pastor who was prominent in anarchist and pacifist circles. Van Doesburg wrote to Kok on December 8, 1918, about de Ligt: "The latter has become a new and beautiful revelation in my life; it is a real delight to work for him." The same letter tells us that van Doesburg was to create a color design for six rooms and a corridor in de Ligt's small country house in Lage Vuursche. Robert van 't Hoff was to contribute to the architectural aspect of the interior alterations. However, these plans were never realized, because the de Ligt family moved to Katwijk. There, van Doesburg got another opportunity at the end of 1919, and this time his design was indeed realized. Large color planes were applied to the walls and the doors, and to the ceiling of one small room. In addition, furniture by Gerrit Rietveld was installed.

A heavily retouched photograph of this interior was published in *De stijl* in November 1920, with a short explanation by van Doesburg. He did not find the result optimal, because he had had to work in an existing building with large architectural deficiencies; no sympathetic architect had entered into the project. Nevertheless, he wrote, "the painter succeeded in combining the five painted planes (ceiling and walls) with the furniture into a compositional unity."[47] Van Doesburg's pride was justified, for the room looks much more exciting than his earlier painted interiors. The architectural divisions certainly were taken into account in the application of the color planes, but the latter seem to detach themselves from their background; an effect of suspension is created, and this is repeated in the small dark planes on the endgrain sections of Rietveld's white furniture. The photograph in *De stijl* does not show the colors, but according to the legend the walls and the ceiling were done in blue, green, red, white, and black—the same colors that appear in the drawing shown here as figure 29 (although the red in the drawing is markedly orange). Curiously, some years later van Doesburg exhibited and published a photograph of the interior which was filled in with red, yellow, and blue (figure 30). Apparently he found this color combination more in line with the image that De Stijl had acquired in the interim.

The pictures of the de Ligt interior give a good impression of the spatial effect that the color planes must have had in the original room, but there also is an eyewitness account by Rietveld. In a letter of February 28, 1920, he compliments van Doesburg, who he says has succeeded in "showing the space at one glance (through the color)." The formulation suggests that van Doesburg had told Rietveld that this was his aim. The "seeing at a glance" of the space seems to eliminate the time factor; van Doesburg does not talk about that in his explanation in *De stijl,* but it can be ascertained that his pictorial intervention was temporal-spatial in character. A viewer in this interior must have experienced a dynamic interchange between the color planes around him.

In 1920 and 1921 van Doesburg designed color solutions for some fairly large projects, including a number of housing blocks by Oud in the Spangen quarter of Rotterdam and a row of houses and a school by the architect C. de Boer in Drachten.[48] Much of van Doesburg's work on these projects was transmitted from Weimar, Germany, where he moved in May 1921.

A number of van Doesburg's drawings for the Rotterdam project have been preserved, and these give a good indication of the process by which he arrived at decisions about the color applications for the facades. Auxiliary lines indicate how he activated, as it were, the whole street front by relating distantly spaced architectural details to one another by means of color. In the caption of the drawing shown here as figure 31 he talks about a "dynamo-static color effect," and he adds as an explanation that "whereas the yellow as a color in itself already militates against the static principle, the other colors do so by their position in the facade." If these designs and those for the interiors had been realized, the blocks of dwellings in Spangen would have been a real sight. However, after a positive first reaction, Oud backed out in the course of 1921. Apparently he thought that van Doesburg had gone too

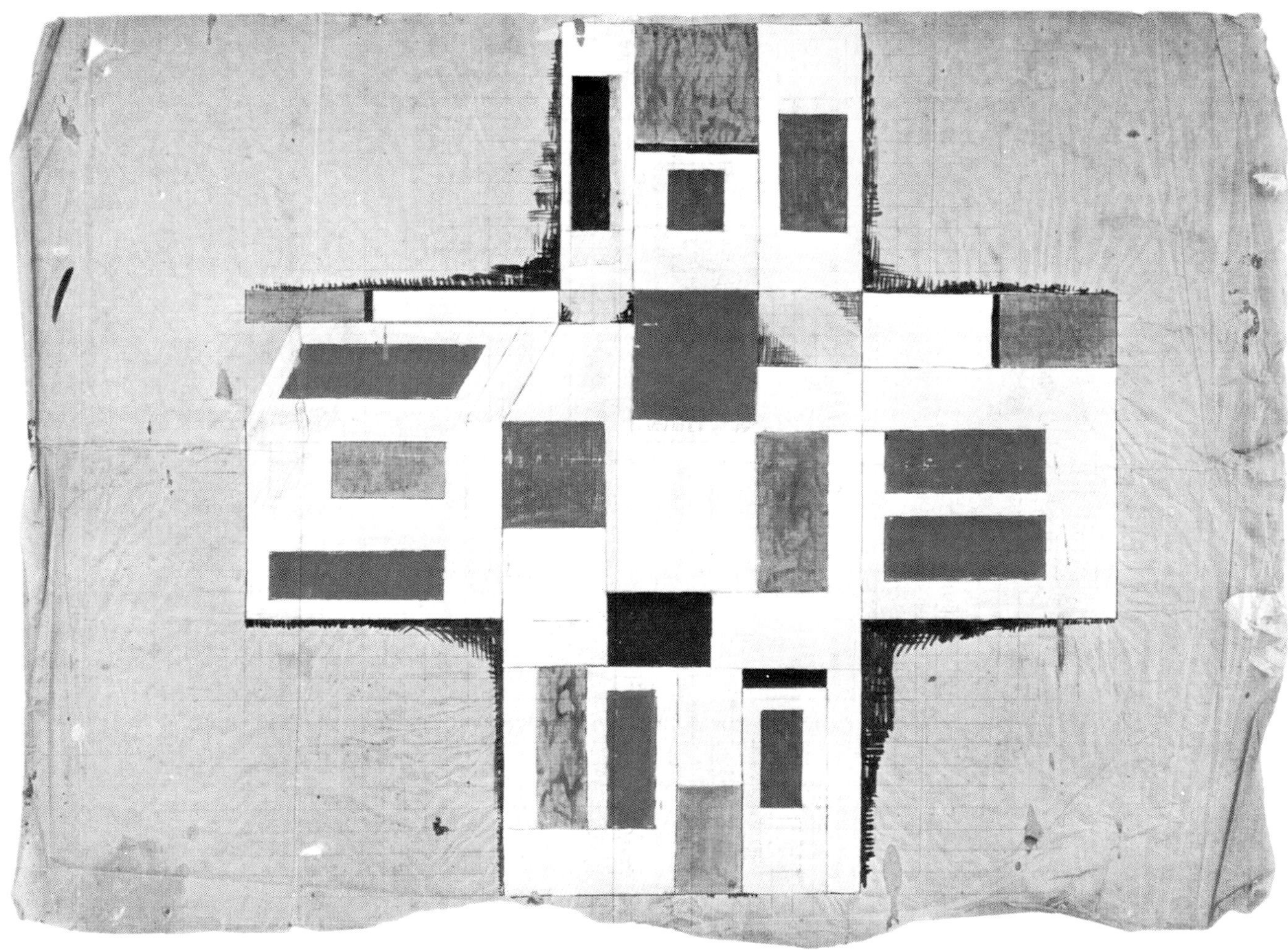

29 Van Doesburg, design of color applications for a room in the de Ligt house, Katwijk, 1919. Pencil and watercolor on paper, 60.5 × 43 cm. Rijksdienst Beeldende Kunst, The Hague. (Color plate on page xiv.)

30

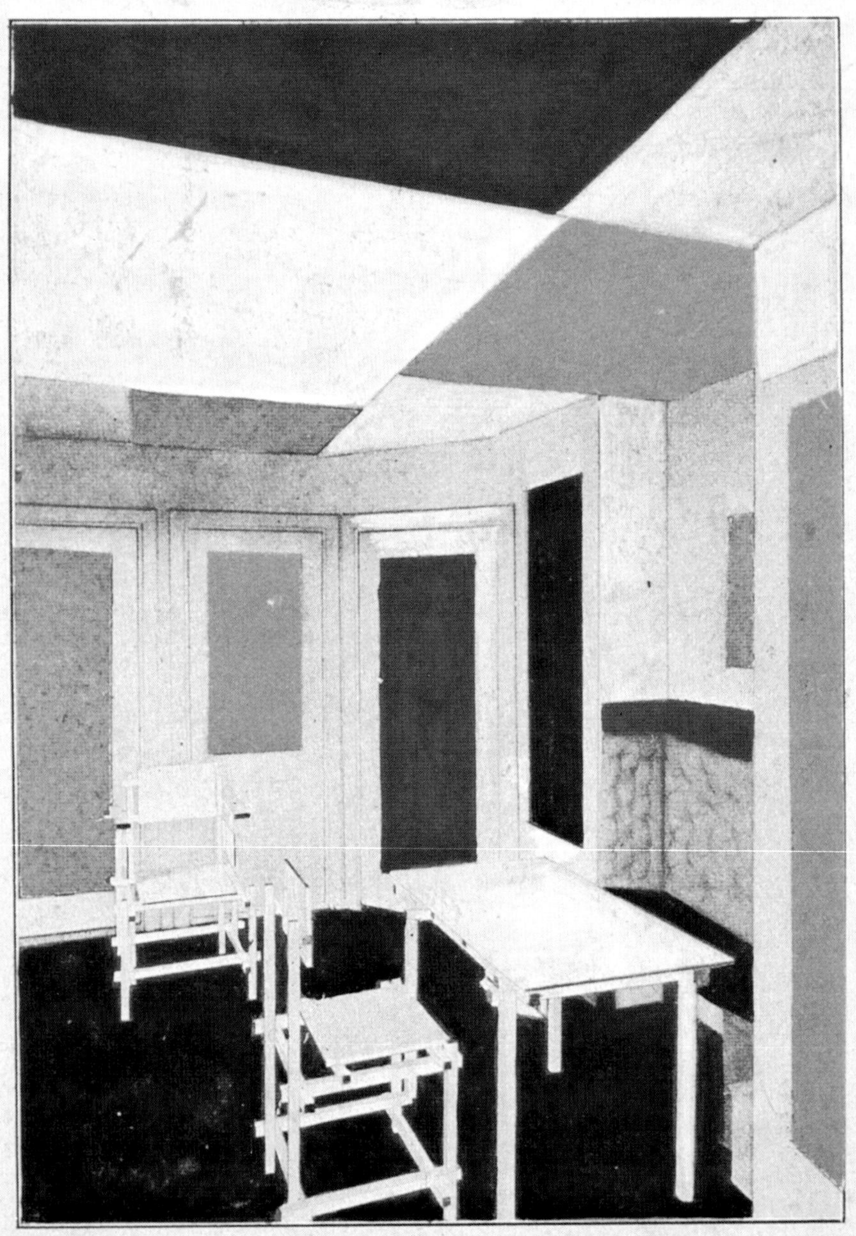

THEO VAN DOESBURG. PROEVE VAN KLEURENCOMPOSITIE IN INTÉRIEUR (1919). MEUBELEN VAN G. RIETVELD. BIJLAGE XIV VAN „DE STIJL" 3E JAARGANG No. 12.

far in his visual destruction and dynamization of architecture. So bitter was van Doesburg about the cancellation of the project that he came to a parting of the ways with Oud, in which he involved Mondrian as a supporter. Thus Oud's contribution to De Stijl came to an end. Wils and van 't Hoff had already taken their leave, and Rietveld had not yet asserted himself as an architect; with Oud's departure, the architectural side of De Stijl collapsed for a time. This must have been a painful blow for van Doesburg, for his ambitions had become more and more directed toward architecture.

After some time, van Doesburg found a replacement for Oud in the young architect Cornelis van Eesteren. They met in Weimar in the spring of 1922, and a year later an intensive and fruitful collaboration started between them. When van Doesburg moved to Paris in the spring of 1923 and started preparing an exhibition of architectural works by De Stijl artists, van Eesteren joined him and brought a few designs. Together they produced drawings and models of three houses for the exhibition: a dwelling with adjoining gallery for Léonce Rosenberg (at whose gallery the exhibition was held), a "maison particulière" [private house], and a "maison d'artiste" [artist's house].[49]

The maison d'artiste is particularly striking. The model was made with the help of a plumber, who welded a skeleton from metal strips; painted plates and pieces of colored glass were mounted onto this. In this house there is no longer a strict division into floors or a clear delineation of the different spaces; they flow into one another. In a building such as this, one would strongly experience a spatial continuity, divided rhythmically by the shifting primary colors of the walls. This project differed completely from the other projects in which van Doesburg had collaborated, such as the Spangen housing blocks, where the architecture was heavy and static. In the maison d'artiste, both architecture and painting have a dynamic character, and the building gives an almost floating impression (figure 32). Different lines from van Doesburg's work over the years are combined: on the one hand, the maison d'artiste is a paradigm of collaboration between painter and architect as equal partners; on the other hand it is a concretization of van Doesburg's dynamic conception of the world.

In 1922 and 1923 the fundamental differences in artistic perspectives and views on life between van Doesburg and Mondrian surfaced. Up to then van Doesburg had been able to keep his preoccupations with space, time, and movement more or less quiet. He expressed these ideas in periodicals other than *De stijl*—periodicals that Mondrian did not read. Statements about these topics in *De stijl* were mainly clad in literary or philosophical form and attributed to Bonset and Camini. This situation could not endure. When van Doesburg came to live in Paris and talked to Mondrian much more frequently than in former years, it soon became apparent how much they had grown apart. When personal irritations arose, a split between the two main protagonists of De Stijl became inevitable. (The split was not caused by van Doesburg's introduction of the diagonal in his work, as is often said; that was a consequence of the split.) Thus, from 1924–25 on, van Doesburg once more expressed in his paintings his preference for dynamism and change over harmony and peace—a preference that had grown over the years.

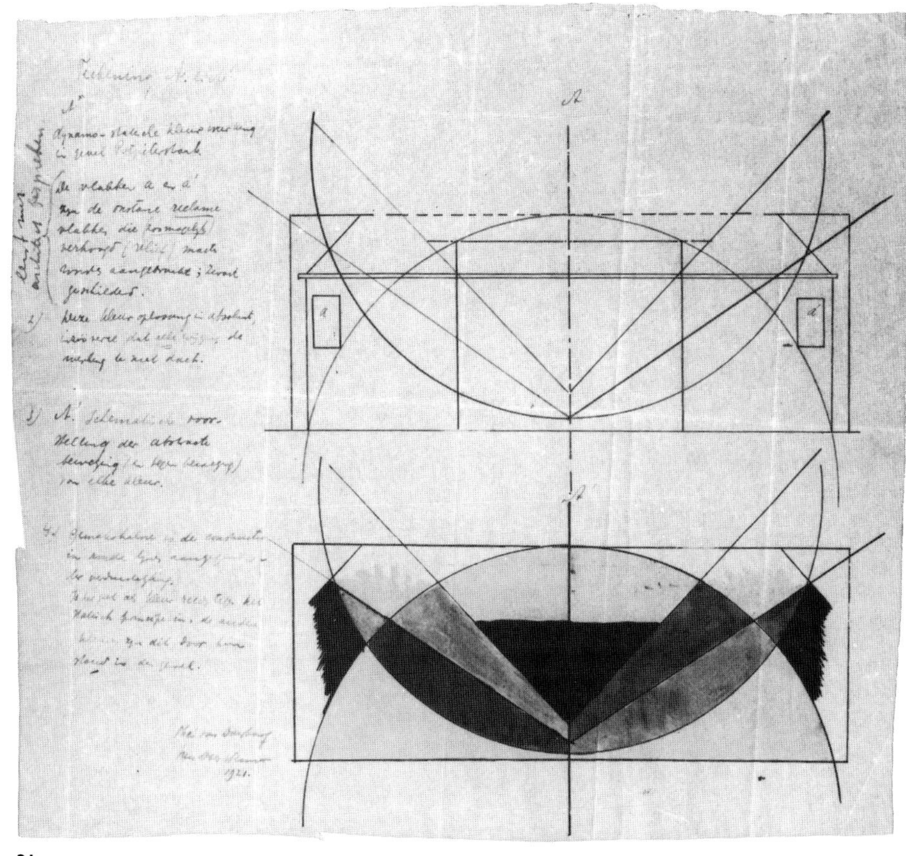

31

30 Van Doesburg, retouched photograph of a room in the de Ligt house, Katwijk. *L'architecture vivante* 3, no. 9 (1925), p. 12. The legend reads: "Theo van Doesburg. Specimen of color composition in interior (1919). Furniture by G. Rietveld. Appendix XIV of *De stijl* 3rd volume no. 12." (Color plate on page xv.)

31 Van Doesburg, design for color application for housing block on Potgieterstraat, Rotterdam, 1921. Ink and watercolor on paper, 28.5 × 32 cm. Fondation Custodia, Institut Néerlandais, Paris. (Color plate on page xvi.)

32 Van Doesburg and Cornelis van Eesteren, model for maison d'artiste, 1923, as illustrated in *De stijl* 6, no. 6–7 (1924), between pages 84 and 85.

32

1

The most important general literature on van Doesburg is the following: *Theo van Doesburg 1883–1931* (exhibition catalog, Van Abbemuseum, Eindhoven, 1968–69); J. Baljeu, *Theo van Doesburg* (London, 1974); *Theo van Doesburg, scritti di arte e di architettura*, ed. S. Polano (Rome, 1979). The last of these volumes contains an extensive bibliography and a tentative catalogue raisonné of van Doesburg's works, to which I refer below with the abbreviations "Polano P" (for paintings and drawings) and "Polano A" (for architectural works). Two more recent books are *Theo van Doesburg 1883–1931, een documentaire op basis van materiaal uit de Schenking Van Moorsel*, compiled by E. van Straaten (The Hague, 1983), and H. L. C. Jaffé's *Theo van Doesburg* (Amsterdam, 1983). On the current status of studies on van Doesburg, see S. Ex and E. Hoek, "Theo van Doesburg 1883–1931/1931–1983, een bibliografisch overzicht," *Wonen/TABK* 24 (1983), pp. 23–28.

2

Anon. (T. van Doesburg), "10 jaren Stijl algemene inleiding," *De stijl* 7, no. 79–84 (1927), pp. 2–9.

3

Until recently, most of the literature was based on the rather distorted picture of his early work and ideas that van Doesburg gave later in his life. A good, concise survey that corrects this is A. de Jongh's "De stijl," *Museumjournaal* 17, no. 6 (1972), pp. 262–282; see particularly pp. 263–264 and 269–270.

4

On van Doesburg's literary work, see H. L. Hedrick, *Theo van Doesburg, propagandist and practitioner of the avant-garde, 1909–1923* (Ann Arbor, 1980).

5

Van Doesburg's correspondence with Evert Rinsema and his brother Thijs has been published in K. Schippers's *Holland dada* (Amsterdam, 1974); see pp. 161–186. His correspondence with Antony Kok has not yet been published; it is with the van Doesburg estate in the Rijksdienst Beeldende Kunst, in The Hague.

6

In the original Dutch edition of this book, I dated the painting 1915 and interpreted it as a psychological portrait of Helena Milius. That has been proved incorrect. Evert van Straaten pointed out to me an unpublished literary text by van Doesburg, "Fifth letter to Bertha," dated December 10, 1914, in which he calls this painting "the last work I made in Amsterdam." Thus, it must have been made before van Doesburg became acquainted with Helena Milius.

7

The drawing *Straatmuziek I*, too, is probably incorrectly dated 1914; see the picture in *Kunstenaren der idee, symbolistische tendenzen in Nederland ca. 1880–1930* (exhibition catalog, The Hague, 1978), p. 68.

8

T. van Doesburg, "De ontwikkeling der moderne schilderkunst," *Eenheid*, May 27, June 17, June 24, July 15, July 22, and August 12, 1916. More than half a year passed between the lecture and its publication; it is possible that van Doesburg added the name of Huszár in the interim. Since the publication of the first edition of the present book, an analysis of van Doesburg's early texts relating to his visual work has been published: J. M. Joosten, "Rondom van Doesburg," *Tableau* 5 (September–October 1982), pp. 49–61.

9

For general information about Wichman, see I. Spaander, "9 biografieën," *Museumjournaal* 17, no. 6 (1972), pp. 294–297, and the exhibition catalog *Erich Wichman 1890–1928* (Utrecht, 1982).

10

Van Doesburg's poetry has been collected in the following volume: I. K. Bonset, *Nieuwe woordbeeldingen, de gedichten van Theo van Doesburg*, ed. K. Schippers (Amsterdam, 1975).

11

T. van Doesburg, "Kunst-kritiek," *Eenheid*, November 6, 1915.

12

For general information on de Winter, see Spaander, "9 biografieën" (note 9 above), pp. 297–302.

13

On van Doesburg and Feis, see the postscript by W. de Graaf in the 1981 edition of A. H. Feis's *Verzen in staccato* (Woubrugge, n.d. [1981]).

14

Quoted in the catalog of an auction of part of Kok's estate; see Schippers, *Holland dada*, p. 134.

15

Van Doesburg's use of a regular geometric pattern is discussed extensively in R. P. Welsh's "Theo van Doesburg and geometric abstraction," in *Nijhoff, Van Ostaijen, "De Stijl": Modernism in the Netherlands and Belgium in the first quarter of the 20th century*, ed. F. Bulhof (The Hague, 1976).

16

On the basis of different data, the numbering can be ascertained as follows: *Stilleven I* (Polano P97), formerly owned by Huszár and now in a private collection, is the painting pictured as appendix X in *De stijl* 1, no. 5(1918); *Stilleven II* (Polano P96) had already been bought by Bremmer at the exhibition of De Anderen, and is now in the Museum Kröller-Müller in Otterlo; *Stilleven III* (not in Polano; see figure 9 of the present volume) is in a private collection. Huszár's painting can be seen in van Doesburg's interior in a photograph that dates from 1917 or later; subsequently it was lost in a fire in the home of Helena Milius.

17

The painting with the tree motif (Polano P94) is in the Portland (Oregon) Art Museum. *Stilleven IV* (Polano P98) was destroyed by fire and is known only by means of a reproduction in the journal *Feuer* [5 (1921), p. 269]; a study (Polano P95) has been preserved and is in a private collection. It is remarkable that *Stilleven IV* makes a less abstract impression than I, II, or III. The pastels are unknown to me.

18

T. van Doesburg, "Expressionistisch-literaire komposities," *Het getij* 4 (1919), pp. 37–39.

19

For more information about this commission, see J. Beckett, "'De Vonk,' Noordwijk, an example of early De Stijl cooperation," *Art history* 3, no. 2 (1980), pp. 203–217.

20

R. W. D. Oxenaar, *Bart van der Leck tot 1920, een primitief van de nieuwe tijd* (The Hague, 1976), pp. 119–120.

21

On these and subsequent architectural projects, see N. J. Troy, *The De Stijl environment* (Cambridge, Mass., 1983), passim. See also C. Blotkamp, "Mondriaan—architectuur," *Wonen/TABK* no. 4–5 (1982), pp. 12–51, particularly pp. 31–32.

22

J. J. P. Oud, "Glas-in-lood van Theo van Doesburg," *Bouwkundig weekblad* 39, no. 35 (1918), pp. 199–202.

23

On the development from dance and music themes into work connected with architecture, see N. J. Troy, "Theo van Doesburg: From music into space," *Arts magazine* 56, no. 6 (1982), pp. 92–101.

24
In the original Dutch edition of the present book I suggested that *Compositie V* might represent the Three Graces, after Carpeaux's sculpture. After further consideration, this suggestion seems rather arbitrary . It is certain though, that van Doesburg used that motif in 1917 for a painting; see note 34 below. As long as figurative studies are lacking, it is impossible to propose a new interpretation of the motif of *Compositie V*.

25
Oud, "Glas-in-lood" (note 22 above), p. 201.

26
T. van Doesburg, "De nieuwe beweging in de schilderkunst," *De beweging* 12, no. 9 (1916), p. 234.

27
J. Leering, "De architectuur en van Doesburg," in *Theo van Doesburg 1883–1931* (note 1 above), pp. 19–25. See also Troy, *The De Stijl environment* (note 21 above), pp. 50–55.

28
This glass mosaic (Polano A10) is often incorrectly called a second commission for Villa Allegonda. Van Doesburg made a little sketch of it in the quoted letter; therefore, it is certain that it was meant for the villa in Alkmaar.

29
See Beckett, "De Vonk" (note 19 above); Troy, *The De Stijl environment,* pp. 41–48; and Esser's chapter on Oud in the present volume.

30
A photograph of Theo van Doesburg and Helena Milius at home, which shows the mantelpiece, is reproduced on page 31 of Baljeu's *Theo van Doesburg* (note 1 above).

31
Line and movement (exhibition catalog, Annely Juda Fine Art, London, 1979), p. 22.

32
Another variant of this sketch is reproduced in the exhibition catalog *Zu gast bei Käte Steinitz* (Galerie Gmurzynska, Cologne, 1977).

33
The development of the still-life motif is pictured and discussed on pages 93 and 94 of van Doesburg's *Drie voordrachten over de nieuwe beeldende kunst* (Amsterdam, 1919). The woman-in-interior motif is discussed and illustrated in van Doesburg's "Van 'natuur' tot 'compositie,'" *Hollandsche revue* 24, no. 8 (1919), pp. 470–476.

34
In a letter to Kok dated May 9, 1917, van Doesburg reported that he was working on the Graces. In July and August of 1917, he showed a work under this title at an exhibition in Domburg. This work was probably *Compositie VII.*

35
See *The Guggenheim Museum collection, paintings 1880–1945,* volume I (New York, n.d. [1976]), pp. 118–123. A picture of the exhibition label on the back of the painting is given.

36
See Polano P136 and P137. Later the title *Tango* was attached to these works, probably incorrectly; this led to confusion with other paintings that have dance motifs. *Compositie in grijs* was called *Ragtime* in the periodical *A bis Z* (15, 1931). Van Doesburg mentioned creating a painting called *Ragtime* in a letter to Kok dated April 22, 1919.

37
Schippers, *Holland dada,* p. 164.

38
It may be that van Doesburg also put the center outside the picture in *Peinture pure* (figure 25); see Welsh "Theo van Doesburg and geometric abstraction" (note 15 above), pp. 91–92.

39
L. D. Henderson, *The fourth dimension and non-Euclidean geometry in modern art* (Princeton, 1983), passim. For a more detailed account of the notion of the fourth dimension in Dutch visual art, see A. Gasten, "Pseudo-mathematica en beeldende kunst," in *Kunstenaren der idee* (note 7 above), pp. 59–66.

40
Van Doesburg used a quotation from Apollinaire's book as the epigraph of an article in *Eenheid,* October 18, 1913.

41
Gasten, "Pseudo-mathematica" (note 39 above), pp. 63–64.

42
G. Severini, "La peinture d'avant-garde," *De stijl* 1, no. 4 (1918), pp. 45–47; 1, no. 5 (1918), pp. 59–60.

43
Baljeu, *Theo van Doesburg* (note 1 above), pp. 28–29.

44
Half a year later, in April 1919, there appeared in *De stijl* an extensive list of books which the subscribers could get on loan from the editor. That list mentions, apart from these books, other publications about topics in mathematics and physics (of scientific as well as pseudo-scientific characters); however, no publication by Lorentz is mentioned. Consequently, van Doesburg's allusion in his letter to Kok is not clear, and exactly what he had learned at that moment about relativity theory is uncertain. In this respect it is important to relate here that Einstein had published his theory of general relativity recently, in 1916. Popular versions of his revolutionary ideas (to which Lorentz had contributed significantly) found their way to a vast public—including Van Doesburg, no doubt.

45
Bonset, *Nieuwe woordbeeldingen* (note 10 above), p. 83. There are also extant several painted studies (naturalistic as well as extremely abstract ones) of the motif of this poem, which is the view from van Doesburg's studio. Van Doesburg developed the abstract ones into the seemingly completely abstract stained glass windows for Oud's housing blocks in Spangen (Polano A16) in 1919.

46
I. K. Bonset, "Het andere gezicht," *De stijl* 3, no. 11 (1920), pp. 90–92.

47
Anon. (Theo van Doesburg), "Aanteekening bij de bijlage," *De stijl* 3, no. 12 (1920), p. 103.

48
On the crucial significance of these projects, see Troy, *The De Stijl environment,* pp. 109–120, and Troy, "Theo van Doesburg: From music into space" (note 23 above), pp. 95–98. Van Doesburg met de Boer through Evert Rinsema. In the Drachten houses, van Doesburg determined not only the colors of all the interior and exterior woodwork but also the choice of the wallpaper and even the plants in the front yards.

49
The three houses are discussed extensively in Leering's "De architectuur en van Doesburg" (note 27 above) and on pages 128–140 of Troy's *De stijl environment.*

33 Piet Mondrian, 1922.

Piet Mondrian

Els Hoek

Mondrian's biography will be familiar in broad outline to many readers. An extensive literature describes in detail his youth, his education, and the various stages in his career as an artist. In these writings, Mondrian's development is always presented as a gradual process, with every step a logical consequence of the previous one. The discussion of his works in terms of evolution conforms closely to the retrospective ideas put forth by Mondrian himself.

In describing the origin of Neo-Plasticism (as he called his abstract art), Mondrian always took his early landscapes as a starting point. These, he said, contained all the characteristics of the new art, albeit somewhat blurred. Alluding to the modern artists, of whom he considered himself to be the prototype, he wrote in 1918: "Was it by chance that they found a most appropriate subject matter through which to express their feeling for determinate relationship in an unforeshortened (non-perspective) view of a farmhouse with its mathematical articulation of planes (its large doors and groups of windows) and its primary (basic) colors? Was it by chance that they were attracted to straightness and—to the chagrin of habitual vision—dared to represent a wood simply by its vertical tree trunks? Was it surprising that, once they had abstracted these trunks to lines or planes, they spontaneously came to express the horizontal—hardly visible in nature—thus creating equilibrium with the vertical? Or that, in a rhythmic linear composition of the predominantly horizontal sea, they again expressed the—unseen—vertical in appropriate opposition? Did they do more than exaggerate what all painting has always done? Again, was it by chance that they were more deeply moved by the leafless tree, with its strong articulation of line or plane, than by the tree in leaf, where relationship is blurred? And is it surprising that in the course of their work they abstracted natural appearance more and more, so as to express relationship more and more explicitly? And that the ensuing composition was more mathematical than naturalistic? Was it, finally, by chance that, after abstracting all that was capricious, they abstracted curvature completely, thus achieving the most constant, the most determinate plastic expression of equilibrated relationship—composition in rectangular planes?"[1]

The transition from one style to another really was not always so obvious, however. At several points Mondrian could have chosen to go in an entirely different direction. In 1908, having seen Sluyters's and Gestel's paintings, he made the transition in a fairly short time from a soberly impressionistic to a symbolic-luministic manner of rendering. In 1911 his style again changed rather abruptly, influenced by cubism, and the following years saw a development toward a virtually abstract rendering of the subject. His abstract compositions from 1917–1922, the formative years of De Stijl, show vast differences from one to another; these differences resulted from his repeated attempts, in consultation with his colleagues, to bring theory and practice into line with each other. Bart van der Leck's, Theo van Doesburg's, Vilmos Huszár's, and Georges Vantongerloo's ideas, especially their criticisms, appear to have had a very stimulating effect on Mondrian's search for new pictorial solutions. His paintings reflect the influence of his discussions with the painters connected with De Stijl—discussions that can be retraced, in part, from preserved letters.

Thus, Mondrian was to a certain extent susceptible to new pictorial developments, and he could appreciate the work of others even if they did not apply the principles of Neo-Plasticism as thoroughly as he himself would have. On the other hand, he could be opinionated and even dogmatic. He judged other artists more on the validity of their intentions than on their implementation of these intentions. For example, in a letter to van Doesburg dated December 10, 1918, he took a moderate stand toward the other signers of the De Stijl manifesto: "I myself am of the opinion that one can certainly agree with the concepts without necessarily carrying them to extremes." Against this background, it is understandable that Mondrian felt more of an affinity for the artistically vacillating van Doesburg than for the more consistent Huszár.

The years up to 1910

Mondrian's fame has grown beyond all proportion in the years since his death. Not only does the angular monogram with which he signed his later works command a small fortune; nowadays even the curlicued signature on his earliest artistic products brings a high price. Sometimes excessive sums are paid for his early paintings, although most of them are mediocre and lacking in individual character. In the beginning, Mondrian was not yet quite able to fuse different influences into an individual style; some of his works from this period are rather academic, while others show influences of the impressionism of Amsterdam and The Hague. (For instance, Mondrian's admiration for Breitner is evident in the handling of paint and the composition of a number of his works from around the turn of the century.[2]) According to an exhibition review in the *Arnhemsche courant* of September 9, 1898, Mondrian "treads the golden middle way"; he does not depict his objects purely realistically, but neither does he deform them by "extraordinary color effects or affectation in drawing." Thus, Mondrian was at the outset a fairly old-fashioned painter in comparison with his contemporaries—perhaps as a result of his upbringing and education.

34 Mondrian, *Devotie [Devotion]*, 1908. Oil on canvas, 94 × 61 cm. Gemeentemuseum, The Hague.

Mondrian was born March 7, 1872, at Amersfoort, into a strict Calvinist family. His father was headmaster of a Dutch Reformed elementary school, first at Amersfoort and later at Winterswijk. The artistic talent of the son came to light rather early, but his parents expected him to prepare for a more conventional career than that of an artist. He met this requirement by enrolling in a program leading to a degree in art education. During his student years, his uncle Frits Mondriaan, a semi-professional painter in the Hague School tradition, often came to Winterswijk to paint studies of the rural scenery. Piet Mondrian accompanied him, and it was in this way that he learned the first fundamentals of painting. After obtaining his certificate as a teacher of drawing in secondary schools, he enrolled in the National Academy for Visual Arts in Amsterdam.[3]

When at age 20 Mondrian came to Amsterdam, he must have acquainted himself with the latest developments in visual arts; however, these hardly influenced his work. While Toorop and Thorn Prikker made a stir with their symbolist paintings, he associated himself with the older, more established impressionist landscapists.[4] Perhaps Mondrian was somewhat more conservative than his peers because of his training as a drawing teacher, which was more technical than artistic. Perhaps, though, his restraint also had a psychological background; he may have refrained from experimenting in order to prove himself an artist to his relatives.

For whatever reason, Mondrian began to deviate perceptibly from the "golden middle way" by deforming shapes and using nonrealistic colors in his paintings in 1908, at the age of 36. One would not expect that an artist who had produced traditional works for sixteen years would change his approach so radically. Mondrian, however, put all conventions aside and in a short time became one of the most progressive artists in the Netherlands.

Although from 1905 on some paintings already hint at a changing approach, it can be stated generally that Mondrian's primary aim in his paintings before 1908 was to represent the mood of the Dutch scenery. With muted colors and an impressionistic use of paint, he tried to give an impression of the play of light and shadows through the foliage of the trees, or the spacious, hazy atmosphere of the polders. After he came to know the works of Jan Sluyters and Leo Gestel, who were influenced by the fauvists, he used bright colors and stylized forms that were not suitable for depicting a quiet atmosphere. From this moment on, Mondrian used the effects of line and color to convey symbolic meaning.

There are indications that Mondrian used color for the conveyance of meaning in his earliest known letter, written in the summer of 1909 as the result of a review of his work by Israel Querido in the weekly *De controleur.* In his article (clearly based on information procured from the artist), Querido had given an overview of Mondrian's development from a "conventionally color-expressing tonalist" to a "bright colorist."[5] The development of other moderns could have been described similarly, but Mondrian's work, Querido had written, distinguished itself by the special meaning color had for him: "The color has become symbolically expressive, has a visionary meaning." Of Mondrian's recent painting *Molen bij zonlicht* [*Mill in sunlight*], Querido had written: "One realizes that this seer wanted to capture in color-expression and color-harmony something symbolic of that mighty summer-mill, blazing in the sun's fire." In his reaction to this review, Mondrian was very explicit about the way he had used color. Of the painting *Devotie* [*Devotion*], he said that he had intentionally given the girl's hair a red color "to tone down the material side of things . . . and to stress the spiritual."[6]

Color was only one means of stressing the spiritual side. The choice of certain subjects, and particularly the way in which he depicted these, suggests that Mondrian attributed deeper meaning to his work. For instance, he painted church towers and lighthouses from very close by, so that they rose as mighty beacons against the sky. Along with *Devotie,* the depiction of church towers could be related to traditional Christian symbolism; however, Mondrian emphatically dismissed that. In his response to Querido he objected for this very reason to Querido's use of the Christian term "praying" in connection with *Devotie.* He said that he had not wanted to depict such a specific act as praying, but more a general idea of devotion: "Once more I must admire your deep sensitivity to so much, but I seem to have expressed myself to you incorrectly if I made you believe that I wanted that girl to express a prayerful act. With that work I only envisaged a girl conceptually devoted, or perceived devotedly, or with great devotion. . . . I had intended rather, as I said, to convey the very deepest sources of the action 'prayer,' among other things that to pray could just as well be to thank, etc." This wording suggests that Mondrian's depiction of the spiritual element was based not so much on traditional Western religion as on Theosophy.

In 1909 Mondrian became a member of the Theosophical Society.[7] His interest in Theosophy, the "spiritual science" founded by Madame Blavatsky and based mainly on oriental religions, probably went back to the turn of the century. Some ex librises which he made in the years just after 1900 show lotus flowers and six-pointed stars,[8] which could be interpreted as Theosophical symbols; however, in the free work from this period we can find no traces of Theosophical influence. It is difficult to trace precisely when this influence began to play a role. As mentioned, it is clearly discernible in the 1908 painting *Devotie;* however, in the landscapes from about the same time it is more hypothetical. A good example is *De rode wolk* [*The red cloud*], shown as figure 35. This work can be considered as a realistic image of a rosy-red sky at dawn, but also as a mystical vision of nature in the tradition of the nineteenth-century Romantics;[9] other paintings from this period also suggest that Mondrian wanted to express in his art the fact that he viewed nature with new eyes. His change in point of view may be explained in terms of his becoming acquainted around 1908 or slightly earlier with the ideas of Rudolf Steiner, which were based not only on Theosophy but also on the scientific writings of Goethe. In his lectures, books, and articles, Steiner devoted much attention to the possibility of gaining insight into hidden natural laws through conscious observation of the natural surroundings. In Steiner's terms, *De rode wolk* could be interpreted as a mystical vision of nature: light conquering darkness.[10]

The Moderne Kunstkring

The changes that appeared in Mondrian's work around 1908 were closely related to his changing ideas about the role of art in human awareness. From that time on he tried, influenced by the Theosophical literature, to free himself more and more from visible reality and to visualize the essence of things in a manner strongly influenced by the newest trends: luminism, fauvism, and expressionism. It is no wonder that he soon made connections with the Dutch avant-garde.

In 1910 Mondrian took part in the founding of the Moderne Kunstkring [Modern Art Circle]. Jan Toorop was president, Conrad Kickert was secretary, and Mondrian and Jan Sluyters were regular board members.[11] In a communication about the founding of the Moderne Kunstkring, Kickert explained why the development of modern art required the founding of a new society: Every time period has its own manner of expression, and this should not be impeded by conventions of whichever kind. Only artists who sought to "work in the spirit of their times" were allowed to join the new society, and submissions for exhibitions would be judged according to Delacroix's statement "le moderne, il n'y a que cela!"[12] No doubt Mondrian was in agreement; for him, too, "le moderne" was the only true way, not only in art but also in life. He must have already felt that his vision of art was different from that of others. As he had written to Querido in 1909, most modern artists ignored the relationship between philosophy and art, which in his opinion were inseparable. "And further," he noted, "you write at the end that what I have achieved was obtained through my talent as a painter, etc., and you consider my work like that of the others, who do the same. And yet I know that—despite much similarity—there is a great difference. It seems to me that you too recognize the important relationship between philosophy and art, and it is exactly this relationship that most painters deny. The great masters grasp it unconsciously, but I believe that a conscious spiritual knowledge will have a much greater influence on a painter's art."

Besides working in Amsterdam, Mondrian in these years also worked regularly in the small seaside resort of Domburg.[13] There he moved in different circles. Through Toorop, who also had a somewhat mystical inclination, he had contacted colleagues who shared his interest in Theosophy, including Jacoba van Heemskerck and Mrs. Elout-Drabbe. Through Mondrian, their works were exhibited next to those of the younger Amsterdam artists at the exhibition of the Amsterdam artists' association St. Lucas in 1910. Jan Sluyters was not very happy about this; in a letter to the painter Kees Spoor he objected to the way in which Mondrian had hung the "limp unsubstantialities" of his "male and female friends" from Domburg next to his own paintings, and in another letter of the same year he expressed his astonishment that Mondrian wanted to let Gust van de Wall Perné, who painted very traditional symbolistic images, exhibit his works with those of the moderns. He thought that Mondrian was acting rather strangely, and that his work was more "trendy" than temperamental; he probably meant that Mondrian's modernism sprouted more from preconceived ideas than from a spontaneous need.[14] Sluyters had seen the difference very clearly.

35 Mondrian, *De rode wolk* [*The red cloud*], 1907. Oil on cardboard, 64 × 75 cm. Gemeentemuseum, The Hague.

In the autumn of 1911 the Moderne Kunstkring organized a large exhibition in the Stedelijk Museum in Amsterdam. This was the first showing in the Netherlands of cubist works by Picasso, Braque, and Le Fauconnier. A large number of Cézanne's paintings from the Hoogendijk collection were also shown. Mondrian exhibited recent works, such as *De rode molen, Kerk te Domburg* [*Church at Domburg*], *Duinlandschap* [*Dune landscape*], and *Evolutie* [*Evolution*]. In comparison with his earlier works, these paintings are remarkable for their strong emphasis on composition; they are constructed from large, rather flat geometric shapes in bright colors.

Most critics reviewed Mondrian's works without pointing out the differences between him and the other moderns. Because of his extreme use of color, his paintings were compared to those of Sluyters and Gestel. In general, they met with disapproval; for example, G. H. Marius wrote in *Het nieuws van de dag* of October 25, 1911: "Truly, everyone could imagine a landscape more highly colored than ours; but imagine partitioning the dunes into those colorful planes in which the character of their ruggedness and barrenness, their shape and their beautiful roundings get totally lost—one certainly must have an ultramodern taste in order to enjoy this."

Some discerned symbolic meaning in Mondrian's paintings. That is not too surprising, for at the Moderne Kunstkring show his triptych *Evolutie* was on exhibition—the only work in all of Mondrian's output that unequivocally shows the influence of Theosophy. (It depicts the most important Theosophic dogma—the spiritual awakening of mankind—through a combination of stylized female figures and Theosophic symbols.) J. H. de Bois, who was not only a critic but also a prominent art dealer, objected to this triptych, in the *Haarlems dagblad* of October 26, 1911, as an example of the profundity of "a tailor who subscribes to *Vrije gedachte.*" (*Vrije gedachte,* meaning *Free thought,* was a spiritualist-anarchist periodical.) After 1911 Mondrian never again used directly recognizable Theosophic symbols in his paintings. Perhaps he heeded the press reactions and agreed in principle with de Bois that the triptych was more of an illustration than a convincing depiction of profound ideas.

At the Moderne Kunstkring exhibition Mondrian saw works by the cubists Picasso and Braque that impressed him deeply. He realized that the natural shape could be pushed back farther by abstraction than by stylization. Shortly after the exhibition, he decided to move to Paris.[15] There he would acquaint himself further with the work and the ideas of the French cubists.

1912–1914: Cubism

The period 1912–1914, which Mondrian spent in Paris, was of great importance for his further development. In this period he resolved to publish his ideas about art in due time. For the time being, he began to write them down for his own use in notebooks and sketchbooks, some of which are extant.[16] These books offer a wealth of information about Mondrian's nascent ideas. The center of his attention is the question of art's role in the Theosophical idea of the evolution of humanity. Thus, he also tried to define his function as an artist in society. In Paris he not only developed his theory, but he also laid down the basis for his work of the De Stijl years.

Influenced by cubism, Mondrian proceeded to abstract his subjects drastically. In the very first paintings this method is not yet so completely radical. He reduces the volume to geometric forms, but the objects—a still life with a ginger pot, a woman's head, a tree—still have a clear contour; they contrast like a silhouette against the background, which also is divided into geometric forms. In the paintings from the end of 1912 and the beginning of 1913, the whole canvas is partitioned with dark lines, which enclose rather sketchily forms such as arcs and triangles. They are filled in with the brown and gray shades of the cubist palette. During 1913 and 1914 the character of the line pattern changes to more stair-like shapes and rectangles. The colors also become much more marked; besides brown, gray, and ochre, pastel blue and pink occur regularly. The subject, most often a tree or a facade, is recognizable in these later paintings only with difficulty, and sometimes not at all; at most, some diverting lines (oblique or arched) or a concentration of colored shapes indicate the motif that was Mondrian's starting point. Sometimes an extant study clarifies the motif.

The unrecognizability is the consequence of Mondrian's rigorous manner of abstraction. He breaks the contour open and disperses the forms and colors over the whole canvas. For instance, the rectangular planes of the facade paintings of 1914 (e.g., figure 36) are not a "tightened" version of the motif; it remains unclear where the facade ends and the sky starts. This method is reminiscent of the cubists' aim of simultaneously rendering an object from different sides. This kind of representation is based on the idea that the subject interacts with the space around it. One could also speak about such an interaction in Mondrian's work; the motif flows out into the background or, conversely, it is penetrated by the background. However, Mondrian always shows only one of the motif's sides.

Mondrian's choices of subject, too, differ from those of the French cubists. They painted mainly portraits and still lifes—traditional subjects, which they could arrange in their studios. Mondrian, on the other hand, always chose outdoor subjects: at first trees, and later, as a result of his intense interest in the phenomenon of the metropolis, facades of buildings. His rapid adoption of the formal solutions of the cubists suggests that he must have studied their paintings thoroughly; he must have known that they used neutral motifs in order to direct their full attention to the solution of formal problems.

In a letter of January 29, 1914, to the critic H. P. Bremmer, Mondrian wrote about his ideas in relation to cubism and futurism: "Futurism, although one step beyond naturalism, occupies itself too much with human sensations. Cubism (whose content is still based too much on earlier aesthetic considerations and therefore is less timely than futurism) has made the great stride to abstraction, and therefore it does belong to these and future times: so not modern in its content but yet modern in its effect. I judge myself as belonging to neither, but feel the spirit of the time in both and in myself."[17] Mondrian thought it very important that an artist be conscious of "the spirit of the time." As for choice of subjects, he felt that the cubists fell back on the past too much; the futurists, he thought, relied too much on the experiences of the moment—speed, bustle, and noise; moreover, their depiction of these was too illustrative. The architecture of a large city also expressed the spirit of the times, but was less anecdotal.

Another subtle difference with the French cubists lies in Mondrian's use of the oval form. Just as they did, Mondrian, during the years 1912–1914 and also afterwards, often let the composition fade out toward the borders of the canvas, so that it was not cut off suddenly. Thus he avoided the "window effect." At the same time, he emphasized the center of the composition by giving the composition within the plane of the painting itself a clear boundary (figure 36).

It is likely, however, that there were deeper reasons for Mondrian's use of the oval form—reasons related to his demonstrable interest in the androgyne myth. In Plato's philosophy, original man is described as a spherical being in which both sexes were united. The same idea is found in the Tantra of Hindu mythology, where the "cosmic egg" stands for the original unity.[18] In Theosophy, which is in part based on the Tantra, the idea of "egg of the universe" is used,[19] and Rudolf Steiner's evolution theory describes very extensively the androgyne myth, the original unity of both sexes in one egg-shaped body.[20] Among the symbolist artists of the late nineteenth century the literal depiction of the hermaphrodite,

36 Mondrian, *Compositie in ovaal* [*Composition in oval*], 1914. Oil on canvas, 113 × 84.5 cm. Gemeentemuseum, The Hague.

37

the physical combination of male and female, was particularly popular. The growing interest in Oriental religions in the beginning of the twentieth century resulted in a shift of attention to the abstract concept of the unity of opposites. This shift can also be seen in the visual arts. In the works of Marc Chagall and Constantin Brancusi there are several endeavors to depict the reunion of man and woman. In *Hommage à Apollinaire* (1913) Chagall put a figure, split into male and female parts, within an oval. The famous sculpture *The kiss,* in which two figures are amalgamated, shows that Brancusi was already interested in this theme in 1908. The small oval sculptures Brancusi made afterward (figure 37) can be viewed as abstract renderings of the idea of unity.[21]

Later, in *De stijl,* Mondrian stressed the difference between the visual duality of the sexes and the universal concept of the "spiritual hermaphrodite." He wrote that the physical combination of both sexes in one body only seemed to manifest a unity of opposites; the male and female elements remained on the surface: "More or less external femininity and masculinity are a duality of external appearance and therefore cannot form the true unity. We see this in the unsatisfactory situation of the relatively physical hermaphrodite. The physical hermaphrodite is a unity of an apparent duality, whereas the spiritual hermaphrodite (the ideal of the Old Sages) is a unity of a real duality."[22]

That Mondrian was already occupied with this idea in his first years in Paris is evident from the notes in his sketchbooks. It is remarkable how often he tried in these short notes, in which the key words are abbreviated to a few letters, to articulate the essence of the relation between the male and the female element. He viewed the female element as stationary, horizontal, and material, the male as the moving, vertical, and spiritual element.[23] These two opposites, Matter and Spirit, attract each other like positive and negative: the man covets the material element because he himself is spirit, and the woman covets the spiritual because she herself is matter. A well-balanced ratio between these two principles gives durable and unchangeable happiness. Because the human being is split into male and female, the original status of peace and happiness is transformed into a situation in which everything is constantly susceptible to change. Mondrian, in his sketchbook notes (figure 38), articulated this as follows: "The conflict between Matter and Force exists in everything; between the male and female principle. . . . The balance between the two means happiness. This is difficult to achieve, partly because the one is abstract and the other is real."[24] A few pages later, having described the male element as opposed to the female as the positive opposed to the negative, he wrote: "The positive and negative states of being

37 **Constantin Brancusi, *The beginning of the world,* 1920. Marble, glass, and stone. Norton Simon Museum of Art, Fullerton, Calif.**

38 **Mondrian, two pages from a sketchbook, ca. 1914. Pencil on paper, 11.4 × 15.8 cm. Private collection.**

38

bring about action. They bring about the loss of balance and of happiness. They bring about the eternal revolutions—the changes that follow one upon the other. They explain why happiness cannot be achieved within time."[25]

Mondrian tried to rediscover these very general cosmic ideas in the functioning of the world around him. He was primarily concerned with the function of art. It was, he thought, the task of art to help humanity attain a higher step on the ladder of evolution. Art must hold out a prospect for the future unity of the opposites Matter and Spirit. Therefore art must stand above reality, and those who create it have special qualities which ordinary man has not yet attained. According to Mondrian one of the most important of those qualities is that in an artist there is a better-balanced relation between the male and the female element, which enables the artist to approach the ideal status of unity more closely than an ordinary human being. Mondrian seems to have been talking primarily about himself when he wrote: "The man-artist is female and male at the same time; therefore he does not need a woman. The female artist is never completely an artist; thus one cannot say that she does not need a man."[26] And a few pages later: "The oneness of positive and negative is happiness. Therefore, the more the positive and the negative are united in one nature, the greater the happiness. This unity is pronounced in the artist, in whom both male and female elements are found. Thereby, however, he is no longer purely male."[27] In view of these ideas, the oval form of the compositions from this time should not be considered a purely formal, cubist element. It is a meaningful element, a reference to the happiness that will befall humanity in the distant future through the reunion of Matter and Spirit, the female and male elements.

1914–1917

In July 1914 Mondrian returned to the Netherlands for a short visit. Caught unawares by the outbreak of the First World War, he was forced to stay and live there for the next five years. During his stay in Paris he had hardly had any contact with the Dutch art scene, and during the first years of the war he did not show much interest in it. Although he exhibited a few times, he kept rather aloof from the well-known art associations.[28] He had never felt very close to the Dutch moderns. Once, he had experienced superficial affinities with their work; now that he had taken quite another direction, even that superficial connection was gone. This somewhat isolated position may be part of the reason for his scanty artistic output during the years 1915 and 1916. Letters from these years to the painter Lodewijk Schelfhout and the minister H. van Assendelft, who was also a collector of modern art, betray his homesickness for the French capital[29]—the artists with whom he felt close worked there, and from the cosmopolitan life he drew inspiration for new solutions in his own work.

As a theoretician, Mondrian was less solitary in the Netherlands. He regularly exchanged philosophical views with the Reverend Mr. van Assendelft, and the composer Jacob van Domselaer, with whom Mondrian lived for some time in Laren, shared his interest in Theosophy. Moreover, in the beginning of 1915 he came into contact with Dr. M. H. J. Schoenmaekers. Their conversations in particular must have prompted him to extend and publicize the theories he had developed in Paris.[30] Thus, another explanation for the small number of paintings produced by Mondrian during those years is that he was spending a lot of time working out his theory of art. He wrote a number of essays about the new painting, elaborating on the ethical ideas he had jotted down in his sketchbooks.[31] (Later these appeared in *De stijl,* in reworked form, under the title "Neo-Plasticism in painting.")

The basis of Mondrian's theory is a faith in a higher reality—"the universal"—which can be found in all things and which is independent of accidental external qualities. The task of the arts is to depict this universal element through beauty. Beauty is not something that manifests itself in the external appearance of things; rather, it is the essence of art, just as truth is the essence of philosophy. Beauty and truth both result from a well-balanced relation of opposites. Similar ideas had been formulated by the neo-Hegelian G. J. P. J. Bolland of Leiden, whom Mondrian quoted in this respect: "The beautiful is the true in the perceptual mode. And truth is a multiple unity of opposites. . . . The concept of beauty is a relational one—of aesthetic relations, of perceptually agreeable and thus emotionally satisfying relationships."[32]

The beauty of a work of art suffers, Mondrian believed, when the individual characteristics of the rendered object dominate the universal element; they must be brought into equilibrium with it. However, to see this equilibrium requires an uncustomary attitude in the artist and in the spectator: the suppression of their individual emotions. In this respect Mondrian adopted Schopenhauer's concept of "disinterested perception": "Since perception springs from the universal (within us and outside us), and completely transcends the individual (Schopenhauer's perception), our individual personalities have no more merit than the telescope through which distant worlds are made visible."[33]

Up to this point, Mondrian's ideas do not differ in essence from those of the Romantics (at the beginning of the nineteenth century) and of the Symbolists (at the end of the century). These artists also viewed reality as a misleading manifestation of the Idea they wanted to represent. Notwithstanding these similarities, there is also a big difference: The Romantics and the Symbolists were mainly grounded in the Western Christian tradition, whereas Mondrian extended the universalist theory with elements from Theosophy.

As mentioned above, from 1909 on Mondrian was a member of the Theosophic Society. He was acquainted with Madame Blavatsky's *Secret doctrine.* Moreover, his ideas were probably influenced strongly by the writings of Rudolf Steiner, who made less use of abstract symbols than Madame Blavatsky. Steiner's starting point is that man can influence his own development and can attain a higher level of consciousness. One can "awaken the soul" when—starting from the everyday wakeful consciousness, not from a trance—one engrosses oneself in a certain image. Not all images have the power to influence the soul; the most suitable are those that have no other primary function—that is, representations that do not depict some external appearance.[34] This idea corresponded beautifully to Mondrian's ideas about the universal and the individual. Moreover, it underlined the importance of the artist's function. By surrounding humanity with abstract representations, one could influence the awakening process of awareness. Thus the universal would be able to manifest itself in an increasingly pure state in the future, not only in painting but in man's entire environment.

Mondrian's interest in metaphysics and mysticism was shared by the aforementioned Dr. Schoenmaekers, a former Catholic priest who called himself a Christosophist because he combined Theosophy and the Christian doctrine. Both lived in Laren, and for some time they met frequently. Mondrian's articles on "Neo-Plasticism in painting" appear to be based largely on Schoenmaekers's theories.[35] However, on closer scrutiny it appears that Schoenmaekers's influence is mostly limited to Mondrian's terminology. Mondrian copied the names Schoenmaekers had used for certain phenomena in the books *The new image of the world* and *Plastic mathematics* but ignored ideas Schoenmaekers had taken from physics.[36] The ideas that Mondrian put forward in his articles were his own, and they predate his meeting Schoenmaekers. His Paris sketchbooks and other evidence make it clear that he had developed these ideas long before he met Schoenmaekers. One could say that Schoenmaekers was, by chance, present in the right place at the right moment in order to help Mondrian focus and smooth out his formulations.

Mondrian's interest in Schoenmaekers did not last long. In a letter to van Doesburg dated May 21, 1917, he mentioned him as a possible contributor to *De stijl,* but by then he already regarded him as a "miserable fellow" and doubted the sincerity of his intentions. A month later he proposed to ask Frits van Hengelaar (a student of psychiatry) for an article, instead of Schoenmaekers. It is clear from a passage in a letter which is difficult to date but which may have been written in December 1917 that Schoenmaekers's authority was not so great any more. Mondrian wrote to van Doesburg: "I do feel to be justified about this orthogonal position. I have everything from the Secret Doctrine (Madame Blavatsky), not from Schoenmaekers, although the latter says the same." In January 1918, after the publication of Schoenmaekers's lecture "Kunst en gedachte" ["Art and thought"] in the literary journal *Het getij,* he was officially written off by van Doesburg as a possible contributor to *De stijl,* with the approval of Mondrian and van der Leck.

In May 1917 the plans for the new periodical were already well underway. The initiative, however, had been born as early as 1915. In October of that year van Doesburg contacted Mondrian, having seen his work at the exhibition of the Hollandsche Kunstenaarskring. Within a month Mondrian was informed of "the plans for a periodical to be founded." He did not react very enthusiastically at first. On November 20 he warned van Doesburg not to proceed too hastily in promoting new things: "First more should be accomplished in art in this direction. I hardly know of anybody who really produces art in our direction." Not long afterward he met Bart van der Leck, who came to live in Laren in April 1916. Mondrian found in him "a man striving in the same direction," as he wrote on August 1 to the critic Bremmer, who knew and financially supported them both.[37] Thus an exchange of ideas with kindred artists got underway, which gave Mondrian enough confidence to promise his collaboration in the journal. It must also have stimulated him in his artistic work, for in 1917 and 1918 he produced a fairly large number of paintings, finding new solutions to certain problems.

1916–17: Abstraction

One of the most important consequences of Mondrian's view of art was that the subjects of his paintings became unrecognizable. The individual qualities of the motif (size, shape, and color) were indeed merely accidental circumstances; they were subject to change and therefore a misleading manifestation of the universal.

The later paintings from Paris were abstractions of a tree or a facade. The two paintings made in 1915–16 when Mondrian was in the Netherlands had as their subjects the sea and the church tower of Domburg, respectively, but the identification of these subjects is possible only because there are some extant studies.

Compositie in lijn [*Composition in lines*], shown as figure 39, is an example of a painting whose starting point cannot be discerned with certainty. There are no recognizable elements, and no studies to provide clarification. This has often been called Mondrian's first abstract painting, yet the term *abstract* in the sense of "without subject" is not suitable here. Similarities in shape and color between this painting and *Compositie X* (figure 40) suggest that these two works deal with the same subject. The vertical concentration of lines that can be interpreted in *Compositie X* as an abstract rendering of a pier is missing in *Compositie in lijn,* in which Mondrian left the pier outside the picture and depicted only the water's surface (which blends into the sky at the horizon).

There are no indications that Mondrian considered motifs very important. He had stopped using explanatory titles a good while ago. He was concerned primarily with the idea represented by the work; he did not think it important for the viewer to know what motif had inspired him. This is apparent in a letter to Bremmer, dated January 5, 1916, in which Mondrian approves of Bremmer's characterization of *Compositie X* as having a "Christmas mood"; for Mondrian there was no essential difference between the idea of Christmas and the tranquility and equilibrium he wanted to express in the abstract sea image.[38]

In the works made after *Compositie in lijn,* reality as it manifests itself in nature is not recognizable. Nevertheless, this does not mean that these paintings lack a subject. In a letter to van Doesburg dated April 18, 1919, Mondrian says explicitly that he still bases his paintings on certain motifs from reality: "Also about starting from a natural subject or not. . . . I do agree with you on the main point that the natural element should be destroyed and reconstructed in a spiritual way, but let us take that in a very broad sense. For the natural doesn't have to be a definite representation. I am now working on a thing which is a reconstruction of a starry sky, but still I make it without a natural given. Therefore someone who says that he starts from a natural element may be right, and at the same time he who claims to start from nothing is also right!" The painting with the starry-sky motif must be the dark version of *Dambord compositie* [*Checkerboard composition*], with which he was occupied until June 1919. According to the correspondence, the original idea was to reproduce this painting next to the night scene of the trialogue "Natuurlijke en abstracte realiteit" in *De stijl.*[39] However, Mondrian was not satisfied with the photograph: "The photographer . . . put his camera on an angle, so that [the planes] became trapezoids," he wrote in August 1919 to van Doesburg. Because of the photographer's error, a photo of the diamond-shaped painting *Lozangique met vlakken in oker en grijs* [*Lozenge with planes in ochre and gray*] had to be substituted. Thus, in 1919 Mondrian could not yet free himself completely from the world as it manifested itself to him. The connection was no longer strong, however; he readily abandoned his plan to use the *Dambord compositie* as an illustration of the third scene of the trialogue ("because a starry sky was exactly the occasion for its creation"[40]) when the photograph failed to meet his approval.[41]

In 1916 and 1917 Theo van Doesburg, Bart van der Leck, and Vilmos Huszár were also abstracting their subjects to compositions of lines and rectangular color planes. They, however, proceded much less radically, and they chose lighter and more commonplace subjects, such as figures and still lifes. One explanation for the difference is that Mondrian's aspiration to diminish the recognizability of the subject had a long history. As early as 1908 he had given objects different colors than they had in reality; he had painted trees in red and blue in order to "dematerialize" them. Then, under the influence of cubism, an abstraction process had set in; he had opened up forms and reduced them to their essential horizontal and vertical lines. Just before Mondrian met van Doesburg and van der Leck, this process had culminated in *Compositie X* (1915) and *Compositie* (1916). For some time, van Doesburg remained under the influence of Janus de Winter's lyrical abstractions; in 1916–17, via Huszár, he crossed over to a geometric form language. Van der Leck had already been using geometroidal forms for some time when he met Mondrian, although not as a result of an interest in recent international developments in the visual arts; his preference for geometrical forms originated with his ideas about monumental art. The not very expressive character of Mondrian's paintings appealed to van der Leck, and shortly after he met Mondrian (probably in the spring of 1916) he began to abstract his motifs by opening up the contour and "destructivizing" the form. Still, van der Leck's paintings have quite a different effect than Mondrian's; they give a more anecdotal and naive impression. This is connected with the manner in which van der Leck abstracted the figurative subject. In many cases it remains possible to retrace the starting motif by connecting the blocks. In Mondrian's work, however, putting the blocks together never produces a tightened version of the motif. Influenced by cubism, he had developed a method of viewing the subject and the background as an inseparable unity. It is because of this that his starting motifs are often much more difficult to recognize.

The acquaintance between van der Leck and Mondrian stimulated Mondrian, too, as his *Compositie in lijn* shows. A photograph of this painting in its first state (figure 43) shows many similarities

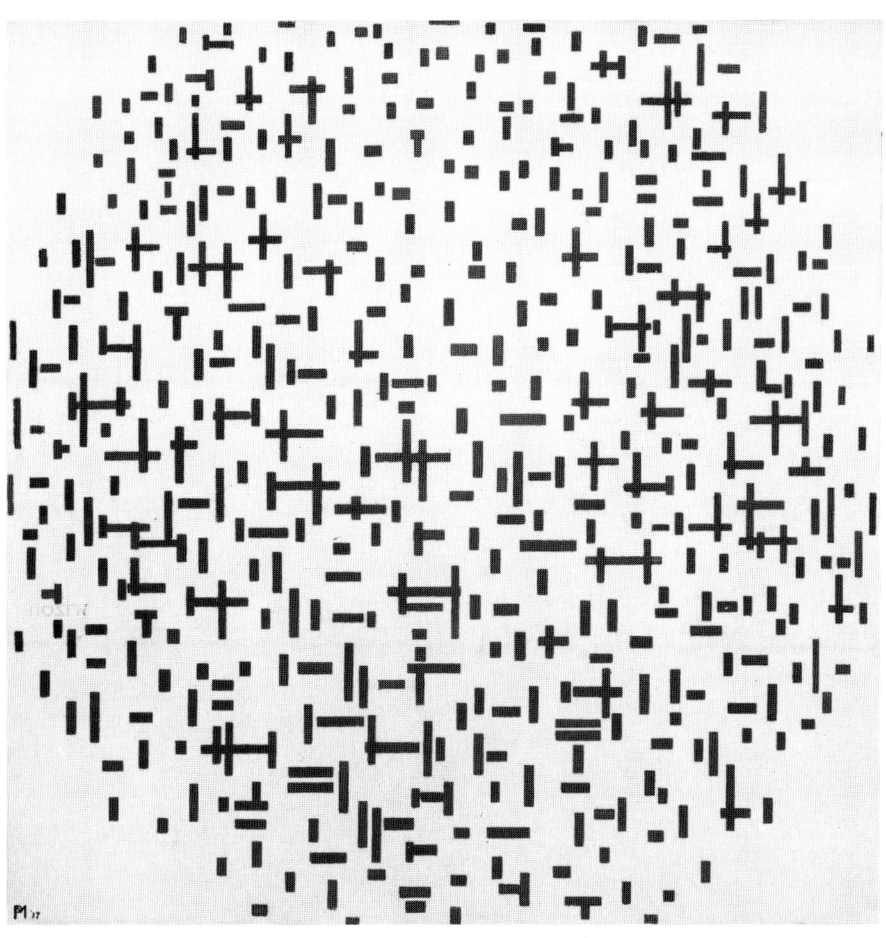

39

40

39 Mondrian, *Compositie in lijn* [*Composition in lines*], 1917. Oil on canvas, 108 × 108 cm. Rijksmuseum Kröller-Müller, Otterlo.

40 Mondrian, *Compositie X,* 1915. Oil on canvas, 85 × 108 cm. Rijksmuseum Kröller-Müller, Otterlo.

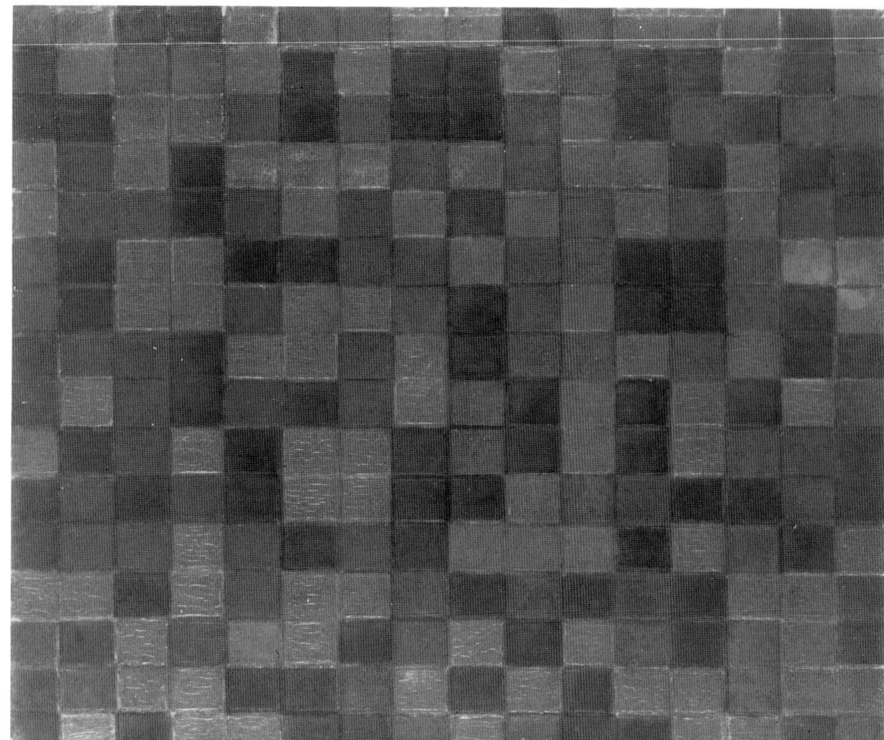
41

42

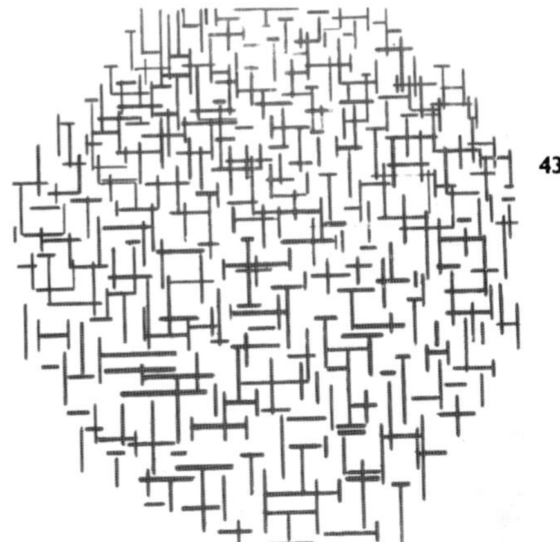

43

with *Compositie X* (figure 40). The relatively long and thin lines form a sort of lattice over the plane of the picture. In the finished painting the line fragments are shorter and thicker, with the result that they resemble small blocks. They are also more isolated, sometimes without any mutual contact. Moreover, Mondrian decided to make the background a solid white. He had also done that in *Compositie X,* but he had accounted for that with the nonartistic argument "lack of time."[42] In 1917 the white background was an intentional choice, probably after van der Leck's example.

1917: Color

An important question that the De Stijl painters asked themselves and each other was: Which colors should be used in abstract compositions? Mondrian, in his texts, always pleaded for primary colors, on the ground that they are much less material than natural colors. In "Neo-Plasticism in painting" (1918) he states that the basis of the new painting is "color brought to determinacy," and he explains what he means: Volumes must be reduced to planes; these planes must be rectangular; and natural colors must be converted to primary colors. The pictorial means a modern painter can use are thus restricted to red, yellow, and blue rectangles.[43]

At the beginning of 1916, Bart van der Leck was the only one who was already juxtaposing the primary colors, unmixed, on canvas; his interest in monumental art probably played an important role in this not very painterly approach. Neither van Doesburg nor Huszár nor Vantongerloo was limiting himself to the primary colors; green, purple, and orange occur in their paintings. Mondrian is usually considered to have been dogmatic in his use of color, but the colors in his paintings became forceful only after 1920, and they did not become purely primary until even later. At first, he reduced the intensity of the primary colors by mixing in white or gray. Contemplation of some paintings from 1917 suggests that this restraint probably originated from his aim to achieve a well-balanced proportion between the elements of the composition. He was, in point of fact, not concerned with color as a phenomenon in itself, but with the relations between the different colors and the way they were dispersed over the picture plane.

In the year when *De stijl* was officially founded, Mondrian painted five "compositions with color planes" on white backgrounds. One of those (by way of exception a gouache) was reproduced in the periodical in January 1918. The small planes are in yellow, red, and blue of a forcefulness hitherto unusual for him. Mondrian mentioned the gouache several times in letters to van Doesburg. In August 1917 he had photographs made of it, which he sent to van Doesburg. In the accompanying letter of September

41 Mondrian, *Compositie dambord, donkere kleuren* [*Checkerboard composition, dark colors*], 1919. Oil on canvas, 84 × 102 cm. Gemeentemuseum, The Hague.

42 Mondrian, *Lozangique met vlakken in oker en grijs* [*Lozenge with planes in ochre and gray*], 1919. Oil on canvas, 84 cm in diameter. Rijksmuseum Kröller-Müller, Otterlo.

43 Mondrian, *Compositie in lijn,* initial state, 1916–17. Photograph in Bremmer Archive, Gemeentearchief, The Hague.

5 he points out that the color balance is impaired in the print; the yellow is too light, the blue too dark. He wrote the same on the back of the photograph of the gouache which he sent to Louis Saalborn a few weeks later (figure 44). This observation probably prompted him to look at the gouache again to scrutinize its color proportions. Mondrian clearly found it difficult to get used to the forceful colors of this painting; in any case, he had difficulty finding the equilibrium for which he was striving so hard. "I myself do want equilibrium, but the color makes it real again," he wrote about the composition in his next letter to van Doesburg.

In the other "compositions with color planes," executed in oil, the three primary colors were mixed with a lot of white and were approximately equal in tonal value. Therefore, Mondrian was able to change the size and the position of a color plane without disturbing the equilibrium. It is not as difficult to achieve a well-balanced proportion with pastel colors as it is with pure colors, which have a strong optical effect. A large dark-colored plane recedes from white and "punches a hole" in the composition; a light color has, for the eye, a protruding effect.

The search for equilibrium played an important part in Mondrian's use of color, but in a letter to van Doesburg he also mentioned another reason for reducing the intensity of the color. Although van Doesburg was rather free in his choice of colors, he often pointed out that one should not "pollute" colors by mixing them with gray; he was of the opinion that doing so caused "tone." He associated that word with old (impressionist) art; it did not have a very favorable meaning for him, as is apparent from the following passage from a letter to Anthony Kok dated May 3, 1917: "Painters of old used to attempt to express their emotions through tone. Music had already done that before they did. Therefore the term 'tone' has been derived from music; tone is, in connection with painting: breaking of color. In music, tone is: breaking of sound. In the art of painting this has led to painting with dirt. That was called art of sentiment." In a few paintings from 1918 Mondrian did, nevertheless, "pollute" colors in this manner. Van Doesburg saw these paintings at the 1919 exhibition of the Hollandsche Kunstenaarskring. He must have vented his displeasure immediately, because on February 13 Mondrian wrote a letter in which he defended his use of colors. Mondrian's defense indicates how much the view of the world he had formed via Theosophy influenced his formal decisions: Most people had not yet reached that level of evolution at which one is able to digest colors of optimal force; therefore, it was still necessary to use colors nearer to nature than the purely primary ones. "Furthermore," he wrote, "I use those mute colors for the time being, adjusting to the

44

present-day surroundings and the world; this does not mean that I would not prefer a pure color."

Mondrian's words make it clear that in 1919 he still took the natural environment into account, in respect to motif as well as color. The two checkerboard paintings from that year provide insight into the manner in which he wanted to incorporate natural colors into abstract painting. That the paintings differ only in color may mean that Mondrian took the sky as his starting point in both cases, and that he wanted to depict it at different times of day; the dark blue, red, and orange of the one painting may have been meant to suggest the night sky, and the pastel hues of the other are not far from visible reality if it is interpreted as a rose-tinted morning or evening sky. There is yet another argument that supports an interpretation of the light-hued composition as a morning or evening sky with clouds. In a 1923 article about Mondrian, the artist Herman Hana relates the "checkerboard blocks" in this painting to the cumulus clouds that occur regularly in Mondrian's paintings of church towers and lighthouses from 1909 and 1910: "The 'cumulus clouds'—a predilection of Mondrian's—are sailing around it in cloudlike unawareness. How could they suspect that they are the prototypes of the master's famous 'checkerboard' blocks?"[44] It is not certain, however, that Hana was referring particularly to the lighter of the checkerboard compositions of 1919; he may have been talking about all Mondrian's compositions with rectangular color planes.

1918: Grid paintings

In 1918–19 Mondrian no longer made up a composition from separate color planes against a solid background; now he divided the canvas into compartments with a pattern of horizontal and vertical lines—a grid—and filled the compartments with different colors. These grid paintings are related to a problem which was of concern to several of the De Stijl artists and for which they tried in mutual consultation to find a solution. In their theory, the new painting was characterized as flat, without any illusion of space or perspective. In practice, however, it appeared not to be easy to completely eradicate spatial effects.

Mondrian's "compositions with color planes" from 1917 still have a somewhat spatial effect; the colored blocks seem to float in front of the white background. In the last two paintings of this series, Mondrian attempted to link the foreground and the background more closely by dividing the background into rectangular planes of different shades of light gray. (See figure 45.) Even then, however, the result was not completely planar; the distinction between colored planes (foreground) and gray planes (background) still remained.

45

44 Mondrian, *Compositie met kleurvlakjes* [*Composition with color planes*], 1917. Gouache on cardboard, 48 × 60 cm. Shown here are the front and the back of a photograph sent by Mondrian to Louis Saalborn, dated September 24, 1917. The photograph and the painting are now in private collections.

45 Mondrian, *Compositie met kleurvlakjes* [*Composition with color planes*], 1917. Oil on canvas, 47 × 60 cm. Private collection.

Huszár tried to solve the problem in 1917 by a kind of interweaving of foreground and background; as he formulated it himself, "What is first in front goes to the back, and vice versa." (In the chapter on Huszár in the present volume, this method is illustrated by figures 82 and 83.) Mondrian, however, did not consider Huszár's "weaving" a solution, as is apparent from a letter to van Doesburg dated January 8, 1918: "The last photograph which Huszár sent me I thought rather beautiful, but still the background stays background with him, just as with me; even in his Hammer and Saw."

Mondrian's 1918 paintings show a new attempt to bring all compositional elements to one level. Colored and uncolored (white and gray) planes are treated in the same manner; they are pushed together and set within a grid. The dark gray, nearly black lines of the grid mark the boundaries of the planes. The suggestion of color planes floating in front of a white background is, for the most part, suppressed. In a passage from a letter to Bremmer dated February 27, 1918, Mondrian states emphatically that it had indeed been the problem of figure and ground that had motivated him to try another method of dividing the picture plane: "Those 8 pieces are once more a development in which I found a better solution for color planes on a ground. While I was working it appeared to me that the color planes on a solid plane in my work do not form a unity. With van der Leck this does indeed happen, but he works differently, after all."[45] Huszár, too, used grids in the first half of 1918. Perhaps he arrived at this solution by way of his stained-glass compositions, independent of Mondrian; however, it may also be that Mondrian's first grid paintings, which were exhibited in March 1918 by the Hollandsche Kunstenaarskring,[46] gave him the idea. Van Doesburg made his first grid paintings later in the year, Vantongerloo in 1919. The problem played no role at all for van der Leck.

All the paintings made by Mondrian in 1918 are grid paintings in the sense that the picture plane is divided by wide horizontal and vertical lines. The method that brought about the division, however, changed in the course of that year. In the beginning Mondrian placed the lines intuitively, but from about June on he used a simple mathematical system.[47] Mondrian took no pains to disguise this method. Two of his lozenge compositions (e.g., figure 47) show regular patterns of lines; in two other lozenges and two perpendicular works, some parts are covered with color but the paint is somewhat transparent (see, e.g., figure 42).

The correspondence reveals that early in 1919 Mondrian had to defend the regular division of planes against van Doesburg, whose own paintings show a strong similarity to Mondrian's compositions

46

46 **Mondrian, *Compositie met kleurvlakken en grijze lijnen* [*Composition with color planes and gray lines*], 1918. Technique, dimensions, and whereabouts unknown; photograph in Vilmos Huszár's estate.**

47 **Mondrian, *Lozangique met grijze lijnen* [*Lozenge with gray lines*], 1918. Oil on canvas, diameter 121 cm. Gemeentemuseum, The Hague.**

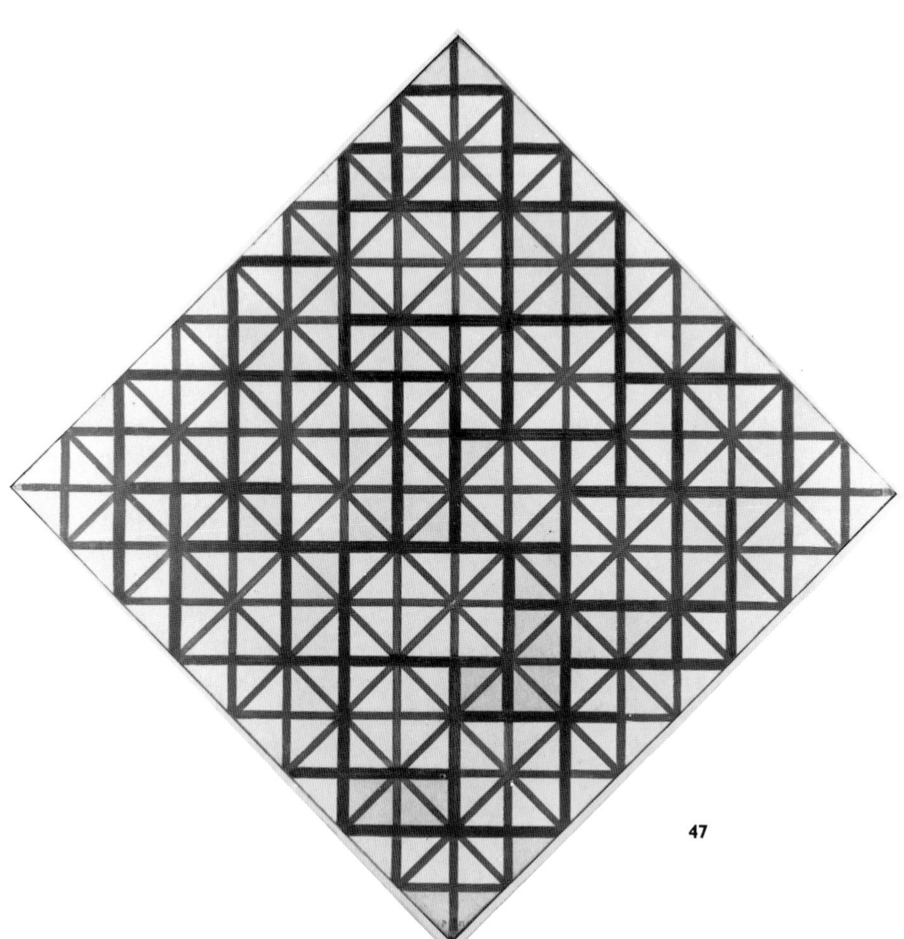

47

from the beginning of 1918 (when Mondrian's grids were not yet systematic). Van Doesburg probably objected less to the use of a systematic grid in itself than to the fact that Mondrian showed the system so clearly. He pointed out to Mondrian the danger of repetition in a painting, and he tried to convince him that he could eliminate most of the repetition by making the planes differ more in size, so that the composition would not show so clearly that it had been derived from a system.[48] Mondrian did not pay much attention to this criticism. In the two checkerboard paintings from 1919—the last ones he made before his departure for Paris—he let the system determine the composition; each comprises 256 small rectangles of the same size, albeit of different colors. Van Doesburg now began to really worry about the way Mondrian put his theories into practice. On June 24, 1919, he wrote to J. J. P. Oud: "Maybe his departure for Paris was necessary to give him new possibilities in his work. Refreshment. His most recent works are lacking composition. The division of the plane is uniform. Hence ordinary rectangles of the same size. Contrast has only been achieved by means of color. I find it at variance with his theory of dissolving position and size. This is equality of position and size."

Use of mathematics

Mondrian's idea of explicitly presenting a systematic division of the plane was also difficult for Huszár to accept. His 1918 paintings in which he did divide the plane systematically do not show this method explicitly. Mondrian's, van Doesburg's, and Huszár's different views on the use of mathematics in the visual arts probably account for this difference.

Of course, working according to mathematical principles was nothing new in itself. Through the ages artists had used mathematics to construct perspective and to determine the correct proportions between depicted objects. It was a tool, and rarely was a deeper meaning attached to it. Van Doesburg and Huszár, too, considered mathematics primarily as a tool; in their collaborations with architects they had to follow certain rules regarding sizes and proportions.

Such rules had the additional advantage of curbing the artist's individuality. The contributors to *De stijl* aspired to a universal validity; a work, although the result of intuitive decisions by an artist, must never be individual or arbitrary. Once, the extent to which a work of art was a true-to-life representation of the subject could be used as a measuring stick; now, the general validity of an abstract work could be checked mathematically. Against this background, it is understandable that van Doesburg and Huszár

48 Mondrian, *Compositie met kleurvlakken en grijze lijnen* [*Composition with color planes and gray lines*], 1918. Appendix IX of *De stijl*. Technique, dimensions, and whereabouts unknown.

accepted the use of a system. Huszár even went so far as to plead not only for uniform proportions of size but also for standardized colors; this explains his enthusiasm for Ostwald's color theory, about which he wrote in *De stijl* in August 1918: "We painters must use the colors that are inspired by our intuition, but this (subjective) intuition is (objectively) controllable. Whereas we, up till now, had the experience of nature (primitive) as a standard of control for the objectivity of the presentation, now we get control of colors through science."[49]

Van Doesburg and Huszár saw in the systematic method two advantages of the combination of the idealistic with the practical: When they were collaborating with other artists, the system served as a guideline according to which they could, apart from all personal artistic decisions, realize a work of monumental art in one style. Moreover, they could lay down the design exactly in terms of the codes of the system, so that others could undertake the execution. Huszár wrote: "When a painter makes a design for an interior he nowadays must discuss everything with the house-painter and select and mix the colors etc. in order to get the desired shade in the end—all this with much trouble and loss of time, while when in possession of the atlas he can send a statement of the codes to the housepainter, who can find the colors in his atlas and mix them accordingly. This seems to us a modern, practical method."[50]

Mondrian had a very different view of the role of science and mathematics in art. His paintings were self-sufficient; he never had to take requirements from the outside world into account. A mathematical system was for him not a tool but an artistic solution to a formal problem—a solution that, however paradoxical this may sound, had an intuitive origin. He found the irregular grid paintings from the beginning of 1918 unsatisfactory because of the disorderly manner in which the lines divide the plane. When a vertical line is cut off at the intersection with a horizontal one, sometimes another vertical line continues along from a point a few millimeters to the left or the right of the intersection. The same thing happens horizontally; there the lines shift up or down. Apart from an untidy zigzag effect, it gives the illusion, particularly at the borders, that the planes overlap one another. (See figure 48.) A regular plane division, in which the lines continue from top to bottom and from left to right (or at least can be thought to do so), brings order to the chaos.

For some time, Mondrian elected to use a regular plane division based on mathematics because he wanted to represent order and harmony. Like many other Dutch artists of the early twentieth century, he based his use of mathematics on a belief that there is a higher reality, with a systematic logical structure, behind the natural appearance of things. This thinking was influenced greatly by Neo-Platonism and Theosophy. A remark in a letter of June 13, 1918, reveals that Mondrian, because of this philosophical background, looked at mathematics very differently than Huszár and van Doesburg, who praised it mainly for its exactness. In that letter he told van Doesburg that he did not see the regular plane division in his paintings as mathematical in the literal sense: "As for this pure proportion, I think that when one talks about that in art, it is already a foregone conclusion that that cannot be a pure mathematical proportion." Mondrian was convinced that art stood on a higher spiritual level than the pure rationality of empirical science. Mathematics in art could therefore never be ordinary mathematics, for something had been added that lifted it to a higher level. Theosophy sometimes refers to a "holy mathematics," which reveals fundamental truths whereas "profane mathematics" is strictly linked to the intellectual powers of man.[51] In these terms, Mondrian's interpretation can be described as "holy mathematics," and Huszár's and van Doesburg's, with some reservations, as "profane mathematics."

At first, Mondrian did not understand why van Doesburg objected to a completely systematic division of the plane. Mondrian thought that an artist who determined the proportions intuitively could just as easily fall into repetition. Only when he saw the reproduction of *Lozangique met vlakken in oker en grijs* in *De stijl* in August 1919 could he understand why van Doesburg discerned too much repetition in it. According to Mondrian, the repetition was not nearly as striking in the original, because the planes were in different colors; in the black-and-white reproduction, though, they all had the same gray tone, so it seemed as if the whole canvas was uniformly colored and was divided only by dark lines. This was the second time that Mondrian became aware of problematic aspects in one of his works through a black-and-white photo. Both cases concerned the precarious relation between the size of a plane and its color value. In the case of the gouache, the equilibrium had been labile because of the force of the colors; the photo motivated Mondrian to return to the use of muted colors so that he could differentiate the sizes of the planes better without disturbing the balance. In the case of the *Lozangique,* the photo made Mondrian realize that well-balanced color values created a monotonous effect and that a regular line pattern offered little opportunity for variation. Thus, in the first works he created after his return to Paris in June 1919, Mondrian tried different color solutions and a new way of dividing the plane. Within a year his colors became very strong, and he began to use lines to divide the canvas into compartments of greatly differing sizes and shapes.

1918: The diagonal[52]

In 1918 the De Stijl painters discussed, apart from the aforementioned subjects, the use of oblique lines juxtaposed with, or instead of, horizontal and vertical lines. Van der Leck's work and that of his friend and follower Peter Alma[53] provided the immediate occasion for this discussion.

The opinions on the use of the diagonal differed greatly. Mondrian took a less dogmatic position than is usually thought. He did not make the fundamental assumption that a vertical line in opposition to a horizontal one is the only way to represent a well-balanced proportion; rather, he looked, with the others, for a way to use oblique lines. Letters to van Doesburg show that he tried to justify this implementation theoretically. These letters also make it possible to reconstruct the history of the diamond-shaped paintings Mondrian made in 1918 and 1919, which can be regarded as his artistic contribution to the discussion.

It was at the end of 1917 that Mondrian first mentioned his disagreement with van der Leck about the shape of color planes. He had shown van der Leck his article "Beeldingsmiddel en compositie" ["Means of representation and composition"], which would appear in January and February 1918 in *De stijl.* Van der Leck had disagreed with Mondrian's contention that color planes had to be rectangular and had pleaded with him to offer more options in the choice of shapes by replacing "rectangular" in the article by "rectilinear." Mondrian held to his opinion that the rectangular enclosure was the most exact expression of equilibrium, particularly since he saw that opinion confirmed in *The secret doctrine*[54]; however, he did not peremptorily dismiss the use of different geometric figures.

Mondrian had always placed the rectangles parallel to the borders of the painting. Apparently van der Leck's comments caused him to rethink this, because not very long afterward he started on a composition wherein the planes were placed diagonally on the canvas. He wrote to van Doesburg about this on April 4, 1918. Van Doesburg, who then probably was working on his article about Alma's painting, had asked Mondrian for his opinion on the use of oblique lines. The problem was apparently of current interest to several De Stijl artists, and Mondrian dealt with it extensively: ". . . on the oblique line I agree with you: if combined with the perpendicular I think it is to be rejected. In van der Leck's case I am not sure: his works still don't seem individual; I think that is because he works in a way totally different from ours. Some time ago I started a thing completely in diamonds. . . . I'll have to see if this is possible; intellectually I would say yes. There is something to say in favor of it, because the vertical and the horizontal can be found everywhere in nature: with diagonals I could dissolve that. But I think in that case there can never be added horizontal or vertical lines, or any sort of oblique lines [i.e., other than diagonals]." (Van Doesburg had severely criticized the combination of oblique and straight lines in Alma's *Saw and goldfish bowl;* see note 53 below. According to him, the painting had an effect of perspective, because of the domination of one oblique direction, that disturbed not only the equilibrium of the work itself but also that of the environment in which it would hang—it contrasted with the horizontal-vertical proportion of architecture.)

Thus, the painters differed considerably on the use of oblique lines. Van der Leck wanted to use all kinds of geometric forms. Van Doesburg took architecture into account and therefore found the domination of oblique lines unacceptable. Mondrian, who presumed that his paintings were autonomous, was not unsympathetic to the oblique position, but the shapes had to be rectangular and could not be combined with planes or lines in a different orientation. Huszár's opinion about this is not clear. Since his paintings from this period show only horizontal and vertical lines, and since like van Doesburg he wanted to integrate painting and architecture, it is plausible that he shared van Doesburg's opinion.

The "thing completely in diamonds" to which Mondrian referred in his letter to van Doesburg must have been one of the four lozenge paintings he had in progress. (See, e.g., figure 49.) During the course of 1918 he encased the diamond-shaped color planes in a grid, using a system of horizontal, vertical, *and* diagonal auxiliary lines. According to a letter to van Doesburg written in February 1919, Mondrian suddenly got the idea to rotate the square paintings 45 degrees: ". . . I now hang several pieces like this: ◇, in order that the composition becomes like this +; whereas in this way □ the composition is like this × (à la van der Leck for example)."

The literature on Mondrian has offered several explanations for the hanging of paintings in the "diamond shape." The diamond shape has been said to be a Theosophic symbol for the well-balanced proportion between matter (the downward-pointed triangle) and spirit (the upward-pointed triangle).[55] Mondrian is also said to have copied it from escutcheons which were hung on columns in churches in the seventeenth century; therefore, it could have a religious connotation.[56] The shape could also have been chosen in order to obtain a certain spatial effect, comparable to what the impressionists achieved by close-up cutoffs.[87] For the first diamonds none of these explanations are plausible, because they are based on the presumption that Mondrian had a preconceived notion in creating them. There is not a single indication that he had

49 Mondrian, *Lozangique met kleurvlakken* [*Lozenge with color planes*], 1919. Oil on canvas, 49 × 49 cm; shown in original, upright position. Rijksmuseum Kröller-Müller, Otterlo.

contemplated making diamond-shaped paintings; on the contrary, his words indicate that the diagonal hanging was a spontaneous inspiration, due to his unhappiness with the diagonal direction of the original composition. The exhibition of the Hollandsche Kunstenaarskring in which he wanted to participate would open on February 22, and there was little time to make drastic changes; the most obvious solution was to turn the canvas.

Personal motives probably also played an important part in Mondrian's change of opinion about the diagonal. Apparently, he associated oblique composition with van der Leck's work. During the course of 1918 their friendship had cooled considerably, mainly because of van der Leck's critical attitude toward *De stijl.* When Mondrian heard that van der Leck was to exhibit his work in Utrecht in the beginning of 1919 without having told him anything about it, this meant the definite end of their friendship, as is apparent in a letter to van Doesburg dated January 3: "My friend! van der Leck is having an exhibit in Utrecht, so I heard from somebody else. A short while ago he told me that he had no work ready yet! I shall visit him sometime. I never talk to him about De Stijl any more, not after I discovered that he was not sympathetic to it."

After the split with van der Leck, Mondrian's opinion concerning the use of oblique lines reversed. Wanting to keep his paintings from being connected with those of van der Leck, he hung his canvases in such a way that they showed a composition of vertical and horizontal lines. He withheld the two diamonds (e.g. figure 47) that showed oblique lines.

1919–20: Paris

After the war, Mondrian returned to Paris at the first opportunity, in June 1919. He stayed for a short time in the studio of Conrad Kickert on the Rue du Départ, which he had used before the war and where he had left a part of his work from those years. In November he found a studio of his own in a building on the Rue de Coulmiers. Exactly two years later he had to look for new lodgings, and so it happened that he returned to the Rue du Départ, where he got the use of two rooms on the third floor. There he would live for more than fourteen years, until the beginning of 1936.

Mondrian's departure from the Netherlands did not keep him from contributing to *De stijl,* and he also continued writing to van Doesburg to report on current matters and to discuss his ideas at length. (The two had never visited very frequently anyway, so the distance did not make much of a difference.) Van Doesburg stayed with Mondrian in Paris for several weeks in February and March 1920 (alone) and in the spring of 1921 (with his new girlfriend Nelly).

Mondrian's contacts with the other *De stijl* contributors (except van der Leck) were more sporadic. He did not begin a correspondence with the architect J. J. P. Oud until early 1920, and they did not meet in person before the summer of that year. He did not meet Georges Vantongerloo until April 1920 in Paris, nearly two years after the latter had associated himself with *De stijl.*

Vantongerloo was very theoretically inclined. He tried to analyze the visual appearance of things in his own pseudo-scientific way, and to record the cosmic order in numbers and diagrams. A major part of his ideas stemmed from Schoenmaekers's books, but, whereas Mondrian was attracted to Schoenmaekers's general philosophy, Vantongerloo paid particular attention to his physical and mathematical ideas.

At first Mondrian had some interest in Vantongerloo's ideas, but his attitude changed when the two got into an argument about color. It appears that Vantongerloo did not appreciate Mondrian's use of color and that he had a quite different approach. Before I go deeper into this, I will describe how Mondrian's new color compositions originated and how they differ from his previous works. In order to do this, I have to take up the thread in the summer of 1919, at the moment when Mondrian got to see the reproduction of *Lozangique met vlakken in oker en grijs* in *De stijl.* As I have said, this was what motivated him to think about the effect of color. Now he became aware why van Doesburg had criticized the regular division of the plane and the muted colors. On September 6, 1919, Mondrian sent van Doesburg a postcard, on which he wrote about the painting: "I now agree with what you wrote in the past: that there is indeed something of a 'repetition' in it; it was much less so in the original, I daresay because of the color values. But still I try to avoid that in my new things."

Mondrian had tried to create an equilibrium in his painting between what he called "the rhythm" and "the invariable proportion." The latter was apparently brought on by the mathematical system, the former by the planes of different size and color derived from that system. All colors had been given about the same value by means of strongly detoning them with white. In this way all impression of depth was avoided, but the effect was rather monotonous. The harmony was based on the unity of equal parts, not on the unity of opposites. Mondrian realized this and tried to do something about it. His colleague Jacob Bendien, who published an article about him in 1932, also appears to have had a sharp eye for this sort of thing. Bendien was probably referring to the abstract paintings of these years when he wrote: "In striving for equilibrium all unity through equality must be avoided. . . . At first Mondriaan's colors, however different externally, had many internal similarities. That is to say that these colors, however far apart they may be in the spectrum, still evoked about the same feeling. Thus his work had a pleasant decorative tranquility, without much depth, but very accessible. However, this tranquility has nothing to do with the living balance of the—also internally—strongly contrasting colors of his later work."[58]

The most important aim was, as Mondrian formulated it in a letter dated September 16, 1919, to represent rhythm and proportion in a living harmony. In order to achieve this, he decided to vary the dark colors of the lines, and not to adhere to the regular division of the plane any longer. He wrote about this in a letter dated October 11, 1919; the formulation shows that he was seeking a solution to the problem in consultation with van Doesburg: "I also had already noticed that not all lines must always be equally dark. I think you are right. Now again I do not always stick to the regular division." But a glance at the works Mondrian must have started in the second half of 1919 makes it evident that the most important innovation was the coloration. Red, yellow, and blue are detoned with white only slightly or not at all; they are strong, clear, and contrastingly juxtaposed.

For many months Mondrian worked to perfect the equilibrium in these paintings. They were not finished until 1920, and therefore they are dated accordingly. Nevertheless, it is all but certain that Mondrian had already arrived at his method before the beginning of the new year. In a letter dated December 4, 1919, he tells enthusiastically about a painting that pleases him more than all previous ones, and he is very eager for van Doesburg's opinion: "I would gladly send you a photograph immediately, but I will let it sit for a while before I apply the last paint, and see how it stands up." The same letter contains a passage about the furnishing of Mondrian's studio. On November 1 he had moved to the studio on the Rue de Coulmiers, and this move had, according to him, a very favorable influence on his work, because he now was not bothered by Kickert's antique furniture. Moreover, he told van Doesburg, he had furnished his new surroundings stylishly by painting the furniture and putting cardboard rectangles on the walls.[59] There is no extant photograph of the furnishings of the studio on the Rue de Coulmiers, but the portion of the trialogue "Natural reality and abstract reality" that was published in the May 1920 issue of *De stijl* probably gives a fairly accurate description of the room. In the text, Mondrian tells precisely what colors he used. For instance, the part of the wall next to the window was divided by a red, a gray, and a white piece of cardboard, a shelf with a gray box and a white jar, and an ivory-colored curtain underneath which was a small orange-red cabinet. For the rest, the space contained a gray-white worktable, a yellow stool, and a sofa, upholstered with a black pelt, against a dark red wall panel. In a description of this room in the newspaper *Het vaderland* of July 9, 1920, every wall is called "a kind of painting with blocks." The reporter also mentions the bright colors in the painting on the easel, "the latest one the painter is working on": "It is divided into rectangular blocks, filled in with . . . bright red, blue, and black."[60]

Less than a year earlier, Mondrian had used muted instead of pure colors, because he still wanted to adjust to his environment. Now, by implementing the principles of Neo-Plasticism in the interior of his studio, he could liberate his surroundings from the old atmosphere, and in these liberated surroundings he could use more intense colors without conflict.

The new harmony

In May 1920 the first six paintings in the new style were completed. Mondrian immediately sent three to the Netherlands for the exhibition of La Section d'Or[61]; these are now known as *Compositie A, Compositie B, and Compositie C,* as they were called in the exhibition catalog. The other three were originally to go to Brussels, where a simultaneous exhibition of La Section d'Or would take place. This plan fell through, however, and Mondrian must have kept the works in his studio for some time. Letters reveal that the new plane-and-color divisions in these paintings were judged rather unbalanced and inharmonious by Georges Vantongerloo and by the painter Leopold Survage. Both these men had very specific ideas about the way in which equilibrium should be represented in a work of art, and they tried to persuade Mondrian to use more mutually harmonizing colors and to divide these evenly over the canvas.

At their very first meeting, in April 1920, Mondrian and Vantongerloo got into a discussion about colors. Their talk was centered on the concept of harmony. Vantongerloo had recently become convinced that an artist could only bring equilibrium into his work by starting with seven basic colors. He had developed an ingenious method for determining and checking the division of these colors in a composition. With the help of a disk, he computed the necessary quantities and intensities of the separate colors for a painting so that all the colors added together would yield a neutral gray. At first Mondrian did not understand exactly how this method worked, and was rather impressed by Vantongerloo's theoretical expositions. "He has a circumstantial manner of explaining, but I believe he is very clever in technical matters," he wrote to van Doesburg on April 19, a few days after the visit.

50 Mondrian, *Compositie II*, 1920. Oil on canvas, 63 × 56 cm. Private collection.

When Wilhelm Ostwald's article "Die harmonie der farben" ["The harmony of colors"] was published in *De stijl* in May, Mondrian got the idea to ask Vantongerloo for his opinion on the subject. He more or less expected that Vantongerloo would be able to put the new division of colors, which he had been implementing since his return to Paris, on a theoretical basis, as Ostwald had done for what Mondrian called "the old harmony." Mondrian believed that the "new harmony" was visible in his own paintings. In a letter dated June 12 he suggested to van Doesburg that a commentary on Ostwald's article be published in *De stijl,* and he mentioned Vantongerloo as the obvious person to write that article. "I remember," wrote Mondrian, "that he thinks Ostwald is wrong in his detoning with black and white, and that he thinks his method 'with the schijruif [disk]' (as he says) is better. You know more about that; I just do it intuitively, as I said to Vantongerloo, but I do think that the theoretical element can be of great importance for Neo-Plasticism in general."

Mondrian's admiration for Vantongerloo's technical and theoretical knowledge disappeared at once when he got a letter (around the end of August or the beginning of September) in which Vantongerloo—probably in answer to Mondrian's question about the theory of the new harmony of colors—set forth his method in detail. Only then did it dawn on Mondrian that Vantongerloo computed the color proportions within a composition by a rational method. Mondrian's aversion to such a method is evident from the following sarcastic passage in a letter to van Doesburg dated September 5: "I already wrote to you that I corresponded with him about colors. And now he writes me that he has invented a whole system about eternity—o no, I mean about unity—based on the seven colors and seven tones!!! You know, he uses all seven of them too, damn it, just like the rainbow. You already told me it was ugly. Now he, with his Belgian intellect, sets up an auxiliary system which is, in my opinion, based on nature. He has not the faintest idea of the difference between in the way of nature and in the way of art. I now see how well I discriminated between the unconscious and the conscious: he is computing everything with his ordinary consciousness. . . . I had only expected something of him as a sculptor, and to tell me technical things about color. . . . He behaves like an ordinary Theosophist."

Leopold Survage, with whom Mondrian was in regular contact after his return to Paris, also was of the opinion that there was no evidence of a harmonious color division in the new paintings. Although Survage did not rely on a pseudo-scientific system, and although his ideas about harmony were, like Mondrian's, purely intuitive, there was an important difference between Mondrian's and Survage's starting points. Survage, a rather orthodox cubist, considered the center of the canvas as the center of the composition, around which the shapes and colors were to be evenly distributed. Mondrian, on the other hand, tried (in part because of his search for flatness) to avoid compositions in which one could point out a center, which might have the effect of a vanishing point in perspective. In a letter dated June 15, Mondrian told van Doesburg in what respects Survage had found his paintings unbalanced: "I first showed him the little square one that you and I think so good [figure 50]. He thought that it was not well balanced. The yellow was not harmonious against the red, etc. And the two small blues at the top had no counterpart in blue at the bottom (I tend to think that this, among other things, makes it so off-centered). I then said that we were looking for another harmony; he contended that there was only one. . . . He also began to talk very theoretically about colors. I then saw that, on the contrary, a well-balanced proportion does not always require harmonizing colors, and have taken care to write down some things about that."

Because of the criticism he received from Survage, in whose vision the traditional element could more easily be exposed than in Vantongerloo's, Mondrian became more strongly aware that the term *harmony* was always used to denote the equilibrium between *equivalent* parts. In the trialogue in the June issue of *De stijl* he had already called that "the old harmony" in regard to Ostwald, and had introduced "the new harmony" in opposition to that. The well-balanced proportion of opposites was the most important goal of the new painting: "Natural harmony, the 'old' harmony, doesn't express itself according to the concept of pure equilibrium. It expresses itself as a relative equilibrium. In it the 'repetition' that characterizes nature still dominates: it expresses antithesis, but not the process of one thing continually canceling another. Precisely for this reason, Neo-Plasticism goes against the old harmony. It is the difficult task of the modern artist to realize the new harmony."[62]

It was still not quite clear to Mondrian in the first half of 1920 how this new harmony should look on canvas, and it seemed better to him not to go into the problem of achieving harmony through color contrasts more deeply in his texts.[63] But in September, after Vantongerloo's letter and after van Doesburg had stated his ideas on harmony, Mondrian gained the insight that he could use the effect of strongly contrasting pure colors to achieve a new harmony. In an undated letter that must still have been written in the same month, Mondrian told van Doesburg that he was pleased by his remarks, and also with Vantongerloo's letter, because through them he had gained insight into how the new harmony distinguished itself from the old one in practice: "Since the new harmony has to be totally different, I too am partial to dissonants, and now I remember that Survage and Vantongerloo again and again found fault in disharmony in my most recent pieces (paintings). I believe that equilibrium can exist with dissonants; you do too, eh? All this goes straight against Vantongerloo, and it is just because of him that my mind has cleared up, particularly after what you write. I have great confidence in your clear view."

After this discovery, Mondrian must have set to work immediately, with enormous energy. He wrote van Doesburg in the beginning of 1921 that he had twenty or thirty new canvases ready. He would gladly have exhibited all of them in April at Léonce Rosenberg's gallery, but since he shared the exhibit with Léger and others there was no room for such a large entry. In the end, Rosenberg chose five of Mondrian's paintings, and they ended up hanging near the back of the room. One of them—the piece visible in the center of the wall in figure 51—would, to Mondrian's great astonishment, be bought by his old patron Bremmer for the collection of Mrs. Kröller-Müller.[64]

Methods of composition

The paintings with very irregularly distributed, eccentrically located lines and color planes can be regarded as Mondrian's reaction against the use of mutually harmonizing colors and shapes, for which both Vantongerloo and Survage had pleaded. With his new ideas about harmony, Mondrian strove to achieve a well-balanced composition through the contrasting effect of the colors and through variation in the sizes and shapes of the planes. The strongly asymmetric compositions in which a white square takes up almost the whole plane of the picture and the color planes have been reduced to a few narrow strips at the borders of the canvas are good examples of this method. (See figures 54 and 55.)

Mondrian must have had certain standards according to which he determined whether a composition was well balanced. As his reaction to Vantongerloo's system reveals, these standards were not objective, controllable rules that had evolved according to certain laws. Mondrian worked from his artistic intuition, as of old. In the new harmony the main focus was the visual effect, which was determined by the shape, size, quantity, and intensity of the color planes. The standards Mondrian set himself in composition were thus connected with the suggestive force of the pictorial means he used. The new manner in which Mondrian handled these means can be seen in four of the many canvases he painted between 1920 and 1923. The choice of the pieces is based primarily on the distribution of lines, which is representative of most of Mondrian's compositions from these years. Apart from that, the fact that two of these paintings were reproduced in *De stijl* suggests that Mondrian himself considered them successful.

From 1921 on, Mondrian developed two standardized methods of dividing the canvas, which I will call the central and the peripheral way.[65] The first method is shown in the large *Compositie met rood, geel en blauw* [*Composition with red, yellow, and blue*] that now hangs in the Haags Gemeentemuseum (figure 52) and in the equally large composition of the same name that was pictured in *De stijl* in December 1922 (figure 53). In these paintings, Mondrian quartered the picture plane with a horizontal and a vertical line, which intersect around the center of the canvas. He brought variation to the plane division by subdividing the rectangles thus created in different ways with short line segments. He colored some of those small planes red, blue, yellow, and black. Both works have a red and a blue plane in the left half of the canvas, and a yellow and two black planes in the right half. By varying only the place and sizes of the blue and the black planes, Mondrian achieved two different kinds of equilibrium. In figure 53 all the dark planes have been placed in the bottom half, two of the three at the very bottom. They act visually as "weights," anchoring the lines securely to the base of the canvas. In figure 52 the blue plane is situated somewhat below the center, at the intersection of the lines, and there is a small black block in the upper right corner; therefore the composition seems to radiate from the center.

The peripheral method can be seen in the small *Compositie met rood, geel en blauw* shown as figure 54 and in a painting of the same dimensions and title (figure 55) which was reproduced in *De stijl.* In these two paintings the lines were positioned almost identically, in such a way that a large square was created away from the center of the canvas. Mondrian left this square without color and placed all the colored planes along the borders. The 1921 painting has a small strip of red at the upper left, a small black block and an oblong plane of yellow at the bottom left, and at the right next to the square a small bar of blue. Though small, the black block appears indispensable for the equilibrium of the composition. The

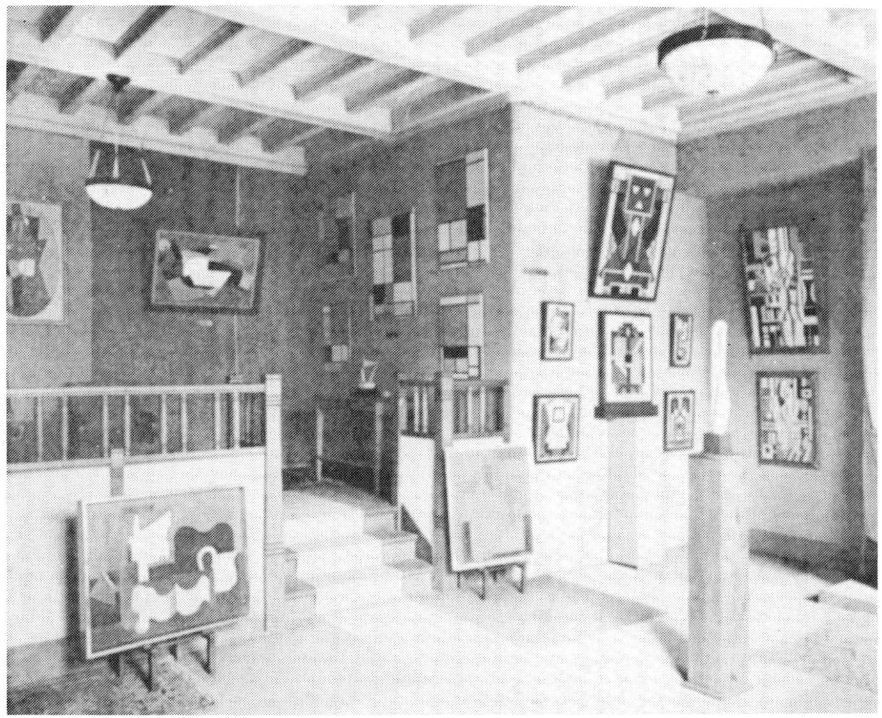

51

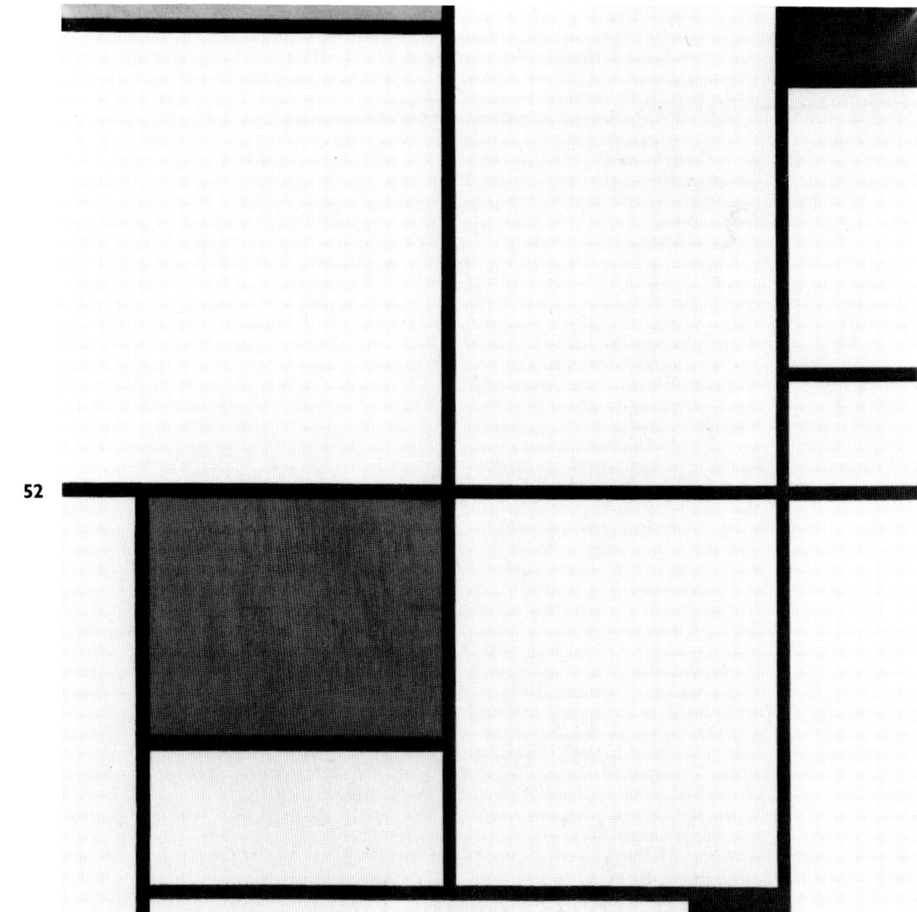

52

51 The exhibition Maîtres du Cubisme, at the Galerie de l'Effort Moderne, in Paris, 1921.

52 Mondrian, *Compositie met rood, geel en blauw* [*Composition with red, yellow, and blue*], 1921. Oil on canvas, 103 × 100 cm. Gemeentemuseum, The Hague.

53 Mondrian, *Compositie met rood, geel en blauw,* 1921. Oil on canvas, 103.5 × 99.5 cm. Private collection.

54 Mondrian, *Compositie met rood, geel en blauw,* 1921. Oil on canvas, 39.5 × 35 cm. Gemeentemuseum, The Hague.

53

54

light yellow color at the bottom of the painting has little optical weight; it is not a solid basis for the line pattern, which would be afloat without the black as point of support. Moreover, the small dark block accentuates the left side of the composition, which keeps the visual center of gravity from being situated at the right side in the blue bar; that would give the illusion that the canvas tilted to the right. In this case, equilibrium was brought about mainly by a precisely balanced distribution of the small red, yellow, blue, and black planes.

In the 1922 painting, the small black block is missing; instead, a short line divides the column at the left into two parts. The colors have been shifted counterclockwise: the yellow to the site of the blue, the blue to that of the red, and the red to the bottom, to the site of the yellow and the black. In terms of color, the center of gravity is clearly situated in the left half of the canvas; only the light yellow is on the right. The whole is stabilized by the large square, which, bordered by yellow instead of blue, seems less enclosed and therefore larger and "heavier." In this painting the planes without color are more involved in the creation of the equilibrium.

Thus, Mondrian knew how to bring about a different kind of equilibrium by making only small changes, changing the atmosphere of the painting drastically. The way a spectator experiences a painting, of course, depends partly on his personality, and sometimes even on his state of mind at the moment, yet there exists a certain collectively experienced emotional value of the pictorial means. Habits of looking at things are deeply rooted in the traditions of one's own culture.[66] Mondrian always manipulated the pictorial means consciously, as is evident from the formal discussions among the De Stijl painters, and he himself must have experienced his paintings as different in character. However, he never made public statements about the specific meaning of the colors, lines, and white planes in the individual paintings. His letters to his colleagues likewise contain only sporadic remarks in this direction. Yet the correspondence with Oud occasionally reveals that Mondrian connected a certain expression with the appearance of a painting and, on that basis, discerned different types in his work. For instance, he sent four paintings to the Netherlands in the beginning of 1927 in hopes that Oud, who had important connections in the art world, would perhaps be able to sell them. In a letter of May 13 he stressed that he had intentionally chosen four different types: "All of them are different in expression." It is a pity that Mondrian did not add what those different paintings expressed.

From the correspondence with Oud it is also evident that when a painting was commissioned, Mondrian made the kind of composition the buyer preferred. For instance, some acquaintances of

55 Mondrian, *Compositie met rood, geel en blauw,* 1922. Oil on canvas, 39.5 × 35 cm. Reproduced in *De stijl* 7, no. 78 (1927), p. 82.

Oud's saw a Mondrian painting in his house and were so impressed by it that they wanted to have something like it themselves. Mondrian's matter-of-fact reaction to this commission, in a letter dated May 22, 1926, indicates that he was not at all offended: "Because of all those exhibitions I have not had time yet to make a painting in the spirit of the one which you own, and which those acquaintances of yours wanted to have." When in 1929 both the Museum Boymans in Rotterdam and a private buyer (the architect Karsten) were interested in a painting that was being exhibited in the Stedelijk Museum in Amsterdam,[67] Mondrian sold the painting to the museum and suggested that Karsten just hang another work for the time being "until I have one ready in the spirit of the painting in the Museum Boymans."[68]

Mondrian pointed out the different options to one of his friends, the Swiss architect Alfred Roth, in a letter dated September 7, 1929. Here he made no secret of the fact that the various types had different meanings, which apparently were particularly related to the colors: "Write to me whether you prefer blue and yellow, white and gray, or rather red, a little blue and yellow and white and gray. These last works with red are more 'real,' the others rather more spiritual."[69] Thus, Mondrian saw paintings with red as more real—closer to nature—than paintings with only blue and yellow or paintings without any colors at all. The less color had been used, the more "spiritual" was the expression. (A related term, which Mondrian used a few times to characterize the paintings with a lot of white and few lines and colors, was *quiet.* "The last ones are still quieter; for you such a one would be preferable, I think," he wrote in 1926 to Oud.) For Roth, who replied that he would like a painting with all three colors, Mondrian made a painting with an extraordinarily large red plane. If in doing this he took Roth's personality into account, he must have thought Roth particularly earthy. However, it may also be that Mondrian was only playing on Roth's name; the German word for *red* is *rot.*

The first author to point out the importance of the color distributions in Mondrian's paintings was the painter Jacob Bendien, who was very conscious of the factors that play a part in the creation of an abstract composition. Bendien had already, in 1912, developed a form of abstract painting in which the course of the lines and the colors expressed thoughts and feelings.[70] It is not surprising that in an article written in 1932, on the occasion of Mondrian's sixtieth birthday, he went into the emotional value of the colors in Mondrian's paintings. He expressed the suspicion that Mondrian had mostly adhered to the general psychological effects of the colors. This would mean that yellow was related to activity and blue to passivity; that red stood for the natural life, black for death, and white for the potential of life; and that gray mostly expressed the feeling of lifelessness. In his article Bendien gave several examples of color combinations and discussed their meanings in terms of these often contrasting concepts. For instance, a combination of red, white, and black suggested life in contrast with the not yet living and the no longer living; yellow and gray "active fierceness, bordering on frenzy, opposite the sober, calm neutrality." There were also some combinations that were not very expressive, such as red and blue or red and yellow. The effect not only depended on the choice of colors but was also strongly determined by their quantity and their location on the canvas; a color plane at the top had a very different value from the same one at the bottom of the composition, and one on the right side had a different effect from one on the left.[71]

Mondrian's paintings and a few remarks in his letters suggest that he probably took meaning into account when creating his compositions. Yet the paintings are never diagrams in which every shape and color has a specific symbolic meaning. Nobody would dare to describe a painting in which a small blue plane is positioned opposite a large, empty white field as expressing "modest passivity in contrast to large life possibilities," to use Bendien's terms. It was not Mondrian's intent to juxtapose different feelings; on the contrary, he was always searching for an equilibrium in which all specific meanings would cancel one another. Bendien knew this. Having given a number of examples of color combinations and their meanings, he emphatically pointed out at the end of his article that it was impossible to completely explain Mondrian's paintings in such terms: "It seems very understandable to us that Mondrian is very hesitant to express the feelings which the various primeval elements evoke in us separately, because he aims . . . to bring these feelings into such close and active contact with one another that they cancel one another out in a higher equilibrium. Therefore the issue is not to understand the elements, but to understand the equilibrium. Understanding of the separate elements can help us to grasp the equilibrium, but it also can, if we dwell on them too much, hamper us in experiencing the equilibrium, the more so since often all kinds of allegoric meanings and associations of thoughts which have nothing to do with their direct emotional effect are being attached to the elements."[72]

1920–1923: Architecture[73]

From the start, *De stijl* promoted a synthesis of painting and sculpture with architecture. The other painters and the architects involved with the periodical devoted their energies to the development of a universal image language for the various arts. But Mondrian, in his first three years as a contributor, had very little interest in architecture and applied art.

After his return to Paris, in the same period when he was developing a definite style in his paintings, Mondrian became more interested in the problem of applying the principles of Neo-Plasticism, which had been developed in the field of painting, to other fields. The design of his studio, the last installments of the "Natural and abstract reality" trialogue, and the brochure *Le Néoplasticisme* (which he wrote during the course of 1920) testify to that.[74]

Mondrian's ideas about architecture contributed to the deterioration of his good relationship with Theo van Doesburg, and consequently to the end of his contribution to *De stijl.* Mondrian, Oud, and van Doesburg had rather different ideas about the implementation of certain principles of form in architecture, as their discussions reveal. Moreover, these discussions made Mondrian realize that van Doesburg, up to that moment his most important supporter, held an opinion that differed in principle from his own.

This discovery may have embittered Mondrian somewhat. Later in his life, he repeatedly stated that he had always had to find "the true way" on his own.[75] That was not quite the case; in the early years of De Stijl he had found support and inspiration in the work and ideas of others. As we have seen, the ideas for his abstract compositions were gained from dialogues with Bart van der Leck, Theo van Doesburg, Vilmos Huszár, and Georges Vantongerloo. Of course, there was not always consensus. The opinions of the painters often remained opposed, and then Mondrian demonstratively opted for a solution of his own. Remarkably, van Doesburg's opinion and approval were always very important to Mondrian in these cases. Several remarks in Mondrian's letters show that he had his doubts about the existence of a likeminded De Stijl group; however, it does not seem to have occurred to him that he and van Doesburg might find themselves in disagreement. "The two of us must make the whole movement," he wrote on June 12, 1920, and in many other letters there are words of the same tenor. Mondrian's sense of solidarity with his colleagues found its clearest expression in a letter dated April 4, 1922. On the occasion of his fiftieth birthday he had been interviewed by a reporter of the *Nieuwe Rotterdamsche courant,* who had asked Mondrian about his contacts with other artists and whether he belonged to a "circle."[76] This question appears to have been painful and difficult to answer. "I have also emphasized that this method was not peculiar to me alone," Mondrian wrote to van Doesburg. "I have represented it as a 'movement,' but those guys always know better! . . . He has put something of it across when he writes about you. I have not put Vantongerloo on the same level with you, but I also did not want it to be a movement of two people. Huszár I could not mention at all. It was difficult!"

Although Mondrian was still convinced in the beginning of 1922 of his and van Doesburg's unconditional unanimity, van Doesburg already felt in 1919 that there were important differences of opinion about some topics. This emerges from a letter he wrote to Oud on June 24 of that year. Mondrian had visited van Doesburg just before his departure for Paris, and they had "talked about a lot of things." Van Doesburg told Oud in this letter that he had gotten quite a different view of Mondrian because of the latter's "Theosophical avowals." He found it particularly odd that Mondrian did not consider Neo-Plasticism a transition to something else again but saw it as an endpoint of painting; somewhat baffled, he quoted Mondrian's explanation: "When I look through the canvas—when I pass through a wall—what will I then still see on that canvas or that wall?" Van Doesburg was also disappointed that Mondrian could not muster more interest in the practical problems that he found so important: "He is indifferent to many subjects, such as architecture, communism etc."

Mondrian and Oud met for the first time (and probably the last) in the summer of 1920.[77] It is understandable that van Doesburg at first did not encourage a meeting between these two important contributors to De Stijl, because Mondrian displayed little interest in architecture. However, when van Doesburg came to Paris in February of 1920, he noticed that in the meantime Mondrian had enthusiastically begun to experiment with colors in his studio, and consequently he advised Oud to visit Mondrian during his summer trip to France.

Around the middle of 1921, a debate arose between Mondrian and Oud about architecture. Van Doesburg soon joined in. He was furious because Oud had rejected his color designs for the housing at Spangen, and he tried to secure Mondrian's support in this dispute. Thus it came to a split between Oud, on one side, and Mondrian and van Doesburg on the other.

The connection between van Doesburg and Mondrian was not unseverable either. This came to light in 1923, the year after their split with Oud. In that year, when Mondrian and van Doesburg still had only sporadic contact with each other, Mondrian withdrew (though not officially) as a contributor to *De stijl.* His letters make it possible to follow the course of this dispute.

In the summer of 1921 Oud sent Mondrian the text of a lecture entitled "Over de toekomstige bouwkunst en hare architectonische mogelijkheden" ["On future architecture and its architectonic possibilities"] that he had recently delivered to the Vereniging Opbouw [Society of Architects] in Rotterdam.[78] This text gave Mondrian cause to doubt Oud's commitment to the new architecture, because in it Oud did not state explicitly that Neo-Plasticism was the basis for all renewal. On August 17 Mondrian wrote to Oud, thanking him for forwarding the lecture and chiding him gently: "You are writing very cautiously that a new, purer art is developing from cubism. Would it not have been better to state openly that Neo-Plasticism is the principle of all artistic expression (of these times). Solely by starting from the one and only firm principle that Neo-Plasticism discovered in painting we can speed up new things. If the people of De Stijl do not stand up together for this one thing, everything will go more slowly."

Oud must have answered that the strict rules formulated for painting could never be implemented in architecture, because architecture was restricted by practical requirements. For Mondrian, however, the fact that some ideas were not immediately practicable was no reason to eradicate them from the theory. Artists should work with an eye to the future—a future which in any case would be different from the present, and where things that seemed impossible now could very well be realized.[79]

At this point van Doesburg joined in the discussion. His disappointment with the failed Spangen collaboration was his main motive for attacking Oud's ideas, and he more or less forced Mondrian to choose sides. In a two-part article titled "De realiseering van het Neoplasticisme in verre toekomst en in de huidige architectuur" ["The realization of Neo-Plasticism in the distant future and in present-day architecture"], published in the March and May 1922 issues of *De stijl,* Mondrian proved his loyalty to van Doesburg. Moreover, in an undated letter written in August or September of 1922, he broke off his friendship with Oud. For van Doesburg, just as for Mondrian, the greatest objection to Oud's ideas was that Oud let utility prevail over the aesthetic principles of Neo-Plasticism. In two articles in the *Bouwkundig weekblad,* van Doesburg emphasized that these principles should be the basis of the new architecture.[80]

Whereas Mondrian thought that Neo-Plastic architecture could not yet be brought about because architecture was too subservient to the public and to money,[81] van Doesburg thought that Neo-Plastic ideas could already be put into practice. Thus, Mondrian could continue to create paintings "free from architecture" without any qualms. Van Doesburg, however, could not accept that Neo-Plastic architecture was out of the question for the present, and devoted himself to the task of realizing his ideas through collaboration with the young architect Cornelis van Eesteren.

During the course of 1923 Mondrian came to the conclusion that the argument with Oud had not been important enough to justify cutting off the friendship so abruptly. In August he cautiously reopened contact; in doing so he told Oud that he did not collaborate with van Doesburg any more, because the latter believed that an architectural environment in which all principles of Neo-Plasticism were applied could actually be realized.

Van Doesburg had noticed Mondrian's reserved attitude toward his grandiose architectural schemes. In a letter of September 1923 to Antony Kok he expressed disappointment that Mondrian was staying aloof from the organization of the architectural exhibition of De Stijl, to be held in October and November at the Galerie de l'Effort Moderne in Paris: "Mondrian . . . is not very interested, since he is of the opinion that it is still 'too early.' In addition he is not a good judge of architecture, as I noticed."

At first, Mondrian wanted to persuade himself as well as Oud that van Doesburg's practical atittude was the only reason for his reserve toward the architectural exhibition. However, van Doesburg's theoretical starting point also differed fundamentally from his. He became aware of this through a statement made by van Doesburg in his lecture "Der wille zum stil" ["The will to style"], which was published in *De stijl* in 1922.[82] Up to that moment, Mondrian had always been able to avoid discord with his most important supporter by dismissing a difference of opinion as "not a matter of principle." Even now, he at first perceived the contradiction in their words as merely apparent, and he explained it as a consequence of the fact that van Doesburg was working more with an eye to practice, and that he himself viewed the matter more theoretically. "Basically we are saying the same thing," he wrote.[83]

But the ideas van Doesburg put forth in "Der wille zum stil" are evidence that he and Mondrian were not saying the same thing any longer in 1922. He pleaded for a synthesis of the various fields of art on a monumental scale. Just as space in a painting should be represented not by perspective but by a system of planes, space within a building should be determined by the planes of the walls, whose form and color had to be in equilibrium. These requirements, for the most part, agreed with the principles Mondrian had formulated in his theory of Neo-Plasticism. Van Doesburg's theory, however, differed strongly in one respect. He was of the opinion that an artist should take into consideration the new scientific discovery that perception is dependent on place and time: "As a result of the new scientific and technical widening of vision, a new and important problem has arisen in painting and sculpture beside the problem of space: the problem of time."[84] Thus van

Doesburg integrated the phenomenon of change over the course of time into his theory; he had a dynamic picture of reality. Movement in space and time implied that there was no constant, fundamental idea any more; with time, the standard according to which reality could be tested changed. Mondrian's theory was based on the opposite principle. He was convinced that there existed one universal reality, which was the same in all places and at all times. Because things assume different aspects at different points in time, mankind was, according to him, no longer aware of the cosmic unity. Natural appearance, bound to place and time, disguised reality. In order to create a purely abstract image of the universal, it was necessary to do away with the aspect of time in the presentation.

Mondrian reacted to van Doesburg's lecture in a letter dated May 25, and one can sense from his words that he particularly objected to the introduction of the time element: "Now about your remark. Of course we are also basically of the same opinion in this. Only I do not agree at all with the positioning in time of architecture, because the new principle does away with time. . . . because I want, on the contrary, to eliminate time in the contemplation also of arch.[itecture]. . . . The sentence on page 32 I find unfortunately phrased. One could read in it that you take time into consideration, although I believe that that is not your intention and that you only want to say as I also said that space and time act (as one and the same). . . . (The sentence on p. 32 to which I am referring is this one: '. . . besides the problem of space another important problem: the problem of time.')"

It is a pity that the correspondence stops at such an important point. After the famous dada tour, in early 1923, van Doesburg came to live in Paris. He and Mondrian must have discussed their differences in person, and Mondrian must have concluded this time that they were fundamental and important.

In the aforementioned letter to Oud of June 24, 1919, van Doesburg showed an awareness that he had different views about some things than Mondrian; in fact, he already sensed where the difference lay. Mondrian was of the opinion that the paintings they were making were the end of painting; that something more spiritual was unthinkable. Van Doesburg opposed this: "I defended the concept that we were a transition, just as Cézanne was to us—we again to something else. Everything is in perpetual motion! Mondrian is in fact a dogmatic."

Thus, the seed of the conflict between van Doesburg and Mondrian already existed in 1919. That the difference of opinion did not come to the surface until a few years later is related to the fact that the contact up till then had been mainly by correspondence. Van Doesburg probably wrote little about matters he knew would not interest Mondrian. For that matter, Mondrian did not exactly immerse himself in the ideas van Doesburg was propagating in *De stijl,* which from 1920 on were more associated with international developments than with Mondrian's rather esoteric views.[86]

In 1923, just at the moment of the difference of opinion about the factor of time, van Doesburg moved to Paris. A split became all but inevitable. In August 1924, Mondrian and van Doesburg agreed not to meet any more and to correspond only when necessary. They turned against each other more and more in their writings.[87] In 1928 their relationship was patched up when Mondrian met the van Doesburgs by chance in a café. As he wrote to Oud, they approached him so cordially that he could not remain angry any more. Van Doesburg was, according to Mondrian, "despite his faults . . . about the only one besides me who paints purely abstract art."[88] But in 1930 Mondrian had to sever contact again because of his friendship with Michel Seuphor, against whom van Doesburg had lashed out rather ferociously.[89] After van Doesburg's death a year later, the correspondence between Mondrian and Oud became much less intensive; apparently van Doesburg had been the cementing factor. The only original contributor to *De stijl* whom Mondrian still visited with some regularity was Georges Vantongerloo, but they probably did not often speak about De Stijl. For both of them, that period in their lives was long since closed.

Notes

1
P. Mondrian, "Het bepaalde en het onbepaalde," *De stijl* 2, no. 2 (1918), p. 17.

2
J. M. Joosten, review of C. Blok's *Piet Mondriaan: Een catalogus van zijn werk in Nederlands openbaar bezit,* in *Museumjournaal* 20, no. 2 (1975), pp. 81–82.

3
For more information on Mondrian's youth see H. Henkels, *Mondriaan in Winterswijk: Een essay over de jeugd van Mondriaan, z'n vader en z'n oom* (The Hague, 1979); H. Henkels, "Mondrian in his studio," in *Mondrian: Drawings, watercolors, New York paintings* (exhibition catalog, Stuttgart, The Hague, and Baltimore, 1980–81).

4
On the early landscapes see R. P. Welsh, *Piet Mondrian's early career: The "naturalistic" periods* (New York and London, 1977); R. P. Welsh, "Piet Mondrian: Landscapes before mid 1908," in *Mondrian and The Hague landscape painting* (exhibition catalog, Regina, 1969).

5
I. Querido, "Piet Mondrian" *De controleur,* May 29, 1909.

6
Letter from Mondrian to Israel Querido, *De controleur,* October 23, 1909, published in English in R. P. Welsh and J. M. Joosten, *Two Mondrian sketchbooks, 1912–1914* (Amsterdam, 1969), pp. 9–10.

7
R. P. Welsh, "Mondrian and Theosophy," in *Piet Mondrian centennial exhibition* (exhibition catalog, Solomon R. Guggenheim Museum, New York, 1971).

8
These ex librises are reproduced on page 42 of Henkels's *Mondriaan in Winterswijk* (note 3 above).

9
On cloudy skies as a theme for Romantic painters, see A. C. Esmeyer, "Cloudscapes in theory and practice," *Simiolus* 9, no. 3 (1977), pp. 123–148. On Romantic influences in other works by Mondrian, see R. Rosenblum, "Mondrian and Romanticism," *Art news* 64 (February 1966), pp. 33 ff.; R. Rosenblum, *Modern painting and the Northern Romantic tradition: Friedrich to Rothko* (London, 1975), pp. 173–194.

10
See R. Steiner, "Die zwei grundgesetze der farbenlehre im morgen- und abendröte und in der himmelsbläue—Gesundheit und krankheit in zusammenhang mit der farbenlehre," in *Das wesen der farbe* (Dornach, 1973), pp. 147–148.

11
A. Venema, "De stormachtige beginjaren van de 'Moderne Kunstkring,' 1910–1915," *Tableau* 1, no. 2 (1978–79), pp. 34 ff.

12
C. Kickert, "Kunstberichten," *Onze kunst* 10 (1911), p. 35.

13
Mondrian was in Domburg from September through the autumn of 1908, in the summer, autumn, and winter of 1909 (with interruptions), and from the end of August 1910 to the end of October. In the summer of 1911 he lived in Veere. See C. Blok, *Piet Mondriaan: Een catalogus van zijn werk in Nederlands openbaar bezit* (Amsterdam, 1974), p. 23.

14
L. van Ginneken and J. M. Joosten, "Documentatie: Kunstenaarsbrieven Kees Spoor," *Museumjournaal* 15, no. 5 (1970), pp. 264–265.

15
Mondrian was recorded in the municipal records of Amsterdam to have ceased to be a resident of that city on December 20, 1911. This indicates that his resolution was then already firm. See Welsh and Joosten, *Two Mondrian sketchbooks* (note 6 above), p. 11, n. 20.

16
Two sketchbooks have been reproduced in facsimile; see Welsh and Joosten, *Two Mondrian sketchbooks.* On the remnants of a third and a fourth sketchbook, see J. M. Joosten, "Mondrian's lost sketchbooks from the years 1911–1914," in *Mondrian: Drawings, watercolors, New York paintings* (exhibition catalog, Stuttgart, The Hague, and Baltimore, 1980–81).

17
Letter from Mondrian to H. P. Bremmer, quoted in J. M. Joosten, "Documentatie over Mondriaan (1)," *Museumjournaal* 13, no. 4 (1968), p. 211.

18
R. Knott, "The myth of androgyne," *Artforum* 14 (1975–76), p. 41.

19
Welsh, "Mondrian and Theosophy" (note 7 above), p. 50.

20
R. Steiner, *Het occultisme in groote trekken* (1910; facsimile reprint published in The Hague, 1979), pp. 88–226.

21
Knott, "Myth of androgyne" (note 18 above), pp. 38–45.

22
P. Mondrian, "De Nieuwe Beelding in de schilderkunst; natuur en geest als vrouwelijk en mannelijk element," *De stijl* 1, no. 12 (1918), pp. 145–146, note 4.

23
Welsh and Joosten, *Two Mondrian sketchbooks,* p. 16.

24
Ibid., p. 24.

25
Ibid., p. 48.

26
Ibid., p. 34.

27
Ibid., p. 47.

28
"I am exhibiting with Schelfhout, Jan Sluyters, and L. Gestel, but I keep out of any association. The Mod. Kunstkring has fallen apart because of Kickert's fanaticism." Letter from Mondrian to H. van Assendelft, published in J. M. Joosten, "Documentatie over Mondriaan (4)," *Museumjournaal* 18, no. 3–4 (1973), p. 218. On the history of the Moderne Kunstkring see Venema, note 11 above.

29
"I am still at the old work here. I hope through that to be able to lay away something "pour rentrer à Paris." [Letter from Mondrian to Lodewijk Schelfhout, February 1, 1915, published in J. M. Joosten, "Documentatie over Mondriaan (2)", *Museumjournaal* 13, no. 5 (1968), pp. 267–268.] "The war gets on only slowly." (September 29, 1914) "I think that the work will take a few weeks, and then I hope that there will come some more work, and that I then can go back to Paris." (September 1915) "I am trying to get money in order to be able to go back to Paris." (September 7, 1915) The letters from Mondrian to van Assendelft are published in "Documentatie over Mondriaan (4)," *Museumjournaal* 18, no. 3–4 (1973), pp. 178–218.

30
On this period see M. van Domselaer-Middelkoop, "Herinneringen aan Piet Mondriaan," *Maatstaf* 7 (1959–60), pp. 269–293.

31
These would later appear, reworked, in *De Stijl:* P. Mondrian, "De Nieuwe Beelding in de schilderkunst," 1, no. 1 (1917) through no. 12 (1918); "Het bepaalde en het onbepaalde," 2, no. 2 (1918). Carel Blotkamp has pointed out that this series of articles is not a closed entity; the introduction and the articles from June 1918 on were

written later. See Blotkamp, "Mondriaan—Architectuur," *Wonen/TABK* 4–5 (1982), p. 34, note 99.

32
Mondrian, *De stijl* 1, no. 9 (1918), p. 103.

33
Mondrian, *De stijl* 1, no. 5 (1918), p. 52.

34
Steiner, *Het occultisme* (note 20 above), pp. 232–233.

35
To compare Mondrian's ideas with those of Schoenmaekers see H. L. C. Jaffé, *De Stijl 1917–1931: The Dutch contribution to modern art* (Amsterdam, 1956), pp. 53–62.

36
This is in contrast with Georges Vantongerloo, who, on the other hand, adopted precisely Schoenmaekers's pseudo-scientific ideas and his method of representing these in diagrams.

37
Letter from Mondrian to H. P. Bremmer, published in J. M. Joosten, "Documentatie over Mondriaan (3)," *Museumjournaal* 13, no. 6 (1968), pp. 322–323.

38
Letter from Mondrian to H. P. Bremmer, published in J. M. Joosten, "Documentatie over Mondriaan (2)," *Museumjournaal* 13, no. 5 (1968), p. 269.

39
P. Mondrian, "Natuurlijke en abstracte realiteit III," *De stijl* 2, no. 10 (1919), pp. 109–113.

40
Letter from Mondrian to van Doesburg, August 1, 1919.

41
Carel Blotkamp has pointed out the possibility that the checkerboard painting in dark colors, not the diamond-shaped painting, is based on the starry-sky motif. See book reviews, *Simiolus* 8, no. 2 (1975–76), pp. 102–104.

42
"I had intended to make it in color, but I had no more time, and I thought that it expressed what it was supposed to express anyway." Letter from Mondrian to Bremmer, October 4, 1915, published in Joosten, "Documentatie over Mondriaan (2)," p. 268.

43
Mondrian, *De stijl* 1, no. 3–4 (1918), pp. 29–31, 41–45.

44
H. Hana, Piet Mondriaan, de pionier," *Wil en weg* 2 (1923–24), pp. 602 ff.; reprinted in *De fakkel* 1 (September 1925), pp. 62 ff. (see p. 63).

45
Letter from Mondrian to Bremmer, February 27, 1918, published in Joosten, "Documentatie over Mondriaan (3)," pp. 325–326.

46
Exhibition of Hollandsche Kunstenaarskring, Stedelijk Museum, Amsterdam, March 16–April 7, 1918. Mondrian's 1917 exhibit consisted of a few paintings with small, separate blocks on a white ground, and some of the new type with lines. See J. M. Joosten, "Abstraction and compositional innovation," *Artforum* 11, no. 8 (1973), pp. 55–59.

47
"I . . . was just working . . . on a regular subdivision. . . ." Letter from Mondrian to van Doesburg, June 13, 1918.

48
Van Doesburg's objections are known mainly from Mondrian's answer in a letter of April 18, 1919: "It is true that with regular subdivision there is a danger of falling into repetition, but that can be eliminated again by contrast. Everything can become a system, the regular as well as the irregular distribution; it all depends on the manner of solution. When I compare the work now reproduced in *De stijl* with, for instance, the diamond-shaped one, which you (and I, too) think best, then I see clearly that the latter one is better put together. It may be that the compartments could differ more in size, but that doesn't bother me here." The paintings Mondrian compares here are those shown in figures 48 and 42.)

49
V. Huszár, "Iets over de farbenfibel van W. Ostwald," *De stijl* 1, no. 10 (1918), p. 115.

50
Ibid., p. 117.

51
A. Gasten, "Pseudo-mathematica en beeldende kunst," in *Kunstenaren der idee: Symbolistische tendenzen in Nederland ca. 1880–1930* (exhibition catalog, Gemeentemuseum, The Hague, 1978), pp. 61–62.

52
Carel Blotkamp discusses the problem of the diagonal and the origins of the diamond-shaped paintings in detail in "What's up? Mondrian 1918/19," *Metropolis M* 2, no. 1 (1980), pp. 43–52, and in "Mondrian's first diamond compositions," *Artforum* 18, no. 4 (1979), pp. 33–39.

53
Theo van Doesburg, "Aanteekeningen bij bijlage XII. De zaag en de goudvischkom van P. Alma," *De stijl* 1, no. 8 (1918), pp. 91–94.

54
"I believe I am justified in this perpendicular position. *I* have everything from the Secret Doctrine (Blavatsky), not from Schoenmaekers although he says the same thing." [Undated letter from Mondrian to van Doesburg (probably from December 1917)]

55
Welsh, "Mondrian and Theosophy," in *Piet Mondrian centennial exhibition* (note 7 above), p. 50.

56
B. Hopkins, letter to the editor, *Artforum* 13 (March 1975), p. 8; M. Schapiro, "Mondrian," in *Modern art, 19th and 20th centuries* (New York, 1978), p. 259, note 7.

57
Schapiro, pp. 233–261. The different views are discussed extensively in E. A. Carmean, Jr., *Mondrian: The diamond compositions* (exhibition catalog, National Gallery of Art, Washington, D.C., 1979), pp. 45–54, and in E. Saxton, "On Mondrian's diamonds," *Artforum* 18, no. 4 (1979), pp. 41–45.

58
J. Bendien, "Piet Mondriaan—60 jaar," *Elseviers geillustreerd maandschrift* 42, no. 84 (1932), p. 171, also published in P. Citroen, *Jacob Bendien, een herinneringsboek* (Rotterdam, 1940).

59
Letters from Mondrian to van Doesburg, one undated (November 1919) and one dated December 4, 1919.

60
Quoted in Henkels's "Mondrian in his studio" (note 3 above), pp. 262–263. On the furnishings of the studio see also N. J. Troy, "Piet Mondrian's atelier," *Arts magazine* 53 (December 1978), pp. 82–87, and C. Blotkamp, "Mondriaan—architectuur," *Wonen/TABK* 4–5 (1982), pp. 35–36 and 44–51.

61
The International Exhibition of Works of La Section d'Or, Paris—organized by Theo van Doesburg, among others—was in Rotterdam from June 20 to July 4, in The Hague from mid July to mid August, in Arnhem in September and October, and in Amsterdam from October 23 to November 7.

62
Mondrian, *De stijl* 2, no. 10 (1919), pp. 109–113; 3, no. 8 (1920), p. 66.

63
Letter from Mondrian to van Doesburg, June 15, 1920.

64
This painting, *Compositie* (1921), is no longer in the Kröller-Müller collection; it is now in a private collection.

65
R. P. Welsh was the first to perceive the existence of a number of standard compositions in the years 1921–1935. The paintings differ mostly in color gradation, width of lines, and size of rectangles. See *Piet Mondriaan 1872–1944* (exhibition catalog, Gemeentemuseum, The Hague, 1966), particularly numbers 98, 100, 103, 107–111, and 113.

66
For an analysis of nonanecdotal visual data and their role in determining the meaning of the image, see M. Schapiro, "On some problems in the semiotics of visual art: Field and vehicle in image signs," *Simiolus* 6 (1972–73), pp. 9–19.

67
The exhibition A.S.B. (architectuur-schilderwerk-beeldhouwwerk, or architecture-painting-sculpture) was held in the Stedelijk Museum in Amsterdam, November 2–24, 1929.

68
Letter from Mondrian to Oud, December 8, 1929. The "composition with red, yellow, and blue" from Karsten's collection is not very similar to the "composition with yellow and blue" in the Museum Boymans van Beuningen, except in dimensions. It is possible that Karsten decided to keep the work that he could hang temporarily.

69
Letter from Mondrian to A. Roth, published in A. Roth, *Begegnung mit pionieren* (Basel and Stuttgart, 1973), p. 150.

70
On Bendien's work see M. Hoogendoorn, "Nederlanders in Parijs," *Museumjournaal* 17, no. 6 (1972), pp. 247–253, and *Kunstenaren der idee* (note 51), items 1, 8, 102, and 103.

71
Bendien, "Mondrian" (note 58), p. 172.

72
Ibid., p. 173.

73
Extensive information on Mondrian's attitude toward his architectural surroundings from his early years on can be found in Blotkamp, "Mondriaan—architectuur," *Wonen/TABK* 4–5 (1982), pp. 12–51.

74
Mondrian, *De stijl* 3, nos. 5–8 (1920), pp. 41–44, 54–56, 58–60, 65–59; Mondrian, *Le néoplasticisme, principe général de l'équivalence plastique* (Paris1920; English translation: "Neoplasticism," in *Mondrian,* exhibition catalog, Whitechapel Art Gallery, London, 1955).

75
See, for instance, J. J. Sweeney, "Piet Mondrian," *Bulletin of the Museum of Modern Art* 12, no. 4 (1945), reprinted in *Mondrian,* exhibition catalog, Museum of Modern Art, New York, 1948.

76
Anonymous, "Bij Piet Mondriaan," *Nieuwe Rotterdamsche courant,* March 23, 1922.

77
As far as I know, their long and intimate correspondence was based on this single visit. The correspondence mentions several times that Oud planned to come to Paris; however, something seems to have interfered each time. Although Mondrian never met Mrs. Oud, he addressed her in a friendly and familiar manner in his letters.

78
J. J. P. Oud, "Over toekomstige bouwkunst en hare architectonische mogelijkheden," *Bouwkundig weekblad* 42, no. 24 (1921), pp. 147–160.

79
Letters from Mondrian to Oud, August 30 and September 18, 1921.

80
T. van Doesburg, "De betekenis der mechanische esthetiek voor de architectuur en de andere vakken," *Bouwkundig weekblad* 42, nos. 25, 28, 33 (1921); van Doesburg, "De taak der Nieuwe Architectuur," ibid. 42, no. 1 (1921).

81
Letter from Mondrian to van Doesburg, undated (March 1922).

82
T. van Doesburg, "Der wille zum stil (neugestaltung von leben, kunst und technik)," *De stijl* 5, no. 2–3 (1922), pp. 23–41.

83
Letter from Mondrian to van Doesburg, May 25, 1922.

84
Van Doesburg, "Der wille zum stil" (note 82 above), p. 32.

85
Blotkamp, "Mondriaan—architectuur," *Wonen/TABK* 4–5 (1982), p. 41.

86
Although his letters of 1920 are larded with "dada" and "merdre," Mondrian was not a very committed dadaist. On December 10 he wrote to van Doesburg: "I won't write Dada any more, for although that was nice for showing *enthusiasm,* we are not even Dada in the long run."

87
A clear example of van Doesburg's criticism can be found in his "Licht- en tijdbeelding (film)," *De stijl* 6, no. 5 (1923), p. 62. In the interview "Het Neoplasticisme in schilderkunst, bouwkunst, muziek, literatuur" (*Het vaderland,* October 17, 1924), Mondrian criticizes van Doesburg openly. For more information see Blotkamp, "Mondriaan—architectuur," *Wonen/TABK* 4–5 (1982), 40–43.

88
Letter from Mondrian to Oud, September 7, 1929.

89
Letter from Mondrian to Oud, July 27, 1930.

56 **Vilmos Huszár in front of his house in Voorburg, ca. 1925.**

Vilmos Huszár

Sjarel Ex

In 1927 Vilmos Huszár concluded his brief contribution to the tenth-anniversary issue of *De stijl* with these words: "My aim is to dictate from a higher level of authority, and I will break the boulders with my head, or break my head on the boulders." This obstinate tone is characteristic of Huszár, and of his collaboration with De Stijl.

Huszár was one of the founders of *De stijl,* and (with some interruptions) he remained associated with it until 1923. Within the group of contributors he was a versatile and dynamic personality, active as painter, applied artist, interior designer, and theoretician. The end of his collaboration was not the end of his artistic development, and in fact he remained loyal to the principles of De Stijl through the 1920s.

The exhibition reviews from Huszár's De Stijl period show that his path was not strewn with roses. Mondrian was hardly understood in those times, but at least his fundamental attitude was appreciated. Huszár was seldom acknowledged as more than a disciple. To some people De Stijl was a scandal; for most it was a farce in which the actors could hardly be taken seriously. In the 1920s there was admiration for this avant-garde movement only within a very small circle, but within that circle Huszár had authority—particularly because of his interior designs.

In the historiography of De Stijl, Huszár has been slighted. His contribution was significant, however. In the first years he was especially close to Theo van Doesburg, who had a great admiration for his work. He took part in the essential artistic discussions, although this is hard to reconstruct because most of his works have been lost and are now known only through reproductions. The first volumes of *De stijl* regularly contained reproductions of his work and articles by him. Though his "aesthetic considerations" did not reach the theoretical level of Mondrian's articles, they certainly were among the most accessible writings in *De stijl.*

The early years

Huszár is the great unknown among the painters of De Stijl. Anyone interested in Mondrian, van Doesburg, or van der Leck can get extensive information, but little about Huszár can be found in the literature. Information about him in the years before De Stijl is even scarcer; for this reason those years will be emphasized here.

That Huszár was born on January 5, 1884, in Budapest, is commonly mentioned; after that the data are scarce. However, his estate contains a handwritten list with autobiographical notes, which he made around 1930. This little list, the information that can be gathered from a few early articles, the exhibition catalogs, the reviews, and the retrieved works give a fairly detailed image of Huszár in the years before 1917.[1]

Huszár was already artistically inclined at an early age, and from 1901 to 1904 he was enrolled in courses in mural painting and decoration at the School of Applied Arts in Budapest. Although he learned much about the technical aspects of painting, he was not happy with the constraints imposed on him. Wanting to become a free artist, he dropped out of school before finishing. This was a big step, but not an ill-considered or rash one, for during his vocational training he had scored some small successes at exhibitions (with a self-portrait, among other things). In 1904 he departed for the art academy in Munich, where he studied with the Hungarian painter Simon Hollosy.

During his studies in Munich, Huszár befriended the Dutch artist Anna Egter van Wissekerke, who also studied in Munich. From her hometown, The Hague, she knew the famous impressionist painter Jozef Israels, for whom Huszár had great admiration. She invited Huszár to visit her in The Hague, and he stayed there from December 1905 until March 1906. He painted a portrait of his hosts, Anna's parents, that was so well received that he began to get commissions for other portraits. Moreover, he had the opportunity to show his work to Israels, who gave him prudent advice. After some wanderings and an unsuccessful attempt to enter the art academy in Düsseldorf, he moved to The Hague at the end of 1906.

Almost immediately after Willy Huszár (as he was then called) settled in The Hague, he must have met the art critic H. P. Bremmer. In his autobiographic notes he listed the period from December 1906 to May 1907 as "The Hague, with Bremmer." It is not absolutely clear how this remark was meant, but it is certain that Bremmer influenced Huszár greatly in his first years in the Netherlands.

In this period Bremmer was prominent in the artistic life of The Hague. In 1906 his book *Een inleiding tot het zien van beeldende kunst [An introduction to the viewing of visual art]*, which he had written for the layman, was published. This book was fairly traditional in its choice of art and artists, and such was also the case with his 1909 book *Practisch aesthetische studies.* However, in the periodicals he published—*Moderne kunstwerken* (1903–1910) and *Beeldende kunst* (1914–1938)—Bremmer paid attention to the art of the Hague School and to modern Dutch and French painters. When Huszár made his acquaintance, Bremmer was promoting Vincent van Gogh, who was not yet so well known and who was certainly not appreciated everywhere. Huszár, too, admired van Gogh greatly. The annotated copy in Huszár's estate is evidence that he had read Mauthner's book *Vincent: Briefe* [*Vincent: Letters*] in 1906, and Huszár's 1907 painting *Zonsondergang* [*Sunset*] shows a strong van Gogh influence.

Huszár felt Bremmer's influence even at a distance. In February 1908, when he was staying in Paris with Anna Egter, he sent Bremmer a letter thanking him for his benevolent criticism. "I quite agree with you about the still life," he wrote; "its failure was caused by the fact that I, besides studying, also wanted to express a thought in this picture; I wanted to stylize and study at the same time, and that cannot be done in the same picture." In the letter he also expressed an interest in Gauguin. He ended by complimenting Bremmer and, at the same time, criticizing the Parisian painters: "Here there are a lot of bad painters who imitate Vincent, Gauguin, and Cézanne, and all the young painters are carried away with this, and I think that I too would have fallen into this pit if you had not opened my eyes to objective viewing. I am very grateful to you for that."[2]

"Objective viewing" was an approach that Bremmer stressed. It applied to the artist as well as the spectator. According to him, it did not matter much whether a work of art was good or bad, beautiful or ugly, or even whether it had been made after nature; first and foremost, the artist should have represented his intention as objectively as possible, and the work was to be judged according to this standard. Huszár's fascination with this way of thinking is evidenced by his copy of *Een inleiding tot het zien van beeldende kunst;* passages about objectivity are underlined and annotated. Even years later the influence of Bremmer's views came out in the "aesthetic considerations" Huszár wrote for *De stijl.*

In his letter from Paris, Huszár talked explicitly about "stylizing." This trend can already be perceived in paintings he made before his journey to Paris. Several paintings from 1907—the year of the van Gogh-like *Sunset*—have a very flat paint treatment, the effect of which is intensified by the use of tempera. One such painting is *Veluws vrouwtje* [*Woman from Veluwe*]. Here Huszár painted large areas in one color, virtually without gradation or detail, and bordered by rigid contours; there is almost no perspective to the surroundings.

During his stay in Paris and his subsequent six-month sojourn in London, Huszár could have seen quite a lot of modern art. In 1955 he stated that Picasso's and Braque's work had already impressed him at that time, and that he had visited Gertrude Stein.[3] In the works Huszár produced after this journey there is not yet a hint of cubist influence. There are, though, traces of the influence of the Nabis group, and particularly of the Hungarian painter Rippl-Ronai. The manner in which these painters juxtaposed soft colors, and

57

58

57 Huszár, *Zonsondergang* [*Sunset*], 1907. Oil on canvas, 57 × 67 cm. Private collection. The landscape is depicted in bright pink and green, and the brush strokes coincide with the rays of the sun.

58 Huszár, *Veluws vrouwtje* [*Woman from Veluwe*] (also known as *Oude vrouw* [*Old woman*]), 1907. Tempera on canvas, 70 × 46.5 cm. Rijksdienst Beeldende Kunst, The Hague.

59

60

59 Huszár, *Zelfportret met echtgenote* [*Self-portrait with wife*], 1910. Oil on canvas, 71 × 61 cm. Gemeentemuseum, The Hague.

60 Huszár, *Le livre*, 1911–12. Oil on canvas, 80.5 × 44 cm. Rijksmuseum Kröller-Müller, Otterlo.

61 Huszár, *Bloementuin te Almen* [*Flower garden at Almen*], 1912. Oil on canvas, 60 × 70 cm. Private collection.

62 Huszár, *Jongen kijkt naar witte wolk* [*Boy looking at white cloud*], 1912. Tempera on panel, 36 × 54 cm. Private collection.

their line treatment (derived from Gauguin), can also be found in much of Huszár's work from the years 1907–1909.

Returning to The Hague, Huszár again worked regularly as a portraitist. In Bremmer's circle he met the well-to-do Jeanne Elisabeth van Teylingen, whom he married in 1909. As his 1910 portrait of himself and his wife (figure 59) shows, he did not always stylize in this period; he also painted in a more naturalistic way. In addition to commissioned portraits, he painted fairly naturalistic landscapes and still lifes.

It can hardly have escaped Huszár that Bremmer was becoming more and more interested in Bart van der Leck, whose paintings he started buying in 1910. Van der Leck's work was then characterized by stylization and the use of bright colors, and in 1911 Huszár too began to use bright colors. An example of the possible influence of Van der Leck on Huszár is the painting *Le livre* (figure 60). It is dated 1911–12, which might indicate that Huszár worked a long time on it. As in his 1907 paintings, Huszár again used stylization here. The contours are heavy and rather rigid; there is a minimum of detail, and the colors are applied evenly. The intense colors can hardly be called true to nature; the woman's hands and face are yellow. She is clad in solid green and blue-black, which contrast against a bright blue background and a purple floor. The book is bright red, and the footwarmer is pink.[4]

Yet Huszár was not consistent in his stylization and his use of bright colors. He was still seeking a style of his own, as is evident from an interesting letter to Bremmer dated February 1911. From the letter it is also evident that their relationship had deteriorated somewhat. Bremmer was something of a despot, and Huszár was too obstinate to tolerate that. Bremmer had apparently said that Huszár should stop showing him his work, to which Huszár replied: "I believe that I am still too much of an artist to show in my work what I have learned from you. . . . During the last years so many new things have come my way that I have to have more peace of mind to be able to concentrate in a pure way, without other thoughts. You may ask yourself why I am writing all this. I am doing it because I feel as if this is a kind of parting with you as a teacher, and yet I believe that to be right. I was unable to be your student, and yet I feel your guidance. Therefore, please accept my gratitude; I hope to remain in contact with you as a human being."

The estrangement between Huszár and Bremmer was not radical, however. Huszár's wife continued to attend Bremmer's courses, and the Huszárs later subscribed to Bremmer's journals. *Le livre* and two other paintings by Huszár were bought by Mrs. Kröller-Müller on Bremmer's advice, and there are more indications of this sort that the contact between Huszár and Bremmer continued into the 1920s.

1912–1914

In 1912 Huszár took part in his first exhibitions in the Netherlands. The first was in March and April at the gallery Artz and De Bois, in The Hague. The other exhibitors were the painters Maxime Dethomas and Simon Bussy, now both forgotten. Huszár showed *Veluws vrouwtje, Le livre,* and some ten landscapes with such titles as *Gezicht op Leidschendam* [*View of Leidschendam*] and *Boerderijen te Almen* [*Farms at Almen*]. His work of this period appears to have been inspired by Gauguin and van Gogh; see, for example, figure 61. The second exhibition, which paired Huszár with the sculptor and potter W. C. Brouwer, took place in September 1912 at the gallery of the Rotterdamsche Kunstkring. In his copy of the catalog,[5] the critic Albert Plasschaert noted "influences of Toorop, Verster, Bremmer and Vincent." Many of the works Huszár had exhibited in The Hague were on view again in Rotterdam, but there also were a few additions. One of these, which was dated 1912 in the catalog and which must have originated between April and September, was *Jongen kijkt naar witte wolk* [*Boy looking at white cloud*]. This painting, shown in figure 62, indicates the direction in which Huszár's style was developing. The forms are still stylized, although there is more attention to details. What is most striking in this painting, though, is the use of colors. The little boy, clad in green, sits in a yellow-ochre space. His hair is red and his shoes are blue. The colors are even brighter than those in *Le livre.* The white frame with yellow dots was specially made for the painting.

In 1913, Huszár took part in two exhibitions of De Onafhankelijken [The Independents] in Amsterdam. This association had been founded in 1912 for the purpose of holding nonjuried exhibitions, after the example of the Indépendants in Paris. The first exhibition took place in May of 1913, and it made a stir mainly because of the presence of abstract works (by Erich Wichman, among others). As was the case during the 1912 exhibitions, Huszár's paintings were hardly mentioned in the press. However, his works were mentioned in several reviews of the second show of De Onafhankelijken, which was held in November 1913. Here Huszár exhibited six paintings, two of which—*Femme couchée* (now in the Museum Kröller-Müller) and *Vieillard* (the whereabouts of which are unknown)—attracted particular attention. These paintings were characterized in *De kunst* of December 1913 by the critic Wolf as "experiments in color." Plasschaert, too, noted Huszár's exhibit. He wrote at the end of November in *De nieuwe courant*: "Willy Huszár of Voorburg probably lives near a cemetery and is possibly plagued by terrible hallucinations in which half-decomposed bodies appear to him. . . . The yellow-ochre 'femme couchée,' lying in bed in a green robe, [and] the 'vieillard' with

61

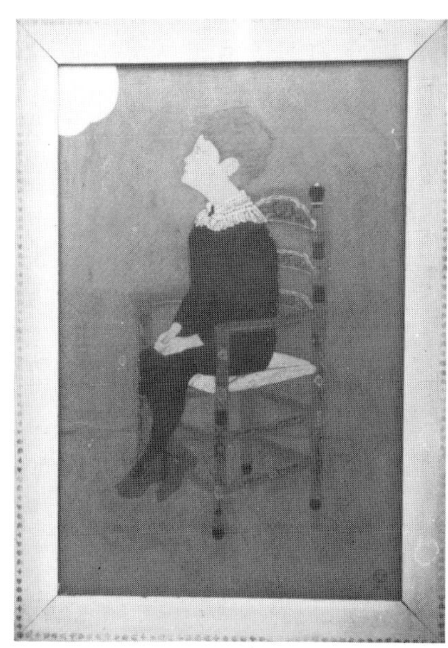

62

light pink eyelids over heavy bags, blue moustache, long pink ears sticking out far from the head, all against a black ground, are a real nightmare." The most interesting reaction is that of Erich Wichman, one of De Onafhankelijken from the very beginning. He wrote a fairly technical commentary expressing his interest in the kind of work Huszár was doing; however, he also offered fundamental criticism: "Although the artist relinquished touch, which is the means for expressing depth, tone, mood, light effects, and dissected his subjects in evenly brushed planes, he seeks to express in such an absolutely inadequate technique just *these* effects. . . . And indeed he often achieves with these pieces such an intensely fierce expression that that must necessarily exceed his intention. Thus, there is in these works *a very strong and individual technique,* thrown away as it were to a tendency which it should express, without being the right one for that purpose."[6] Apparently Wichman liked the flat stylizing and the areas with solid colors, but thought that this technique did not fit Huszár's choice of expressive subjects.

The fierce colors that made people notice Huszár's work at the Onafhankelijken exhibition were not present in all his paintings of 1913. Neither did he always practice the flat technique of painting. He did not consistently work on the adaptation of the image to the two-dimensional plane of the painting, as Bart van der Leck did. Huszár was much less steady in style. His reputation as a portrait painter may have played a part in this. He was popular for his naturalistic portraits, but not for his colorful stylized work. The fact that he exhibited portraits side by side with his more experimental work suggests that he himself attached equal value to both sides of his art.

During 1914, Huszár realized that the differences between his experimental and his traditional work were too great. He wanted to make a choice. This realization was precipitated by a large comprehensive show held in the Stedelijk Museum in Amsterdam from June 16 to July 16, 1914, which involved, in addition to Huszár, the Bremmerites Anna Egter, Truus van Hettinga Tromp, Bertha van Hasselt, Jo Koster, Corrie Pabst, and Jan Terwey. Huszár was represented by 80 works—among them a large number of landscapes, 24 portraits and portrait studies in tempera and oil, and various drawings and etchings. All these works had originated between 1906 and 1914, and according to the catalog many of them were already in private collections. A critic stated in the *Rotterdammer courant* of June 18, 1914, that the works did not show a development toward the so-called modern style, but that the traditional and the modern alternated: "It is most peculiar that anybody who in 1910 makes a piece in pointillé of refined color qualities, such as the lady reclined on the couch, at the same time should be the creator of the disproportioned, rachitic, alarmingly strange-colored small nude no. 66, which hangs above it." A more favorable reaction came from the critic Leonardo in *De controleur* of June 27, who, although he did notice the fluctuations in the work, found the show interesting—particularly because of Huszár's contribution. He had especially good things to say about the painting *Vieillard,* which had already been exhibited at the Onafhankelijken show, and he stated regretfully that Huszár had abandoned that style.[7]

Two weeks after the Stedelijk Museum show, Huszár wrote to Bremmer. The critic had visited the museum and had wanted to buy a few etchings, which Huszár had given him. Perhaps still under the influence of the aforementioned reviews, Huszár wrote: "We have been flooded with ideas which hold us back, and my intellect tells me that that is not yet sufficient, and I also know that it is useful always to point out different matters, and you can do that. At our show I have seen what your students are able to do, because they do not have what for us (I also mean Terwey) is nearly a burden, and therefore they can listen to you. . . . It is very difficult for me to express exactly what I want to say, but on the occasion of the exhibition it has dawned somewhat on me that you have good reason to suggest serious study, although we are not yet ready to do it."

In the next few years, "serious study" was indeed the order of the day; Huszár began to work with more direction, and did not exhibit again until May 1916.

1915–16

Not many works from this period are known, but what is extant shows the influence of cubism. Huszár must also have been acquainted with paintings by Mondrian. He may have met the latter and come to appreciate him at the show at the Walrecht gallery in The Hague in June and July of 1914, which was organized by Bremmer. Because Huszár knew both Bremmer and Walrecht well, he probably visited this show. Huszár's appreciation for Mondrian's Parisian paintings is evidenced by the fact that he bought one himself, albeit a few years later (*Compositie 8,* now in the Guggenheim Museum, in New York). Furthermore, he may have read about Mondrian's work in an article by Bremmer in *Beeldende kunst* in the beginning of 1916.

From the years 1915 and 1916, mainly graphic work is extant. The most important information about this work is to be found in the catalog and in the reviews of the graphics exhibition held by

63 Huszár, *Scheepjes* [*Little ships*], 1915. Lithograph, 26 × 32.7 cm. Collection of B. E. Huszár, Deil.

the Stedelijk Museum in Amsterdam from May 14 to June 11, 1922. Huszár exhibited ten drawings and prints, all dated from 1913 to 1917. Apparently he had no more recent graphic work available in May 1922. The reviews of this show speak of "combinations of planes and lines" and "colorful work."[8] In the catalog, two works are described as "compositions" from 1915; those would thus be his earliest works to have been given such a neutral title. Yet it seems probable that Huszár's work from that time still had some figurative basis. An example of this is the 1915 lithograph *Scheepjes* [*Little ships*], shown as figure 63. Mondrian's influence can be sensed in the 1916 etching *Figuur* (figure 64), particularly in the plane construction of the surroundings. The planes are rather separate from the female figure; they have been hung in front of it as a kind of curtain.

Huszár's most important extant work from this period is his 1915 painting *Vincent* (figure 65), an homage to van Gogh. This work depicts a sunflower (or several sunflowers), constructed from triangular shapes, in blazing colors of blue, orange, yellow, red, and (mostly) green. Unlike the works just mentioned, this painting gives a highly dynamic impression. Huszár's production from 1915 and 1916 shows large differences, but it is clear that he oriented himself toward trends in the international avant-garde, particularly cubism and futurism.[9]

In May 1916, after working more or less in silence for two years, Huszár contributed to a show organized by the artists' association De Anderen [The Others], which had recently been founded by Theo van Doesburg, Louis Saalborn, and Erich Wichman. It is not known how Huszár became associated with De Anderen. Wichman had reviewed his 1913 exhibit at the Onafhankelijken show, and van Doesburg could have seen his work there. In the end of 1915 and the beginning of 1916, when van Doesburg and Wichman were in the throes of founding a periodical and a society, their path crossed that of Vilmos Huszár. Although he did not get a position as a board member of De Anderen, he was considered a prominent member—certainly in the eyes of Theo van Doesburg. That is evidenced by a letter written to Antony Kok on May 18, 1916, by van Doesburg (who was in a rather depressed mood because the attendance at the exhibition was scant): "Nothing has been sold. Much has been written about [the exhibition], [but] all in all the artistic success [has been] less than I expected. The bad feeling I have now stems, I believe, from de Winter's mean attitude. I have seldom met anyone so against himself. In regard to his work, it doesn't matter so much anymore, because we have in Vilmos Huszár a force of the first order."

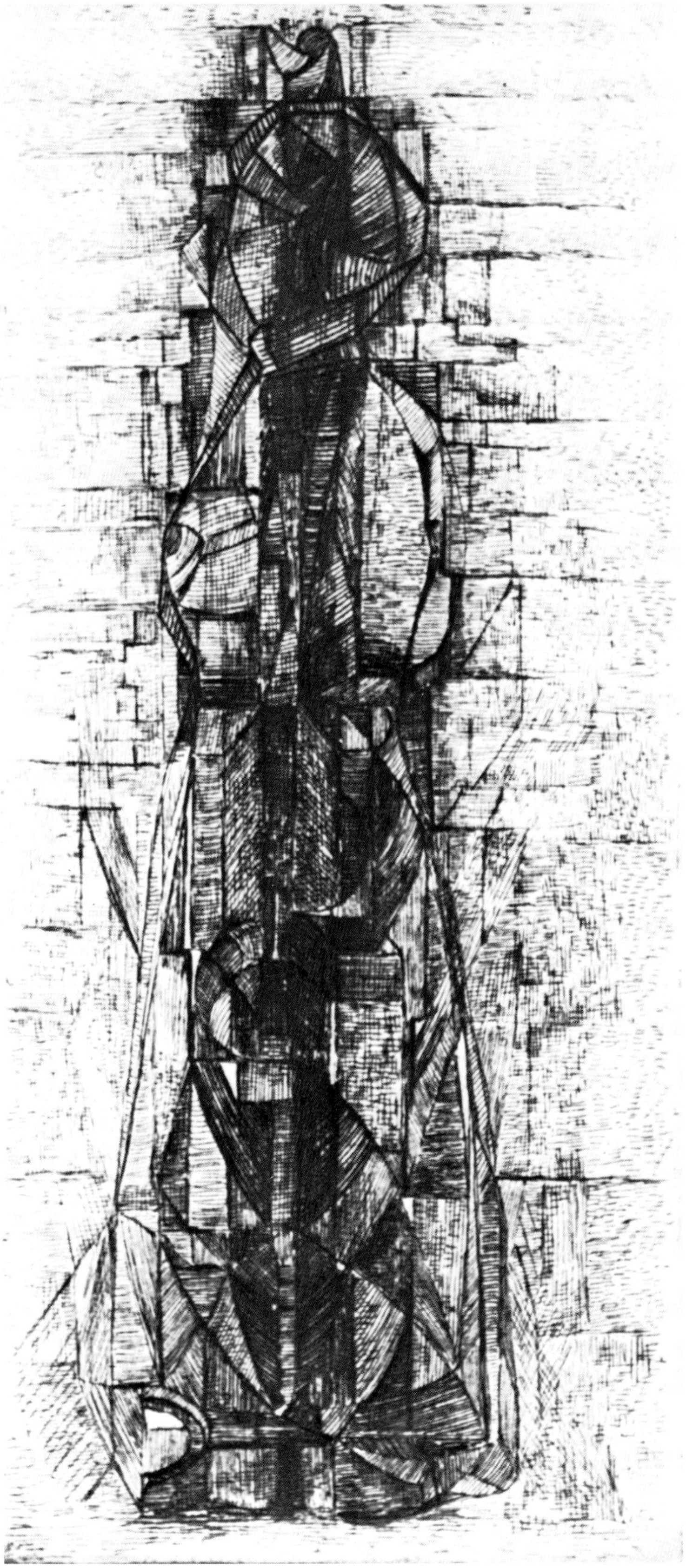

64

65

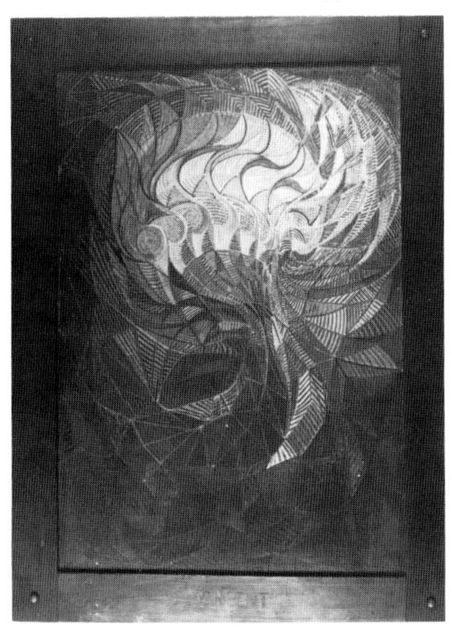

64 **Huszár, *Figuur,* 1916. Etching, 38 × 24.5 cm. J. P. Smid collection, Kunsthandel Monet, Amsterdam.**

65 **Huszár, *Vincent,* 1915. Oil on Eternite (asbestos cement), 69 × 48 cm. J. P. Smid collection, Kunsthandel Monet, Amsterdam.**

66 **Huszár, *Schilderij (geel)* [*Painting (yellow)*], 1916. Technique and dimensions unknown. The painting was acquired by Theo van Doesburg. It was probably destroyed in World War II. This reproduction shows a retouched photograph that is in the artist's estate.**

Huszár had sent five works to the show: *Schilderij (geel)* [*Painting (yellow)*] and *Schilderij (donker)* [*Painting (dark)*], both in tempera, and three drawings, which the catalog mentioned as designs for paintings. The exhibit was small; obviously Huszár showed only his newest work. Only *Schilderij (geel)* is known, and that only from reproductions. Nothing is known about the whereabouts of *Schilderij (donker)* and the drawings.

Perhaps *Schilderij (geel),* shown as figure 66, is completely abstract. At any rate, no starting point in visual reality is evident from the reproduction. The picture plane is filled with transparent angular and round shapes, which are dark at the borders but become lighter toward the center. A comparison between *Schilderij (geel)* and *Vincent* suggests that Huszár had begun to work in a much more orderly and controlled fashion; the varied forms used in *Schilderij (geel)* are purely geometrical, and the dynamism of *Vincent* has given way to symmetry.

In May 1916 Huszár's exhibit was praised in the *Overijsselsche courant* by Bertha van Hasselt, who, as mentioned above, belonged to Bremmer's entourage and was a good friend of Huszár's. It can be assumed that her description and her interpretation closely approximated Huszár's own. "Huszár's work," she wrote, "has more tranquility than the rest, more distance; there is a small painting by him in tempera, singularly delicate in color; there is a crayon sketch for a painting; out of dark hues, lines are wheeling upward and radiating out again in lighter colors: bright yellow and orange, like the depiction of a soul working itself upward from the dark to the light."[10]

The membership of De Anderen comprised a varied lot. It seems that Huszár was not very happy with this and took the initiative to gather a more select group of artists. Van Doesburg wrote the following to Kok on August 16, 1916: "Some moderns want to combine separately, because they do not want to collaborate with the intuitive artists. The latter are the guys who work out of an impulsive urge, but who do not have a rational and conscious foundation. De W[inter] is also counted among them. Perhaps this will result in a split: the very reasoning ones on one side and the intuitive ones on the other. I am in a difficult position in this case, for Huszár rather wants me to resign from the association, because, according to him, I do not belong in there. Huszár and Bremmer called me 'the only important one.' He (Huszár) will perhaps resign from the association and join with Mondrian, van der Leck, and others. I am writing this to you confidentially, of course."[11]

Huszár's plans to form a group came to naught. In the meantime, van Doesburg did make progress with his old plans to found

66

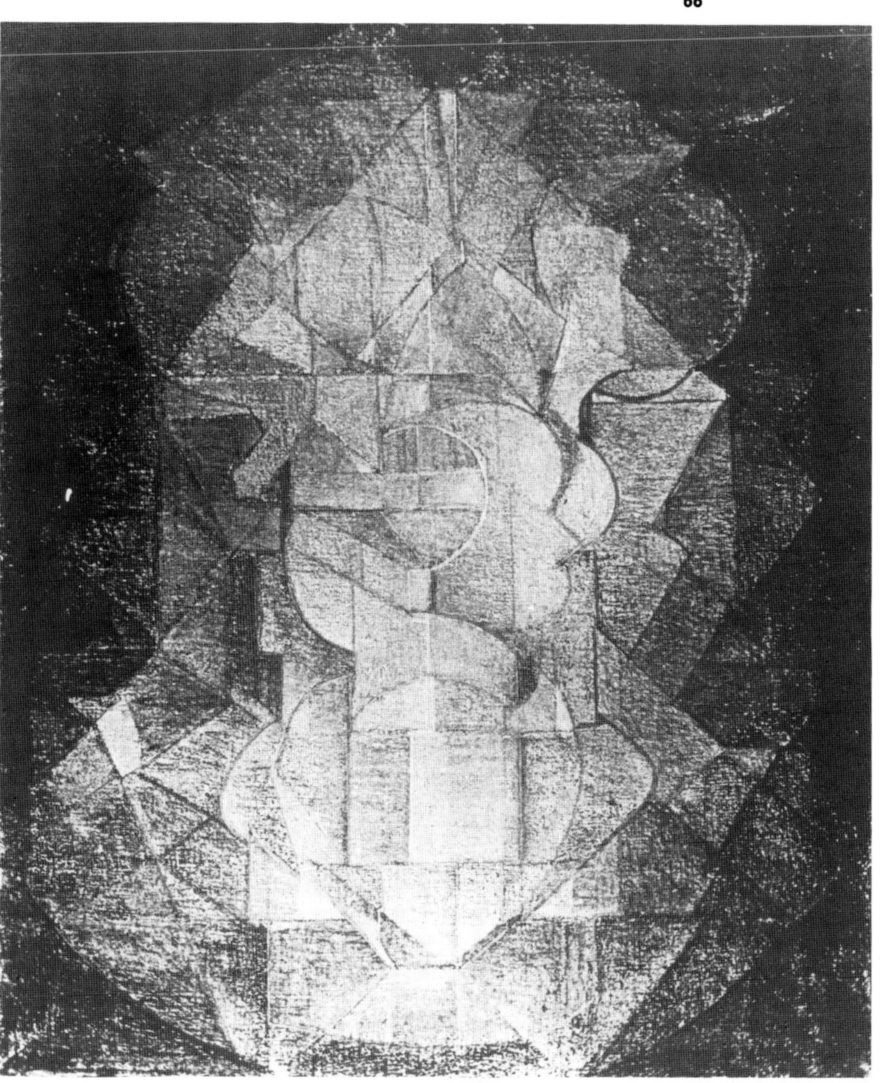

a journal. In a certain sense, van Doesburg "scooped" Huszár by associating himself with Piet Mondrian and Bart van der Leck. In May 1917 he had obtained promises from both of them and was in possession of a contract in writing with the publisher, according to the information he sent to Antony Kok in one of his detailed letters.

Huszár was involved in the plans for the periodical; however, Mondrian did not know him yet and was rather reserved for the time being. On May 21 Mondrian wrote to van Doesburg: "I do not know Huszár's work, and Wichman's work is really not good (I saw De Onafhankelijken). Therefore (I implore you) be more cautious: particularly about the illustrations. Remember the Nieuwe K.K. [Nieuwe Kunstkring] and their woodcuts! There is so little good work." Obviously van Doesburg had recently informed Mondrian of Huszár's participation.

Huszár was involved in the recruiting of advertisers for *De stijl,* as well. The sample copy was ready on August 16, and in the following weeks van Doesburg tried feverishly to find advertisers in order to get the periodical off the ground financially. The first five issues ended up running a full-page advertisement for Bruynzeel's parquet flooring, designed by Huszár. Undoubtedly it was Huszár who had set up the contact with Bruynzeel.

In the letters from Mondrian to van Doesburg, Huszár was again mentioned in August 1917. Mondrian was concerned about the rumors in The Hague about *De stijl.* He was particularly anxious that Huszár would present *De stijl* too much as a competitor of Bremmer's journal.[12] Mondrian had heard about this when he wrote to van Doesburg on August 8, 1917, that he feared a misunderstanding between Bremmer and *De stijl.* Mondrian made the diplomatic suggestion that Bremmer be told that he belonged but that he had not been invited because, after all, he had his own journal. In the end, Bremmer sent word that he would not thwart the plans for *De stijl,* and that he would even take a subscription.[13]

Some rather alarming news emerged in September. Even before the periodical had gotten off the ground, Huszár was thinking about resigning because he thought the plan "impure."[14] Perhaps the later rumors that Huszár planned a journal of his own can be explained by this incident. However, for some time he remained loyal to the cause of *De stijl.* In fact, he tried to organize shows. In December 1917 he proposed a joint exhibition for the coming spring. Mondrian was agreeable to that, but pressed for some haste because otherwise he would make arrangements for participation in an exhibition of the Hollandsche Kunstenaarskring. When he did so, Huszár again proposed a De Stijl exhibition, this time for the autumn. That plan, too, came to naught.

Stained glass

In 1916, besides the drawings and paintings exhibited by De Anderen, Huszár produced designs for stained-glass windows. His interest in this technique may already have existed when he was at the School for Applied Art in Budapest, but it also may have originated or increased during his days as a member of the Haagsche Kunstkring, which he joined in 1916 and in which he was enrolled in the "architecture and applied arts" section. Most of the windows designed by Huszár and van Doesburg were executed by J. W. Gips, whose studio was advertised regularly in *De stijl* until 1928 (perhaps as a return favor).[15]

Huszár's first stained-glass windows are important in the development of his work. As early as 1916, it appears, he was converting reality into a conglomerate of vertical and horizontal planes. Thus, his stained-glass works are harbingers of the abstract paintings of 1917 and 1918. These windows are also interesting because they lead up to Huszár's interior designs, which can be considered among his most important contributions to De Stijl. More than any of the other painters, he tried to realize his ideas in the applied arts. His first stained-glass windows were autonomous additions to architecture; however, from 1918 on he integrated his windows into interiors designed as entities, which he called Ruimte-kleur-composities [Space-color compositions].

Huszár's first window was probably *Compositie (motief zonnebloemen)* [*Composition (motif sunflowers)*]. As far as is known it does not exist any more, but it was reproduced by Theo van Doesburg in 1917 in *De nieuwe beweging in de schilderkunst.* This window is reminiscent of the 1915 painting *Vincent* in theme, though not in design. The four sunflowers represented in mirror images across the diagonals are constructed out of geometric forms—rectangles, triangles, and circle fragments—which show similarities to the picture elements of *Schilderij (geel).*

Huszár's second stained-glass design from 1916 was probably *Meisje* [*Girl*], in which the image is composed exclusively of horizontal and vertical rectangles. This work, too, is known only from a reproduction in van Doesburg's booklet. As a close examination of the photograph (figure 67) shows, this was a design, not a realized window; whether it ever was executed is uncertain. The preliminary study given here as figure 68 shows how Huszár realized the decomposition of the girl's profile.

Another early window composition with horizontally and vertically positioned rectangular planes is *De familie* (figure 69). This important window shows, from top to bottom, a father, a mother, and a child. Huszár made this window for the nursery in his own house in Voorburg. The colors he used were purple, green, yel-

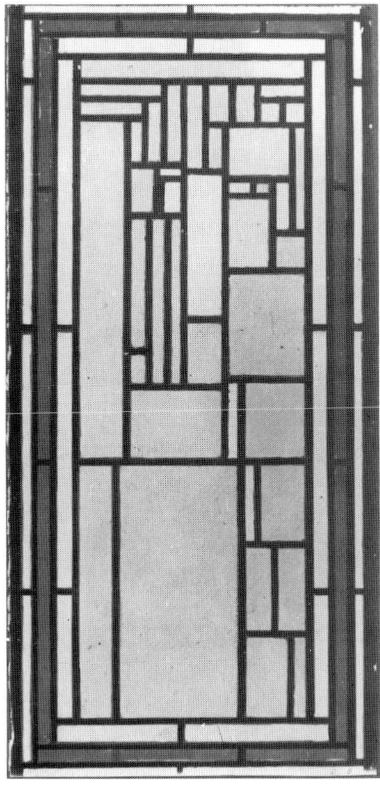

67

68

67 Huszár, *Meisje* [*Girl*], 1916. Designed for stained-glass window. Technique, dimensions, and whereabouts unknown; photograph in collection of Rijksdienst Beeldende Kunst, The Hague.

68 Huszár, preliminary study for *Meisje,* 1916. Technique, dimensions, and whereabouts unknown. Reproduced from T. van Doesburg, *De nieuwe beweging in de schilderkunst* (Delft, 1917).

69 Huszár, *De familie,* 1916. Stained-glass window, ca. 145 × 70 cm. Window in private collection; photograph in the artist's estate.

69

70

low, blue, and red. According to the critic Ro van Oven, who reproduced the window in 1919 in *Levende kunst,* it was still very close to reality. That is true in comparison with Huszár's later work, but it appears that Huszár was already taking the natural shapes into consideration to a lesser degree here than he had in *Meisje*. The planes are generally larger and more regular, and are arranged more or less symmetrically. Aside from its extreme abstraction, this window is also interesting because of its construction. With such a rectangular motif, the supporting iron bars could be fitted in without artifice.[16]

Huszár found a different solution, at least as elegant, for fitting the frame into the image when in 1916 he was commissioned to make a skylight for the house of the Bruynzeel family in Voorburg.[17] Though it is difficult to see from the photograph (figure 70), the skylight had the shape of a hipped roof. The metal support beams, positioned in a double-Y form, were accentuated by parallel color beams. They partitioned the window in four segments, which were positioned in symmetrical order toward the center. In contrast with the previous windows, there were still some beveled planes here; these echoed the oblique beams of the frame. It is hard to say whether Huszár started from any figuration in the composition; I see small figures in it, but that may be an optical illusion.

Finally, we can add to this series of early windows a curious application of "stained glass" to a set for a shadow play put on in 1926 by the Rotterdamsche Kunstkring (figure 71). Huszár's set cannot be dated with absolute certainty, but the small windows in the church nave correspond directly to *De familie* (1916).

That Huszár's stained glass played a trailblazing role in the prehistory of De Stijl is evident from Theo van Doesburg's work. Van Doesburg's high opinion of Huszár's work is apparent in his writings about De Anderen. His appreciation went so far that he adopted Huszár's motifs and followed him in his development. One of the most striking examples of direct borrowing is the window van Doesburg designed in 1916 for the home of the mayor of Broek in Waterland, Mr. de Geus (figure 72). The background of this window, without the swan, shows that van Doesburg took Huszár's *Schilderij (geel)* as his starting point. That was easy, because the painting was hanging over his worktable. Furthermore, van Doesburg's *Vrouwekop* (figure 73) was inspired by Huszár's *Meisje* (figure 67). The similarity in the nose and the eyes is particularly striking. Before 1917, when he made *Vrouwekop,* van Doesburg had not realized any rectangular plane compositions. Huszár's influence on van Doesburg did not remain completely unobserved in those years; in May 1918, during van Doesburg's exhibit of

71

72

70 Huszár, stained-glass window for De Arendshoeve (residence of C. Bruynzeel, Voorburg), 1916. Ca. 200 × 300 cm. Window no longer extant; photograph from Rijksbureau voor Kunsthistorische Documentatie, The Hague.

71 Huszár, set for shadow play *Baron von Münchhausen's trip to Russia.* Dimensions and whereabouts unknown. Shown here is a portion of a photograph that is in the artist's estate.

72 Theo van Doesburg, stained-glass window for home of Mayor de Geus, Broek in Waterland, 1916. Ca. 100 × 55 cm.

73

73 Theo van Doesburg, *Vrouwekop* [*Woman's head*], 1917. 39 × 26 cm. Rijksdienst Beeldende Kunst, The Hague.

74 Huszár, *Compositie II (De schaatsenrijders)* [*The skaters*], 1917. Oil on canvas, 74 × 81 cm. Gemeentemuseum, The Hague.

75 Huszár, clock, 1917. Dimensions and whereabouts unknown; photograph in artist's estate.

76 Huszár, *Ornament XXe eeuwse stijl* [*Ornament in the style of the twentieth century*], 1917. Technique, dimensions, and whereabouts unknown; illustrated in van Doesburg, *De nieuwe beweging in de schilderkunst* (Delft, 1917).

stained glass in a show of arts and crafts and folk art at the Rotterdam art academy, the reporter of the *Nieuwe Rotterdammer courant* wrote: "Theo van Doesburg would perhaps have merited more praise if his admiration of Vilmos Huszár had not been so evident."[18]

The first half of 1917

The stained glass of 1916 was the beginning of Huszár's contribution to the form language which usually is associated with De Stijl. The first paintings of which we can say the same are from the beginning of 1917. While the stained glass shows a rather independent development, namely the abstraction of a natural subject into adjoining geometric forms, the paintings seem to be a direct response to Bart van der Leck's work.

In December 1916, Huszár and van Doesburg visited the collection of Hélène Kröller-Müller on the Lange Voorhout in The Hague, which recently had been augmented by van der Leck's paintings *Compositie 1916, no. 1* (figure 147) and *Compositie 1916, no. 4* (figure 148). The impression these paintings made on Huszár is evidenced by his *Compositie II* (figure 74), which he finished in February 1917 and which is similar to the works he saw in the Kröller-Müller collection in the manner of abstraction as well as in the technique. In *Compositie II,* each of the skating figures is composed of small separate horizontal and vertical rectangles, painted in black and in the complementary colors red and green on a white ground. The figures are distributed fairly regularly over the canvas, without touching the borders. The white area around the skaters recalls Bart van der Leck's painting techniques. The sixteen figures are, as it were, surrounded by rough brush strokes; the planes are painted on the white, just as in van der Leck's work.

There must have been at least six paintings from 1917 to which Huszár gave Roman numerals, but numbers I, IV, and V are unknown. To complicate matters even more, there are also two extant paintings from 1917 without Roman numerals, namely *Stillevencompositie (hamer en zaag)* [*Still life composition (hammer and saw)*] and *Compositie met witte kop* [*Composition with white head*]. Because of the "missing links" and the capricious use of numbers, it is not easy to reconstruct Huszár's development in this important year.

It is probable that after *Compositie II* Huszár experimented further with separate, regularly distributed blocks. No other paintings in this style are known, but there are two works of applied art. The first, shown in a photograph in the artist's estate, is a clock in a sort of triptych (figure 75). The face of the clock, predominantly black with a white border, is flanked by two white panels with black borders. On the side panels are twelve block patterns, the abstracted signs of the zodiac.[19] Huszár dated this photograph 1917; the stylistic similarity with the skating figures of *Compositie II* suggests that it originated in the first months of that year. The second work, *Ornament XXe eeuwse stijl* [*Ornament in the style of the twentieth century*], shown as figure 76, appeared in van Doesburg's booklet *De nieuwe beweging in de schilderkunst,* which was

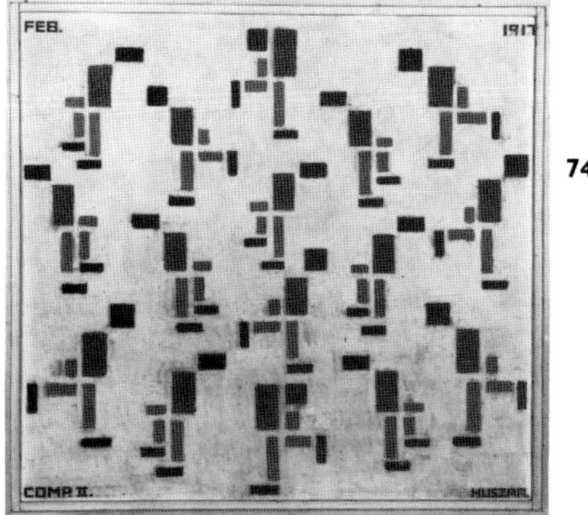

74

75

76

77

77 **Huszár, logo of *De stijl,* 1917. Woodcut, 8 × 6 cm. Private collection.**

78 **Postcard from Huszár to van Doesburg, dated December 4, 1917. Rijksdienst Beeldende Kunst, The Hague.**

published in the second half of 1917. Judging from its irregular contours, it was probably a woodcut. It is plausible that this work also has a figurative starting point, but I cannot identify it.

In the middle of 1917 Huszár worked on the logo for the cover of *De stijl,* and perhaps also on the characteristic blocked letters that appeared above it.[20] In the first issue van Doesburg stated clearly that the "typographical ornament between title and text" was by Huszár. That would mean that Huszár designed the logo only, were there not some reason to doubt the reliability of van Doesburg's announcement. In the first place, the "blocked" work shown above suggests that the design of such lettering was in Huszár's domain, and that cannot be said of van Doesburg, the only other person who may have been responsible. The stylistic similarity with Huszár's other work from the beginning of 1917 is of course no proof, but there is more. In Huszár's estate there is a loose copy of the logo that contains the lettering (figure 77). This copy has the same dimensions as the reproduction on the cover of *De stijl,* 8 × 6 centimeters. The letters and the logo are thus closely connected, a fact which makes Theo van Doesburg's distinction between the title and the logo less plausible. Perhaps van Doesburg wanted to avoid giving the impression that Huszár had invented the name *De stijl.* There is yet another indication of Huszár's interest in the lettering. On December 4, 1917, he sent van Doesburg a postcard (figure 78) on which the letterhead of *De stijl* had been printed. He had filled in the letters with black ink, so that the separate blocks disappeared. At the end of his note he asked van Doesburg: "How do you like the change in De Stijl on this card?"

78

Huszár must have completed the logo in the early summer of 1917, because the specimen copy of *De stijl* was ready on August 16. In the logo he discarded rather rigorously the fairly simple manner of abstraction of the previous months. In his works from the first half of 1917 his method of abstraction had been based on deformation of a natural subject, which was represented by a pattern of small vertical and horizontal rectangles distributed more or less regularly on a white ground. However, the logo shows evidence of formation. The planes are joined together in a fairly complex manner. No contour of a figure or an object is recognizable; the interaction between the planes and the interstitial space appears to dominate.

There is an important passage about the logo in a letter written by Huszár to van der Leck on September 25, 1917: "This is the same procedure I applied on the cover of *De stijl,* namely white and black, giving them equal value, without ground." Apparently Huszár wanted to attribute equal value to black and white, so that neither would serve as ground. The logo was his first attempt to eliminate the difference between figure and ground, one of the formal problems for which the painters of De Stijl tried to find a solution in 1917–18.

It requires some practice and perhaps also a good dose of fantasy to recognize a natural starting point in the logo. Yet I would like to make a suggestion. The two stepped forms resemble those used frequently in the image language of De Stijl for heads of hair rendered in profile, and the rectangles near these could be eyes. The "zebra stripes" in the lower right and left can be interpreted as abstracted hands. The motif of Huszár's logo, then, could be the union of two heads and two hands—perhaps an embrace. (See also figure 13.)

Huszár's *Kop* [*Head*], shown as figure 79 and probably also from the middle of 1917, shows a combination of rectangular forms and groups of stripes. To the left of the center can be recognized a head with a strong chin, lips, eyes, and hair in the same stepped form that appears in the logo. The untitled painting shown as figure 80 also refers to the motif of a head in profile. In this painting can be seen a number of stripes and angular forms, colored in solid white, green, red, and blue, surrounded by black. The white head is visible in the middle of the composition, but it is difficult to interpret the planes around it. Because of the manner of abstraction and the use of forms, I date this painting to the summer of 1917, the same time that the logo and the drawing originated.

The painting shown as figure 80 also bears a strong similarity to Huszár's *Mechanisch dansende figuur* [*Mechanical dancing figure*], which is known only from reproductions. Usually this movable

79

80

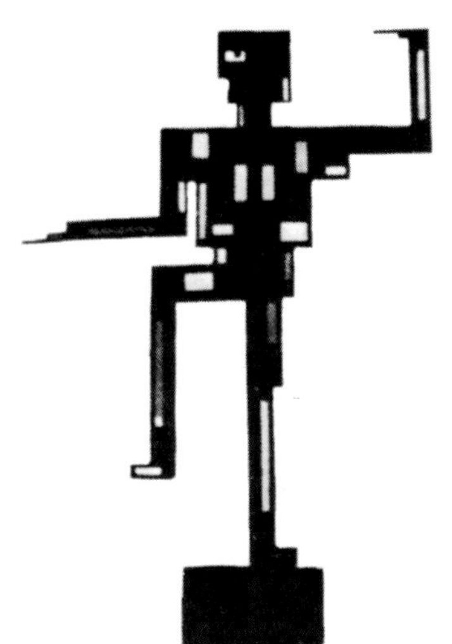

81

79 Huszár, *Kop* [*Head*], 1917. Ink on paper, 15 × 12.5 cm. Private collection.

80 Huszár, untitled painting, 1917. Oil on panel, 50.7 × 45 cm. Gemeentemuseum, The Hague.

81 Huszár, *Mechanisch dansende figuur* [*Mechanical dancing figure*], 1917–1920. Aluminum, paper, and rope; height ca. 1 m . No longer extant; photograph in artist's estate.

shadow puppet is dated 1920; however, that must be a sort of ultimate date, when Huszár finally had mastered the technical difficulties. There are indications that he had already started to work on the puppet in the summer of 1917.[21] On July 14 of that year, Theo van Doesburg wrote to Antony Kok that Huszár had "invented something totally new, a kind of kinetic painting."

The first performances of the dancing figure took place mostly in family circles, such as at soirées of the de Roos family in Voorburg. Mr. de Roos was, like Huszár, a member of the Haagsche Kunstkring, where puppetry and miracle plays were a focus of attention. The shadow puppet had hinges in its hands, arms, and legs and could assume various positions. The head had a plate in the middle that could shift to the left or to the right; when it shifted to the left, a profile appeared on the right, and vice versa, so that one got the impression that the head was turning. The puppet, which must have been about one meter tall, was moved via a keyboard with ten keys to which were attached cords from the limbs and the head. This panel was probably placed behind the pedestal.[22]

Van Doesburg's allusion to "kinetic painting" was a reference to the effect that Huszár wanted to achieve. The puppet had rectangular apertures, in which Huszár had put red and green translucent paper or mica. When a strong light source was put behind it, both shadow and color fell on the white sheet stretched between the puppet and the audience. This procedure was similar to one used in the shadow plays of Indonesia. However, Huszár's representations had no narrative character. As he wrote in an article in 1923, his intention was to have the puppet represent a composition in each position; in these compositions an interaction occurred between shadow, color planes, and background. This puts the puppet in close relation to the *De stijl* logo, where Huszár had aimed at a similar interaction between the white and the black parts. Huszár created a stir with the puppet in 1923 at the legendary dada soirées held in various Dutch cities, and he gave many performances with it well into the 1930s.

1917–18: The figure/ground problem

In the second half of 1917 Huszár made a few paintings in which the characteristic representational elements of his previous work—vertical and horizontal blocks and bars—were arranged in a different manner. No longer separate and dispersed on an even white or black ground, they touched and overlapped one another against a ground that changed color. Although these paintings do not seem to bear any relation to visual reality, their titles indicate figurative starting points–for example, *Stillevencompositie (hamer en zaag)* [*Still life composition (hammer and saw)*] and *Compositie III (stad)* [*Composition III (city)*]. These paintings are among Huszár's most important contributions to De Stijl, particularly because they express so clearly his stand in the discussion about the figure/ground problem.

The painters of De Stijl aimed, as is well known, for a two-dimensional kind of painting, without perspective or depth. They saw flatness as a universal quality, and they found it lacking in the individualistic expressions of traditional painting. In principle, they all agreed that the difference between the form and its surroundings—between figure and ground—should be eliminated in a painting. They differed, however, on the question of how this should be done, how a completely flat painting should look.

The paintings Huszár made between September and December of 1917 showed the solution he thought best for the time being: He eliminated the difference between figure and ground by (figuratively speaking) interweaving the forms. In *Hamer en zaag* (figure 82), yellow, red, and white blocks lie across one another in such a way that now one, then another color is on top. There is no fixed system in this work, but the composition is fairly stringent. It seems that Huszár closely watched the number of overlappings for each color; clearly he wanted to prevent any one color from becoming dominant. Moreover, the field between the planes is divided into three color areas; in the lower half it is white, at top left it is yellow, and at top right it is red. This precludes one color's enclosing all the blocks and thereby functioning as a traditional ground. The frame is in the same colors as the painting and has a yellow band on the red side and a red one on the yellow side. On the panel one can still see the impressions of the lines with which Huszár "pre-drew" the composition. During the execution he obviously changed the design. The horizontal white plane at top left originally extended further to the right, into the red. The execution is not very precise; indeed, between the planes and on the frame thick black lines can be seen in places.

Huszár applied the same interweaving of small color planes in *Stad* (figure 83). Here he used one additional color. The painting has been lost since the 1920s and is known only from black-and-white reproductions. In a review it was described as follows: "There is . . . the canvas full of busy bars and quadrangles, juxtaposed or divergent, in colors which may be beautiful by themselves but are harsh when adjacent to one another."[23] The actual colors of the painting were not mentioned by this critic or by the Hungarian critic Kallai, who devoted an essay to it some years later.[24] Huszár probably painted a second still life in this style, but it is known only through exhibition catalogs.[25]

82

83

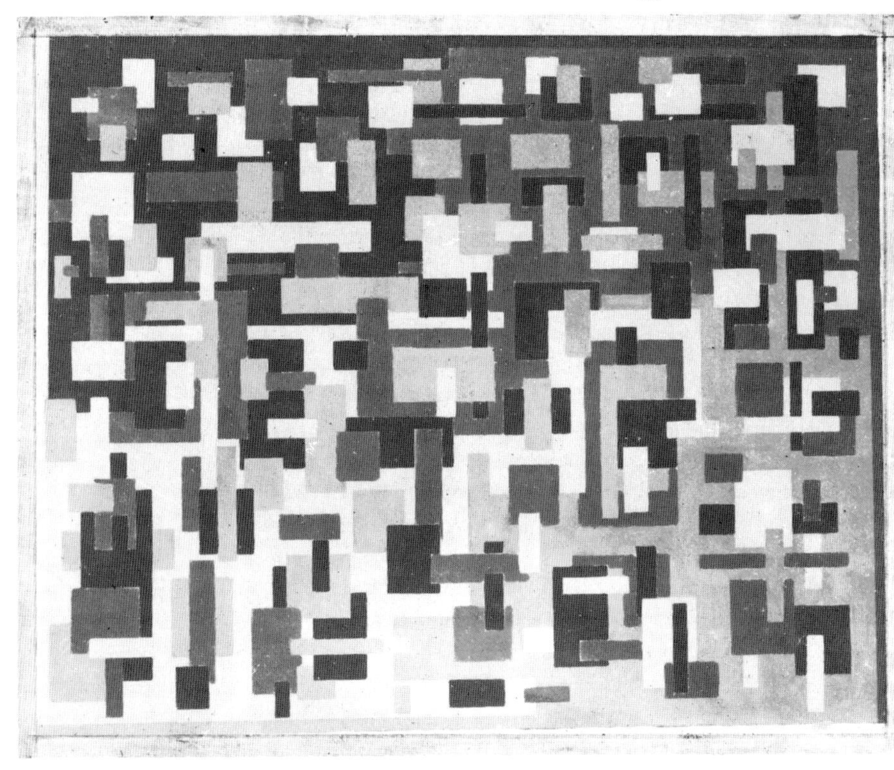

82 Huszár, *Stillevencompositie (Hamer en zaag)* [*Still life composition (Hammer and saw)*], 1917. Oil on panel, 31.5 × 53.5 cm. Gemeentemuseum, The Hague.

83 Huszár, *Compositie III (Stad)* [*Composition III (City)*], 1917. Technique, dimensions, and whereabouts unknown; photograph in artist's estate.

84 Huszár, *Compositie VI,* 1917. Linocut, 11.4 × 14.2 cm. Stedelijk Museum, Amsterdam.

Huszár's solution to the figure/ground problem had a mixed reception among his colleagues. Mondrian assumed an attitude of "wait and see." After seeing photographs of Huszár's work, he wrote to van Doesburg (on January 8, 1918) that the backgrounds of *Stad* and *Hamer en zaag* still remained grounds, but that he believed Huszár's intention to be correct. Some months earlier, Huszár had discussed the new development in his work with van der Leck; his first reaction had not been fully positive either. On September 25, 1917, Huszár wrote to van der Leck: "If we already don't agree, what then about the public? —What you are saying about placing in back / placing in front, whereby the equivalence of the parts is perturbed (because the planes cut through each other)—with me that is just meant as a plastic principle. . . . you therefore should not view it as planes on a ground, but as equal parts, because the background plays the same role as do the planes. What is in front goes to the rear, and vice versa, with the result that absolute planarity is mastered." Van Doesburg, however, was very pleased with Huszár's work. In the January 1918 issue of *De stijl* he published an article full of praise for *Hamer en zaag* in which he interpreted the horizontal planes as sawing movements and the vertical planes as movements of the hammer. The article was illustrated by a reproduction in color, the only one to be published in *De stijl* for years; it was certainly a proof of the exemplary importance which van Doesburg attributed to the work. Van Doesburg also paid attention to *Stad* in his 1919 booklet *Drie voordrachten over de nieuwe beeldende kunst.* He associated the painting with "the bustle of the agitated urban scene, with its changing perspectives," and compared it to *Boulevard,* a cityscape by the futurist Gino Severini.[26] Perhaps this comparison was not made entirely by chance. It is conceivable that Huszár had adopted the theme intentionally from Severini, in order to give De Stijl its own profile vis-à-vis futurism. Huszár must have been familiar with the work of the futurists, and particularly with Severini's work, through private collections (such as that of the Rev. Mr. van Assendelft in Gouda) and through reproductions (for instance in *Der sturm*). He probably also knew Severini personally; in a letter to Theo van Doesburg dated November 3, 1917, Severini sends greetings to "Monsieur Huszár." Nevertheless, there was a considerable difference in viewpoint between Severini and the artists in the Netherlands. Huszár's *Stad* could be described in De Stijl terminology as a pictorial transformation of reality, while Severini's *Boulevard* was viewed as a more or less realistic representation.

84

At the end of 1917, Huszár abandoned the use of overlapping planes. This is evidenced by *Compositie VI* (figure 84), which was

85

reproduced in *De stijl* in April 1918. There was probably also a painted version of this linocut. For Huszár it was an important work, as this was the first time that the image was not derived from visual reality; in any case, the title gives no such indication. From his method in *Hamer en zaag* and *Stad* he kept the color-changing area between the planes and the "overflow" via the frame; however, the planes themselves do not touch or overlap—they are separately disposed next to one another, as if afloat.

How can this development be explained? In the end of November 1917, in his *De stijl* article "Aesthetische beschouwing no. II," Huszár discussed Mondrian's 1917 gouache *Compositie met kleurvlakjes* (figure 44). He reacted very positively to the floating small planes against the white. In his opinion, Mondrian had succeeded in creating a harmonious relation between front and back. Therefore, *Compositie VI* can be regarded as a synthesis of Huszár's own previous work and Mondrian's work from 1917.[27]

In 1918 Huszár explored other possibilities for achieving a flat representation. His method of painting again changed drastically when he began to use a grid, a lattice of lines with color planes in between. Because of this his paintings from that year are reminiscent of his earlier designs for stained glass, and of realized works such as *De familie.* Of course, when one is working in stained glass a grid is necessary for technical reasons; in Huszár's paintings it is only a pictorial means of suppressing the effect of depth.

Six works from 1918 are known from reproductions; they will be discussed in a hypothetical sequence. The composition that may have originated first, shown as figure 85, can be regarded as a transitional work. Square and nearly square color blocks are applied on a black ground. They are more or less aligned. The many gray tones in the photograph indicate the use of a fairly large number of different colors or shades (at least six). The planes are so closely packed that the ground manifests itself as a pattern of irregular lines. From that point it was only a small step to bring the lines to the same level as the planes. In the second composition from 1918 (figure 86), they are completely equivalent. The planes in this composition are arranged more regularly than in the previous one; with some exceptions, they form a checkerboard pattern. It is striking that the lines are painted in different shades; by this method planes are grouped together and more or less isolated from the whole. The colors were exceptionally bright.[28]

These paintings can be regarded as Huszár's first applications of the grid; the second closely approaches a regular grid such as Mondrian, too, started to use in the course of 1918. Huszár arrived at it independent of Mondrian, however; this is evident from

86

a letter Mondrian wrote to van Doesburg on June 13, 1918. Huszár had visited Mondrian for the first time, and to Mondrian's surprise it had turned out that Huszár also used a regular division of the picture plane. Mondrian wrote: "He had told me also about his aspirations, but I got the impression that he definitely still subjectivizes. . . . albeit on a mathematical basis, but nevertheless a relative plasticism. In my opinion that could be all right, because the rhythm continues to subjectivize, even when the division is purely regular. I was also just working on something which I showed to Huszár, and which he judged to be good; also on a regular subdivision without knowing about him. But I am still doing a lot of reworking on that subdivision, and I do think that it will look different from Huszár's work. In my opinion everything depends on the way H. will realize it. But I think that it may very well be possible."

Huszár finished his experiments on the flat surface with a number of more intricate compositions. In these the picture plane was basically divided regularly; however, this regularity was no longer clearly recognizable, because of the differences in size between the planes. Up till this time we know of three compositions of this type, again mostly from photographs. One of them, which belonged to Helena Milius and Theo van Doesburg, can be partly seen in a photograph taken in 1918 or shortly thereafter.[29] A second, similar painting, *Compositie in grijs* [*Composition in gray*], was reproduced in *De stijl* of February 1919. This painting has recently come to light again. As the title indicates, this was as an exception, a painting without color. It shows, like the aforementioned work, contrasts of light and dark. The third painting of this group (figure 88) is known from a photograph in Huszár's estate, on the back of which is written, in Huszár's handwriting, "3 klank + = 3,K. met zwart. Tempera 1918." "3K" means three colors. The word *zwart* [black] can, judging from the photograph, only refer to the dark lines. Finally, the title *3 klank* [Triad] bears upon Ostwald's color theory, in which Huszár was interested during the course of 1918.[30]

Judging from the title, Huszár's *3 klank* is an application of Ostwald's color theory. He made one other composition that can be regarded as an application of Ostwald's color theory; on the back of a photograph he designated this work *4 klank tempera.*

With the tone compositions, Huszár stopped his endeavors toward achieving flatness in his painting at the end of 1918. Though there is very little extant work from those years, the reproductions show that Huszár developed steadily from 1917 on and that his work was an important subject of discussion among the other painters of De Stijl. An explicit example of the influence of Hus-

85 Huszár, *Compositie,* 1918. Technique, dimensions, and whereabouts unknown; photograph in artist's estate.

86 Huszár, *Compositie,* 1918. Technique, dimensions, and whereabouts unknown; photograph in artist's estate.

87

88

87 Huszár, *Compositie in grijs* [*Composition in gray*], 1918. Oil on canvas, 61 × 46 cm. Private collection.

88 Huszár, *3 klank + = 3,K met zwart,* 1918. Tempera, dimensions and whereabouts unknown; photograph in artist's estate. Title discussed in text.

89 W. Ostwald, color circle divided into 100 parts, as illustrated in *De stijl* I, no. 10 (1918), p. 116.

90 Huszár, *4 klank* [*Tetrad*], 1918. Tempera; dimensions and whereabouts unknown; photograph in artist's estate.

90

89

zár's *Hamer en zaag* and *Stad* is van Doesburg's *Compositie IX,* which apart from its overlapping shows a similar interweaving of forms. The frame of *Hamer en zaag* must have served as an example to Georges Vantongerloo; in his early painted compositions he applied interlocking white and black slats to close off the picture plane. Influences of Huszár's work are also traceable outside the circle of direct contributors to *De stijl,* probably mostly because of the reproduction in color of *Hamer en zaag.* Léger applied Huszár-like forms in his paintings from 1918 on, and particularly in his 1924 mural paintings.[31] In those years Huszár's works appeared in several avant-garde periodicals. For instance, *Hamer en zaag* was reproduced in *Het overzicht,* and *Stad* appeared several times in the Hungarian periodical *MA.*

Conflicts within De Stijl

As was mentioned earlier in this chapter, Huszár's relationships with the other members of De Stijl give a fascinating picture of vacillating sympathies and dislikes. Mondrian, until 1918, usually spoke rather reservedly about Huszár's work; however, van Doesburg, from the time of the 1916 De Anderen exhibition, wrote jubilantly about Huszár's work and paid it a great deal of attention in *De stijl* and elsewhere. In June of 1918 this changed. The good relations between Huszár and van Doesburg were upset by a few incidents in quick sequence, with the result that Huszár's involvement with *De stijl* diminished significantly.

The first incident, which occurred in May and June of 1918, has entered history as "the houseboat affair." The architect Robert van 't Hoff had designed a houseboat for himself; he also seems to have intended to present De Stijl exhibitions on it. Van 't Hoff had at first decided to involve van Doesburg in the project as the color designer of the interior.[32] Huszár caused him to reconsider by suggesting that Bart van der Leck was really more entitled to such a commission.[33] Van Doesburg would not accept this. He sought redress from Huszár, and this resulted in a "conflict." A letter to Oud dated May 21, 1918, gives evidence of how seriously van Doesburg took this matter; he stated that the unity within De Stijl was "broken, broken forever." The consequences of this incident were also immediately noticeable in the correspondence between Mondrian and van Doesburg. Mondrian's reaction in the beginning of July was as follows: "I can imagine vividly how unpleasant the houseboat affair is. I have not talked to van der Leck since Huszár and van 't Hoff were here. I had better keep out of it, don't you think so? I would only like to tell you that I myself have not experienced Huszár's untrustworthiness, but I sensed it from what I heard at the time from van der Leck."

After the houseboat affair some smaller differences of opinion occurred. For instance, in the letters from Mondrian to van Doesburg a rumor turned up that Huszár was not very happy about van Doesburg's article in *De stijl* about Peter Alma.[34] After that there was another, bigger falling out, which makes it clear that van Doesburg indeed considered the unity within De Stijl shattered. In the fall of 1917 there had been talk about a collective show by the De Stijl painters. In the end it was postponed to the fall of 1918. Mondrian had sent word early in the game that he would be able to exhibit only a limited number of works because of a lack of time. He saw Huszár in August 1918, and afterwards he wrote to van Doesburg that he had the impression from Huszár's words that a postponement of the show would certainly be "for the best." After Mondrian's letter, van Doesburg became furious and wrote to Oud that the fall exhibition had fallen through because of Huszár's doing; Huszár could not be trusted, he wanted "to be part at one time, and at another time not."[35] Mondrian tried to soothe van Doesburg somewhat in an encouraging letter dated September 3, 1918, in which he took a position against Huszár. He also dwelled on Huszár's objections: "What else does he want? Does he call it 'individual' that you follow and designate a fixed course? But that is exactly the one great difference between *De stijl* and all other writings. If he doesn't want that, he should join *Wendingen.*[36] . . . Somebody else could not possibly have brought about the publication of *De stijl,* I do not think Huszár could have done it either. . . . Huszár never seemed a strong personality or a powerful artist to me (formerly you did not agree with me in this), but he is intelligent and he follows Neo-Plasticism in his work. This, to me, . . . makes up for a lot of his faults. . . . But I gladly accept that he doesn't feel the essence of it, he doesn't experience it. I also think you are the only one who does."

The relation between Theo van Doesburg and Vilmos Huszár cannot have been very good after all this, although van Doesburg's article of praise about *Compositie in grijs,* which was published in *De stijl* in the beginning of 1919, was written during the last months of 1918. This would be the last appearance of Huszár in the periodical for 2½ years. Undoubtedly his absence was the result of a conflict that originated in November 1918. In that month the De Stijl manifesto was published. Huszár objected that the manifesto had been signed by too many people. In particular, Georges Vantongerloo's presence bothered him quite a bit. This is understandable; Huszár probably visited Vantongerloo's shows in The Hague in 1916 and 1917, and he could rightly ask himself what had caused this artist, who until quite recently had had a predilection for folkloristic themes, to suddenly turn to Neo-Plasticism.

Mondrian, who probably knew Vantongerloo only from his first articles in *De stijl,* did not understand the crux of the matter. He suggested that Huszár might have confused Georges Vantongerloo with his brother Frans, who was a conventional painter. Mondrian urged van Doesburg to prevent a split at all costs, and asked whether Huszár by any chance wanted to start a new periodical. Van Doesburg, too, complained about Huszár around the same time: ". . . some five people (exclusively ladies, mostly brought aboard by Huszár) have discontinued their subscriptions. Moreover, Huszár is grumbling terribly because, in his opinion, Vantongerloo does not belong in *De stijl,* and his name should not appear under the manifesto. I have well-founded reasons to doubt Huszár's candidness. His letters give evidence that he is looking for all sorts of reasons to blacken me with the other contributors. Recently he wrote to me that he would suspend his contributions as long as the Vantongerloo affair and my arbitrariness in regard to the editorship have not been cleared up."[37]

In the beginning of 1919, after some additional differences of opinion, van Doesburg became fiercely anti-Huszár. The aforementioned incidents were an occasion for the split, but it is entirely possible that there were other factors. During that period Huszár did not participate in any shows, and therefore van Doesburg got the opportunity to take the stage as the original talent. When van Doesburg exhibited recent works in the fall of 1918 at a show of De Branding in The Hague, Huszár had no exhibit there. Van Doesburg wrote with some satisfaction to Kok on September 22 about the opening of the exhibition: "Huszár was there too; he looked very cross. They had not invited him."

1918: Interiors

Huszár apparently stopped painting for several years and directed his full attention to the painting of walls in interiors. His painted walls, in combination with specially designed furniture, fabrics, and stained glass, resulted in "spatial color compositions." Huszár began to work on these compositions (which often involved collaboration with an architect) in 1918, and remained active as an interior designer until the late 1940s. Like most of his paintings from the early years of De Stijl, his interiors have disappeared without leaving a trace. They are known from reproductions in *De stijl* and in other periodicals. When a "spatial color composition" was executed, either as a model or in reality, photographs were sometimes taken. It is possible to follow the development of Huszár's interior designs through these photographs.

How did Huszár become interested in interiors? In view of his education in Budapest, he must have been familiar with mural painting. In the Haagsche Kunstkring, which he joined in 1916, there was a lively interest in this art form. In this circle Huszár met many of the architects and artists with whom he was to collaborate on interiors including Jan Wils, Herman van der Kloot Meyburg, Kees van Moorsel, Piet Zwart, and Henri Berssenbrugge. The members of the Haagsche Kunstkring had rather traditional expectations of a muralist's activities. Huszár distinguished himself from his fellow members by the form he developed for the mural.[38] The strongest impulse, however, must have come from the De Stijl artists.

In the first issue of *De stijl,* which was published in October 1917, the keynote was collaboration between the arts. This theme comes up in van Doesburg's introduction and in contributions by J. J. P. Oud, Antony Kok, and Bart van der Leck. In the first and the fourth issue, van der Leck formulated his viewpoint that painters and architects should work side by side and not in a hierarchic relation, and introduced new ideas about wall painting. Color planes, he wrote, should be applied to walls in such a way as to create an open impression. His view was that only the painter really creates space in architecture; that the architect only creates a shell, which is destructurized by the painter. Van der Leck considered architecture to be something terrestrial, into which painting should introduce the cosmic value of light.

Huszár's appreciation of van der Leck was apparent in the "houseboat affair" of 1918. Perhaps he was acquainted with van der Leck's earlier interior designs through Bremmer. Huszár undoubtedly read van der Leck's articles in *De stijl* before he began to design his own interiors. Therefore, we may assume that van der Leck's work and ideas influenced Huszár's visual shaping of the interior. However, they had different expectations of the role of painting in architecture. Perhaps part of the difference is plain in their terminology: Van der Leck talked about creating a "space-light relation," Huszár about a "spatial color composition." Huszár intended to evoke a concrete aesthetic experience, van der Leck a nearly mystical experience. This difference is also evident in their remarks about the interaction of the arts. Huszár stated that painting, sculpture, and architecture would be most congenial if they were abstract; in that way they would symbolize the universal. Hence, he interpreted the universal as the communal, while van der Leck connected the universal with the cosmic.

The theoretical difference between Huszár and van der Leck can also be seen in their realizations. Huszár left the architecture intact as much as possible, and painted walls in their entirety so that the spectator appeared to be immersed in a color bath. Van der Leck, who according to his own saying aimed at the destructurizing of architecture, did not create a colorful atmosphere but applied small dispersed color blocks to white walls. Another difference is that Huszár only started applying bright, primary colors in his interiors in 1921, whereas van der Leck had been doing that since 1916.

Everything points to the fact that Huszár focused on form, still partly basing himself on Bremmer's artistic concepts. What counted was the aesthetic experience evoked by the form. To Huszár, an abstract work of art, whether a painting or an interior, could best transmit this experience. He announced this in 1919, in a lecture to the Haagsche Kunstkring.[39] According to him, figurative mural paintings could not evoke an aesthetic experience. The painting of the interior had to be abstract. The gentlemen of the Kunstkring protested loudly against this proposition. Huszár himself always practiced abstraction, but the manner in which he did this changed gradually between 1918 and 1924.

The earliest interiors

In the beginning, Huszár proceeded in a very orderly and methodical manner in his interiors; he applied planes of the same size and color, equidistant from one another. The first designs that can be dated accurately are those for the Bruynzeel company. In February 1918 Huszár made a display stand for the annual industrial fair in Utrecht (figure 91). In this stand, which in a sense was a precursor of his interior designs, he applied a system of regular planes separated by black and white bands. The planes were meant for the display of the company's parquet flooring.

In 1919, Huszár used a much freer working procedure in designing a room in the villa De Arendshoeve for the Bruynzeel sons (figure 92). On this project he collaborated with the architect P. J. C. Klaarhamer, whom he had met through Bart van der Leck.[40] There are several extant photographs of this room which give a good impression of Huszár's radical changes in the interior. He no longer adhered to a regular partitioning into homogeneous elements; instead he used asymmetrically positioned planes of different sizes and colors. In his lecture "Over de moderne toegepaste kunsten" ["On modern applied art"], delivered in January 1922 to the Moderne Kunstencongres [Modern Arts Congress] in Antwerp, Huszár described this interior extensively: "The task of the visual artist is to arrange the spaces [and] the functions rhythmically and at the same time practically. The light of the rooms is continued in the colors, the work of the painters. . . . In that manner I have tried here to join furniture, doors, and walls in space. The door of the closet separates the two beds, and I have tried to find a connection between the two beds by painting the wall white over one bed and gray over the other bed, the planes on the walls the other way around. This practice is continued on the left side wall, where the blue and yellow planes on the white ground form a composition with the red and black bed."[41]

One of Huszár's next designs was the *Ruimte-kleur-compositie voor een zitkamer* [*Spatial color composition for a sitting room*]. This design was fairly symmetrical. The walls, the floor (with rugs and furniture), and the ceiling have to be regarded as compositions in themselves, but there are correspondences, for instance between the floor and the ceiling.

In June 1919 this design was published in the periodical *Levende kunst* [*Living art*], a counterpart of *De stijl*. The critic Ro van Oven, who visited Huszár on this occasion, characterized his endeavors as "obtaining beauty by rhythmical proportions of planes, wherein every perspective is eliminated." She also wrote that Huszár used Ostwald's color theory for his interiors, which may well have been the case in the living room also. Huszár saw particularly good opportunities for its application in the interior, as he already had written in his aforementioned article in *De stijl*. Ostwald's colors were exactly indicated with numbers, and when the artist had no time to realize his design himself he could easily pass them on to the housepainter. Theo van Doesburg was anything but appreciative of Huszár's contributing to this periodical, which had been founded shortly after *De stijl* by the architect Co Brandes.[42] Van Doesburg must have written to Mondrian about this contribution. Mondrian replied from Paris on August 1: "Henceforth I will act as if he doesn't exist. I resent most that he is in league with half-hearted people and collaborates with them. For that is what you told me, isn't it?" Since the difficulties over the manifesto, Huszár had resumed publishing in *De stijl;* however, because of this "unfaithfulness" he would be absent from *De stijl* until August 1921.

Nevertheless, Huszár was not completely excommunicated. In April 1920 van Doesburg, who was trying to put together an exhibit of works by De Stijl artists for a touring exhibition of La Section d'Or, got in touch with him again. Van Doesburg also tried to persuade Bart van der Leck to participate, but the latter did not have any inclination to make another public appearance as a painter belonging to De Stijl. Huszár agreed, however, and this saved van Doesburg from having to present De Stijl as a movement of only two men (Mondrian and himself). As van Doesburg stated in a letter to Antony Kok dated April 25, 1920, the personal difficulties between him and Huszár were forgiven but not forgotten: "At my suggestion Mondrian and Huszár were invited as painters from Holland. Huszár's participation is due to the fact that I do not want to slight him in comparison with the others; when art is involved, I

91

92

91 Huszár, Bruynzeel display stand, 1918. Photograph in artist's estate.

92 Huszár, boys' bedroom, De Arendshoeve, Voorburg, 1919. As illustrated in *De stijl* 5, no. 5 (1922), p. 78. The furniture is now in the Gemeentemuseum, in The Hague.

93 Huszár, *Ruimte-kleur-compositie voor een zitkamer* [*Spatial color composition for a sitting room*], 1919. As illustrated in *Levende kunst* 2 (June 1919).

93

94

94 **Huszár and K. van Moorsel, *Composition en couleurs dans l'espace*, 1920. Technique, dimensions, and place of execution unknown; photograph in private collection.**

95 **Huszár, *Ruimte-kleur-compositie voor een eetkamer [Spatial color composition for a dining room]*, 1921. Technique, dimensions, and place of execution unknown; photograph in artist's estate.**

96 **Huszár and J. Wils, *Ruimte-kleur-compositie voor Berssenbrugge [Spatial color composition for Berssenbrugge]*, 1921. Photograph in Huszár estate.**

cannot dwell on any personal difficulties I have had (with anyone)." Mondrian got word of Huszár's participation only in the beginning of June, just before the opening of the show in Rotterdam.

Huszár showed three works. *Composition en couleurs dans l'espace IV (perspective) [Composition in colors in space IV (perspective)]*, which was reproduced alongside a review in the weekly *Het leven,* was a bedroom designed in 1920 in collaboration with the architect Kees van Moorsel.[43] *Composition en couleurs dans l'espace VII* was a living room designed in 1920 with Jan Wils.[44] The third piece is described in the catalog as "Etude (peinte en caseine)."

The Section d'Or exhibition, which after Rotterdam traveled to The Hague and Amsterdam, received much coverage in the press.[45] Kasper Niehaus wrote in *De telegraaf* of July 20, 1920: "Another adept of Mondrian's is Huszár, who . . . shows some sketches, spatial color compositions. This 'absolute' art, applied to craft (which is very logical), cannot make us forget [the] work of the initiator of this trend, van der Leck, which carried so much more conviction." The review that appeared on July 17 in *De hofstad* is also interesting; here, an unknown reporter wrote: "What strikes us anew in this exhibition is the growing inclination of the exhibitors to realize their intentions in practice. . . . Jan Wils and Vilmos Huszár are among the first to demonstrate this; they seek to point out a certain psyche in the space of the room by means of distinct lines and color planes." A certain T. van Lelyveld wrote a long article in *De loods* of July 29, 1920, in which he presented Huszár and van Doesburg as followers of Mondrian's most recent method—"rectangular colored blocks fitted together." This immediately drew a letter to the editor from van Doesburg, in which he said: "Neither in Huszár's interiors nor in my work is there any question of following Mondrian's most recent method."

After the Section d'Or exhibition, Huszár was not mentioned for some months in the correspondence. The show had improved relations somewhat. In September 1920, a few months before van Doesburg's departure for Germany, he and Huszár officially made peace. Mondrian was informed and reacted as of old: "Nice that Huszár is 'back,' but I would wait and see, I don't know for sure about him (I mean, I would not trust him too much, he is a Tongerloo-like figure)."[46] Huszár corresponded with van Doesburg in Germany, but not until 1921 did he begin to submit contributions to *De stijl* again. In the meantime he published an article in *Bouwkundig weekblad.*[47]

The first primary-color interiors

The 1921 dining-room composition shown as figure 95 was probably the first interior in which Huszár used only primary colors of

95

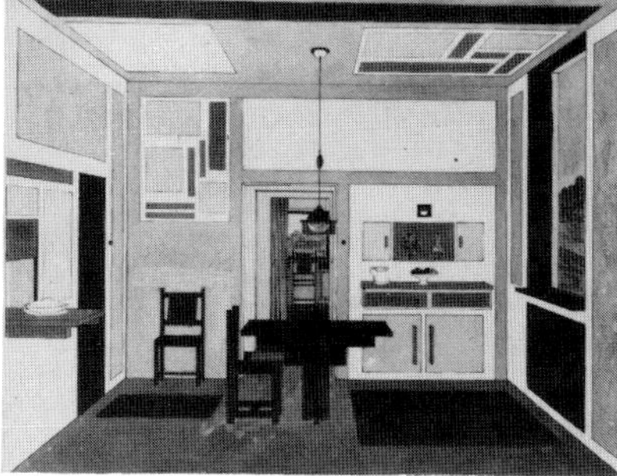

96

maximum brightness. According to his accompanying explanation, he sought in this design to integrate the "needed utensils" into the whole.[48] For instance, the different parts of the sideboard recur as motifs in the small compositions on the walls and the ceiling.

A few of Huszár's interior designs were realized in the homes of his friends and acquaintances. As Huszár himself wrote in his article "De kunst en de leek" ["Art and the layman"] in the *Bouwkundig weekblad* of April–May 1922, he allowed the patron hardly any say in the design of an interior. As an artist, he felt absolutely autonomous. As he had written in 1920 in the same periodical, he also took a position independent from the architect—a concept which Bart van der Leck also nurtured.

The fact that so few of Huszár's interiors[49] were realized can perhaps also be explained by the circumstance that their actual usefulness was deemed to be very slight. The client had to reorganize his household, and what he got was generally considered chilling and not cozy. Another criticism was that the whole composition would collapse like a house of cards if the client dared to move a chair or a rug. Huszár knew these arguments and tried to counteract them by creating special spots in the composition where variation could be tolerated, but that did not make much of a difference. The doubts regarding livability were probably less valid for spaces like halls and stairwells.

Appreciation for Huszár's spatial color compositions gradually increased. The studio of the photographer Henri Berssenbrugge, on which Huszár collaborated with Jan Wils, created quite a stir. Wils built a high, oblong room behind Berssenbrugge's old parlor-studio, and Huszár provided the colors. When the new studio was finished, in June 1921, Berssenbrugge held an open house for the press for a few days. According to the many press reports,[50] the floors had two shades of gray. They carried black, blue, and raspberry-red rugs, the colors of which recurred in the wall planes with the addition of yellow-ochre. A few of the wall planes were surrounded by a gray strip. The basic colors of the walls were white and black. The aesthetic experience that Huszár valued so highly seems to have actually been felt by a few reporters who viewed this studio. The reporter of the *Zeeuwsche courant* described his impressions as follows: "Very curious is the effect of the human figure in this colorful but yet not at all gaudy room. He has much more space and atmosphere around him than in the usual crowded rooms, and because of the large diversity of light elements forming together the harmonic color atmosphere, every conceivable [clothing color] has a pleasant color effect against the walls; therefore it looks much freer than in the usual surroundings. . . . I suspect that someone seeing a color drawing of this interior

97 Huszár (color) and P. Zwart (form), living room of Stormhoek, Zaandam, 1921. Photograph (from Zwart estate) in Gemeentemuseum, The Hague. In this room, green planes on a gray ground were put between the paneling (reported by Mrs. Busschbach-Bruynzeel). The photograph reproduced here is from the archives of the Bruynzeel company in Zaandam.

98 Huszár, *Mechanisch beeldende toneel* [*Mechanical plastic drama*], 1921. Dimensions and whereabouts unknown; photograph in artist's estate.

97

98

would get a wrong impression . . . the colors . . . actually reach our eyes through the space."[51] The architectural critic J. P. Mieras, of *Bouwkundig weekblad,* also attempted a description of the spatial effect. He felt free and light in the space, and wrote that the colors were "form-determining."[52] One reporter asked whether every portrait photograph would now feature the interior as background, but Berssenbrugge answered reassuringly that he could eliminate that by focusing sharply.[53]

In Berssenbrugge's studio, Huszár guided the light into the room by painting light planes next to the windows and dark ones opposite the windows. The planes were applied in such a way as to accent the direction of the wall. The color intensity was proportioned to the sizes of the planes; the large planes were probably painted in less forceful colors. Opposite planes were situated on the same level and always at a constant distance from the corners of the room. Wils kept the walls flat, without cumbersome interruptions, and he kept the furniture to a minimum in order to impede the spatial effect as little as possible.

In 1921 Huszár designed at least three other interiors (including the living room of Cornelis Bruynzeel's house, which by the way does not completely fit into the development outlined above) and a puppet theater, the *Mechanisch beeldende toneel [Mechanical plastic drama]*.[54] The puppet theater can be regarded as a synthesis of Huszár's plans for "kinetic painting" and his interior designs. The movable parts of the set were painted in "primary and secondary colors."[55] The two wooden puppets, which appeared one after the other, also could change positions. In the drawing (figure 98) they are shown in the position they occupied at the end of the show. Specially composed music was to accompany the performance. Although this design was never realized, in 1925 Huszár did make other puppets in different variations.

Return to De Stijl

Although Huszár reconciled with van Doesburg in September 1920, he did not publish another article in *De stijl* until August 1921. This delay may have been caused by a disagreement about the new logo, which Mondrian and van Doesburg had designed in close consultation and which featured "NB"–the abbreviation of "Nieuwe Beelding" [Neo-Plasticism]—in large red letters. The replacement of his logo upset Huszár, which in turn elicited from Mondrian the remark that he really was a null. Mondrian wrote on February 7, 1921: "Resigning now that his picture is not on it any more! Instead of going forward with us and rejoicing that you brought about a better appearance. This Huszár may well fizzle out like a damp candle. But really he was never a 'candle'—maybe a cloudy mirror."

This matter was over and done with in the summer of 1921. In August *De stijl* published the *Mechanisch beeldende toneel,* and in the beginning of 1922 Berssenbrugge's studio and the Bruynzeel dining room also appeared in the journal.

The successful realization of the Berssenbrugge studio must have provided an impulse for van Doesburg. His interest in interiors and architecture escalated in late 1921. In his lecture "Der wille zum stil," which he gave in Weimar, Jena, and Berlin, he presented the Berssenbrugge project as an exemplary collaboration between painter and architect. Mondrian reacted with reserve to van Doesburg's new enthusiasm: "I completely agree with what you are writing, namely that the interior has to become 'it.' But only in the future."[56] He complained about Huszár's interior designs to Oud, as well, calling them "the wrong execution of the wrong concept of [Neo-Plasticism]."[57]

In February 1922 Huszár organized an exhibition in Groningen for the association Pictura. He had connections there because he was a contributor to the journal *Blad voor kunst* of the artists' group De Ploeg. Until shortly before the opening, he tried to get work by others to Groningen; for instance, in the end of January he wrote to Peeters in Antwerp asking if he would like to exhibit "up to ten paintings and [twenty] graphic works."[58] In the end, the show included only Huszár's works and a few by van Doesburg and van der Leck.

The Pictura exhibition can be regarded as a survey of Huszár's work since 1916. There were seven of his paintings in the show, three stained-glass works (one of these was a design), thirteen designs for interiors, the *Mechanisch beeldende toneel,* a clock, and some free and applied graphic works. The paintings were all from the years 1916–1918, except one. Among them were *Stad, Hamer en zaag,* and *Compositie in grijs.* A review in *Blad voor de kunst* gives the colors of the 1921 painting (*Studie*) and thus enables us to identify this work with one of the few extant paintings by Huszár from these years.[59] The two executed stained-glass works that were on view were *Compositie (motief zonnebloemen)* [*Composition (motif sunflowers)*], from 1916, and a 1919 window with a regular distribution of planes. Huszár gave the most prominent place to his spatial color compositions, the oldest of which was the Bruynzeel boys' bedroom (1919) and the most recent of which was Berssenbrugge's studio. The composition of the exhibition suggests that during the years 1919–1921 Huszár created hardly any other work besides interior compositions. This suggestion is strengthened by the fact that on other occasions he did not exhibit any paintings from this period either, with one or two exceptions (*Etude,* 1920; *Studie,* 1921).

In 1922, communication between Huszár and Theo van Doesburg—then residing in Weimar, Germany—depended principally on the mail. A letter from the end of January gives evidence that Huszár was again taking a strong role within De Stijl. He had been at the Moderne Kunstencongres in Antwerp. "By chance Oud was there, and instead of van 't Hoff he read his own lecture, which you also know. It is a pity that you are at odds with him too, and from van Tongerloo's brother I heard this is also the case with V.T. How can *De stijl* ever amount to anything when you break off with everybody? You write asking me if I would promote *De stijl;* how is that possible if all those good collaborators (except v. Tongerloo, I never cared much for his work) . . . , Oud, and I hear Mondrian now also, don't contribute to *De stijl* any more, and you replace them with German expressionists. I think that the last issue with the A.B.C. poems is miserable, but that may be only my opinion. I thought that the tinny container and some other verses were yours. There will have to be quite a few changes in order to firm up the people in *De stijl.* You are complaining that you have no contributors, but that is not possible if you break off with everyone. . . . Perhaps you will resent this letter, but if you want to collaborate with me I have to say what I think."[60] This letter indeed went down the wrong way with van Doesburg. He wrote to Antony Kok on February 9, 1922, from Weimar: "Now Oud and Huszár met at the 'kunstenaarscongres' in Antwerp (Oud was not to speak there, van 't Hoff was, but Oud was there anyway and stood in for van 't Hoff, who was ill). I had visited Huszár and spoken to him. He had often hinted that he wanted to review his relations with me and *De stijl.* From here I had asked Huszár to send me the proceedings of the artists' congress, because I am very much interested. Now I get a terribly mean letter from Huszár in return. Inspired by and as a result of a talk with Oud! Full of reproaches, saying that I pick a quarrel with everybody and that *De stijl* doesn't amount to anything at all any more, etc. In one word: terrible. I am dumbfounded. For five years I have served the idea with all my powers, neglecting my own interests, always deciding between individual petty interests of others with an eye to the general concept, and now the result is that they start to agitate against me. A dirty mess. I will not write to anyone any more, and just let them talk."

This correspondence promised the worst, but it did not turn out to be very serious. In August 1922, Huszár made a trip to

Weimar and visited van Doesburg there. After his return to the Netherlands, he wrote a particularly vehement article against the Bauhaus. This article—written in German—was published in *De stijl* in September, and must have pleased van Doesburg, who had great conflicts with the management of the Bauhaus.

Huszár's renewed involvement with *De stijl* is evidenced by what he did to his copy of the issue in which the aforementioned article was published. Obviously wanting to have something of his work on the cover again, he added two black rectangles to van Doesburg's and Mondrian's layout—an amusing parallel with the black square by Malevich on the first page of that issue.

Next Huszár occupied himself with the organization of the dada tour in the Netherlands. On September 4, 1922, he wrote to van Doesburg: "You should prepare the dadaists for a cool and sober public. . . ." To have Huszár participate with his *Mechanische dansfiguur* probably was planned just before the first dada soirées[61] took place; it is not mentioned in the letters.

That Huszár wanted to write about architecture is evidenced by his letter of September 4, 1922, to van Doesburg. During the last months of 1922 he was working on a study about "the wall plane and planar painting through the ages." The publication fell through, but he did give lectures on the subject to the Kunstkring in The Hague and the one in Rotterdam.[62]

Interior designs after 1922

In October 1923 Huszár was represented at the architectural exhibition of De Stijl in the Galerie de l'Effort Moderne in Paris by four interior designs. He exhibited the *Composition en couleurs dans l'espace,* the Berssenbrugge studio, and two interior designs from 1921 for a home for women, on which he had collaborated with Piet Zwart.

Also in October, Huszár exhibited at the Juryfreie Kunstschau [Nonjuried Art Exhibition] in Berlin. For this show, he and Gerrit Rietveld produced a model with wall paintings in primary colors (figure 100). The model contained two pieces of furniture by Rietveld, the so-called Berlin Chair and a small table. The wall painting was no doubt Huszár's work. A photograph from his estate (figure 101) shows that the wall planes consist of painted thin cardboard; because of this, the totality gives the impression of a study. (The collaboration of Huszár and Rietveld probably did not amount to more than the exhibition of furniture by Rietveld in Huszár's interior, just as would be the case a year later in Til Brugman's house.) Huszár wrote under the photograph: "Model for the Berlin exhibition, executed in Berlin." The first half of this legend suggests that the model was the real exhibit by Huszár and Rietveld; on the

99

99 Huszár's copy of the September 1922 issue of *De stijl,* to which he applied black planes. Private collection.

100

100 Postcard from Huszár to J. J. P. Oud, November 24, 1923. Private collection.

101

other hand, the second half mentions realization in Berlin. No photographs of a "real" room have ever been found, however.[63]

The Berlin model shows that Huszár's method of creating an interior had changed rather drastically. In the Berssenbrugge studio, he had tried to create a cohesive totality by coordinating the planes according to their relative positions on the walls. Such a method of composition can be called friendly to architecture. In Berlin, however, the planes continued through the corners of the room and behaved as if they were more or less independent of the architecture. Huszár now worked with primary-colored planes against a white ground, just as Bart van der Leck had done five years earlier (figure 165). The difference was that Huszár's planes were much larger and that they overlapped.

Huszár had used overlapping vertices in paintings in 1917, but he relinquished this when he started working with a grid. In the Berlin model he took this up again; he placed the ends of the planes on top of one another. He also did this in other works. Around the time when he was designing the Berlin interior, he was developing the so-called monotypes, which until now were incorrectly assigned to 1918. At the earliest, the monotypes could have originated in the fall of 1923. They were first exhibited in October 1924 at the d'Audretsch gallery in The Hague.[64] On October 25 he wrote a note to Oud about the exhibition, in which he described the mixed printing technique he had used: "Dear Oud, I am at the moment having an exhibition of colorprints (woodcut technique) at the gallery d'Audretsch in The Hague. I would like to hold the same show in other cities. Can you provide a place in Rotterdam where I can show them? There are 31 pieces on gray passepartout 47 × 33 cm., so you can conclude from this that I don't need much space."[65]

It is sometimes assumed that Huszár's monotypes were inspired by H. N. Werkman's prints. There are also other possibilities. The prints of the Bauhaus, which he must have seen during his visit to Weimar, were a more direct source. It is possible that an exhibition of Thuringian artists that he reviewed in *De stijl* played a role. The works of the Hungarians Forbat (a student of Gropius) and Moholy-Nagy are very close to Huszár's monotypes.

There is a clear correspondence between the monotypes and the Berlin model. In both, Huszár used overlapping forms. The prints, however, show a new element: mixed color in the overlaps. Huszár also used this transparency effect in 1924 in a realized design for the living room of the author Til Brugman (figure 103). A series of photographs of the old room, the new room, and the design have been preserved.[66] The back of the photograph of the design contains the title "Compositie grijs," so it is probable that

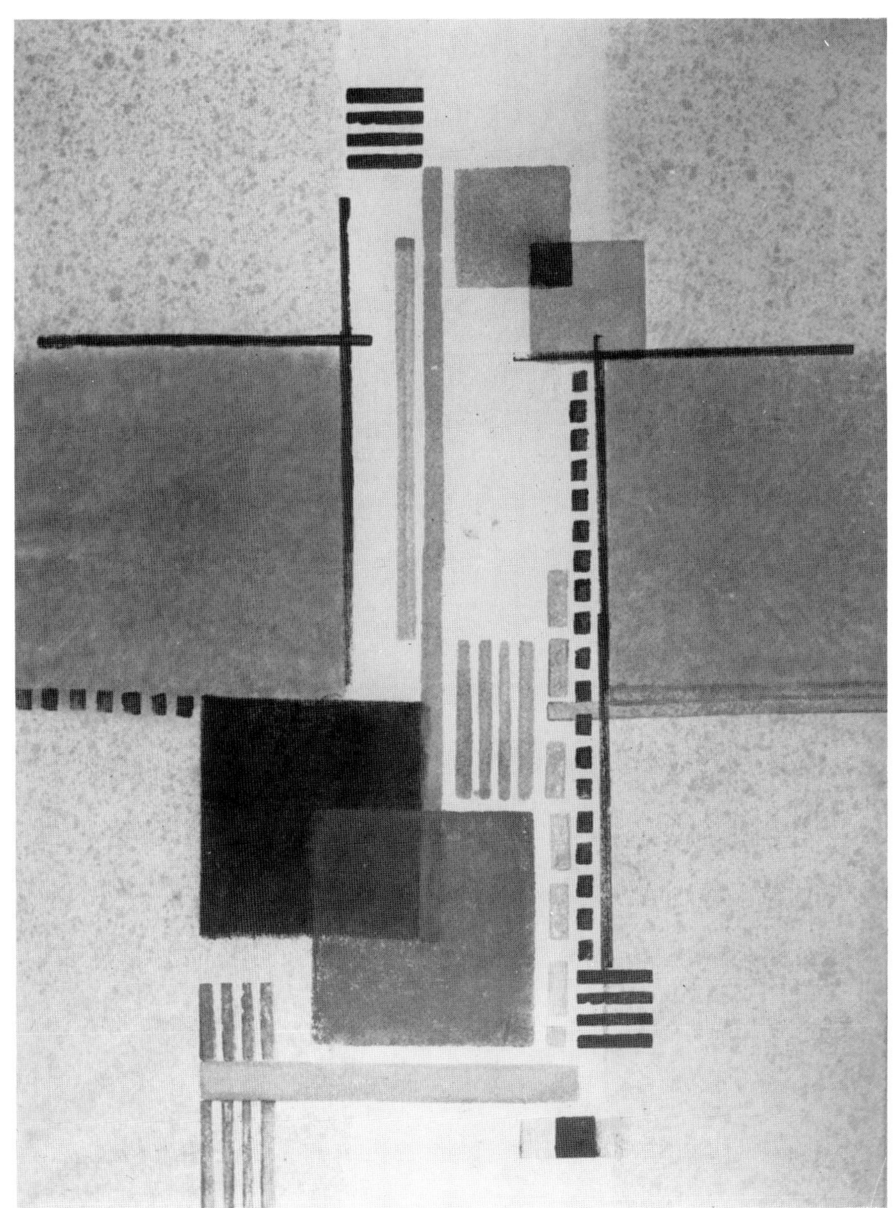

102

101 Huszár and G. Rietveld, *Maquette, ruimte-kleur-compositie voor een tentoonstellingsruimte* [*Spatial color composition for an exhibition*], 1923. Photograph in artist's estate. (Color plate on page xvii.)

102 Huszár, *Monotype*, 1924; 23.3 × 30.5 cm (without passe-partout). Rijksmuseum Kröller-Müller, Otterlo.

103 Huszár, *Compositie in grijs* [*Composition in gray*], 1924. Destroyed; photographs in Stedelijk Museum, Amsterdam.

the whole composition was executed in shades of gray. Just as in the Berlin model, the planes in this living room continue across the corners. The spatial color composition negates the shape determined by the architecture. Obviously Huszár had to work around the presence of the piano; the color plane on the bottom panel is the result of his endeavors to incorporate it in the composition. It appears that Rietveld's furniture was not originally taken into account, but the lamp and the clock (designed by Huszár himself) were.

In the mid 1920s, Huszár produced new paintings and theater experiments. He was then staying in Paris, where he sometimes met with Mondrian. The latter wrote to Oud in 1925 that Huszár, on nearer acquaintance, was quite a bit nicer than he had expected. The fact that both of them had severed their relations with Theo van Doesburg and *De stijl* must have contributed to their mutual affinity.

Dilemmas

Huszár's participation in the formative years of De Stijl was fairly extensive. However, his paintings and interior designs from the years up to 1923 are nearly all known solely from reproductions. The originals have been lost, or their whereabouts are unknown. On the other hand, quite a few of Huszár's paintings have been preserved, and in museums, exhibitions, and galleries these are invariably dated circa 1918.

It is improbable that Huszár created so much in or around 1918; it is still more improbable that in a single year he painted such different works as *Compositie in grijs* (figure 87) and *Danspaar* [*Dancing couple*] (figure 105). The question remains: When could this last painting, and many others, have been created?

This question can be answered only partly. The dating of Huszár's work is a knotty problem that cannot be unraveled as yet, except for the years dealt with in this chapter. Huszár dated very few of his works, sometimes belatedly and obviously incorrectly. Moreover, later in life he still created many works in the spirit of De Stijl. In the dating of Huszár's works, it is not taken sufficiently into account that, although he had not contributed to *De stijl* since 1923, he remained unceasingly sympathetic to the principles of the movement throughout the 1920s. Also, in the 1940s and after 1950, when interest in De Stijl was increasing and when Huszár and van der Leck were the only surviving founding painters, Huszár occasionally returned to his work from the De Stijl period. All this work has been dated circa 1918, not only because the actual dates are unknown, but also because owners often find it more inter-

104

105

106

104 **Huszár, lamps for spatial color compositions. Etched plate glass and milk glass. Private collection.**

105 **Huszár, *Danspaar* [*Dancing couple*], ca. 1938. Oil on canvas, 100 × 60 cm. Gemeentemuseum, The Hague.**

106 **Huszár, *De vioolspelers* [*The violinists*], ca. 1927. 82 × 138 cm. Gemeentemuseum, The Hague.**

esting to possess a painting from the De Stijl years. The result is a very confused image, prevailing to the present, of Huszár's contribution to De Stijl.

In dating and placing Huszár's works from the period up to 1923, I have consulted reproductions in early publications, documents concerning exhibitions, letters, and Huszár's own photographs (which must have been very numerous, though now not many are extant). The reconstruction of Huszár's body of work is certainly not complete yet. Much more of his work might be extant, and the source that could reveal the most information, namely the correspondence between Huszár and van Doesburg, has been tapped only to a very small extent because most of the letters are privately owned. In anticipation of other endeavors to catalog Huszár's work from the 1920s and later years, I shall discuss very briefly some well-known paintings which are usually dated early in the De Stijl period.

One of Huszár's few dated paintings is *Compositie 1916* (figure 107). It is not identical with, but it is very close to, the logo on the cover of *De stijl.* As others have already observed, the date at the bottom of this painting must be incorrect, because the name *De stijl* and the open lettertype were not used for the future periodical before the spring of 1917.[67] So the piece was antedated, by Huszár or by someone else. On the other hand, it is also unlikely that the painting stems from 1917, the time of the logo. Its manner of painting does not correspond to that of Huszár's other work from that year. For instance, in *Compositie II* (figure 74) and *Hamer en zaag* the paint was applied rather thickly; in *Compositie 1916,* on the other hand, the paint was applied thinly. Furthermore, *Hamer en zaag* was the only work from 1917 where exclusively primary colors (without blue) were used; in the other paintings, green and purple also occurred, The combination of primary colors with gray, as in *Compositie 1916,* can only be seen in Huszár's works from 1921 on, at least in interior designs. Thus, *Compositie 1916* could have been painted any time after 1921. There are no early reproductions and no listings in exhibition catalogs, and thus no documentation for assigning the painting to the very first years of De Stijl. The catalog of the 1922 Pictura exhibition in Groningen lists a composition from 1916; however, it is unlikely that this was the painting discussed here. The only fact about this painting that can be established with certainty is that it was shown in 1955 in a Huszár retrospective in Gouda.

A second, comparable case is that of *Danspaar.* That painting is usually assigned to 1917, but that cannot be correct, partly for the reasons just mentioned. As far as we know, Huszár did not use diagonals yet at that time. The main reason that *Danspaar* seems

107

hard to fit into 1917, however, is the manner of abstraction, which differs considerably from that in, for instance, *Compositie II* or *Compositie met witte kop.* What was said above about *Compositie 1916* also holds true for *Danspaar:* It does not occur in any of the early literature or exhibition catalogs. Still, there is reason to assume that it was painted sometime in the 1920s or the 1930s. Huszár himself furnished an argument for this opinion when he in 1939 made a kind of documentary exhibit on De Stijl for the New York World's Fair. He constructed a small glass display case (figure 108) which held some paintings of early members of De Stijl in miniature: Mondrian's *Compositie* from 1917, van Doesburg's *Compositie X* from 1918, van der Leck's *Bakje met appels* [*Bowl with apples*] from 1921, and a painting of a dancing couple (albeit not precisely the one in the Gemeentemuseum).

More research needs to be done before we can be sufficiently certain about Huszár's work in the period after his official parting with De Stijl.

108

107 Huszár, *Compositie 1916*. Actual date: after 1921. Oil on canvas, 60 × 50 cm. Gemeentemuseum, The Hague.

108 Huszár, display case for World's Fair, New York, 1939. As illustrated in *The Netherlands participation at the New York World's Fair* (1939), p. 62.

1
The list of autobiographical data is in the possession of the Huszár family. Some biographical information can be found in H. Rodéro, "Vilmos Huszár," *Nederland* 78 (1926), pp. 570–576, and in E. Berkovich, "Het werk van V. Huszár," *Binnenhuis* 13, no. 7 (1931), pp. 63–64. For more recent literature on Huszár see M. I. Gaugham, "Huszár's way into abstraction" (unpublished paper, 1976, copy in Rijksbureau voor Kunsthistorische Documentatie, The Hague), and C. Passuth, *Magyar múvészek az Európai avantgardeban* (Budapest, 1974). In 1985 a monograph on Huszár was published on the occasion of a retrospective at the Gemeentemuseum in The Hague: S. Ex and E. Hoek, *Vilmos Huszár, schilder en ontwerper, 1884–1960* (Utrecht).

2
The letters from Huszár to Bremmer are in the municipal archives of The Hague.

3
"Op twintig minuten lopen," *Provinciale Overijsselsche courant*, February 18, 1955.

4
A color reproduction of the painting can be found in S. Ex, "V. Huszár en de toegepaste kunsten," *Bijvoorbeeld* 13, no. 4 (1981), p. 28–32.

5
This copy of the catalog is in the Rijksbureau voor Kunsthistorische Documentatie, in The Hague.

6
E. Wichman, "Willy Huszár bij De Onafhankelijken," *Memorandum voor de schilderkunst*, December 22, 1913. Frans van Burkom informed me about this.

7
Huszár was also mentioned in reviews in the newspapers *De maasbode* (June 28, 1914), *Haagsche post* (July 27, 1914), and *De telegraaf* (July 28, 1914).

8
De hofstad (newspaper, The Hague), May 20, 1922; *De kunst*, May 27, 1922, p. 416.

9
See A. de Jongh, "De Stijl," *Museumjournaal* 17, no. 6 (1972), p. 270.

10
Judging from the description, this sketch had the same character as *Schilderij (geel)*. Bertha van Hasselt's talk about the soul's pursuit of the light is remarkable. Theo van Doesburg, who reproduced and discussed *Schilderij (geel)* in his 1919 booklet *Drie voordrachten over de nieuwe beeldende kunst*, interpreted the yellow as light but did not dwell on its possible symbolic meaning. There is no other indication that Huszár had any interest in mystical and esoteric matters, as did van Doesburg and Mondrian. Bertha van Hasselt's interpretation was probably meant in a poetic sense.

11
This letter raises many questions. We know from Mondrian's correspondence that he was not yet acquainted with Huszár's work in May 1917. Therefore, it is very unlikely that he would have wanted to associate himself with Huszár in August of 1916. Huszár may have known Bart van der Leck personally by then, and he certainly knew his and Mondrian's work via Bremmer. Bremmer may have tried to bring van der Leck, Mondrian, and Huszár together. At any rate, it is striking that van Doesburg's letter refers to "Huszár and Bremmer."

The distinction between "reasoning ones" and "intuitive ones" can probably be traced back to Spinoza, whose writings Huszár had studied some ten years earlier. In his *Ethica*, Spinoza discerns people driven by their passions and people who let themselves be guided by their intellect. Huszár quoted this later, in his "Aesthetic considerations" in *De stijl*, in an attempt to clarify the difference between rational and irrational artists.

12
If Huszár did mean to compete with Bremmer, he certainly had some reason for this. He had known Bremmer for at least ten years, but Bremmer had never published an article about him. Huszár's satisfaction with a periodical of his own is evidenced by the fact that he started a drive for subscribers among Bremmer's circle.

13
The circumspection with regard to Bremmer is understandable. Bremmer had contracts with both Mondrian and van der Leck, and in the past he had bought works from Huszár and van Doesburg. Because of his close relations with collectors and potential subscribers, he was a man to be reckoned with.

14
Letter from Mondrian to van Doesburg, September 1, 1917. Mondrian mentions the difficulties that arose with Harms Tiepen, the publisher of *De stijl*, as an explanation for Huszár's attitude.

15
When Gips started an advertising agency with a man named Kerling, around the end of the 1930s, Huszár became the aesthetic adviser.

16
In 1918, Oud credited van Doesburg wth thls innovation. See "Glas-in-lood van Theo van Doesburg," *Bouwkundig weekblad* 39, no. 35 (1918), pp. 199–202.

17
See W. F. Gouwe, *Glas-in-lood*, in the series *De toegepaste kunsten in Nederland* (Rotterdam, 1932), pp. 58–59. For general information on Huszár's stained-glass works see R. van Oven, "Moderne glas-schilderkunst in Holland. I. Vilmos Huszár," *Levende kunst*, 1919, pp. 48–57.

18
This review, from the May 10 issue, is in the Piet Zwart archive of the Gemeentemuseum in The Hague.

19
Huszár also visualized the correlation between the signs of the zodiac and the hours of the day in 1937, in a clock for the interior of Mesd. Bouwens in Nijmegen.

20
Every attempt to attribute to Huszár a share in the layout of the journal has failed, however.

21
Theo van Doesburg said of Huszár in the newspaper *Het vaderland* of February 23, 1923: "He already advocated the possibility of a mechanical theater piece in 1917, and has executed it fragmentarily. For instance, his dancing figure is the result of years of study and planning. The fact that this figure was shown at the dada soirées does not necessarily mean that it is immediately connected with dadaism."

22
I received information on the dancing figure from B. Huszár of Deil and W. de Graaf of Haarlem. Vilmos Huszár wrote a short article about it in *Merz* 1 (January 1923), p. 13. Another short description was published on page 32 of Otto van Tussenbroek's *Speelgoed, marionetten, maskers en schimmenspelen* (Rotterdam, 1925).

23
Anonymous, *Nieuwe Rotterdamsche courant*, May 8, 1919.

24
E. Kallai, *Neue malerei in Ungarn* (Leipzig, 1925), pp. 103–111. Kallai was of the opinion that the intended flatness was not achieved in *Stad* because of the intense colors.

25
See, for instance, the catalog of the 1922 Pictura show at Groningen, in which Huszár exhibited some works. This catalog lists still lifes from 1917 under the numbers 2 and 4. Number 2 is probably *Hamer en zaag*; number 4 is unknown.

26
T. van Doesburg, *Drie voordrachten over de nieuwe beeldende kunst* (Amsterdam, 1919), pp. 86 and 92-93. Severini was *De stijl*'s Paris correspondent.

27
Mondrian reacted with reserve to Huszár's work. When *Compositie VI* was published in *De stijl* he wrote to van Doesburg: "I found what Huszár accomplished something; I do agree with you; I only wrote that I thought it had not been solved yet" (undated letter, spring 1918). Huszár himself was probably not quite satisfied with the result, because to a certain extent a figure-ground relation still existed.

28
This painting is reproduced and discussed extensively in Kallai's *Neue malerei in Ungarn* (note 24).

29
This photograph is reproduced on p. 31 of Joost Baljeu's *Theo van Doesburg* (London, 1974).

30
In August 1918, Huszár published an article titled "Iets over die farbenfibel van Wilhelm Ostwald" ["Something about the color circle of Wilhelm Ostwald"] in *De stijl* (1, no. 10, pp. 113–118).

Ostwald was a German chemist who tried to create a scientific color classification. His publications, which appeared in the Netherlands from 1916 on, included an appendix of color cards and a disk with 24 different colors. By mixing these colors and by using white and black, 2,535 colors, tints, and shades could be produced.

Huszár regarded Ostwald's color theory primarily as a tool. In his article he warned against an indiscriminate use of the results of science: "After all, the individual must possess the ability to use the right color proportions, which results from the capacity to transform aesthetic values into visual art. Just as the notes on the staff determine tonal values, and there everybody produces something else with those tones, so objectively determined colors can be the guide for the modern painters, used by everyone in his own way. . . . We painters must use the colors which our intuition tells us to use, but this subjective intuition is (objectively) *controllable*." He also gave an example of application of the color theory: "00 is pure yellow, namely the yellow that has no blue nor red within it. One can start randomly from every color in order to form a 3, 4, or 6 chord, provided one determines the other color geometrically, that is to say every time equidistant from each other, in the form of a triangle or quadrangle etc. One can also form dissonants in this manner, by omitting one, two or more from the chords." We can conclude from this remark that Huszár definitely did not limit himself to the three primary colors.

31
See C. Green, *Léger and the avant-garde* (New Haven, 1976), p. 212.

32
Postcard from van Doesburg to Oud, May 9, 1918.

33
Letter from van Doesburg to Oud, May 21, 1918.

34
Letter from Mondrian to van Doesburg, July 9, 1918.

35
Letter from van Doesburg to Oud, September 10, 1918.

36
The journal *Wendingen* was the mouthpiece of the Amsterdam school, and a competitor of *De stijl.*

37
Letters from van Doesburg to Antony Kok (December 5, 1918) and from Mondrian to van Doesburg (December 10, 1918). On the artistic disagreements between Huszár and van Doesburg see S. Ex, "Nagekomen kopij voor De Stijl," *Jong Holland* 1, no. 2 (1985), pp. 27–33.

38
Evidence for this is the 1919 competition for a mural; the method was not prescribed, but only figure compositions were allowed. See about this also R. Eggink and P. Fuhring, "2e afdeling: Architectuur en kunstnijverheid," in *Haagsche Kunstkring: Werk verzameld* (The Hague, 1977), p. 64. Noortje van Hellemond and Chris Rehorst of Leiden furnished me with documentation about Huszár's interior designs.

39
Huszár talked on "modern art in general," and discussed questions such as "What is monumental art?" and "What is the aesthetic value of monumental art?" The lecture took place on February 27, 1919. Piet Zwart reacted on March 6 with a criticism of this lecture; a synopsis of this is in his archive.

40
The information about Klaarhamer was furnished by P. Luykx of Utrecht.

41
Second Congress for Modern Arts, Antwerp, January 21–23, 1922. Huszár's lecture was published in *Bouwkundig weekblad* 43, no. 6 (1922), pp. 59–69, and 43, no. 8 (1922), pp. 72–77. In spite of the colors he mentions, it cannot be said that this was an interior painted in the primary colors. In the same lecture, Huszár called the function of the yellow "complementary." The red he used was very dark.

42
The articles in *Levende kunst* were less dogmatic than those in *De stijl*, but they were often in the same field; sometimes they were even written as reactions to articles in *De stijl.*

43
Perspective drawings were made of this bedroom from two sides; these drawings were probably exhibited at the 1922 Pictura exhibition in Gromingen as Bedroom I and Bedroom II (no. 16 in the catalog). An early reproduction of one of the designs was published in *Het leven,* November 2, 1920, pp. 1412–1414.

44
The colors used in this living room were, for the lower part, black, purple, and gray with a single shot of orange; in the upper part the colors were lighter. The colors are mentioned in the newspaper *Provinciale Overijsselsche en Zwolsche courant* of July 27, 1920, in a review signed "H." This review is in Theo van Doesburg's book of clippings on La Section d'Or, which is in the collection of the Rijksdienst Beeldende Kunst in The Hague.

45
Huszár's exhibit was mentioned in the newspapers *Algemeen handelsblad* (June 30, 1920), *Haagsche courant* and *Dagblad voor Zuidholland en 's-Gravenhage* (July 15, 1920), *Het vaderland* (July 20, 1920), and *De hofstad* (November 7, 1920). These reviews are in the book of clippings mentioned in note 44.

46
Undated letter from Mondrian to van Doesburg; probably written in the beginning of September 1920, immediately after Mondrian met Oud for the first time.

47
V. Huszár, "Over de organisatie in de ambachts-kunst," *Bouwkundig Weekblad* 41, no. 30 (1920), pp. 182–184.

48
Huszár, "Ruimte-kleur-compositie voor een eetkamer," *De stijl* 5, no. 1 (1922), pp. 7–8. It is not certain whether the furniture for this interior was designed by Huszár as well. Some pieces of furniture designed by him (clocks, lamps, chairs) are known; however, the furniture for this dining room may have been designed by Piet Zwart, although his name is not mentioned in the publications.

49
During the years 1919–1921 he designed at least thirteen interiors.

50
Reviews appeared in the following newspapers and journals, among others: *De residentiebode* (June 28, 1921), *De Hollandsche lelie* (June 5, 1921), *Lux* (issue unknown, 1921; 33, 1922), *De hofstad* (date unknown, June 1921), *Het vaderland* (June 25, 1921), *Bedrijfsfotografie* (3, no. 14, 1921, p. 238), and *Focus* (July 14, 1921). Ingeborg Th. Leijerzapf made these reviews from the Berssenbrugge archive in the Prentenkabinet at Leiden available to me.

51
F. N., "Atelier Berssenbrugge," *Zeeuwse courant*, June 23, 1921.

52
J. P. Mieras, "Het atelier van Berssenbrugge te 's Gravenhage," *Bouwkundig weekblad* 43, no. 15 (1922), pp. 150–152. Huszár's reaction to this article was published in no. 27 of the same year.

53
F. N., "Atelier Berssenbrugge."

54
This was also known as *Das gestaltende schauspiel* (the German translation of the title).

55
Huszár, "Kurze technische erklärung von der gestaltende schauspiel, komposition 1920–1921," *De stijl* 4, no. 8 (1921), pp. 126–128.

56
Undated letter from Mondrian to van Doesburg (from late March 1922).

57
Letter from Mondrian to Oud, July 13, 1922. Mondrian also expressed his disapproval of Huszár's interiors in letters to van Doesburg and Oud dated April 4, 1922.

58
Marie-Hélène Cornips called my attention to this correspondence; the letters are in the Archive for Modern Art of the Royal Museums of Arts in Brussels (no. 980).

59
J. Wiegers, "Exhibition of V. Huszár and Theo van Doesburg in Pictura, Groningen," *Blad voor kunst* no. 6 (March 1922). This painting is similar to the textile patterns Huszár designed around 1924 for Metz & Co.

60
The issue of *De stijl* about which Huszár could find nothing good to say was the "Anthology-Bonset-issue": 4, no. 11 (1921). Obviously, Huszár did not know that van Doesburg was hiding behind the pseudonym I. K. Bonset. "Tinny container" is a reference to "Blikken Trommel," a Bonset poem.

61
Through these soirees Huszár befriended Kurt Schwitters, who in the mid 1920s stayed with him as a house guest a few times.

62
A synopsis of Huszár's lecture "Het wandvlak voor vlakbeelding in de beeldende kunst" is in the archives of the Haagsche Kunstkring (annals 1921–1923, inv. no. 25), in the municipal archives of The Hague. An extensive commentary on Huszár's lecture in Rotterdam was published under the title "De wand" in *De bouwwereld* 12, no. 13 (1923), pp. 101–102.

63
Pages 129–134 of Nancy J. Troy's *De Stijl environment* (Cambridge, Mass., 1983) give more information on this project.

64
Reviews of this exhibition appeared in *Algemeen handelsblad* (October 27, 1924), *Het vaderland* (October 25, 1924), and *Elseviers geillustreerd maandschrift* (35, no. 69, 1925, p. 80).

65
Postcard from Huszár to Oud, October 25, 1924. Of the 31 compositions mentioned by Huszár, 19 are known to me.

66
Joop Joosten called these photographs to my attention. They are now in the Stedelijk Museum, in Amsterdam; at one time they were in the Instituut voor Sier- en Nijverheidskunst.

67
Robert P. Welsh, "Theo van Doesburg and geometric abstraction," in *Nijhoff, van Ostayen, "De Stijl," Modernism in the Netherlands and Belgium in the first quarter of the 20th century*, ed. F. Bulhof (The Hague, 1976), p. 83.

109 J. J. P. Oud, ca. 1920.

J. J. P. Oud

Hans Esser

The architect J. J. P. Oud has received much attention over the years.[1] His work, however, is generally treated out of context; the discussions are limited, with a few exceptions, to formal descriptions of his projected and realized designs. Oud's interest in the practical and social problems of building is recognized, but usually in only a casual relation to his works.[2] Such a one-sided approach is an injustice to Oud, to whom architecture was not an autonomous phenomenon but was directly related to the exigencies of the time.

Oud is also slighted in the literature that deals with his place in De Stijl. His designs are generally evaluated in relation to Mondrian's and van Doesburg's principles of painting, and then they are considered less interesting. In his collaborative projects with van Doesburg, Oud often is presented as having been a pragmatist who kept the painter from realizing his ideal.

After all this time, Oud must be reconsidered. It is too often forgotten that the painters and architects of De Stijl—in spite of such common ideals as the integration of art and life and the harmonic interaction between the diverse fields of art—had differing aims.

Artistic intentions certainly were important to Oud; however, he was also intensely involved with the technical and social aspects of architecture. He tried to achieve a new aesthetic by making use of modern techniques and building materials; he linked this to his striving to improve the housing conditions of the masses. He saw standardization as something like a magic formula—the industrial production of construction parts would offer a solution to the great need for housing.

In the beginning of 1918, after the founding of *De stijl,* Oud got a job with the municipality of Rotterdam as an architect. He was given the task of quickly and inexpensively putting up as many dwellings as possible. Not surprisingly, financial constraints left little leeway for exalted aesthetic accomplishments.

There were often discrepancies between the architectural ideas Oud professed in his free designs and the theories he published in *De stijl.* Put into their historical context, the apparent inconsistencies become more understandable. Oud's relation to De Stijl is nearly identical to his relationship with Theo van Doesburg, which dates from 1916.[3] Here I shall focus on their artistic collaboration and their ideological interaction as architect and painter. The correspondence in van Doesburg's estate, which has now become accessible, gives a clear picture of this. Until the end of 1921 Oud and van Doesburg were great friends, but this came to an end when van Doesburg submitted color "solutions" for the second phase of the Spangen housing project in Rotterdam. In Oud's opinion, these designs impaired his architecture. A split was inevitable. Oud's connection with De Stijl spans the period covered in this book: 1917–1922.

Youth, education, and early works

Jacobus Johannes Pieter Oud was born on February 9, 1890, in Purmerend. The milieu in which he grew up was not particularly artistic, but he began to draw at an early age. During his secondary education he took private lessons in freehand drawing and painting with H. van der Worp. Moreover, the municipal architect J. Faber instructed him in architectural drawing. The Oud archive in the Nederlands Documentatiecentrum voor de Bouwkunst contains a letter written by Oud (probably in 1926) to the American architect H. R. Graf[4] in which he relates the course of his life; my biographical data are mostly based on this letter. Oud wrote that his decision about his further education was the result of advice from a friend of his father's, the architect Jan Stuyt: "Stuyt said that one could become an architect in two ways: by means of education in secondary school and subsequently the Institute of Technology or via the School for Arts and Crafts and practice. In my youthful enthusiasm I was interested only in art, while I did not enjoy studying subjects which had no direct relation to architecture. Therefore I insisted on going to the School for Arts and Crafts." Oud was enrolled in the School voor Kunst en Kunstnijverheid in Amsterdam from 1902 until 1906. He got his first practical experience with Stuyt, who had an architectural firm in Amsterdam together with Joseph Cuypers. Under Stuyt's supervision, Oud designed and built his first house when he was only 16 years old. Meant for his aunt, Mrs. Hartog-Oud, it still stands in Purmerend.

Oud worked with the architectural firm in Amsterdam from October 1907 until May 1908, when he left to continue his studies. He explains this decision in the above-mentioned letter to Graf: "My lack of a solid theoretical foundation started to bother me more and more. Therefore I left Cuypers and Stuyt, and enrolled in the 'Rijksnormaalschool voor Teekenonderwijzers' [National College for Teachers of Drawing]." This did not satisfy Oud's need for a firmer theoretical basis. He continued his studies in building and mechanics, and eventually landed at the Technische Hogeschool in Delft. His autobiography gives evidence that he was not very happy there: "As a mere auditor I had too little contact with student life. . . . My initial zeal gradually diminished, and finally I sat in my room by the stove for days, thinking only of the misery in the world and mine in particular." Yet this period was very important in Oud's development as an architect, because it was then that he met H. P. Berlage.

In 1911 Oud dropped out of the Technische Hogeschool and went to work for the architectural firm of Theodor Fischer in Munich, probably on Berlage's recommendation. Though he was more impressed with Munich than with Fischer, this sojourn was very beneficial to Oud; it broadened his outlook considerably. Oud was "overwhelmed with the tremendous pep, pluck and confidence" of the German architects A. Messel and J. M. Olbrich, who were experimenting with new methods of construction and building materials.[5] When he returned home, he tried to make use of his German influences in "a completely Dutch manner."

In Oud's native town, Purmerend, a movie theater, a block of workers' dwellings with a common room, and a number of houses were built to his designs in the period from 1911 to 1913. In the movie theater he experimented with reinforced concrete. These experiments were limited, however, to details such as the marquee, the stairs to the balcony, and the projection room; the load-bearing structure was not of concrete. The potter Willem C. Brouwer was commissioned to create terra-cotta ornaments for the facade. Oud's interest in murals, which can be traced to a study trip he had taken through Italy, is evident from the frescoes over the paneling in the common room.[7]

In 1913 Oud moved to Leiden. Only a few of the designs he created around that time were executed; because of the outbreak of the World War, most building activity ceased. However, in collaboration with the architect Dudok, Oud realized a complex of 24 inexpensive workers' dwellings in Leiderdorp and a house in Blaricum.

In 1914 and 1915, Oud tried to get work through participation in contests. He created designs for a bathhouse, a vocational school, a home for the military, and a home for the elderly. These differ considerably in style. The first two designs are reminiscent of Berlage, but the homes for the military and the elderly are much more decorative and are closely related to the architecture of the Amsterdam School, against which Oud took a pronounced stand only a year later. (In retrospect, Oud used the lack of commissions as an excuse for this aberration.)

Oud's work from the time prior to the founding of De Stijl does not show a consistent development. Nor was there an awakening tendency to group cube-shaped volumes, as is suggested in the literature. Rather, the work gives evidence of a search for a form language, in which search Oud was susceptible to various outside influences and did not shrink from using other people's works as examples. He was particularly influenced by the architecture of Berlage.

The concept of monumental collaboration

The first known written contact between Oud and Berlage dates from September 16, 1910. After that an intensive correspondence ensued, and Oud visited the Berlage family regularly, finding with them not only peace but also support in his search for a theoretical basis. According to Berlage, architecture had a social task: building a better society. In his opinion, his era was depressed by the lack of communal pursuits. His ideal was to bring new life to the concept of community by integrating the various arts, with architecture in the lead. This, however, was not to lead to the copying of architectural forms; modern times were entitled to their own style. Berlage did not furnish a set pattern for the new architecture, but he did formulate some requirements to which he stated good architecture should conform. One of these was that an architectural composition had to be founded on basic geometric forms; this would then result in simplicity, order, and regularity. He preferred brick as a building material, on the principle of "unity in multiplicity": "The brick itself, which separately is trivial but as a mass is powerful, is the paradigm for the spiritual social image, to which it has to contribute color and form."[8] Berlage was of the opinion that brick could also fulfill a decorative function.

Berlage's ideas had a strong influence on Oud, who began to submit articles to student publications and to local newspapers such as *Schuitemakers Purmerender courant.* Like Berlage, Oud pleaded for a combining of forces. He suggested that architects, like painters, get together to discuss the philosophy of art—in this case, the art of building—and to formulate a spiritual ideal. From this ideal, "style" could originate. Oud also adopted Berlage's ideas about collaboration among visual artists, which in turn harked back to nineteenth-century ideas about communal art. Oud mentioned Berlage's Amsterdam Stock Exchange as an example of a project in which this "spiritual ideal" had been realized, and as an example of what modern architecture should look like.

A design for a bathhouse created by Oud in 1915 gives evidence of his appreciation of Berlage's work. The front of this never-realized bathhouse shows great similarities with the southern facade of the stock exchange: a main entrance consisting of three arcs, flanked by two low corner towers. Oud agreed with Berlage's idea that the outward appearance of a building should be as simple as possible. In his articles the phrase "to build simply" occurs regularly. He was opposed to added ornamentation. It was better to let the brick speak for itself, "with its colorful sparkles and its effect of simple braiding." An example of this kind of thinking about brick is the facade of the house shown in figure 110.

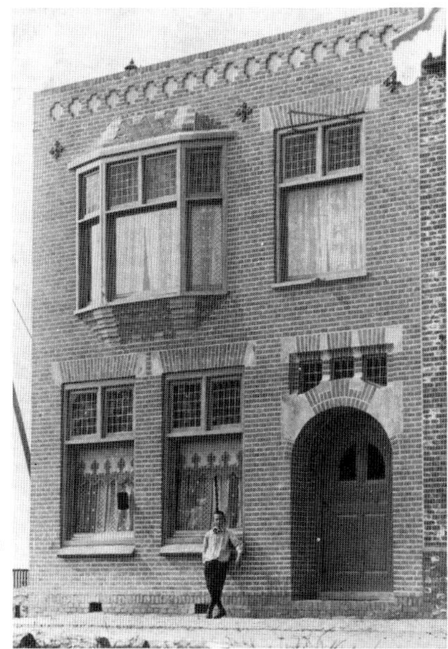

110

110 Oud, house in Purmerend, ca. 1912.

111 Oud, design for villas in Velp, 1916. 7 × 19 cm. Nederlands Documentatiecentrum voor de Bouwkunst, Amsterdam.

112 Menso Kamerlingh Onnes (designer) and J. J. P. Oud (architect), Villa Allegonda, Katwijk, 1916–17. The photograph, which is from a private collection, shows the inland-facing side.

Oud meets van Doesburg

Oud and van Doesburg met in 1916, mainly because of their common interest in the coalescence of the various arts (although at first their ideas were rather vague and diffuse). Van Doesburg had not yet freed himself completely from the way of thinking about art that had prevailed around the turn of the century. He was of the opinion that "it expresses our deepest feelings in a clear, monumental form."[9] In Berlage's 1905 book *Gedanken über stil* [*Thoughts on style*] and his 1910 book *Studies over bouwkunst, stijl en samenleving* [*Studies on architecture, style, and society*], too, van Doesburg found a theoretical basis for his idea that a synthesis between life and the arts could be achieved by collaboration between artists.

Oud looked at collaboration in a traditional way, from the viewpoint of his own field of specialization: the architect should make room for the painter and the sculptor. Van Doesburg, on the other hand, took modern painting as his starting point. In his opinion, an enduring style could originate if applied arts and architecture would focus on the "new European painting."[10] Painting, he thought, could spiritualize architecture, which was materially bound. From the beginning, this difference surfaced in their articles. In June 1916 Oud published an article in the architectural journal *Bouwkundig weekblad* in which he called abstract painting "architecturally speaking . . . *the* applied painting par excellence."[11] Van Doesburg reacted indirectly to this view in a series of articles under the title "De nieuwe beweging in de schilderkunst" ["The new movement in painting"] in the periodical *De beweging.* "Many are agreed," he wrote, "that the art of this time 'lends itself eminently to applied art.' Nothing is farther from the truth."[12]

This difference of opinion did not keep Oud and van Doesburg from becoming friends in May and June of 1916. Both men were then members of the Leiden association De Kunst om de Kunst [Art for Art's Sake], but they had not yet met in person. In May, Oud got hold of the issue of *De beweging* that contained the first installment in van Doesburg's series. (In this article van Doesburg outlines the origins of abstract painting and pleads for the representation of emotion rather than naturalistic representation.) After reading this article, Oud wrote to van Doesburg (on May 30) that he had heard from the painter Kamerlingh Onnes of van Doesburg's plan to found a modern-art association in Leiden. In this letter Oud proposed a collaboration of visual artists and architects within the new organization. The organization became the Leidsche Kunstvereniging [Leiden Art Association] De Sphinx; its date of foundation was recorded as May 31, 1916. Oud became president, van Doesburg assistant secretary.

Soon after their personal meeting, the first opportunity for collaboration between Oud and van Doesburg arose. In July 1916 Oud designed a dwelling for the mayor of Broek in Waterland, and van Doesburg was asked to create a stained-glass composition for the rear door.[13]

In 1916 Oud created two designs for a row of villas in Velp. In one of these designs there is a brick gable over the entrance, and the roofs are high-pitched; however, in style the compact mass of the buildings was far from Oud's designs of 1915. The second design is still more outspoken. The small sketch given here as figure 111 shows a conglomerate of block-shaped volumes, receding and protruding, covered with a flat roof. In the aforementioned article in *Bouwkundig weekblad,* Oud himself cited his encounter with cubism and futurism as the cause of this change. His intensive contact with van Doesburg undoubtedly helped Oud bring his views on visual art into a more definite form.

In 1916, van Doesburg's approach to the relation between painting and architecture was still predominantly theoretical. However, this changed drastically in the next year. His contacts with Piet Mondrian and particularly with Bart van der Leck were essential in this respect. Van der Leck had experienced the problems

111

112

arising in the interaction of painting and architecture in practice during his collaboration with Berlage in 1915–16. Like van Doesburg, van der Leck emphasized the independence and the equal status of the painter, but he went a step further and imposed restrictions on the architect. Painting should visually destroy [*destructiveren*] architecture; by this van der Leck meant that it should annihilate the material character of a building. He saw architecture as a neutral background for pictorial additions. On the basis of these theories and Mondrian's ideas about modern painting, van Doesburg's ideas about monumental collaboration became more concrete. Oud did not catch up with him in this respect. His ideas were limited by what had been realized in the way of decorations, particularly in Berlage's and de Bazel's buildings. He did emphasize the importance of trends like cubism and futurism for modern architecture, because of their simplification of forms; however, Mondrian's plea for rectangular forms and primary colors had probably hardly gotten through to him at that time.

Even before the founding of De Stijl, Oud and van Doesburg had a difference of opinion about color. The occasion for this was the renovation of the Villa Allegonda in the seaside resort of Katwijk (figure 112).

In the extant literature the Villa Allegonda is always dated 1917. However, the renovation request in the municipal archive of Katwijk has a blueprint attached which gives evidence that the design originated in 1916. Oud's name is not mentioned, but the document does include the name of the painter Menso Kamerlingh Onnes, who lived in Katwijk. Kamerlingh Onnes had been deeply impressed by the block-shaped white houses on the coast of North Africa, and, when his neighbor Trousselot expressed a desire to renovate his home, Kamerlingh Onnes saw an opportunity to enjoy such a view from his own house. He proposed his ideas for a renovation to Trousselot, and Oud was commissioned to execute the plan.[14]

The Villa Allegonda became a light gray plastered building with austere lines. A tower, loggias, and a basement were added to the original house, giving it a very different appearance. Oud kept the facade on the land side closed in order to emphasize that the boulevard on which the house was situated ended at that point. The floor plan of the basement tapered, so that the eye was drawn to the closed mass of the tower. The living quarters looked out to sea. There, the large windows, terraces, and loggias formed a beautiful transition from the inside to the outside. A modest amount of space was left for the work of visual artists: Harm Kamerlingh Onnes designed a nameplate, and van Doesburg a stained-glass window which was placed in the stairwell. (Van

Doesburg's window, which was based on the "rhythmically rising motion of the surf," is shown in figures 10–12 of the present volume.)

Van Doesburg would have liked to have been consulted in other aspects. This is suggested by his mention of a falling-out with Oud in a letter to Antony Kok dated April 17, 1917. Presumably the disagreement was over the use of color in architecture, for in the letter van Doesburg also pleaded for the use of bright colors: "They had forgotten what color means, they were color-phobic. Used as they were to living in dirt, colors like yellow, blue, red had an irritating effect on the retina. We want to build with colors, not with dirt." Van Doesburg must have considered the color Oud had applied to the woodwork of the Villa Allegonda—a shade of purple mixed with gray—a "dirty" color. Oud defended the use of what he called "the color of shadow" with the argument that this was the color that would break up the large wall planes the least, and that it therefore would foster harmony with the picturesque environment.[15] His attempt cannot be considered fully successful; the sober architectural forms contrasted with the rolling dune landscape more than they harmonized with it.

It is not easy to attribute a place to the Villa Allegonda in Oud's work, because his part in the project cannot be pinpointed. There is no doubt that he was a collaborator, but apparently he thought Kamerlingh Onnes's contribution so extensive that he would not present the design as his own. In a commentary on the house in the *Bouwkundig weekblad* of February 2, 1918, Oud wrote: "The renovation was technically executed by me after the painter Kamerlingh Onnes's design."[16] When the German critic Adolf Behne wanted in 1920 to devote a publication to Oud's work, he requested some photographs from Oud. Behne expressed disappointment when it appeared that there was no photograph of the "house in the dunes near Katwijk," which he had visited. When he asked for the reason, Oud answered: "As you suspected, I purposely did not include a photograph of the house in the dunes. In the first place this is a renovation of an old building (some parts had to be preserved, which resulted in requirements influencing the design); secondly I architecturally executed the house according to the directions of Mr. Kamerlingh Onnes, a painter; therefore it does not appear appropriate to me to count it as my own work. Also, it only partly conforms to my views, and consequently it could evoke a wrong impression of my work. Although, like you, I enjoy looking at the house, I would rather not see it illustrated in your article for the reasons mentioned above."[17] The same letter suggests that Oud did not want to claim a larger share in the design than he was entitled to: "I would be happier—if you agree—if the judgment of my work would not be influenced by someone else's merits." Thus, by Oud's own choice, Villa Allegonda was left out of most reviews of his work, or was discussed very summarily, although the project was very important in his further development.

Surely, Menso Kamerlingh Onnes's interest in North African architecture stimulated Oud and provided an impetus for him to develop a form-language of his own. A number of connections can be made between Villa Allegonda and early De Stijl designs; some of the common elements are block-shaped architectural volumes, plain plaster walls, and flat roofs.

First projects within De Stijl

During the argument about color, van Doesburg apparently thought that collaboration with Oud was impossible in every way. His anger did not last long, however. Despite the difficulties, he was convinced of the integrity of Oud's intentions.

The plans for a periodical were already in an advanced stage, and Oud was closely involved in them. In an announcement of the founding of *De stijl* in the August 1917 issue of *Eenheid,* Berlage and Wils are also mentioned as founders, the first probably through Oud's mediation.[18]

Because van Doesburg and Oud lived in Leiden, Huszár and Wils in Voorburg, and Vantongerloo not far away, in The Hague, it is assumed as a matter of course that they kept in touch. The correspondence gives no evidence of this. The only one of these men with whom Oud kept in fairly close contact was van Doesburg.

In the early issues of *De stijl* the participating artists all expressed their opinions on interaction between the arts, and particularly on the relation between painting and architecture. These expressions were rather contemplative, except for van der Leck's. Mondrian continued to view collaboration with architects mainly as theoretical; practical implementation would, in his opinion, be possible only in the distant future. Van Doesburg's and Huszár's ideas became more concrete in the course of 1918 as they gained experience. Van der Leck doubted from the beginning the willingness of the architects to grant the painters an equal position. At first Huszár and van Doesburg had less difficulty in adjusting to the restrictions posed by architecture; they enthusiastically provided stained-glass windows, tile floors, and color solutions for walls and woodwork. In the meantime, the "destructive" effect of color on architecture became more and more important for van Doesburg. Theoretically Oud had no great objections to this; however, their collaboration had in practice been limited to innocuous additions (such as an occasional stained-glass window), and he did not know

113 Oud, design for housing complex on seaside boulevard, 1917. Whereabouts unknown; photograph in private collection.

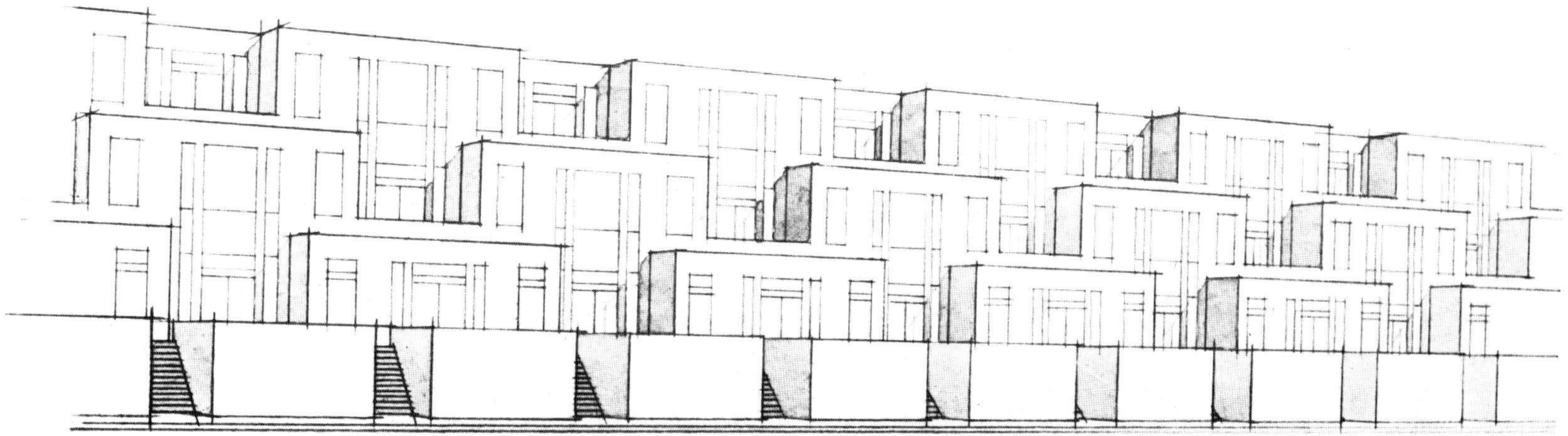

what van Doesburg had in mind with the word *destructie.* When in the fall of 1921 van Doesburg submitted facade designs that really impaired his architecture, Oud was extremely unhappy.

In the literature about De Stijl, Oud is discussed mostly in connection with the aesthetic ideas of the painters, especially Mondrian and van Doesburg. For the painters, the crucial thing was the optical effect of color on a building; for Oud, the function of the building was the most important thing, and this function was primarily social. Oud's aim was twofold. On the one hand, the living circumstances were to be improved by the use of a clearly arranged floor plan and a greater access to light and air; on the other hand, an architecture founded rationally on the circumstances of modern life could not help but spread a morally uplifting influence. Oud tried to encourage the use of modern materials, such as plate glass, and new construction techniques, such as concrete skeleton construction and standardization. Because the application of these materials and techniques in the construction of community housing was still in the beginning stages, the execution of his ideas was impeded, and when Oud went to work for the government in 1918 he was even more confronted with restrictions (financial, economic, and political).

The first issue of *De stijl* contained an article by Oud entitled "Het monumentale stadsbeeld" ["The monumental image of the city"] and a design by Oud for a housing complex on a seaside boulevard (reviewed by van Doesburg). In the article (written on July 9, 1917),[19] Oud formulated his ideas on street scenes in future cities: Separate dwellings should no longer be constructed. The disappearance of private initiative would mean mass construction, most desirably of blocks of dwellings grouped around a courtyard. Modern materials, such as iron and concrete, were the tools with which such housing blocks would be realized.

Oud's "seaside-boulevard" design (figure 113) can be considered an attempt to visualize these ideas. The aforementioned design for villas in Velp shows a rudimentary use of block-shaped construction volumes; in the seaside-boulevard design Oud further detailed this principle. The complex consists of a row of blocks which can be expanded without limit. Each unit consists of three apartments, stacked in a stepped manner. The design suggests that from the start standardization was the basic idea. The floor plans for all dwellings are the same, but because of the stepped construction the upper apartments are smaller than the lower ones. The functions of the different spaces are not specified, and the design should probably be considered not as a plan ripe for execution but as an attempt by Oud to express his ideas about more comfortable and more economical living conditions on paper. The lack of a design for the rear facade confirms this suspicion. The fact that Oud mentioned an actual site, namely a seaside boulevard, can be explained by his remark that such a construction with plastered walls and flat roofs was particularly appropriate for the seaside.

Van Doesburg, in his commentary, was enthusiastic about the seaside-boulevard design.[20] He called it an excellent example of style-conscious construction—particularly because of the interaction between the inside and the outside, the use of the square as a basic module, and what he called the architectural rhythm, the "spatial movement"—and compared it to the work of the good modern painters. Until 1926 Oud never wrote about the design in *De stijl* or in any other periodical. He mentioned it for the first

114

115

time in his 1926 biography, where he confirmed that his contacts with modern painting had greatly influenced his work.

There exists another drawing, of uncertain date, which is related to the seaside-boulevard design. This four-story complex (figure 114) appears to have been intended for an urban setting, perhaps in Rotterdam.

Simultaneously with the seaside-boulevard design, Oud produced a design for a vacation house in Noordwijkerhout to fulfill a commission from a foundation called Het Leidsche Volkshuis.[21] Berlage, who was a friend of Emilie Knappert (see note 21), was asked to submit a design; however, he could not spare the time, and he recommended Oud. The house, named De Vonk [The Spark], was opened on February 8, 1919. It still exists today, and is in use as an educational center.

The exterior of De Vonk is rather traditional, particularly in comparison with Oud's seaside-boulevard design. Oud probably had to accommodate the wishes of his clients, and he may also have been influenced by the knowledge, that the project had originally been offered to Berlage. There are three floors. The central part of the house is flanked by two wings. The front and rear facades are completely symmetrical, and the sides are almost entirely closed. The roofs are steeply pitched.[22] Aside from the little annex in back, the plan is symmetrical. The rooms are grouped around a spacious hallway, which Oud conceived not as a passageway but as a place "for the children and their escorts to sit down for a moment with a book or needlework."[23]

Financial gifts to the foundation made it possible for Oud to involve his friends in the De Vonk project. Van Doesburg's share in the work is clearly evidenced by a correspondence that began after Oud moved to Rotterdam in the beginning of 1918. As early as 1917 van Doesburg designed three compositions in glazed brick for the facade, where Oud had planned to use traditional brick decorations. The asymmetrical pattern of green, blue, and yellow (figure 117) relieved the strict symmetry of the facade. Early in 1918, van Doesburg was commissioned to brighten up the hall and the stairwell. This must have appealed greatly to him, because the architecture of the stairwell in particular had a very plastic character (figure 118). The spare forms and the smooth finish were an ideal starting point for van Doesburg's plastic solution. He created for the floor of the hall a composition of black, white, and yellow tiles. At first glance no system is apparent in the composition, but on further contemplation it appears that van Doesburg repeated certain sections, rotated or in mirror image. This dynamic pattern was also used in the hallway of the second floor. Van Doesburg showed this project at an exhibition of the Academie van Rotter-

114 Oud, design sketch for a street facade, 1917 or 1918. Collection of Mrs. A. Oud-Dinaux, Wassenaar.

115 Oud, back of De Vonk, Noordwijkerhout, 1917–1919. Photograph in private collection.

116 Hall on second floor of De Vonk, as illustrated in *De stijl* 2, no. 1 (1918), appendix 1.

117 Theo van Doesburg, three compositions in glazed brick for facade of De Vonk, as illustrated in *Klei* 12, no. 2 (1920), p. 17.

116

117

118 **Hall and stairwell of De Vonk.**

119 **Oud, design sketch for Spangen housing blocks I and V, Rotterdam, 1918. As illustrated in *Bouw* 34, no. 5 (1979), p. 73.**

118

dam. The exhibition was held from April 27 to May 27, 1918, but the design was not on view there for all that time—the workmen in Noordwijkerhout needed it.

After the floor was completed, the doors were also drawn into the color composition. In connection with the colors of the floor, they were executed in black, white, gray, and yellow. In his 1926 biography, Oud described the manner in which van Doesburg filled the doors with color: "When a door was black in the center and yellow around the frame, then the inner part of the frame was gray. In the case where it was yellow in the center, and had a gray frame, the inner part of the frame was black." Van Doesburg was probably trying here, as he had six months earlier in Wils's Villa de Lange in Alkmaar, to "free" the planes by using contrasting colors. To set them apart, the two doors to the directress's rooms were executed in black, white, and gray.

The way in which van Doesburg had decorated the hallway and the corridor of De Vonk evoked enthusiastic reactions. Huib Hoste, who criticized the exterior of the house, found the floors very beautiful, although he did not recognize in them the "direct contact with God" that van Doesburg claimed was there.[24] Many people came to look at the house. It showed, more clearly than could possibly be done in theoretical essays or the exhibition of the designs, what the De Stijl artists had in mind. When Robert van 't Hoff took Bart de Ligt to Noordwijkerhout in October 1918, the latter was so charmed by De Vonk that he asked van Doesburg to make a design for his home in Lage Vuursche.

But van Doesburg did not decide completely on his own what the interior of De Vonk was going to look like. Harm Kamerlingh Onnes was asked to determine the colors of the rooms and to design five stained-glass windows for the stairwell. It is evident from the conflict that arose that van Doesburg was not consulted very much. The rooms were painted in green, which in van Doesburg's opinion clashed frightfully with his tile floor. The doors could not remain open, because then the effect of the floor would be destroyed "by the bright color radiation." In a letter to Oud dated July 6, 1918, van Doesburg already expressed fear that the windows would completely ruin his composition. In August the windows were put in place, and they appeared to be even less compatible with his principles than he had expected. On August 29 he vented his frustration: "The Light is Space. Since now a thoughtless dilettante has obscured the windows here with monstrous glass shapes in a gaudy disorder of gloomy colors, which even have been covered over with oil paint, it is obvious that the little space that we created with much care and difficulty is completely ruined, and the hall has been transformed into a gloomy corridor where tiles are lying in a hodgepodge on the floor. Since the light is lacking, nothing makes sense any longer. In every spot of this hall one finds oneself in the gloom of a medieval chapel." Van Doesburg wrote that he would rather see a flowerpot on every step of the stairs, and rugs everywhere, than the situation as it had come to be. "I did try," he wrote, "to recapture something of the clear, pure atmosphere by closing a door or changing the position of some object, but I felt quite soon that I bumped into the corpse of an uncommunal idea." He concluded that in the future he alone would designate all colors; otherwise he would not enter into such projects.

Municipal architect of Rotterdam

In the beginning of January 1918, Oud, who had been recommended by H. P. Berlage, went to work for the city of Rotterdam as municipal architect. There was a lot to be done in Rotterdam.[25] Between 1900 and 1915 the population had grown by 50 percent. There was a great need for low-income housing, in particular. Although private construction had continued at a reasonable tempo until 1917, public housing was started later there than in other cities. The city council had kept rather aloof from it until that time. In November 1917 an autonomous Municipal Housing Authority was instituted and public housing was set in motion through subsidies.

Oud faced the difficult task of building dwellings for the poorest classes as quickly and as inexpensively as possible. He must have been aware of the restrictions inherent to his position of municipal architect; after some doubts, ethical considerations proved to be more important to him than aesthetic ones.

Immediately after he started in his new position, Oud designed two blocks of dwellings for the Spangen district. There is an extant design sketch which does not give any details but whose composition is close to the final execution (figure 119). The blocks were situated on one side on the Spaansche Bocht [Spanish Curve]. The facades (eighteen and fourteen units wide, respectively) followed the curve. Each unit contained three dwellings; the two blocks amounted to 242 dwellings. The complex, constructed of brick, had (particularly along the Spaansche Bocht) a fairly closed front, which was completely flat. This effect was reinforced by the uniformity of the windows and doors. The horizontality of the facade was emphasized by a continuing roof gutter and by three horizontal bands at the bottom. The oblong windows were grouped to provide a vertical counterbalance. The front on Potgieterstraat was executed in the same way, but there the receding parts and the protruding entrance to the inner yard enlivened the totality. The houses had sloping tiled roofs with dormers.

Oud could not design all four sides of the blocks, because the middle part of the site, around the Bilderdijkstraat, had already been contracted to the housing association Onze Woning [Our Home]. The architects Meischke and Schmidt were responsible for that part. Oud had to come up with a completely detailed design within a very short time. The lot was ready for development in the beginning of 1918; it had been filled with sand recently dredged from harbors. Oud's designs were approved by the city council on July 25 and the first stone was laid in September.

The Spangen complex gives a fairly traditional impression because of the use of brick and the sloping roofs. This is not surprising, for Oud had to adjust to many exigencies in working on the project. The minutes of the city council meetings during 1918 mention that the designs of Meischke and Schmidt were approved on May 16, two months earlier than those of Oud. Because the project ultimately had to be an entity, we may assume that there

119

were consultations between the different parties. Oud was forced to use as a starting point the ground plans dictated by the municipal authorities, and he adjusted his corner solutions to those of Meischke and Schmidt. On the other hand, Oud wrote in his review of the project in *Bouwkundig weekblad* that, after consultation, Meischke and Schmidt were willing to "amalgamate the height of the stories, the three black bands of the plinth, the roof with the fascia etc. in their design in such a way that the blocks of buildings were completed without interruption of the facade walls."[26] Oud arranged the windows in such a way that the arrangement of the rooms was evident from the outside; three windows close together indicated the living room, a single window the bedroom.

It is hard to relate the architecture of the Spangen housing blocks directly to Oud's contributions to *De stijl;* however, he did collaborate with van Doesburg here, as he had on De Vonk. Van Doesburg designed two types of glass windows to be installed above the doors. The first type, used over the single doors at the corners, had red, yellow, blue, orange, purple, violet, black, and transparent glass. The other doors are grouped in fours; the second type of window, used above these doors, had pale blue, yellow, and green glass. Both kinds of windows show an abstract composition of rectangular color planes of diverse dimensions. The correspondence reveals that the first models were finished in late February 1919.

Van Doesburg also designated the colors for the exterior woodwork of the dwellings. He worked from what he called, in Ostwald's terminology, a "triad" of gray, green, and yellow.[27] Besides those colors he used black and white. The fascias of the dormers he painted in black; thus, they correspond with the black bands at the bottom of the plinth. The fascias of the gutters, the rabbets of the windows, and the center planes of the doors were colored yellow. Green and gray were used for the frames of the yellow center part of the doors and for the stained-glass windows, respectively. By this manner of applying colors to the facade, van Doesburg tried to cancel out the "material heaviness" of the architecture. He himself attributed a "destructive" effect to it. Oud imposed few aesthetic requirements on the color applications for the facade; financial considerations appeared to be more important. In a letter to van Doesburg dated August 4, 1919, he wrote: "I have no money: please no expensive (bright) colors."

The interior color solution for the Spangen housing was circumscribed somewhat by Oud. In the living rooms there were wooden mouldings at the level of the tops of the doors, from which paintings could be hung. Oud thought that the wall planes over those mouldings should be white. Moreover, van Doesburg was asked to keep the totality in mind, and to avoid treatment of separate details. He had not taken these requirements sufficiently into account in his first design, and Oud had turned it down. Apparently van Doesburg had overlooked the fact that the apartments were to be lived in. In a letter of September 8 he conceded that his first color solutions had been "too unilaterally aesthetical."

The correspondence about the Spangen housing blocks also gives evidence that Oud as well as van Doesburg decided on the use of primary colors (mostly yellow and blue) and the noncolors gray, black, and white in the interiors. Exactly how these colors were ultimately applied is not clear, but we do know that the wall planes under the wooden mouldings were yellow, the doors yellow and blue, and the mantels blue and gray. Van Doesburg paid special attention to the mantel in order to highlight the hearth underneath. He wanted to discourage the occupants from putting "junk" up against it and spoiling the effect. Oud had designed the hearth especially for Spangen. Refusing to be satisfied with the usual plate behind the stove, he had designed a plastic entity of receding and protruding block shapes. The spare lines were accentuated by the square tiles in black, red, and yellow with which van Doesburg furnished the mantelpiece.

Even before the delivery of the Spangen housing blocks, in June 1920, a model apartment in the complex was furnished with furniture by Gerrit Rietveld. This furniture was not specially designed for Spangen, but it completed the image of a De Stijl interior. (See figure 257 below.) Neither Rietveld nor Oud considered this furniture especially well suited for workers' dwellings. Rietveld viewed it primarily as experimental, and absolutely did not want to force it on people as a paragon of good and modern taste.

Soon after the occupants moved into the Spangen complex, Oud discovered that they were not very pleased with the mural paintings that had been forced upon them; in short order, the walls in most of the apartments were covered with wallpaper. Therefore, he did not expect the tenants to be enthusiastic about Rietveld's furniture. In furnishing a subsequent model home, in September 1920 in the garden village of Vreewijk in Rotterdam, Oud used standard, inexpensive, readily available furniture; an article in the *Nieuwe Rotterdamsche courant* on the occasion of the presentation praised his efforts to make the living quarters of "people with modest means" cozy.[28]

It is remarkable that the interiors and the exteriors of these buildings in Spangen were not executed in the same colors. The primary colors plus black, white, and gray were used in the interiors; however, the exterior colors were somewhat more reserved.

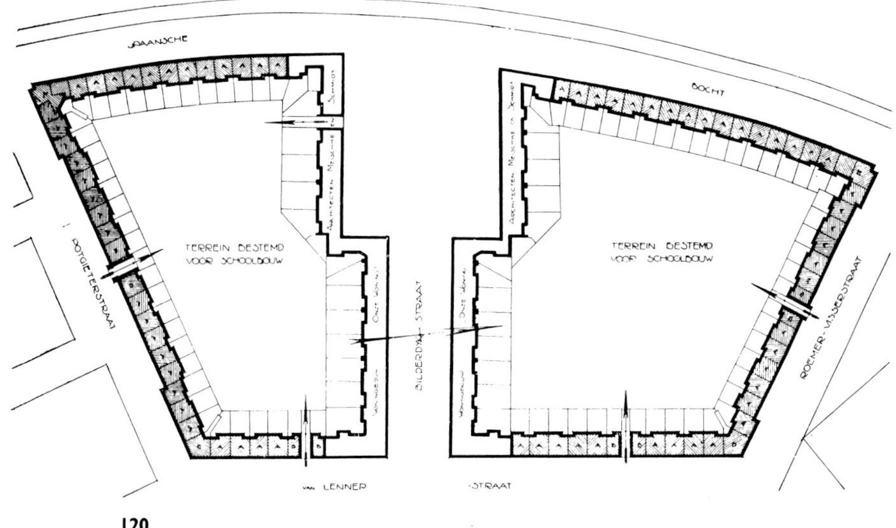

120

120 Site plan of Spangen housing blocks I and V, as illustrated in *Bouwkundig weekblad* 41, no. 37 (1920), p. 220.

121 Oud, Spangen housing block V. Photograph in private collection.

121

Oud had specifically asked van Doesburg to keep the colors on the outside muted. He stated as his reason that bright colors were expensive, but probably another consideration was that he did not feel justified in turning his first commission as municipal architect into a gaudy spectacle.

In spite of his cautious attitude, Oud was criticized for the Spangen buildings. He was cheered up by van Doesburg, who wrote to him on December 18, 1919, that he should not be upset by this criticism: "They are in fact very good, considering the circumstances, and I would be happy to discuss them aesthetically in an architectural journal." Van Doesburg did not think (contrary to what is commonly assumed) that the architecture was fundamentally contradictory to the principles of *De stijl.* If Oud wanted to see the project reproduced in the periodical, that could be done: ". . . if you want them in *De stijl,* fine. I have to take many blows too."

Standardization and reinforced concrete

The problem of standardization was discussed at a housing congress that was held in Amsterdam in early 1918. Many architects objected to standardization as a threat to their artistic freedom. Tenants, too, feared its aesthetic implications.

Oud formulated his ideas about standardization in two articles in the May 1919 issue of *De stijl.*[29] In the first of these he argued that standardization in mass construction would have a cost-saving effect, so that it would be possible to get by with less economizing in other aspects. Besides, he wrote, the use of standard elements would speed the construction process. Construction would be more efficient, and thus the shortage of specialized labor would be less of a problem. Finally, standardization would promote a new kind of beauty related to that of modern painting. The possibility of grouping identical parts (such as windows and doors), and even complete dwellings, in varying juxtapositions would make architecture an "art of proportions," like painting. Standardization in mass construction meant, by definition, that the individual element was subordinated to the whole, and therefore it fitted beautifully into the context of De Stijl. In his second article, Oud integrated the principle of standardization into his views on city planning. Just as a modern dwelling consisted of standard elements, a housing block was a series of units of the same form—the houses. A series of such housing blocks formed a street, which again could be seen as a building element of the modern city.[30]

In the second half of 1918 Oud attempted to elaborate these ideas on paper. One of his designs, which he called a "street composition," was reproduced in *De stijl* with the second of the two articles mentioned above. In this design, standardization is carried through most thoroughly. It shows a facade that can be extended on both sides with an unlimited number of dwelling units. The facade is predominantly flat; it only recedes somewhat at the bedrooms. In the floor plan Oud used a system of square modules; there he worked from the creed "maximal requirements in minimal spaces," a slogan that would return again and again in the following years. A design for emergency housing units under a viaduct (figure 122) gives evidence that in some instances Oud could not work according to his creed and neither could he realize his ideal of "light, air, and hygiene." This design was created after a decree for emergency housing was proclaimed in 1918. In it Oud still tried to use something of the form language of De Stijl; note the window arrangement. Oud may have been somewhat embarrassed by these drawings, for he never counted them among his artistic output.

Mrs. Oud, née Dinaux, still possesses a second design, unknown till now, for a street front (figure 123). This too is a series of identical facades; however, the composition is more complicated. Each unit consists of three parts, one of which is higher than the others; on top of that part Oud put a very high, closed attic. In the central construction unit, which probably was to contain the living rooms, the facade was handled differently than in the side parts. Here Oud seems to be less thorough in using standardized elements than in the design published in *De stijl.* Perhaps he had this drawing in mind when he wrote, in his article on street architecture, about a less radical form of standardization. This, then, would be an example of what he called a "melodic-visual street front."

It is not surprising that Oud, who expressed himself so enthusiastically about new technical developments in general and about standardization in particular, also pleaded for the use of modern materials. He saw many possibilities—constructional as well as aesthetic—in the use of reinforced concrete.[31] Construction with concrete had the advantage that large, smooth, uninterrupted wall planes could be realized, and this offered an ideal opportunity to paint the facade white and to accentuate the various parts with colors. The constructional advantages were closely connected to the aesthetic ones. Reinforced concrete made possible extensive horizontal spans, and hence flat roofs. Also, in Oud's opinion, a greater plasticity could be achieved with the use of reinforced concrete, which made it much easier to have parts of a building recede and protrude. Finally, concrete would facilitate standardization; prefabricated concrete elements would allow faster and more economical construction.

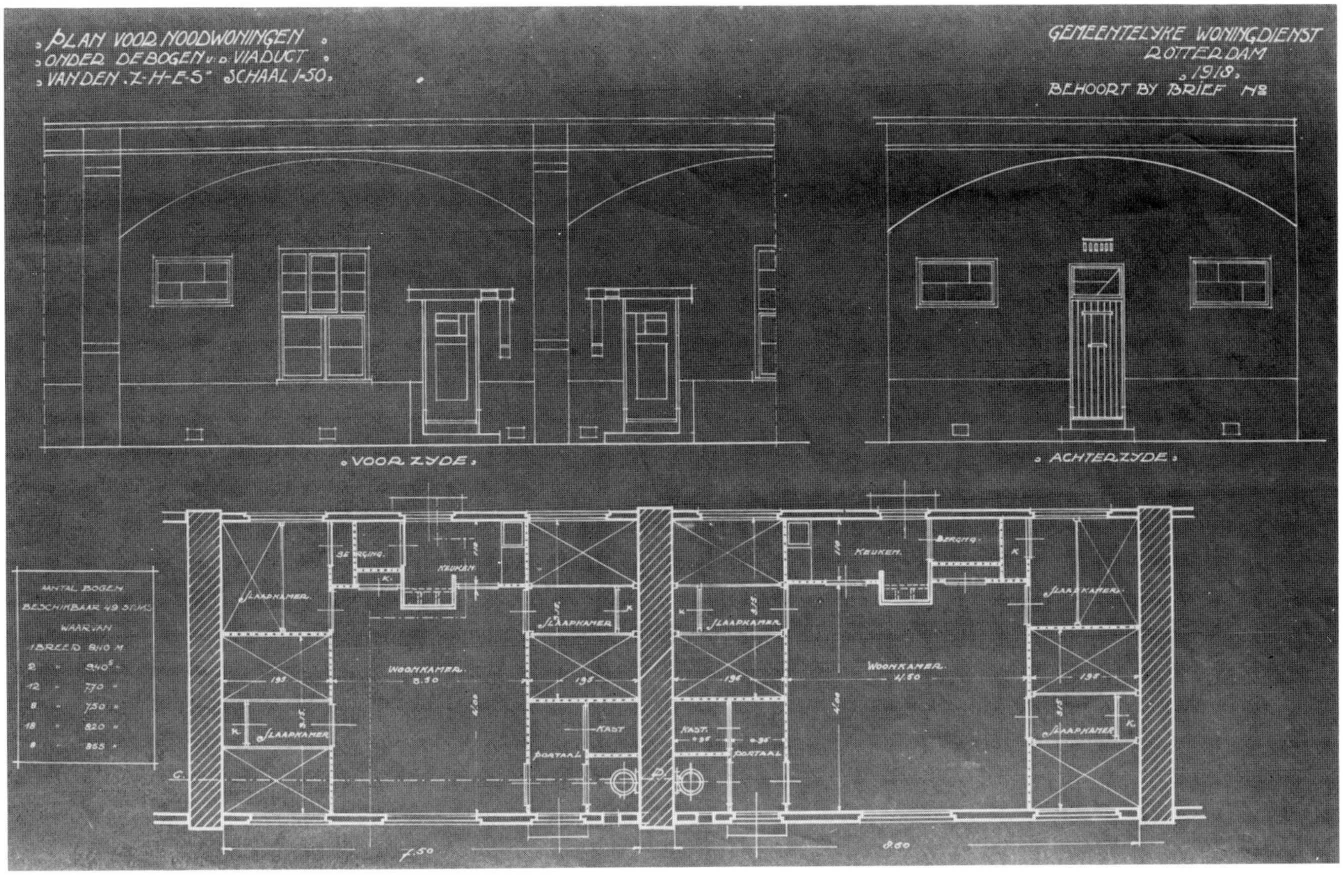

122

122 **Detail of Oud's plan for provisional housing, 1918. Nederlands Documentatiecentrum voor de Bouwkunst, Amsterdam.**

123 **Oud, design for a street front, 1918. Mrs. A. Oud-Dinaux, Wassenaar.**

123

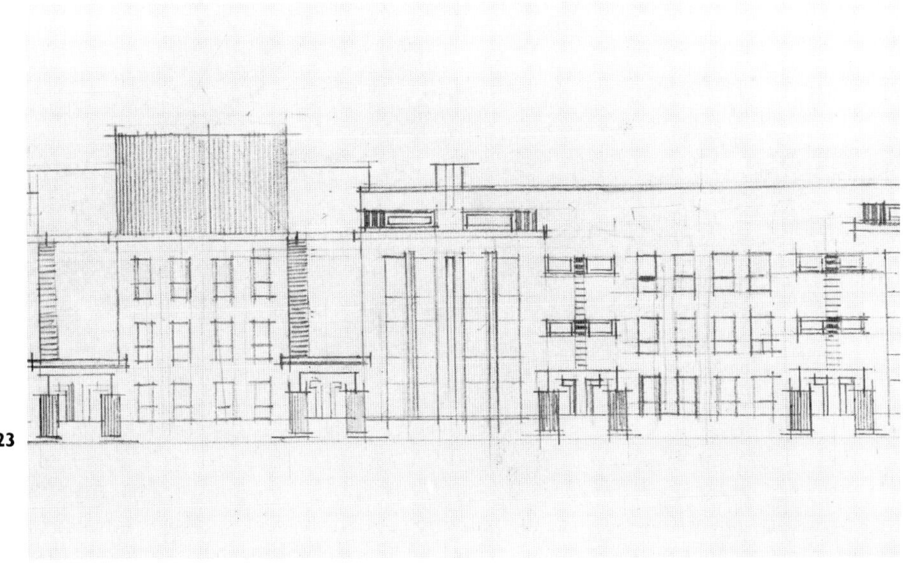

124 **Oud, detail of design for double workers' dwelling in reinforced concrete. Mrs. A. Oud-Dinaux, Wassenaar.**

125 **Oud, design for double workers' dwelling in reinforced concrete. Mrs. A. Oud-Dinaux, Wassenaar.**

124

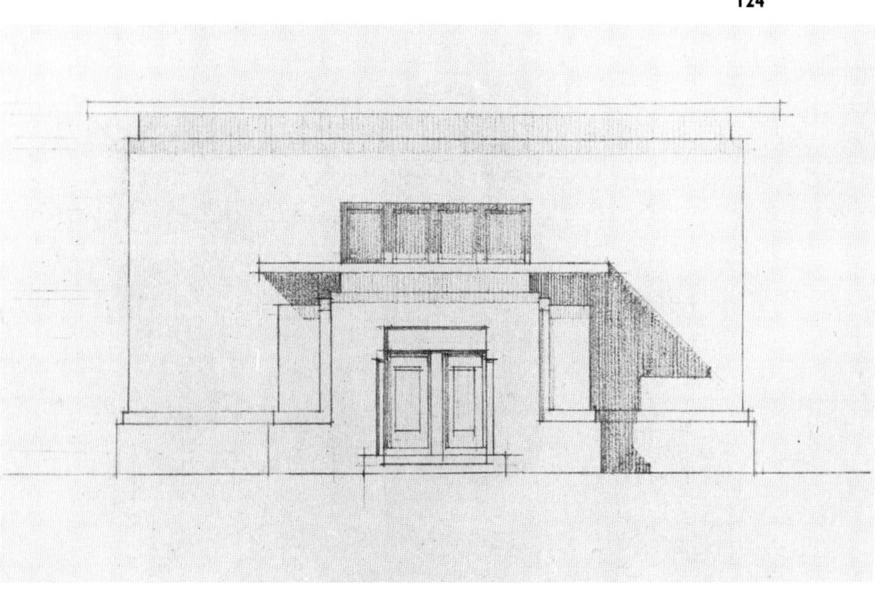

In the end of 1918 Oud created a design for a house that was called a "double workers' dwelling in reinforced concrete" in *De stijl* (figure 124). He sent drawings to van Doesburg, who responded on February 22, 1919: "I am very enthusiastic about it! Elevation magnificently quiet. I also think the floor plans are excellent. Nice that they vary, and are differently arranged. I will be very happy to reproduce them in *De stijl.*" The building can be considered a large, closed concrete box. It contains two dwellings positioned symmetrically in relation to each other. The facades on the side and the back are completely flat; only the front entrance is strongly profiled, and therefore it draws all the attention. Oud's statement that construction in concrete is eminently suitable for a plastic, three-dimensional architecture is definitely not applicable to this design. It is even less applicable to the design shown here as figure 125. When Oud created these drawings is not quite clear. It is plausible that they originated in 1919, because they were meant for the Municipal Housing Authority, and because Oud clearly took into account the practical possibilities at that moment—in fact, he made a trip through Germany to study the possibilities of concrete.[32] Like the first design published in *De stijl,* the double dwelling was block-shaped and completely symmetrical. The floor plans were practically identical. Traditional windows and doors were set into flat facades. Oud had not used windows with this kind of mullions for years, and at first glance it is incomprehensible that he did so now, in a dwelling constructed in concrete. Perhaps he was forced to use standard windows; most of the concrete dwellings that were realized in the Netherlands around 1920 have such windows.

Thus, from 1918 on Oud actively occupied himself with the design of concrete dwellings, but it was some time before he got the opportunity to realize his plans within the context of the Municipal Housing Authority. The reasons were that many technical problems still arose in the implementation in housing construction, and that concrete was more expensive than brick. After the war this situation changed. Because of the paucity of coal, the prices of bricks and roof tiles rose very quickly. Moreover, a large part of the Dutch brick supply was destroyed by floods during the winter of 1919–20. In 1921 the first concrete dwellings in Rotterdam were built after the design of the architect J. M. Hardeveld. Oud's first housing in concrete was realized in Hoek van Holland as late as 1927.

Warehouse and factory in Purmerend, 1918–19

Beside working for the city of Rotterdam, Oud was also working on a private commission. In a letter to van Doesburg, which can be

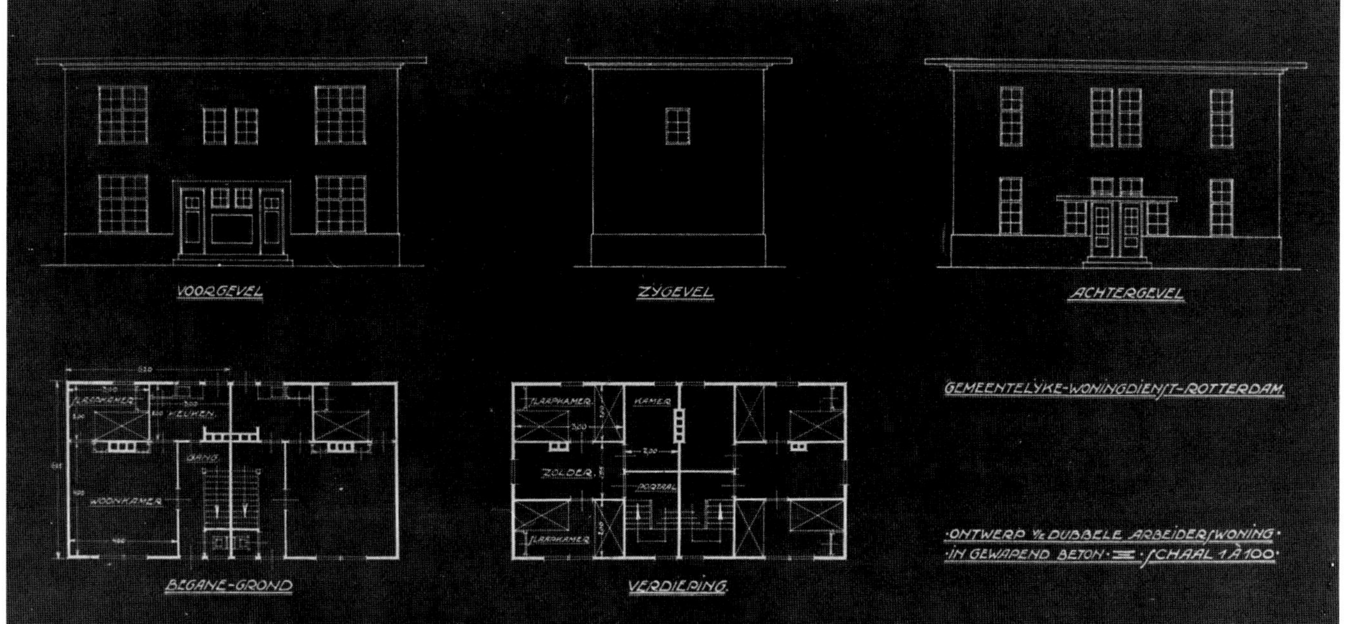

125

dated mid 1918, he wrote rather cryptically about this: "Again I have beautiful things in concrete to look forward to! So I hope that we soon will be able to really get busy together. In September I will hear definitely about something very large!" Van Doesburg inquired of Oud on October 12, 1918: "A new private commission? I am very curious, particularly if it is something where both of us can create new things."

The commission came from Wed. G. Oud Pzn. en Co. [The Company of the Widow of G. Oud, the son of P. Oud] in Purmerend, a wine distillery. In 1918 part of the company's business was still carried on by J. J. P. Oud's father, and therefore it is not surprising that Oud was asked to create a design. He had been asked to do so once before. Around 1915 he had designed a "warehouse with rinsing space." (This design has been preserved in the Nederlands Documentatiecentrum voor de Bouwkunst.) At the time, the company's expansion fell through; however, the plan for the warehouse became of interest again when the family bought land in the beginning of 1918. Whereas the first design would have had to be incorporated in the existing building complex, there was now a possibility for a separate complex. Again Oud was asked to make designs.

From a letter from van Doesburg to Oud dated January 7, 1919, it appears that the commission encompassed two parts, for van Doesburg wrote about a warehouse and a factory: "It is nice that your factory is progressing and that bids have already been invited for the warehouse." This warehouse (figure 126), which has always been regarded as a second, simplified version of the factory, thus appears to have been a separate design that predated the design for the factory. It was a large, oblong space whose front had two extensions, one extending on top and another protruding forward. The entirety was conceived symmetrically. The higher part was intended as office space; the low annex functioned as a distillery. The warehouse itself had no windows because distilled spirits have to be stored in the dark.

After this simple, probably less expensive extension of the distillery, Oud created another design for a more grandiose complex (figure 127). Van Doesburg also became involved. From June 1919 on, he and Oud corresponded extensively on this project. He periodically sent new sketches, so that van Doesburg could get an idea. The preliminary studies, six of which are in the Nederlands Documentatiecentrum voor de Bouwkunst, are all based on the same principle. This might be a result of the fact that Oud always started from the same floor plan.[33] As of June 1919 it still is not clear exactly what van Doesburg's contribution encompassed. However, he hoped that he and Oud would soon be able to begin. On June 24 he wrote: "When it comes through financially, I would like to know in advance whether your cousin insists on figurative representation, or whether I can work in a purely abstract manner. In the former eventuality there are many possibilities as well. By the use of proportion it may still be so compositional that it expresses the new." A few months later the plans were in an advanced stage, and in the beginning of November Rietveld appears to have been involved in the project; he was waiting for the latest drawings in order to construct a model. Oud's final design looks very striking. It shows an asymmetric series of block-shaped building volumes. Two of these blocks, the store and the warehouse, had completely closed wall planes, as a result of the function of those spaces. The office space, at the right on the drawing, was opened up by a long series of windows. The middle part was the most striking. In the preliminary studies Oud paid no particular attention to this part, but he gradually elaborated it until he arrived at its ultimate appearance: a composition of intersecting horizontal and vertical building elements. For instance, a flat beam, seemingly without function, rose far above the complex. A narrow horizontal series of windows cut through this element at about half its height. The other parts were interwoven in the same manner. Thus, the factory was asymmetrical not only in its floor plan but also in the treatment of the facades—a phenomenon that had not appeared so outspokenly in Oud's work before.

In retrospect, Oud himself saw the design for the factory as a turning point in his career. Furthermore, he was praised by some *De stijl* contributors. In a letter to Oud dated December 16, 1920, Mondrian called the factory design "the best thing I have seen in this field"; this, coming from him, was a great compliment.

Van Doesburg had ambitious plans for the factory design. He wanted several posters made to promote *De stijl* (figure 128), and he proposed to have Oud's factory design and one of Mondrian's diamond-shaped paintings reproduced on them. He had gotten the idea from the English vorticist artist Wyndham Lewis, who had sent him his publication *Architects! Where is your vortex?* and a poster of the *Daily mirror.*

In the middle of November 1919, the news came that the construction was canceled. It appears that, because of the economic crisis, Oud's cousins looked for a more secure investment and put the family capital into houses in Haarlem.[34] Van Doesburg tried to cheer up the disappointed Oud in a letter of November 18: "Well, dear fellow, be of good courage. Your time will come, too."

In 1922, it seems, the first design—the one for the warehouse—was yet to be realized. This is evident from a letter from the architect Saal (see note 33) to Oud, dated May 9, 1922: "I received a request from the Company de Wed. G. Oud Pzn. en Co. to state my conditions, in order to execute the construction of the Warehouse together with you. I had not expected this offer after more than 2 years." But even then the construction plan fell through.

According to van Doesburg's letter about the posters, at the time of the factory design Oud was engrossed in the architecture of Frank Lloyd Wright.[35] His interest in Wright's work is evident in the design. Like Wright's country houses, it shows a wide, asymmetric layout and is predominantly horizontal in character. The long series of windows and their overhanging marquees, which emphasize this horizontal effect, are motifs which were often used by Wright. Oud derived certain details, particularly the decorative edges between the windows, directly from Wright.

Wright's influence can be seen not only in Oud's factory but also in earlier designs. A 1913 drawing of a house shows an entrance with a round sectional brick arch much like that of Wright's Dana House at Oak Park, Illinois, which Oud had probably seen pictured in Berlage's 1913 booklet *Amerikaansche reisherinneringen.* After this one derivation, Oud seems to have put aside his interest in Wright until 1918, when he not only wrote about him in *De stijl* but also adopted elements of his formal language, such as long lines of windows and overhangs. It is possible that Oud's interest in Wright was stimulated by his contacts with Robert van 't Hoff, whose 1915 design for a Concrete Villa was in the Wright style. Van 't Hoff had translated Wright's formal language into concrete, and Oud's designs for concrete housing in particular show Wrightian motifs.

Cracks in the collaboration, 1920–1922

It should be clear from what has been said above that the contacts between Oud and van Doesburg were very friendly during the formative years of De Stijl. Van Doesburg also collaborated with the other De Stijl architects; however, in 1919 he broke with Wils and van 't Hoff, which left Oud as the only architect with whom he would be able to realize the living ideal of monumental collaboration.

In the course of time, van Doesburg became much more intensely involved with architecture than before. He simply had to. There was no editor for architecture in *De stijl,* and Oud refused to fill that role. Wanting to learn more about the technical aspects of architecture, van Doesburg wrote a letter on August 8, 1918, asking Oud to send him the notebooks of his "course on construction" and the addresses of the editors of architectural journals.

Van Doesburg also was thinking about standardization, but he looked at the matter from an aesthetic perspective whereas Oud was interested primarily in the practical advantages. Van Doesburg viewed standardization in mass construction generally in the light of the idea that the individual element had to be subordinated to the collective. When it came to the signing of the De Stijl manifesto in November of 1918, Oud and van Doesburg interpreted this idea differently. For van Doesburg, at that moment it also included politics; he saw in it parallels with communism. Oud did not want to go that far, and he did not sign the manifesto.

The correspondence reveals that in the second half of 1919 van Doesburg hoped to go into building himself, with the support of Oud. In July 1919 he negotiated with a man named Hagemeijer who had asked him to renovate office buildings. Van Doesburg did not see many possibilities in renovation, and he wrote to Oud on July 6: "I have sketched an image for him of a harmonious con-

126

127
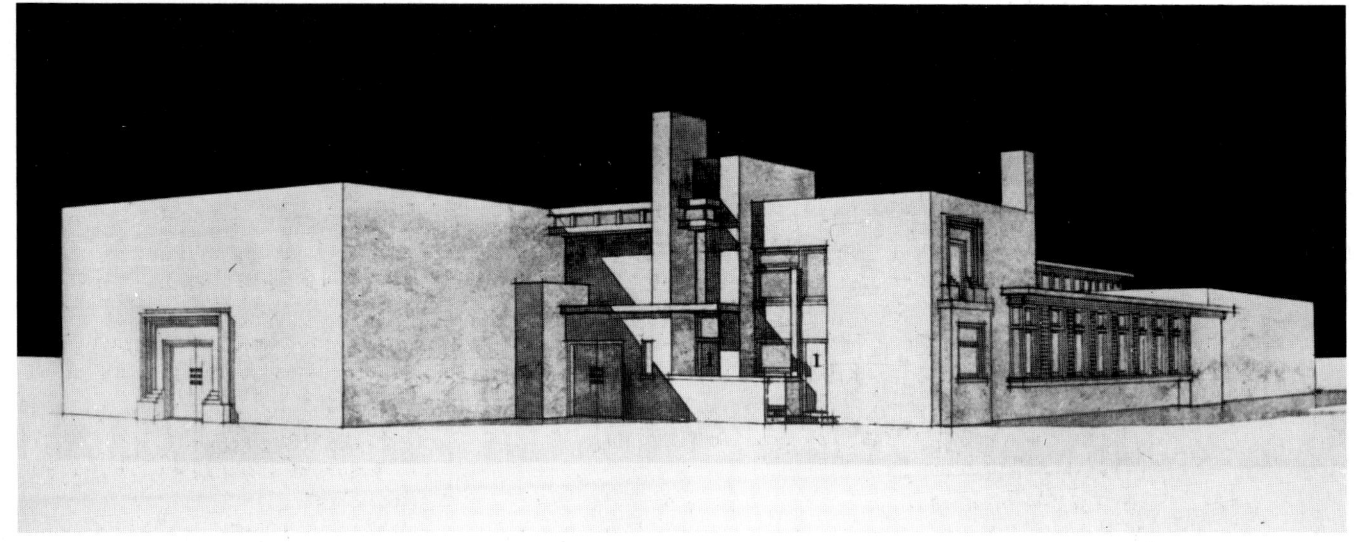

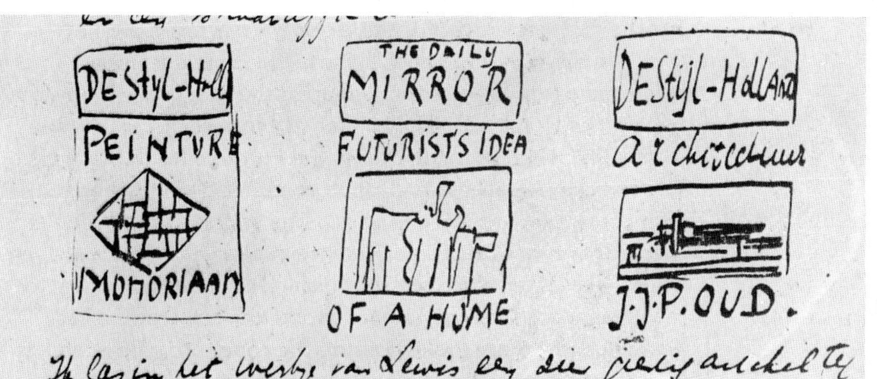
DE Styl-Holl
PEINTURE
MONDRIAAN

THE DAILY
MIRROR
FUTURISTS IDEA
OF A HOME

DE Stijl-Holland
architectuur
J.J.P. OUD.

Ik las in het [illegible] van Lewis een [illegible]
de skyscrapers en de city-architectuur in London.

128

126 Oud, design for a warehouse in Purmerend, 1918. Whereabouts unknown. As illustrated in *De stijl* 3, no. 11 (1920), appendix 12.

127 Oud, design for factory in Purmerend, 1919. Nederlands Documentatiecentrum voor de Bouwkunst, Amsterdam.

128 Detail of a letter from Theo van Doesburg to Oud, December 16, 1920. Rijksdienst Beeldende Kunst, The Hague.

129

130

struction from the ground up for new, modern offices! But he hesitated." Van Doesburg stated further that the offices should be constructed in concrete. Nothing came of all this; Hagemeijer even refused to pay for the sixteen designs on which van Doesburg had worked for nearly half a year.

Van Doesburg had still other plans in 1919. In November he asked Oud's advice on the building of a wooden house with a studio. Oud sent him a drawing (figure 130) and technical data. Remarkably, Oud did not want other people to see the design, because he thought it too sketchy. The plan fell through, probably for financial reasons.

Van Doesburg's ideas about the relation between painting and architecture became more and more pronounced in the course of 1919. His opinion that collaboration between artists should result in "an interlocking unity of the house and its belongings, extending even to notepaper"[36] would later lead to conflicts in the collaboration with Oud on blocks VIII and IX of the Spangen housing project. These blocks (figures 131 and 132) were designed in 1919–20. Just as with the first project in Spangen, the dwellings were grouped around an inner court and were constructed out of brick. The street facades give a still flatter and more sober impression, because the standardized windows are distributed uniformly. There is a slight vertical articulation at the stairwells, but horizontal lines predominate. The entire structure is bordered at the top by a wide frieze, and again three black bands are found at the bottom. Oud viewed the corners of the housing blocks as terminations that were to contrast with the protracted facades.

In block VIII the corners have the character of a compromise; forced to bring about a transition to the existing, more conventional architecture, Oud created sloping roofs at the short side, while the long facade had a flat roof. The facades are connected visually by two concrete slabs which continue around the corner. For the rest, concrete only returns in the overhang over the doors. In block IX, Oud could adhere to his own principles of form more consistently. The corner solution shows a simple, completely symmetrical composition of horizontal and vertical building elements. (In his design for the factory in Purmerend, Oud had been able to realize a much more varied composition in a similar way, with concrete as his starting point.) The balconies of the corner apartments are squeezed between vertical accents of unequal height. The other apartments had balconies in back; contrary to the usual procedure, the "front" rooms were also at the back. Consequently, these looked out on the courtyard, while the less important spaces were situated on the street side. Oud implemented this principle because of his opinions that the streets in a

131

129 Oud, front of house in Aalsmeer, 1913, as illustrated in folder. Private collection.

130 Oud, sketch for studio, 1919. Nederlands Documentatiecentrum voor de Bouwkunst, Amsterdam.

131 Oud, block VIII, Spangen (Rotterdam), 1919–1921. Photograph in private collection.

132

modern city were too narrow and that looking into a garden would enhance living. (This ideal was not realized in block VIII because some of the dwellings there were built not by the municipality but by a private developer.)

Preliminary studies show that Oud originally planned for the inner court of block IX to have galleries around the building at the level of the second floor above ground level. Perhaps he got this idea from the architect C. Brinkman, who had implemented it in another housing block in Spangen. In the courtyard Oud had originally planned collective facilities, such as a laundry. These were, however, not realized. Standard floor plans were used for the two lowest levels. The upper dwellings may be called revolutionary, because Oud made "maisonettes" out of them: the living room and the kitchen were downstairs, the bedroom upstairs.

With this second project in Spangen, Oud once again entered into a collaboration with van Doesburg. However, this time van Doesburg's self-assurance led to great tensions between them. On October 1, 1920, van Doesburg wrote to Oud that he was about to design color schemes for the interior and the exterior of block VIII. His move to the German city of Weimar and his travels through Europe engrossed him completely in the following months, however; not until the summer of 1921 did the commission come up again in the correspondence. In a letter of June 12, van Doesburg explained that he wanted to start with the interior and work outward. In contrast with the first project in Spangen, Oud did not give him preliminary guidelines. Van Doesburg determined the colors autonomously—a "dissonant triad" of yellow, green, and blue. The bricks (which were, to his regret, not plastered) were a dark red; therefore, van Doesburg said, he did not want to add that color.

Van Doesburg's choice of colors had a special purpose: to break up the static and symmetric character of Oud's facades. In his opinion, yellow had a dynamic effect in itself, whereas blue and green achieved a "destructive" effect only when positioned in a certain way on the facade. He wanted to make the woodwork, the doors, and the window frames of the living quarters green and blue, the frames of the stairwell windows yellow. The architecturally divergent short facades of block VIII were to be given a separate color treatment; there the different colors would be applied not in a straight line but in a V formation, as shown in figure 31.

Contrary to his intention, van Doesburg created his exterior designs first. He sent them to Oud in the beginning of October 1921. Oud reacted very enthusiastically in his letter of October 7: "I am happy and pleased with them, and I find them magnificent. Much better than in the first blocks, because it now also leaves the architecture intact, is acceptable in practice and painterly—as you write, to your liking. I see no reason why changes would be necessary: it will be as you designated; only some black on the bricks may lead to difficulties in the execution." (By "black on the bricks" Oud meant the black rectangles van Doesburg wanted on the short facade of block VIII.) Oud went on to caution van Doesburg against applying too much color in the interior; his experience had taught him that otherwise the occupants would paper the walls. After that, Oud retrenched bit by bit. His approval already appeared to be somewhat conditional when he suggested executing the design in part as an experiment before deciding definitely. Van Doesburg was indignant when Oud advised against using yellow on the doors; in his opinion that color had proved to soil too easily. The bomb exploded when Oud started to object to the black rectangles. In late October 1921 he stated his objections as fol-

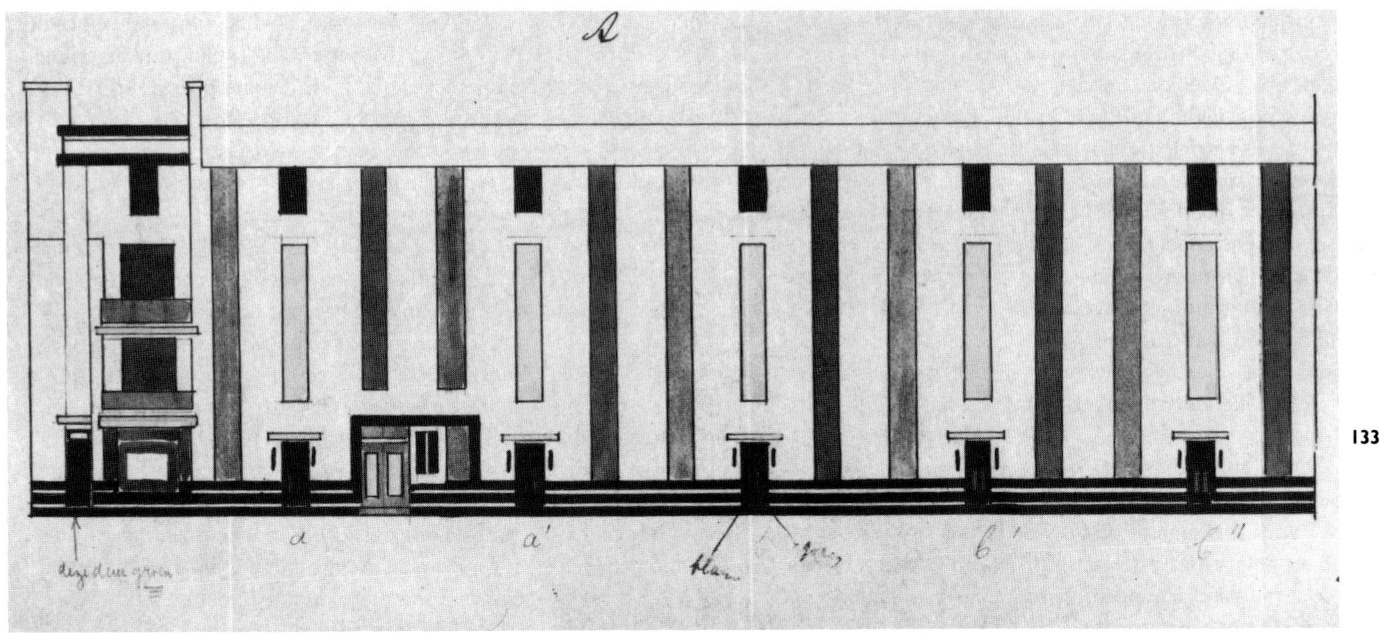

133

132 Oud, block IX, Spangen (Rotterdam), 1919–1921. Photograph in private collection.

133 Theo van Doesburg, color solution for facade of block IX, Spangen (Rotterdam), 1921. Fondation Custodia, Paris.

lows: "Architecturally they have the effect of holes, or pictorially the effect of decoration, so they are undesirable from both points of view." In this same letter he called the application of yellow to the dormers childish and unsuitable for such a serious project.

"Entweder so—oder nichts"

In November, van Doesburg reacted furiously to Oud's objections: "Entweder so—oder nichts" ["Either this way—or nothing"]. He had taken the plans very seriously, and now he felt that he was being treated like a common house painter. Subsequent letters from Oud give evidence that Helena Milius tried to patch up the differences. For a short while there was talk of an alternative plan with gray. However, when Oud maintained that bright painting juxtaposed with drab brick would not show to full advantage anyway, further collaboration became impossible.

Oud's relationship with Mondrian, which had been very good since their first meeting, in 1920, chilled as well. The reason for this was the lecture "Over de toekomstige bouwkunst en hare architectonische mogelijkheden"[37] ["On the future of the art of building and its architectonic possibilities"], delivered in February 1921 to the architectural society Opbouw in Rotterdam, in which Oud held up modern developments in the visual arts as an example to architects. He mentioned cubism and futurism, but to Mondrian's great disappointment he did not say one word about Neo-Plasticism. Oud had intentionally avoided using this term because he was of the opinion that the starting points of Mondrian's Neo-Plasticism were purely aesthetic, whereas in architecture practical matters had to be taken into account. Mondrian conceded that indeed that was still the case, because mankind was still too attached to material things. The ideal architecture could only be realized in the far future, when life would have become spiritualized. Oud disagreed with this separation between life and art. He wrote to van Doesburg in late 1921: "Exactly that which was always De Stijl's aim—to let life and art appear inseparable again . . . —he solves in this way! I now see that Piet really searches for the home and the interior for its own sake (just as the erstwhile painters searched for the painting). That may be a further step, but it still remains very individualistic."

The disagreements between Oud and the two painters had always been latent. It was inevitable that they would explode sometime. From 1922 on, Oud no longer considered himself a contributor to *De stijl*. However, the relations proved not be severed irrevocably. A friendly exchange of letters between Oud and Mondrian started anew in the summer of 1923 and was maintained until the 1930s.

Although Oud's lecture to Opbouw did not please the painters of De Stijl, it was widely appreciated. In Germany there was great interest in the lecture, and Oud was asked to repeat it in several cities. Its text was published in 1926 as part of the tenth of the Bauhaus Books—a book dedicated to Oud.

By 1921 Oud had reached a dead end, not only in his collaboration with van Doesburg but also in his own activities. As municipal architect he had so little creative leeway that he complained to van Doesburg immediately before their split: "At present I am looking around seriously for private commissions. The municipal authorities and the perpetual workers' dwellings bore me. It has no future: standardization in housing construction in this form is also nonsense. For many people brick is death, and it spoils every hour of the day for me. Here I saw a white house in between brick houses and against that everything else looked dingy and drab."[38] Oud wrote this in connection with his work on a plan for eight housing blocks in the new Rotterdam district of Tusschendijken, adjoining Spangen. In all, 1,005 dwelling units were to be built. Oud's design was approved by the city council on October 8, 1920, and blocks I–IV and VI were constructed over the next year. The other blocks could not yet be realized for a while because of financial problems; block V was ultimately built in 1924.

In its plan as well as in the facades, Tusschendijken recalls block IX in Spangen. The main difference between the complexes is visible in the corner solutions. In Spangen the corners had a decorative treatment, but in Tusschendijken they were very sober and completely void of decoration. Here standardization was carried to the extreme. The Tusschendijken project was greatly appreciated and much publicized, particularly in German architectural journals.[39] Yet, understandably, Oud felt that his artistic imagination was being squelched.

In March 1921, the Parisian art dealer Léonce Rosenberg conceived the idea of organizing an architectural exhibition around De Stijl. Oud readily accepted the opportunity to design a house for this show; however, he withdrew in disappointment when it appeared that Rosenberg only wanted to exhibit a model.

A second commission which Oud got in 1921 was, in his opinion, more realistic. On the invitation of the architecture critic Adolf Behne, he made sketches for a house for a Mrs. Kallenbach, of Berlin, who wanted to have a house designed by a "young, truly modern and still unknown architect"—perhaps Adolf Meyer, Richard Döcker, or Ludwig Hilbersheimer. Behne knew Oud's work and thought that he deserved consideration. He had also published an article on Oud in the journal *Feuer*. Mrs. Kallenbach's confidant, Laszlo Moholy-Nagy, had seen this publication. Like

134 Oud, housing project in Tusschendijken (Rotterdam), 1921–1924. Photograph in private collection.

135 

135 Oud, courtyard of Tusschendijken housing block. Photograph in private collection.

136 Oud, detail of design for Kallenbach house, 1921 or 1922. Mrs. A. Oud-Dinaux, Wassenaar.

137 Oud, design for Kallenbach house. Dimensions and whereabouts unknown; photograph in private collection.

138 Oud, design for "corner house," 1923. Nederlands Documentatiecentrum voor de Bouwkunst, Amsterdam.

136 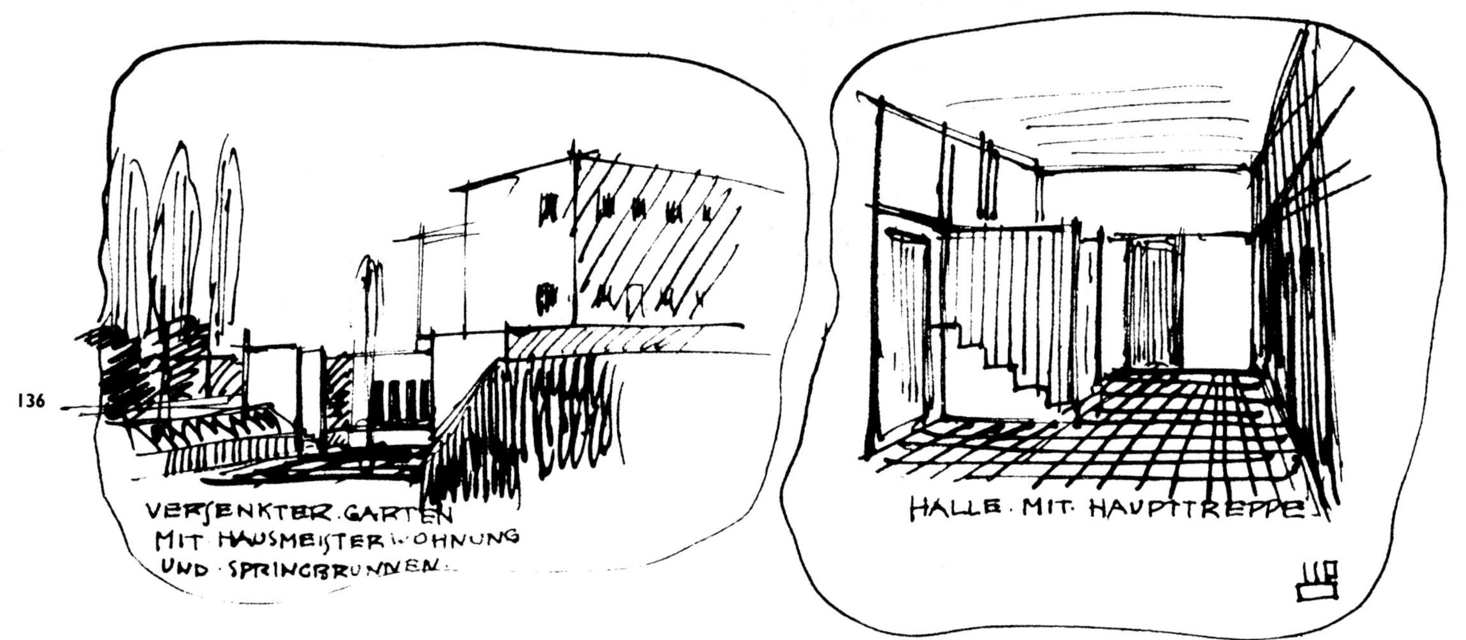

Behne, he found the pictured Villa Allegonda very beautiful, and he wanted a design in the same style. On October 29, 1921, a detailed list was sent to Oud containing wishes concerning the arrangement of the house. He sent sketches to Berlin. The design progressed, and on March 17, 1922, Oud traveled to Berlin in order to study the site and talk over details. According to the design, the villa was to be composed of two blocks situated in an L. The very closed treatment of the facades is remarkable; the windows were to be small and smoothly finished. Oud also designed a garden, with the flowerbeds partitioned into rectangles.

This commission, too, turned out disappointingly for Oud. On May 21, 1922, Moholy-Nagy sent word that the Kallenbach family had put off the construction, possibly for financial reasons. In his letter he mentioned another reason: Mrs. Kallenbach had not been able to persuade her husband to adopt the "modern ideology."[40] The matter was "definitely dead."

In the following years, Oud gradually distanced himself from De Stijl. He no longer accepted its principles, which he thought dogmatic; rather, he developed a new form language of his own. In 1923 he began to use rounded shapes and to experiment with color solutions that, rather than destructurize architecture, accentuated its constructional and functional parts.

137

138

1
The most complete bibliography up to 1956 can be found in H. L. C. Jaffé's *Dutch contribution to modern art* (Amsterdam, 1956). Two recent monographs are Hans Oud's *J. J. P. Oud, architect, 1890–1963* (The Hague, 1984) and Günter Stamm's *J. J. P. Oud, bauten und projekte 1906 bis 1963* (Mainz and Berlin, 1984); the former has an extensive bibliography.

2
B. Rebel makes an attempt to do this in "De volkswoningbouw van J. J. P. Oud," *Nederlands kunsthistorisch jaarboek* 28 (1977), pp. 127–168.

3
For more on the collaboration between van Doesburg and Oud, see the following: N. J. Troy, *The De Stijl environment* (Cambridge, Mass., 1983), passim; *Het nieuwe bouwen. De Stijl. De nieuwe beelding in de architectuur* (exhibition catalog, Gemeentemuseum, The Hague, 1983), passim.

4
Letter in English from Oud to H. R. Graf, undated (1926). Part of this letter has been published in a Dutch translation in *Architectuur van J. J. P. Oud* (exhibition catalog, Lijnbaancentrum, Rotterdam, 1981–82), pp. 6–8.

5
J. J. P. Oud, "Naar aanleiding van 'Van de scheepvaarttentoonstelling,'" *De wereld,* July 18, 1913. This clipping is in the archive of Mrs. A. Oud-Dinaux, in Wassenaar.

6
J. J. P. Oud, "Duitsche kunst," *De wereld,* October 3, 1913 (clipping in archive of Mrs. A. Oud-Dinaux, Wassenaar).

7
These frescoes were executed by the artist Jac Jongert, a student of the painter R. N. Roland Holst. In the periodical *Klei,* Oud wrote that this project was the first example of fresco painting executed in the Netherlands in modern times. See J. J. P. Oud, "Schoorsteen in het gebouw der werkmansvereeniging 'Vooruit,' te Purmerend," *Klei* 4, no. 22 (1912).

8
M. Bock, "Bouwmateriaal," in *Berlage* (exhibition catalog, Gemeentemuseum, The Hague, 1975), p. 17.

9
T. van Doesburg, "Over moderne kunst," *Eenheid* 129 (November 23, 1912).

10
T. van Doesburg, "De ontwikkeling der moderne schilderkunst," *Eenheid* 323 (August 12, 1916).

11
J. J. P. Oud, "Over cubisme, futurisme, moderne bouwkunst, enz.," *Bouwkundig weekblad* 37, no. 20 (1916), pp. 156–157.

12
T. van Doesburg, "De nieuwe beweging in de schilderkunst," *De beweging* 12, no. 9 (1916), p. 234.

13
However, this window (discussed in the chapters on van Doesburg and Huszár) can hardly be considered a real example of collaboration.

14
This commission was mediated by Menso Kamerlingh Onnes's son Harm.

15
Oud, "Over cubisme . . ." (note 11 above).

16
J. J. P. Oud, "Verbouwing huize 'Allegonda,' Katwijk aan Zee," *Bouwkundig weekblad* 39, no. 5 (1918), pp. 29–30.

17
Letter from Oud to Behne, in German, dated November 14, 1920; cited in Dutch in C. Blotkamp, "Mondriaan—architectuur," *Wonen/TABK* 4/5 (1982), p. 32.

18
The correspondence reveals that Oud tried to interest Berlage in the periodical by inviting him to hear van Doesburg lecture. Berlage never contributed, however, In the 1927 commemorative issue of *De stijl,* Wils is not listed as a founder; it may be assumed that he was less involved than Oud.

19
J. J. P. Oud, "Het monumentale stadsbeeld," *De stijl* 1, no. 1 (1917), pp. 10–11.

20
T. van Doesburg, "Bij de bijlagen, II. J. J. P. Oud, ontwerp voor een complex van huizen voor een strandboulevard," *De stijl* 1, no. 1 (1917), pp. 13–14.

21
In the 1890s a wave of social concern spread from England to the European continent. This resulted in the Netherlands in the foundation of community centers. In 1894 Emilie Knappert, a feminist who was actively involved in the Netherlands Christian Socialist Movement, opened the community center Geloof, Hoop, Liefde [Faith, Hope, Love] in an industrial neighborhood of Leiden. There children of laborers were instructed and vacations were organized. In 1899, Het Leidsche Volkshuis [The Leiden Community Center] took over the organization of events. From the very beginning there were attempts to bring the children from the town in close contact with nature in the nearby seaside resorts of Katwijk and Noordwijk. In recent years several authors have discussed this project—see J. Beckett, "'De Vonk,' an example of early De Stijl co-operation," *Art History* 3, no. 2 (1980), pp. 201–217; Troy, *De Stijl environment* (note 3), pp. 17–23.

22
Oud got a lot of comments on his high, steeply pitched roofs. Huib Hoste, a Belgian architect and critic, disapproved of them in a review in the newspaper *De telegraaf* of March 1, 1919. He was an advocate of the principles put forth in *De stijl,* and he found, to his regret, that an architect who was involved with De Stijl did not adhere to those principles: "We just spoke of gabled facades, i.e. facades which are bounded by two tapering oblique lines ending in a point. For van Doesburg an oblique line is evil because it lacks stability: it is in fact not vertical anymore, and not yet horizontal either. I respect that opinion, but I cannot understand why they are not objecting to these gabled facades and roofs." Oud's pitched roofs embarrassed van Doesburg, who as editor of *De stijl* felt responsible for maintaining the modern principles. In a letter to Oud dated March 13, 1919, he suggested antedating the design to the time before the founding of *De stijl:* "You could for instance add that it is a design from 1916, and that concerning the exterior you are not standing completely behind it any more, just as Mondrian and van Doesburg will not be completely behind their work from that time either."

23
Oud, quoted in J. Gratama, "Vacantiehuis te Noordwijkerhout," *Klei* 12, no. 2 (1920), p. 14.

24
H. Hoste, "Het vacantiehuis te Noordwijkerhout," *De telegraaf,* March 1, 1919.

25
A good survey of public housing in Rotterdam, and in the Netherlands in general, can be found in *Architektuur en volkshuisvesting,* by M. Casciato et al. (Milan and Delft, 1980).

26
J. J. P. Oud, "Gemeentelijke volkswoningen, polder 'Spangen' te Rotterdam," *Bouwkundig weekblad* 41, no. 37 (1920), p. 220.

27
On Ostwald, see the chapter on Huszár in this volume.

28
Anon., *Nieuwe Rotterdamsche courant,* September 19, 1920.

29
J. J. P. Oud, "Architectonische beschouwing. A. Massabouw en straatarchitectuur," *De stijl* 2, no. 7 (1919), pp. 79–82; "B. Gewapend beton en bouwkunst," ibid., pp. 82–84.

30
As municipal architect of Rotterdam, Oud must have expected to be able to realize public housing over the whole city; because of financial limitations, however, he had to be satisfied with smaller projects. In extension plans, his housing blocks were immediately juxtaposed with those built by housing associations.

31
J. J. P. Oud, "Architectonische beschouwing. B. Gewapend beton en bouwkunst," *De stijl* 2, no. 7 (1919), pp. 82–84.

32
J. J. P. Oud, "Het bouwen van woningen in gewapend beton," *Bouwkundig weekblad* 41, nos. 15 and 23 (1920).

33
In his review of the factory in *De stijl* (March 1920), van Doesburg mentioned the architect D. Saal, who had a part in the floor plan.

34
Communication from Mrs. A. Oud-Dinaux, November 1981.

35
Wright's influence on Dutch architects is discussed by A. van der Woud in "Variaties op een thema," in *Americana, Nederlandse architectuur 1880–1930* (exhibition catalog, Rijksmuseum Kröller-Müller, Otterlo, 1975), pp. 28–40.

36
Letter from van Doesburg to Oud, July 6, 1919.

37
J. J. P. Oud, "Over de toekomstige bouwkunst en hare architectonische mogelijkheden," *Bouwkundig weekblad* 42, no. 24 (1921), pp. 147–160.

38
Undated letter from Oud to van Doesburg (October 1921).

39
A. Behne, "Von holländischer baukunst," *Feuer* 5 (1921), pp. 171–192; Behne, "Holländische baukunst in der gegenwart," *Wasmuths monatshefte für baukunst* 6, no. 1–2 (1922), pp. 1–33; E. Stockmeyer, "Monumentale mietshaus-architektur in Holland," *Schweizerische bauzeitung* 80, no. 23 (1922), pp. 257–259; M. Stam, "Holland und die baukunst unserer zeit," ibid. 82, no. 18 (1923), pp. 225–229.

40
Letter from Moholy-Nagy to Oud, May 21, 1922.

139 **Bart van der Leck, ca. 1920.**

Bart van der Leck

Cees Hilhorst

"There will come a time when collecting art will be considered rather vacuous," wrote Bart van der Leck to Hélène Kroller-Müller on December 18, 1916. An artist must be rather self-confident to utter such a statement to the only collector who is buying his work regularly. However, in the same letter van der Leck explained why he had broached such a sensitive issue: "The organic integration of the beauty of contemporary artworks into the everyday environment of life will prove its greater vitality in the long run." This is the basis of van der Leck's artistic development; it also characterizes his contribution to the theories of De Stijl.

From the start, van der Leck occupied himself with "monumental" art. He could not envision his work as separate from its environment, nor did he want to, and he went to great lengths to integrate his work into the environment. Besides murals, he created designs for rugs and packaging materials, and he experimented with ceramics.

That van der Leck is known primarily for his easel paintings is due more to the public than to him. At first he worked in a rather traditional style, but later he became so radical that he was appreciated only within a very small circle. Moreover, as a monumental artist he needed patrons who were willing to let him realize his ideas in an architectural environment. Yet a good number of projects were realized during his long life. Unfortunately, almost all of them have been destroyed—van der Leck put such a stamp on the domestic environments he designed that subsequent users generally did not have much affinity with his work, and they often covered it with wallpaper.

In the Netherlands, van der Leck is known mainly for his 1914 painting *De kat* [*The cat*]. He is further known as a painter who provided the viewer with a kind of visual puzzle—one usually needs the title as a clue to what is represented. Although the average musuem visitor often gains little insight into the underlying motivations, it is one of van der Leck's merits that he made abstraction intelligible to the public.

Van der Leck's international reputation has remained limited. He is represented only scantily in collections outside the Netherlands, and not until 1959 was a comprehensive exhibition of his work held abroad (in Recklinghausen, West Germany). France had an opportunity to get to know his work through a similar exhibition in Paris in 1980.

Van der Leck's image has been defined mainly by three authors: H. P. Bremmer, W. C. Feltkamp, and R. W. D. Oxenaar. Bremmer evaluated van der Leck's work from the viewpoint of an art critic. He transmitted his views to Feltkamp, who wrote an admiring monograph on van der Leck just before the artist's death. Thorough research began only later; Oxenaar gave a very detailed account of van der Leck's development up to 1920, based on data from diverse archival sources and highlighting his relation to the other artists of De Stijl.[1]

From tradition to identity

Bart Anthonij van der Leck was born in Utrecht on November 26, 1876, the fourth of eight children of B. A. van der Leck, Sr. (a housepainter) and Hendrika Gathier.[2] At the age of 15 he went to work in a stained-glass studio. At the time, stained-glass work was flourishing because of the construction of Roman Catholic churches, which had been stimulated by a revival of Catholicism in the Netherlands in the second half of the nineteenth century.

Van der Leck's schooling was primarily vocational, but he wanted to be an artist. His first step in this direction was to join the Genootschap Kunstliefde [Art Lovers' Association], which afforded him the opportunity to practice life drawing. He also joined the club Niets zonder Arbeid [Nothing without Work], a rather obscure organization headed by the young architect P. J. C. Klaarhamer. From 1893 on, van der Leck maintained a close friendship with Klaarhamer—a friendship that was to last until his De Stijl years. Probably as a result of Klaarhamer's influence, van der Leck began to improve his general education; he studied French and read political and theological writings.

However, van der Leck wanted to be more than just an amateur artist. After moving to Amsterdam in 1899, he was accepted at the Rijksschool voor Kunstnijverheid [National School for Arts and Crafts, also called the Quellinusschool] for the 1900–1901 academic year. He took the painting course and the "practical morning classes," receiving thorough training not only in his own field (stained-glass work) but also in various techniques of wall painting. For the next academic year he was also accepted to take an evening course in drawing at the Rijksacademie voor Beeldende Kunsten [National Academy for Visual Arts], where he studied with August Allebé among others. Van der Leck successfully completed his studies in both fine and applied art in 1904.[3] Apparently, he was offered a fellowship for an additional year of studies in Germany, but he turned this down along with another offer of a grant to establish his own stained-glass studio because he wanted to be free and look after himself.[4]

The works van der Leck created during his studies and immediately thereafter show the strong influence of Antoon Derkinderen and Jan Toorop, both in style and in choice of subjects. These two men were the major artistic exponents of the Catholic revival. In addition, van der Leck did not escape the influence of the interest in Egyptian art that swept through Dutch art circles. Judging from the few extant works, van der Leck in this period was representing figures very flatly, in rather even colors, and within pronounced outlines. In some cases he used primary colors, but always in combination with nonprimary ones; it is doubtful that he had consciously opted for basic colors.[5] The stylization of the figures recalls medieval miniatures and, particularly, Egyptian reliefs—they stand next to one another in long friezes, represented strictly in profile or full face. Clear examples of this style can be found in the 1905 edition of *Hooglied van Salomo* [*Song of Solomon*], a bibliophile production illustrated by van der Leck and with typography by Klaarhamer. Derkinderen's influence on van der Leck is particularly noticeable in the illustrations in this book.

Van der Leck shared a studio with Klaarhamer soon after returning to Utrecht in 1905. A music cabinet designed by Klaarhamer and decorated by van der Leck is further evidence of their collaboration.[6] However, van der Leck did not remain in Utrecht for long. The years 1906–1910 witnessed a series of moves and visits. He shuttled between Amsterdam, Utrecht, Amersfoort, Enschede, and Glanerbrug (where in 1906 he met his future wife, a teacher named Bertha Teerink). During this period van der Leck developed into an independent, mature artist. He worked in relative isolation, apparently out of contact with the artists who introduced the trends of the moment—cubism and fauvism—to the Netherlands. He did not exhibit, and apparently he sold little. At first there was some influence from symbolism; this can be seen in paintings from 1906 such as *De wijzen uit het Oosten* [*The wise men from the East*] and *Het wonder op zee* [*The miracle on the sea*].[7] The flirtation with symbolism was brief, however.

From 1907 on, van der Leck went his own way in his choice of subjects and his method of working. His portraits of common people and his scenes of everyday life in workers' quarters and factories give him a distinctive place in Dutch painting. He may have been following the works van Gogh produced during his residence in De Peel and the Borinage, economically backward regions of the Netherlands and Belgium—occasionally van der Leck reminds us of his great precursor, particularly in his drawings. Other possible influences are Alexandre Steinlen and Käthe Kollwitz, whose works were exhibited in the Netherlands and were available in several publications.

A fair number of pre-1908 sketches and finished drawings by van der Leck, but relatively few paintings from those years, are extant. Many of the sketches seem to have been made out of doors, on the spot. These rapidly recorded impressions in crayon and charcoal were—in some cases, many years later—elaborated into drawings and paintings. The finished drawings reveal the artist's care for detail and perspective. For instance, in the 1908 drawing *De kramer* [*The pedlar*], both the scene and the background are precisely detailed; the different rolls of fabric in the cart can be distinguished, and in the row of houses in the background every window can be discerned.[8] In the paintings, however, these details were abandoned. Furthermore, many of the paintings are less narrative in character; they are mostly portraits of women, and the exactitude one would expect in a close-up is subordinated to thick, impasted brushstrokes.

Around 1909, van der Leck began to depict faces in such a way that the features of the individuals were no longer recognizable. This was to become a characteristic of his work. In addition, he began to show a clear preference for the depiction of groups of people in motion. Although the choice of subjects appears somewhat anecdotal at first glance, it seems from the uniformity within these groups that van der Leck's intention was to give his work a more general meaning by, as it were, sacrificing the individual to the collective.

One of the first important works in this mode is *Uitgaan van de fabriek* [*Leaving the factory*], shown here as figure 140. This painting shows a strict horizontal partitioning. The upper portion is taken up by a reasonably accurate likeness of a still-extant cotton mill in Glanerbrug, the lower portion by a group of laborers who (as the title indicates) are going home after their day's work. In contrast with the mill, the laborers are scarcely depicted realistically; with the exception of the shorter man and the woman on the right, their heads appear as if they are captured within a narrow horizontal frieze running across the exact middle of the painting. The uniformity in posture is striking—the workers are represented as if they are marching. They do not talk to one another; they look straight ahead. Although it is dangerous to read states of mind from faces in paintings, these people certainly do not present a cheerful impression. By their posture and behavior, they appear to be holding a silent protest-demonstration. Yet the literature on van der Leck often stresses that he was not aiming to take an explicit position in a social conflict.[9] It is true that in his letters to Klaarhamer during these years he did not complain about exploitation or bad working conditions; on the contrary, he gave enthusiastic descriptions of factory halls and new machines—descriptions that, in their optimism, seem to anticipate the ideas and the terminology of futurism. This painting and others from this period do indicate that van der Leck had an involvement with the lower social classes, albeit not in the form of protest or propaganda.[10]

140

141

140 Van der Leck, *Uitgaan van de fabriek* [*Leaving the factory*], 1910. Oil on canvas, 120 × 140 cm. Museum Boymans–van Beuningen, Rotterdam.

141 Van der Leck, *Naar het vliegveld* [*To the airport*], 1912. Oil on canvas, 65 × 115 cm. Private collection.

Van der Leck also saw the depersonalization of the individual in military life. According to him, his interest in this phenomenon prompted him in 1910 to move to Soesterberg, near the large garrison town of Amersfoort. Soldiers play an important role in van der Leck's works, particularly those from 1911 and 1912. When he represented both soldiers and civilians in the same painting, van der Leck placed them in separate friezes; see, for example, figure 141.[11]

First appreciation and commissions for monumental art

Around 1912 van der Leck gradually broke out of his isolation, mainly through the mediation of H. P. Bremmer, a critic and patron in The Hague. Van der Leck had sent Bremmer a number of drawings as early as July 1908,[12] though not until 1910 did Bremmer make a purchase. Perhaps he was struck by the similarities between van der Leck's work and that of van Gogh, whom he admired greatly. By July 1912 van der Leck had a contract to receive financial support from Bremmer, and this arrangement continued (with some brief interruptions, during which others took over the support) until 1945.

In a note dated May 19, 1937, Bremmer explained his support for van der Leck and many other artists. "In order to help an artist, I have started from the assumption that only that kind of support which enables them to work peacefully for a period of time without other concerns would be useful. Thus I have always given them an annuity, and I took the risk of receiving their work in return."[13] Bremmer kept the support going by selling the pieces he received, often to his students. The van der Leck paintings that are now in the collections of the descendants of the "Bremmerites" are evidence of this arrangement. In particular, the 42 paintings and approximately 250 drawings by van der Leck collected by Hélène Kröller-Müller, now in the museum that bears her name, are a monument to Bremmer's support.

Out of enthusiasm for van der Leck and his work (but also, of course, to promote sales), Bremmer publicized the artist, negotiated commissions, and organized exhibitions. He also published many articles on van der Leck in the monthly *Beeldende kunst*, which he managed to fill all by himself for nearly 25 years. In these articles, each of which was devoted to a single painting, Bremmer tried to foster an understanding of van der Leck's motivations and stylistic methods. He almost always warned the reader not to be deceived by the primitive appearance of a painting; the reader, he stressed, could safely believe that the artist had not painted such wooden-looking figures out of a lack of skill. Reactions such as "My nephew PIET can do that, too"[14] were unjustified—nephew Piet had not undergone the gradual development that had led to this conscious simplicity, and he would not be able to create such a well-balanced composition. The rigid forms enabled van der Leck to realize his striving for "monumentality."[15] The hostile reactions of the public were due in part to the unusual stylized flatness; however, one could not accept this in Egyptian and medieval works—merely because they were earlier—and reject it in van der Leck's. After comparisons with other artists' treatments of the same theme, Bremmer invariably concluded that van der Leck had again succeeded in creating a sensitive and significant painting.

As has already been hinted, after 1912 van der Leck strayed farther and farther from realistic representation. Using flat stylization and abandoning pictorial depth, he attempted to make a painting conform to the wall plane where it would eventually come to reside. Between 1912 and 1915, the last vestiges of representation gave way to a gradual process of abstraction. Planes were now evenly colored, without the effects of light and shadow, and were outlined in black. They stood completely on their own, "just as on a map the different provinces are juxtaposed in different colors."[16] Body shapes were represented schematically, and naturally curved contour lines were straightened. Human subjects were twisted into Egyptian postures.

To curb the effect of pictorial depth as much as possible, van der Leck also began to employ other means. Dominant oblique lines of perspective were no longer used, and people and objects were represented only from the front or the side. "Overlap" between figures was avoided. With the introduction of a white ground, the very last traces of depth were abolished. When van der Leck first began to use white grounds, they were interpretable as more or less naturalistic representations of white walls, as in *De zieke* (1912) and *Bij de Gooische haard* (1913); however, later he began to use white grounds in open-air scenes as well, thus lifting the events depicted completely out of their naturalistic contexts. (See figures 142 and 143.) With this same intention, van der Leck broke through the spatial composition of the depicted scene, omitting the common base on which persons and objects were situated. A first, cautious step in this direction was a 1913 still life[17] in which objects were positioned without any apparent interrelation whatever, as if afloat. Later, in such paintings as *Bedelvolk* [*Beggars*], from 1914, and *Arabieren* [*Arabs*], from 1915, human figures were distributed illogically over the picture plane, in such a way that the relationship among them was left for the viewer to determine. In these paintings, because overlapping and size reduction for the

142

143

142 Van der Leck, *De voetballers* [*The soccer players*], 1913. Casein on eternite, 41 × 71 cm. Private collection.

143 Van der Leck, *Arabieren* [*Arabs*], 1915. Casein on eternite, 31 × 57 cm. Rijksmuseum Kröller-Müller, Otterlo.

purpose of creating perspective no longer occur, the upper part of the composition does not serve to represent something in the background; the totality gives a flat impression.

Around the same time that he introduced the white ground, van der Leck began to experiment with a new technique: instead of oil on canvas, he began to paint with casein on the building material eternite (waterproofed asbestos cement cast into a slab). His letters reveal that he investigated the technicalities of this combination of materials and the possible drawbacks. With regard to casein, he made inquiries to knowledgeable people such as Cuijpers, the architect of the Rijksmuseum in Amsterdam. (Apparently, van der Leck knew that the murals in this museum had been executed in casein.) He was told that casein would stick well to plaster or cement, but apparently little was known about the durability or the moistureproof properties of casein on eternite.

Van der Leck's concern for the technical quality of his paintings is evident from a letter to Bremmer, dated February 13, 1914, in which he described one of his experiments. He had immersed a piece of eternite painted with casein in water and had put in in his basement, where it had developed a mold: ". . . after a few months, when the painted side had accumulated a thick layer of mold, I removed that, and the paint came out beautifully. Now, this is not a piece fixed into a wall, but for waterproofing it is still rather a good experiment."[18] The visual qualities of van der Leck's paintings made them well suited to being set into walls. As mentioned previously, he kept the representation very flat, and he kept the image from being cut off by a frame, thereby facilitating a smooth transition from the painting to the wall. The white background would continue imperceptibly into the wall, as white walls were then coming into fashion. The separation between traditional free painting and monumental art was gradually fading.

A good example of van der Leck's style in this transitional period is the 1913 painting *De voetballers* [*The soccer players*]. The choice of subject is perhaps unusual, but it is explicable: Van der Leck was probably fascinated by the depersonalization of athletes playing on teams, as well as by that of soldiers. In *De voetballers,* there is great similarity in posture and appearance among the four soccer players (two from each team). They are discernible mainly by the different colors of their shirts; their personal identities are limited to differences in their profiles and in the length of their sideburns. The rather formally dressed referee occupies the central position. The image looks rather prosaic; however, it can be interpreted as a symbolic reflection of society, in which conflicting interests have to be curbed by laws, rules, and standards.

This interpretation can also be brought to bear upon other works by van der Leck. It is noteworthy that human figures nearly always play the leading role in his works. Still lifes are rare, and motifs derived from nature and from architecture almost never serve as central subjects.[19] Usually van der Leck directed his full attention to the human figures, who appear to be confronted with poverty, illness, calamity, or misery, or to be manipulated by fate. When Bremmer wrote of van der Leck's 1912 painting *De hondekar* [*The dog cart*] that the persons depicted seemed to be trudging along like "puppets without a will of their own, driven by an invisible force," the artist reacted approvingly.[20] His obvious preference for the representation of groups of people on the go can be traced back to the same urge to represent the "fate of mankind."

In 1913, van der Leck received his first important commission. It was for some murals in the building of the insurance company De Nederlanden van 1845, in The Hague. Bremmer had recommended van der Leck to the president of the company, Carl Henny, who had previously commissioned several architectural projects by H. P. Berlage. Though this was van der Leck's first chance to realize his ideal of monumental painting in a public environment, he had no inclination to rely on hackneyed images such as a falling leaf, a half-burnt candle, the "stairs of life," or the wheel of fortune, such as his onetime hero Derkinderen had contributed to the building of the Algemeene Maatschappij van Levensverzekering en Lijfrente in Amsterdam in the late nineteenth century—he called such images "insipid," although he did not mention Derkinderen explicitly.[21] Van der Leck personified the life-insurance company's function in a natty insurance agent carrying a hefty purse. He even planned to make the purse a bit larger, and to label it to make its contents obvious.[22] This lack of subtlety upset some of the company's directors; a few even threatened to resign should the paintings be realized.[23] Van der Leck would not compromise in the least, and the entire commission was shelved.

In 1913, Bremmer arranged van der Leck's first one-man show, which was held at the Walrecht gallery in The Hague.[24] Some twenty drawings and paintings were exhibited. The critic Cornelis Veth expressed little appreciation. The early paintings were barely adequate, he wrote, but the later works displayed "a repulsive monotony." He referred to them as "framed painted things which nevertheless were not paintings."[25] Still, sales went reasonably well, according to the scanty information available. Hélène Kröller-Müller bought six paintings.[26]

It is not known whether van der Leck actually met Mrs. Kröller-Müller during this exhibition. The first indications of direct contact between the two date from March 1914, when Bremmer commended van der Leck to the Müller family's business firm, Fa. Müller & Co. (a holding company of mining and shipping concerns). Soon this company took over the commissioning of van der Leck from Bremmer. The first commission under this agreement was for a large stained-glass window for the office on the Lange Voorhout in The Hague. Van der Leck was offered the opportunity to make a study tour of the company's branches in Spain and North Africa in order to familiarize himself with the operations there, and in the spring of 1914 he traveled around those two regions for 2½ months. He recorded his impressions in many sketches and drawings, building up a reservoir from which he would draw for years.

The design and the execution of the window were interrupted by other commissions (from Mrs. Kröller-Müller as well as from the company), and it was not finished until 1915. In the meantime, in December 1914, van der Leck received a commission to design a poster for the Batavierlijn, a shipping company run by the Müller firm and serving Rotterdam and London. The extant sketches for the poster show that van der Leck struggled with the partitioning of the picture plane.[27] Starting with two horizontal friezes (one with the ship at the top and one with the passengers, longshoremen, and cargo at the top, he arrived at a solution in which the ship was emphasized and the passengers and the cargo appeared in separate small rectangles in the upper corners. Stylistically, the poster resembles van der Leck's uncommissioned work from this period; the postures look Egyptian, there is hardly any depth, and the use of colors is very limited (though not exclusively to the primaries—brown and blue-green occur).

The agreement with the Müller company resulted in so many commissions that in the spring of 1915 van der Leck decided to move to The Hague. Probably around that time, though perhaps earlier, he met the painters Chris Beekman and Vilmos Huszár, both of whom moved in Bremmer's circle.

Van der Leck's commissions from the Müller company also included color consulting for existing buildings and for newly commissioned projects by Berlage, who from 1913 to 1919 was under contract to the company. Berlage was already established as an architect, and he was inclined to keep control over the ornamentation and the color schemes of his buildings. In his interiors he made liberal use of paneling, glazed bricks, and tiles. Although van der Leck had gained a reputation in artistic circles only recently, he was already 40 years old, and he had undergone considerable artistic development. Consequently, he resented the scraps of work that Berlage foisted on him (such as consulting on the interior decoration and the upholstery of the renovated Kröller-Müller house in The Hague, Huize Ten Vijver; designing ceiling decorations for the company's London subsidiary, Holland House; and contributing a tile panel with animals to the model farm "De Schipborg" at Zuidlaren). Early in 1916, when he was once again commissioned to determine the colors of the entire interior of an existing house (the Kröller estate Groot-Haesebroek, in Wassenaar), van der Leck was fed up. In a letter he informed Mrs. Kröller-Müller that he was not about to serve as a kind of glorified housepainter for an environment in which monumental art simply could not be done justice.[28] As soon as an opportunity presented itself, in April 1916, he and his family left The Hague and settled in Laren. His contract with the company was taken over privately by Mrs. Kröller-Müller, and the conditions were modified so that, as in his earlier relationship with Bremmer, van der Leck was to part with his work in exchange for a monthly allowance.

1916: Primary colors

The year 1916 brought a signifcant change in van der Leck's use of colors and forms. In the spring he completed the paintings *De storm* and *Havenarbeid* [*Dock work*], in which he had used only unmixed primary colors—certainly a revolutionary palette. Because the colors in themselves were forceful enough, the contour line that in earlier works might have served to separate pale colors from the white ground could be omitted.

De storm represents a fishing boat on high waves and two fishermen's wives on the beach, a scene that may have been based on Herman Heijermans's play *Op hoop van zegen.*[29] *Havenarbeid* (figure 144) is a continuation of the design sketches for the Batavierlijn poster of 1914–15. In contrast with van der Leck's previous paintings, the scenes in these two paintings are not placed on a white ground, and the overlapping gives them more depth than usual; van der Leck seems to have temporarily regressed a bit in this respect.

As mentioned above, in *De storm* and *Havenarbeid* van der Leck used only pure, unmixed primary colors (red, yellow, and blue), juxtaposed with white and black. No indications of this new use of color can be found in the sketches for his works; in these van der Leck still used brown and green extensively. Statements by the artist about the reasons for this sudden change are rare. One of his few clarifying remarks on this matter was made in 1956, when he described his use of color as "generalized in the three singular colors red, yellow, and blue . . . as essential real values in which every shade of mix of colors is abolished." He characterized his use of forms in similar terms, as "a generalized real design in essential objective values."[30]

144 Van der Leck, *Havenarbeid* [*Dock work*], 1916. Oil on canvas, 89 × 240 cm. Rijksmuseum Kröller-Müller, Otterlo.

After the experiments in which he started from the natural curved line and gradually arrived at the straight line as an elementary form, van der Leck seems to have reduced his colors, too, to their origins. In any case, he chose time and again the primary color closest to the natural one. In *De storm,* for example, the beach is yellow, the sea is blue, and the women wear the colors of the local costume: black and blue. The red of the boat can be interpreted as a "reduction" of brown; the somewhat problematic red color of the horse in *Havenarbeid* can be explained similarly. The rest of the coloring in *De storm* poses few problems when this color-reduction system is kept in mind. The only irregularity here is the blue ship; perhaps this is a reduction of blue-gray. (The smoke in the painting is also blue.) That van der Leck indeed practiced such reduction is evidenced by the fact that human figures and objects in the foreground sometimes "flow" into the background. For instances, the yellow aprons of the longshoremen at the right in *Havenarbeid* continue into the large yellow plane. If van der Leck had not taken the natural colors as a starting point for the primary colors, he could have separated these forms by using a different color arrangement.

The small painting *Kinderspeelgoed* [*Children's toys*], which originated around the same time, is a singular experiment in color. Here van der Leck represented, against a white background, three dolls in the complementary colors orange, purple, and green, and also gray—that is, the mixed shades of the primaries and of the two noncolors. The style of painting here is similar to that of the works that immediately predate *De storm* and *Havenarbeid;* the uniformly colored planes are outlined, and the three dolls are distributed randomly over the picture plane. Apparently, van der Leck was not very happy with these complementary colors; in any case, no further experiments in this direction by him are known. His decision to use primary colors—in tonal qualities balanced separately for each painting—was abrupt but definitive.

The influence of Mondrian

Van der Leck was probably working on the above-mentioned paintings when he met Piet Mondrian. In April 1916, van der Leck moved to Laren, where Mondrian was already living, and a friendly contact soon arose between the two. It is not known whether they had already met, perhaps in The Hague; their connections with Bremmer, Walrecht, and the collector van Assendelft make this seem likely.[31] At any rate, they probably had seen each other's works in Mrs. Kröller-Müller's collection.

The earliest indication that van der Leck and Mondrian knew each other is a letter dated May 17, 1916, in which Mondrian wrote to van Assendelft: "Yesterday I played billiards with v. d. Leck." Another letter, dated August 1 of the same year, suggests that the contact was more than superficial. In this letter Mondrian wrote to Bremmer: ". . . it pleased me to find in van der Lek a man who aims for the same direction."[32]

In paintings such as *Arabieren,* van der Leck had, by using a flat white background and by seemingly distributing the forms carelessly over the picture plane, already succeeded in opening up the composition. Now he made a further step and opened up the form itself. Figures were no longer represented as colored silhouettes, but were reduced to fragments of contour lines and small geometric elements, positioned separately on the white ground. This must have been influenced by Mondrian's work of 1915–16. In his *Compositie X* (figure 40 above), Mondrian had placed black horizontal and vertical line fragments on a white ground, grouped within an oval. Mrs. Kröller-Müller had immediately acquired this painting in 1915, and van der Leck may have seen it in her collection.

Mondrian's influence is perceptible for the first time in van der Leck's design for a poster for the Haagse Volksuniversiteit. With great effort, one can discern four "studying heads" stylized in straight black outlines against a white ground. The eyebrows and the nose of each head are represented by a simple T. Between these heads are three stylized forms representing writing hands.[33] The black lines are placed horizontally and vertically, but also—in a departure from Mondrian—diagonally.

Van der Leck's paintings were consistently called "compositions" until 1918, and that title recurred occasionally as late as 1921. In these paintings, the figures are schematized so drastically that they are nearly unrecognizable. More often than not, one needs the preliminary studies in order to determine what subject served as the starting point. Since in a number of cases entire series of preliminary studies have been preserved, it is possible to follow step by step how van der Leck arrived at his compositions. Some of these studies have been reproduced extensively in the literature.[34]

The process that van der Leck called *doorbeelding* [decomposition] went as follows: Starting from a rather naturalistic study, which he often had made years before, he reduced the subject to flat figures and then to geometric patterns in which the forms were separated by narrow white strips. In successive stages, he gradually covered more and more color with white paint until only small geometric color planes on a white ground remained. This method of abstraction, which van der Leck mastered in 1916, was crucial for his further development. It was to remain his principal working method for many years to come, albeit with some minor changes.

The influence of Mondrian, which is so clearly visible in van der Leck's poster design for the Haagse Volksuniversiteit, can also be traced in his uncommissioned work. Apart from the title of the finished work, the extant sketches of van der Leck's *Compositie 1916, no. 1* reveal Mondrian's increasing influence. In one of the first designs (figure 145), a portrait was drawn in pencil in some detail. Afterward, some planes were colored in gouache—making this the earliest extant preliminary study with bright primary colors—and the nose, ears, jaw, and neckline were painted over with white. In the upper right corner was scrawled one of the dolls' heads from *Kinderspeelgoed;* thus, van der Leck must have made this study while he was working on that painting.

Judging from this first study, the portrait may have been meant to resemble (stylistically) *De storm* and *Havenarbeid.* However, in another study (figure 146) the abstraction became very radical; here the subject was represented only by a number of horizontal and vertical line segments. The choice of these linear elements can certainly be traced to Mondrian's "plus/minus paintings," although van der Leck's lines were red, yellow, and blue rather than black. In the finished painting (figure 147), the beveled edges of the study were eliminated and only rectangular bars remained.

Much confusion has arisen about *Compositie 1916, no. 1.* In van der Leck's preliminary studies, the proportions and the manner of dress suggest an adult woman. Over the years, the painting acquired the subtitle *Noortje*—the name of the painter's eldest daughter. It is not clear exactly when this title came into use, or whether it was due to van der Leck himself; however, the latter is probably not the case—Noortje was only 3 years old when the painting was made, so she cannot have been the model. Recently a small first sketch for this composition was discovered in the artist's estate, and in it the subject can be recognized as his wife, Bertha.

The earliest documentation on *Compositie 1916, no. 1* is a source of more confusion. In Bremmer's 1917 catalog of the Kröller-Müller collection, the work is mentioned under no. 234 as follows: "Composition I. Colored stripes in red, yellow, blue, black. Casein paint on eternite 50 × 44.5. Painted in 1916."[35] No black stripes occur in the painting as it now exists; still, this description must bear on *Compositie 1916, no. 1,* as the technique and the format fit. In the 1921 catalog of the collection, this painting is described in the same manner.[36] However, the 1928 catalog, which is supposed to list only the acquisitions from the years 1921–1927, mentions under no. 802 a work described as follows: "Portrait. Painting in small colored bars of blue, yellow, and red on white ground. Casein painting on eternite, 50 × 45. —Marked in back: B. v. d. Leck '16 No. 1."[37] Can this mean that the painting was acquired twice? One could conclude from the small difference in the descriptions that van der Leck changed the work in the meantime. The changes cannot have been drastic, however; the paint is rather thin, and no reworking is visible. Exactly what went on with

145

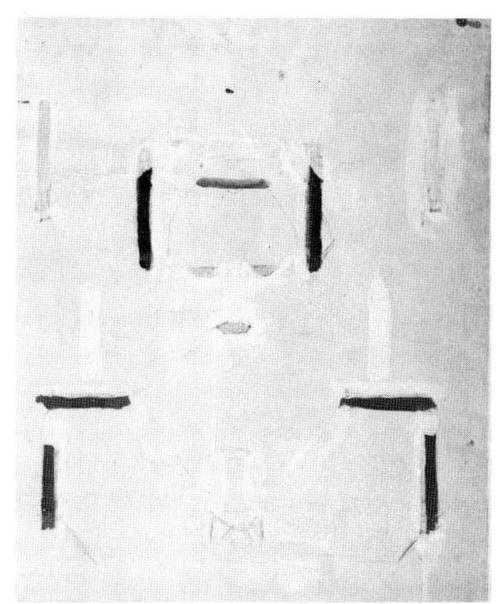

146

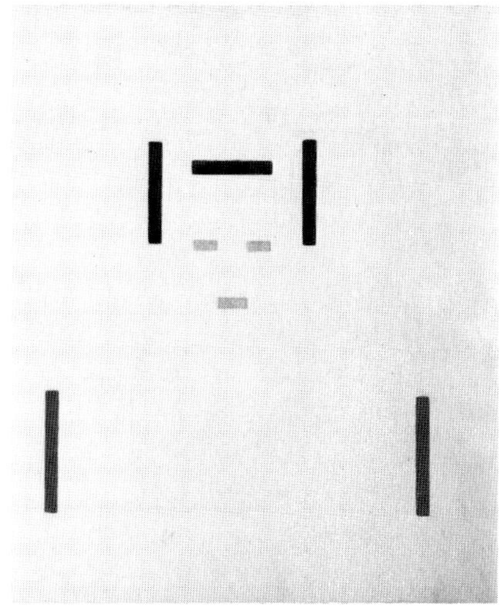

147

145 Van der Leck, study for *Compositie 1916, no. 1*. Gouache on paper, 46 × 48.5 cm. Rijksmuseum Kröller-Müller, Otterlo.

146 Van der Leck, study for *Compositie 1916, no. 1*. Gouache on paper, 46.5 × 40.5 cm. Rijksmuseum Kröller-Müller, Otterlo.

147 Van der Leck, *Compositie 1916, no. 1*. Casein on eternite, 50 × 45 cm. Rijksmuseum Kröller-Müller, Otterlo.

148 Van der Leck, *Compositie 1916, no. 4* (*Mijntriptiek*). Oil on canvas; 113 × 110 cm (center panel), 113 × 56 cm (each side panel). On loan to Gemeentemuseum, The Hague, from Rijksdienst Beeldende Kunst.

Compositie 1916, no. 1 is difficult to ascertain, but there are no real reasons to doubt that this was the first of van der Leck's paintings in which the artist had absorbed the influence of Mondrian.

Whether this influence continued in van der Leck's next few paintings is not known. The 1917 and 1921 catalogs list a *Compositie II* and a *Compositie III* from 1916, but these works have disappeared without a trace; not even reproductions are known. Consequently, we do not know what they looked like, what the subjects were, or when and how they disappeared from the Kröller-Müller collection. From their descriptions in the catalogs it can be deduced only that they were large paintings with stripes in primary colors and black; the color of the ground is not mentioned, but it was probably white. It appears that these were van der Leck's last paintings on eternite; after them he went back to canvas.[38]

The last work van der Leck painted in 1916 was *Compositie 1916, no. 4,* better known as the *Mijntriptiek* [*Mine triptych*]. In the middle panel of this triptych, the entrance to a mineshaft, with mounds around it, is depicted (in very abstract fashion) against a white ground. Starting from a 1914 sketch, van der Leck decomposed the image a number of times[39] until nothing was left but primary-colored and black stripes. By beveling many of these stripes, van der Leck was already distinguishing himself from Mondrian. All but a few of the stripes are horizontal or vertical, yet the middle panel gives a sensation of depth because the bevels follow one another with a certain regularity and because the line segments are grouped according to color. Moreover, the robust diagonal white bands left between the small colored planes work perspectively toward the center of the composition. In the side panels, two human figures—miners—can be recognized with much effort. They are placed against a black ground. This is exceptional for van der Leck—apart from a 1913 still life, this is his only departure from his familiar white ground. In this case, however, the use of black can be readily explained: It suggests the darkness of the mine.

Van der Leck's choice of the triptych format, with its strong religious tenor, seems rather at variance with the secular motif. If the tradition of this format is applied to this work, the mine must be seen as the center of worship, and the miners as saints. It is typical of van der Leck that he brought his usual theme of labor to an apotheosis in a form so heavily laden with meaning.[40]

In accordance with his contract, van der Leck sent his works from the second half of 1916 to Mrs. Kröller-Müller at the end of that year. His patroness' reaction, in a letter dated December 11, was honest but disappointing: ". . . You will certainly not take it amiss when I tell you that I cannot look at them at present. Maybe time will teach me to do so." Two months earlier, in regard to the poster design for the Volksuniversiteit, she had already expressed her concern that van der Leck had been too strongly influenced by Mondrian's "line art." In this letter, dated October 18, she showed a clear understanding of the difference between the two painters: "Mondrian always reveals a mood, and therefore he still fascinates us, although we cannot affix any ideas to his work. But you give us a fact as an abstraction, which you interpret in lines. There is no moment of mood, nor any mystical feeling."[41] Actually, van der Leck still felt a strong commitment to concrete reality. In response to the letter of October 18 he wrote that he "always had a hold on life." He continued: "Fate has always been to me like a strong, inevitable, oppressive force. . . . No illusion, not a mood, no fascination, but a monumental clarity is my aim."[42] He dismissed Mrs. Kröller-Müller's criticism with characteristic stubbornness, and he expressed the hope that she would develop the right insight in due time. This wish never came true, however; Mrs. Kröller-Müller (and Bremmer, for that matter) never completely accepted van der Leck's rigorously abstract works of 1916 and the following years.

Theo van Doesburg, by contrast, was enormously enthusiastic about van der Leck's new work. Although it is not certain exactly where and when they first became acquainted, it is mentioned in a letter of August 31, 1916, from Huszár to Beekman that "Th. van Doesburg . . . visited [van der Leck] in Laren" at least once that summer. A subsequent letter from Huszár, dated September 13, confirms that van Doesburg saw van der Leck's studio during that visit and disputes the gossip that van Doesburg found van der Leck's latest work to be "in the style of Mondrian." On the contrary Huszár stated, "D[oesburg] was very much impressed by the canvas and discerned a different point of view."[43]

In mid December 1916, van Doesburg wrote asking van der Leck to send some photographs for lectures and publications. Van der Leck suggested that van Doesburg make his own choices from the Kröller-Müller collection and take his own photos. Van Doesburg let no grass grow under his feet; on December 31 he wrote to van der Leck that he had viewed the Kröller-Müller collection in the company of Huszár. Van Doesburg was apparently very impressed with the works of van der Leck he had seen there. He particularly praised the definitive version of the *Mijntriptiek* (which he may have seen in an earlier phase during his summer visit to

149

150

151

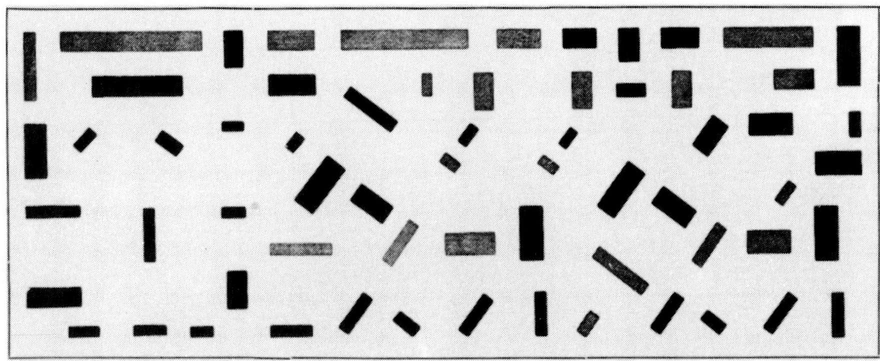
152

149 Van der Leck, study for *Compositie 1917, no. 5/6* (*Ezelrijders*) [*Donkey riders*]. Gouache on paper, 65 × 159 cm. J. P. Smid collection, Kunsthandel Monet, Amsterdam.

150 Van der Leck, study for *Compositie 1917, no. 5/6* (*Ezelrijders*). Gouache on paper, 65 × 150 cm. J. P. Smid collection, Kunsthandel Monet, Amsterdam.

151 Van der Leck, study for *Compositie 1917, no. 5/6* (*Ezelrijders*). Gouache on paper, 61 × 150 cm. J. P. Smid collection, Kunsthandel Monet, Amsterdam.

152 Van der Leck, *Compositie 1917, no. 5* (*Ezelrijders*). Oil on canvas, 64 × 152 cm. As illustrated in *De stijl* 1, no. 1 (1917), appendix I. Now in private collection.

153 Van der Leck, study for *Compositie 1917, no. 1/2* (*Hondekar*) [*Dog cart*]. Gouache on paper, 41.5 × 57 cm. Private collection.

154 Van der Leck, *Compositie 1917, no. 1* (*Hondekar*). Oil on canvas, 45 × 63 cm. Private collection.

Laren). The enthusiasm inspired by van der Leck's works is evident in the works that van Doesburg and Huszár produced shortly thereafter.

In the above-mentioned letter of December 31, 1916, van Doesburg interpreted and evaluated van der Leck's works in the manner of an art critic. He wrote that he "never [had] had the opportunity to admire such a fully developed oeuvre," and he characterized van der Leck's recent work as a "rhythmically visual transformation of universal life." He found the *Mijntriptiek* the best work, because in it "universal qualities of life [were] resolved in harmony with the pure means of painting." Van Doesburg announced his intention to write a "standard work" on van der Leck, but this plan was never realized.

1917: Paired paintings

In the second half of 1916 van der Leck had been working exclusively with colored line segments. In 1917, he began to experiment with lines and planes, as had Mondrian. Mondrian had combined lines and planes in the pair of paintings entitled *Compositie in kleur A* and *Compositie in kleur B,* but van der Leck experimented with them in a very idiosyncratic fashion. Starting from a specific theme, he made two paintings at a time—one with thin lines only and one with planes as well as lines. In 1917 he produced eight such paintings, based on four themes. The compositions were not numbered consistently in the sense that the "thin" version always had a lower number than the "thick" one, or vice versa.

The preliminary studies for three of the four pairs reveal that van der Leck, using the decomposition process, first arrived at the "thin" version. (See figures 149–151.) The representation was opened up into colored bars of different lengths but equal width. Only in the "thick" version (figure 152) was more variation brought into play, through the use of color planes; it addition to somewhat thicker bars, rectangles and squares occurred. In 1917, van der Leck used only rectangular forms (probably at Mondrian's instigation), but unlike Mondrian he sometimes placed them diagonally across the picture plane.

In his choice of subjects for these paintings, van der Leck let himself be guided by earlier themes, which he reused in strongly modified form. For instance, compositions 1 and 2 hark back to the dog-cart theme van der Leck had worked with in 1912. Now, he used a background of a row of trees and a meadow (figure 153). The two paintings that were made after this sketch show how little representation mattered by this time. In *Compositie 1917, no. 1* (the "thin" version of the dog-cart motif), the man is decapitated (figure 154). In *no. 2* (the "thick" version), he is missing a foot. The

153

154

only thing still linking the various parts of a figure or an object was the color, which according to the aforementioned system was always as close to reality as possible. (Thus, in *no. 1* the tree trunks were represented in red and the leaves in blue.)

Like the dog-cart compositions, compositions 3 and 4 hark back to much earlier work. They show a superficial resemblance to the 1910 painting *Uitgaan van de fabriek.* The architectural background in these compositions was derived from that painting, but the workers were positioned differently: They were shown moving from left to right across the canvas.

Compositie 1917, no. 5 was reproduced in the first issue of *De stijl.* Theo van Doesburg revealed the origin ("donkey riders in Spanish landscape"[44]), and apart from a minor geographic error his analysis was quite correct. The preliminary drawings show that this painting (like its counterpart, *Compositie 1917, no. 6)* was derived from *Arabieren.* However, the various elements, which were distributed separately over the picture plane in *Arabieren,* were put on a common plane in the studies for the 1917 paintings; the central rider was more or less crowded out. Of the palm tree, only the trunk was left—a vertical red bar. The well was gone, but the theme of water had returned in the form of a jar carried by a child.

In his comments on *Compositie 1917, no. 5,* van Doesburg stressed that it had not been van der Leck's intention to imitate nature: ". . . the accent is not on reality but on the aesthetic-visual experience of reality." This experience was brought about by the equilibrium between "stability (derived from landscape)" and "movement (derived from the donkey riders)." Because the oblique lines (expressing movement) were enclosed by horizontal and vertical lines, the diagonal did not dominate the composition. A compromise had been reached between stability, movement, and space, causing "the totality to remain *at rest* and the proportions of light (= color) and space to have a purely *pictorial decorative* effect."[45]

Van der Leck's next works, *Compositie 7* and *Compositie 8,* were based on the motif of a mountain scene with a village, which he had recorded in one of his sketchbooks in 1914. In these paintings the subject is much more difficult to recognize, particularly because there are no clear points of focus such as humans or animals.

These four pairs of paintings constituted van der Leck's entire production of 1917. Their number is quite small, but they were of great importance in the development of van der Leck's work and that of the other De Stijl artists. Mondrian, van Doesburg, Huszár, and Vantongerloo all digested the ideas they had received from van der Leck's work, each in his own way.

Contributions to *De stijl*

Van der Leck and Mondrian, out of their mutual appreciation, had thought of forming an association of painters as early as 1916. This can be deduced from a letter to Kok (dated August 6, 1916) in which Theo van Doesburg noted that there was some talk about Huszár's wanting to resign from De Anderen and join up with van der Leck, Mondrian, and other "very conscious ones." In the same letter, van Doesburg said that, at Huszár's instigation, he was thinking of leaving De Anderen himself and joining the new association. During the course of 1917, probably because van Doesburg was encountering more and more obstacles to getting his articles published and because Mondrian thought that the time to publicize his theories had come, the idea of starting a journal began to overshadow the plan for a new association.

However, van der Leck's actual contribution to *De stijl* was very slight. He published only two articles, both in the first volume. These articles reveal an unabated interest in monumental art; both make a plea for linking painting with architecture. This idea regained currency for van der Leck when he received another commission from Hélène Kröller-Müller around the end of 1916. H. P. Berlage was renovating the villa Groot-Haesebroek for the Kröller family, and van der Leck was asked to determine the colors for the "art room." Again, however, the collaboration did not work; there was competition between van der Leck and Berlage. On December 18, van der Leck wrote to Mrs. Kröller-Müller about the roles of the architect and the painter: "The more rigid and plain, without color and line or form, without profiles, without overstepping the essence of his trade, the purer an architect the architect will be. And the architect who wants to work with colors or form or line does so, although unconsciously, in order to disguise his lack of clarity in his own trade. . . . the renewal of painting starts with the treatment of the plane created by the architect." The new impetus of this view of art would emerge through "the organic integration of the beauty of contemporary artworks into the everyday environment of life." At any rate, van der Leck had very little opportunity to introduce his painting into the scheme for the art room at Groot-Haesebroek, since most of the wall space was taken up by paneling, ornamentation, and three enormous display cabinets designed by Berlage specifically for this room. Except for the floor, only a narrow strip on the walls adjoining the ceiling remained for van der Leck to decorate. This he proposed to fill with such overpowering primary-colored bars and planes that it was too much for Mrs. Kröller-Müller or for Berlage.[46] The design was never executed.

One might conclude from reading van der Leck's articles in *De stijl* that they were written in somewhat spiteful reaction to the failure of his collaboration with Berlage. In particular, the second article, "Over schilderen en bouwen" ["On painting and building"], in the February 1918 issue, has this flavor. Here van der Leck, rather uncompromisingly, claims that modern painters—i.e., those whose painting has achieved its "essence"—have a monopoly on the use of color in architecture, and that architecture need only be pure and neutral. In "De plaats van het moderne schilderen in de architectuur" ["The place of modern painting in architecture"], which appeared in the first issue of *De stijl,* van der Leck had tried to analyze the differences between painting and architecture in this manner and had concluded that the two disciplines, if handled in a modern way, need each other and complement each other perfectly—that architecture, which is enclosed, colorless, and space-limiting, is opened up by painting, which is open, colorful, and space-creating. Architecture needs painting in order to create open space. However, this dependence is mutual; painting should "make immediate use of the surface created by *architecture.*" Here van der Leck revealed that it was still his deepest wish to create mural paintings—that is to say, monumental art. It is a justifiable assumption that van der Leck created autonomous paintings as a provisional realization of his ideas; there were still not enough opportunities for the creation of dignified monumental art, and he probably viewed his paintings largely as exercises for the "real thing."[47]

1918: Complete abstraction?

In the last sentence of his first article in *De stijl,* van der Leck wrote that modern painting "converts the representation of visual reality . . . to cosmic values of *space, light,* and *proportion* in which all earthly forms or 'the case' is enveloped and assumed." Van der Leck's use of the terms "earthly forms" and "the case" indicates that in late 1917 he was still starting from reality.

In the literature, the impression has been created that van der Leck relinquished reality entirely for a short time in 1918. In that year (and only then), he is supposed to have created completely abstract compositions of geometric forms, according to the principles endorsed by De Stijl painters. He is supposed to have parted demonstratively with de Stijl in late 1918 with his painting *De ruiter* [*The horseman*] and to have returned definitively to reality.[48] This conception must be reconsidered thoroughly in several respects.

Although the sequence of the 1918 paintings cannot be established with certainty, it may be assumed that the earliest paintings of that year were the compositions numbered from 1 through 5. By title and appearance, these are most closely related to the paintings from 1917. The small color planes are distributed rather randomly, without a clearly discernible system. In 1918, lozenges and parallelograms appeared along with the rectangles and squares; these shapes had not been used in 1917. Apart from this series of five paintings, there appear to be four more paintings bearing only the name *Compositie 1918.* These four works are characterized by more regular arrangements of the color planes. One of the four (shown below as figure 166) can be considered as a transition to the more systematic approach. Apart from a number of seemingly random color planes, this painting has three clusters of black forms, composed of one large and one small square, and two rectangles in varying positions. In the remaining three compositions van der Leck seems to have proceeded in entirely schematic fashion, arranging the small color planes in rotation around the center (as in figure 156). These compositions are nearly mirror images along the orthogonal axes and along the diagonals. Perhaps van der Leck got the idea of such rotations from Huszár, or from van Doesburg (who had been applying this principle to many of his stained-glass windows since early 1917).[49]

In addition to the numbered and unnumbered "compositions," van der Leck made five other paintings in 1918 whose subjects must have been fairly recognizable. These works were exhibited in the spring of 1919 at his one-man show at the gallery Voor de Kunst in Utrecht, and were listed in the catalog as *Naar 'Noortje'* [*After "Noortje"*], *Naar 'Vrouw met koe'* [*After "Woman with cow"*], *Naar 'Boomrooien'* [*After "Pulling up trees"*], *Naar 'Meisje met geit'* [*After "Girl with goat"*], and *Naar 'Man te paard'* [*After "Man on horseback"*].[50]

Thus, van der Leck created three types of paintings in 1918: numbered compositions, unnumbered compositions, and paintings in which the image is fairly recognizable. It is hard to know whether these works were made in the order in which they are described; it is very possible that van der Leck alternated them.

Contrary to the generally held opinion, it appears that at least three of van der Leck's numbered compositions were based on naturalistic subjects. This can again be established from preliminary studies. For example, two studies for *Compositie 1918, no. 2* have been preserved. They show a woman and two children standing in front of a building. To the woman's left is a sort of coal shed. At the right is a tree; in the first drawing (figure 157) only the trunk can be seen, and in the second (figure 158) the leaves are visible. In the process of decomposition, van der Leck painted over large areas with white, deforming and changing the position of some of

155

155 Van der Leck, *Compositie 1918, no. 1.* Oil on canvas, 46.5 × 56 cm. Private collection. (Color plate on page xviii.)

156 Van der Leck, *Compositie 1918.* Oil on canvas, 40 × 32.5 cm. Collection of van der Leck estate, Blaricum.

157 Van der Leck, study for *Compositie 1918, no. 2.* Watercolor on paper, 7.5 × 11.2 cm. J. P. Smid collection, Kunsthandel Monet, Amsterdam.

156

157

158

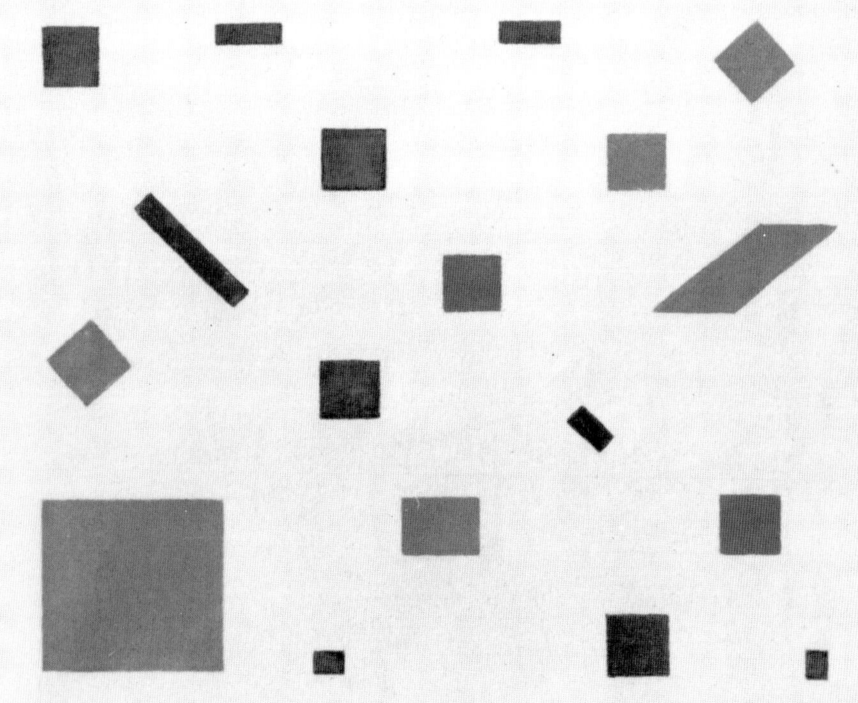

159

the planes. Yet the final painting is clearly linked to the second study, particularly in its colors—for instance, in both pieces the shed is blue, the leaves are also blue (a color reduction of green), the woman's head is yellow, her blouse is red, and her apron is blue. In the painting, the positioning of the color planes was subordinated to the overall composition. This is why the woman and the children came through the process in rather battered condition. The woman's head, her upper body, and her lower body were torn from their natural context, and only one foot remained. The children fared even worse; one no longer had a body, and the other had no head. All the remaining color planes were positioned on diagonal lines. Composition had clearly taken precedence over the representation of the original motif, yet van der Leck apparently was not able, or willing, to relinquish reality completely.

In the case of *Compositie 1918, no. 3,* the relationship between the study (figure 160) and the final painting (figure 161) is indicated by the positioning of the three diamonds and the long diagonal bar. The diagonal bar in the upper corner of the painting is the only form that cannot be traced back to the drawing. The drawing is so abstract that its source is not immediately recognizable, but it is probably based on the same 1914 sketch that van der Leck used as the source for his 1917 *Compositie* 7 and *Compositie 8.*[51] The motif of this sketch is a mountain scene with a village.

Compositie 1918, no. 5 (figure 164) harks back to a farm theme, as is evidenced by a drawing (figure 162) and a gouache (figure 163). In front are two sheep, one standing facing the left and other lying toward the left but with its head turned toward the right. There seem to be two brick walls, a fence, and two peaked roofs. Via decomposition (or, as Bremmer called it, the "unraveling" of the representation), van der Leck progressed from the drawing to the gouache and then to the painting. In the painting, the animals were reduced to six small blue squares and rectangles. The walls recurred as vertical red bars at the sides of the painting, and the fence was transformed into the three black forms in the center. The peaked roofs changed into the two opened-up red triangles under the rectangular forms that border the composition in the upper corners. As in *Compositie 1918, no. 2* and *Compositie 1918, no. 3,* the composition has strong diagonal accents.

Although it has not proved possible to locate preliminary studies for *Compositie 1918, no. 1* and *Compositie 1918, no. 4,*[52] it can be concluded (with some reservation) that in all five of the numbered compositions from 1918 van der Leck still started from a concrete subject, but that the image was of little importance; in the end it only served as a "peg" for the composition. These paintings show a

158 Van der Leck, study for *Compositie 1918, no. 2*. Watercolor on paper, 43 × 55.5 cm. J. P. Smid collection, Kunsthandel Monet, Amsterdam.

159 Van der Leck, *Compositie 1918, no. 2*. Oil on canvas, 45 × 54 cm. Private collection.

160 Van der Leck, study for *Compositie 1918, no. 3*. Pencil on paper, 45 × 54 cm. J. P. Smid collection, Kunsthandel Monet, Amsterdam.

161 Van der Leck, *Compositie 1918, no. 3*. Oil on canvas, 46 × 56 cm. Collection of Mrs. A. R. W. Nieuwenhuizen Segaar-Aarse, The Hague.

160

161

162 Van der Leck, study for *Compositie 1918, no. 5.* Pencil on paper, 51 × 54 cm. J. P. Smid collection, Kunsthandel Monet, Amsterdam.

163 Van der Leck, study for *Compositie 1918, no. 5.* Watercolor on paper, 61.5 × 62.5 cm. Private collection.

164 Van der Leck, *Compositie 1918, no. 5.* Oil on canvas, 70 × 70 cm. Collection of Hannema–de Stuers Fundatie, Heino.

162

163

164

165

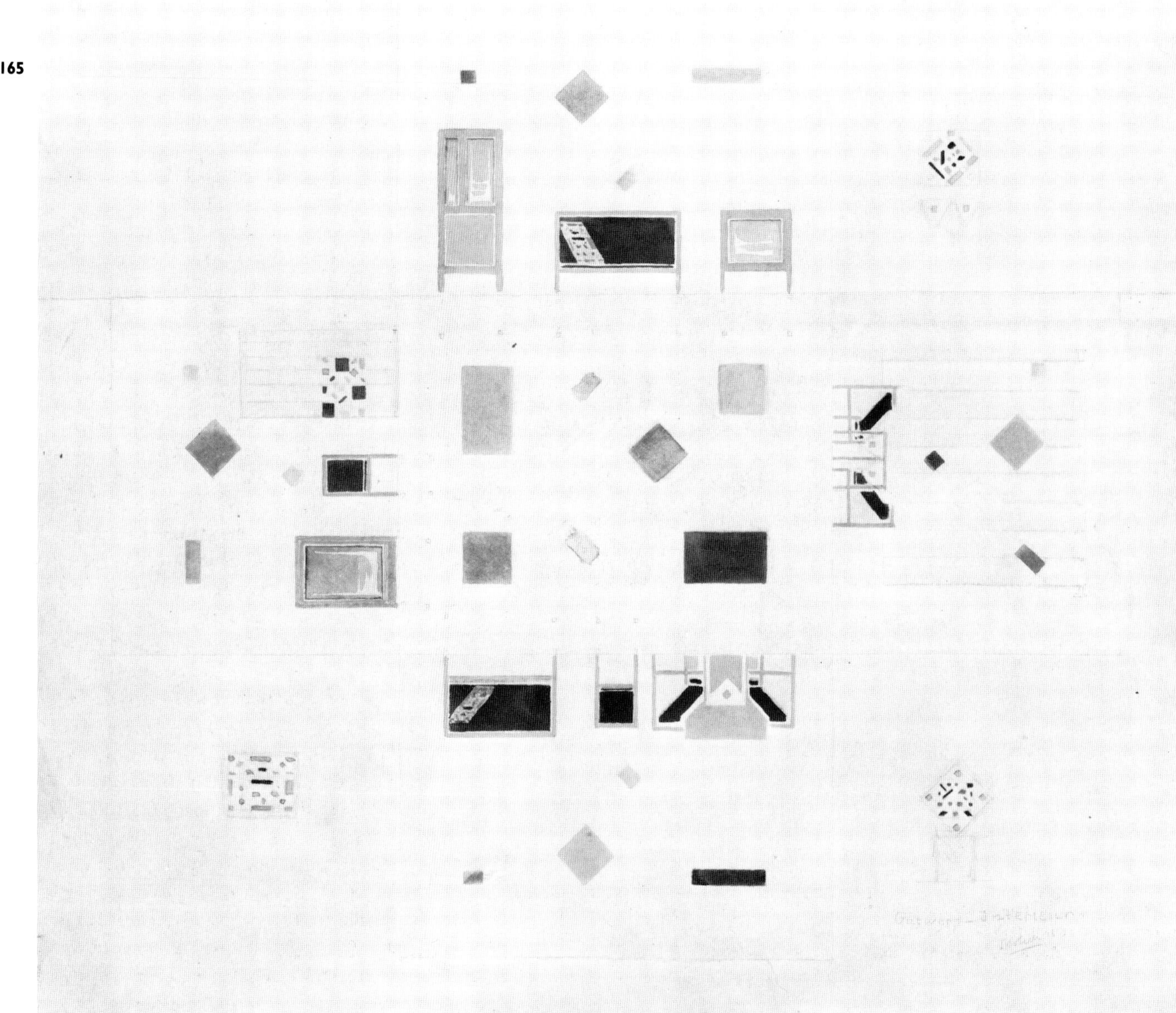

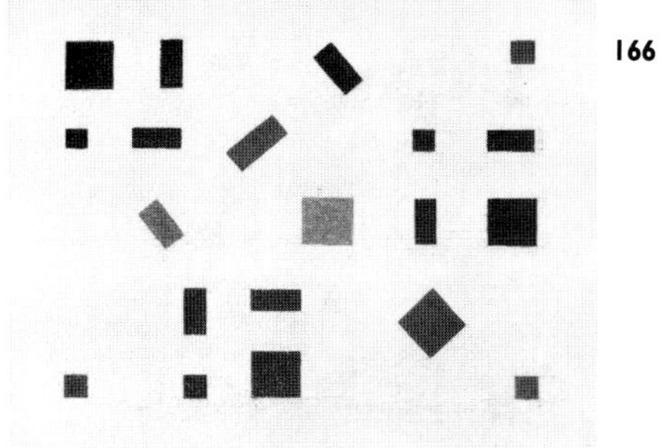

166

167

165 **Van der Leck, *Design-interior*, 1918. Pencil and watercolor on paper, 70.5 × 76 cm. Staatsgalerie, Stuttgart. (Color plate on page xix.)**

166 **Van der Leck, *Compositie 1918*. Oil on canvas, 40.5 × 50.5 cm. Stedelijk Van Abbemuseum, Eindhoven.**

167 **Van der Leck, *Compositie-studie*, 1918. Watercolor on paper, 29 × 31 cm. Collection of McCrory Corporation, New York.**

tendency toward more systematic (diagonal) composition—a tendency also evident, to a much greater extent, in the unnumbered compositions.

It is not clear how the misapprehension of van der Leck's 1918 works as completely abstract compositions of geometric forms came about. Perhaps the fact that no coherent series of designs was preserved had something to do with it. The misconception may also have been caused by an inaccurate interpretation of a term that van der Leck used only once. In the catalog of the Voor de Kunst exhibition in Utrecht, he referred to four 1918 works, somewhat cryptically, as "mathematical images." Van der Leck never used the term again, and it is almost impossible to determine exactly which paintings he meant since neither format nor signature was mentioned. After the four "mathematical images," the catalog mentions a "design-interior" from 1918. The only known interior design by van der Leck from that year is the one shown here as figure 165.[53] This drawing shows a room with the walls, as it were, folded down. The door in the wall at left has a drape over it to keep out drafts, and the right wall is covered with a large drape. Along the walls, a number of cabinets, chairs, sofas, and small tables are projected, with the positions of their legs indicated on the floor. The walls and the drapes in front of the window are provided with compositions in color planes, placed opposite one another like mirror images. On the floor is a composition of larger color planes, probably woven into the carpeting. Aside from the color compositions on the floor and the walls, the drawing also shows four small compositions which are very similar to van der Leck's autonomous work of 1918: The drape hanging over the door is ornamented with small color planes practically identical to those in *Compositie 1918* (figure 166). The upper right corner of the drawing shows, as a tablecloth, a composition resembling an extant gouache (figure 167) which is usually dated ca. 1916–17 but which probably was made in 1918 during the designing of *Compositie 1918, no. 2.*[54] In the lower right corner, *Compositie 1918, no. 3* also recurs as a tablecloth. Finally, at lower left, *Compositie 1918, no. 5* reappears in stretched form as a decoration for the cushions of the sofas. Thus, in the *Design-interior,* three (perhaps four) paintings recur, transformed from autonomous works into patterns for applied art. In an extensive review of the 1919 Utrecht exhibition in the *Nieuwe Rotterdamsche courant,* the critic noted that van der Leck "tends toward applied art" in his mathematical images.[55] Thus, it seems not unlikely that *Compositie 1918, no. 2, Compositie 1918, no. 3, Compositie 1918, no. 5,* and *Compositie 1918* were exhibited by Voor de Kunst under the title *Mathematisch beeld* [*Mathematical image*].

As was mentioned above, several (if not all) of the numbered compositions from 1918 were based on reality. This does not necessarily preclude a mathematical title. In his introduction to the exhibition catalog, van der Leck gives no occasion for thinking that "mathematical images" should be purely abstract. In a rather laboriously formulated creed, he states: ". . . the modern [artist] continues consistently within the substructure of corporal life and arrives at openness of forms within spatial mathematical attachment. . . . In the mathematical truth the entire universal life is expressed. In visual art (painting) the purely mathematical image or gesture is [a] symbol or image of the spiritual experience of the reality of the universe."[56]

Differences of opinion and parting of ways

In the words of van der Leck's creed can be recognized something of the ideas of M. H. J. Schoenmaekers, whom van der Leck had met in 1916 through Mondrian. The sentence "In the mathematical truth the entire universal life is expressed," in particular, seems to be derived from Schoenmaekers's *Het nieuwe wereldbeeld* [*The new image of the world*], in which the universe was defined as a system of forces. Through Theosophy, Mondrian had arrived at a similar theory, and he represented it in his paintings through horizontal and vertical lines. Van der Leck, on the other hand, used diagonal lines as well as orthogonals. These diagonals can be considered the vector sum of forces. Schoenmaekers called them that (embracing the regular laws of mechanics, in which the diagonal serves to calculate the sum and direction of two forces acting together). Although at first Mondrian and van der Leck disagreed about the use of orthogonals and diagonals in the same painting, their difference of opinion was not fundamental. This is evidenced by the fact that Mondrian, in some of his diamond-shaped grid paintings of 1918 and 1919, applied both kinds of lines at the same time. (See figure 47 above.)

However, van der Leck's obstinacy, rather than this minor difference of opinion, was the reason that contact between van der Leck and Mondrian ceased after Mondrian's departure for Paris in June 1919. Van der Leck did not appreciate Mondrian's abandonment of the "openness of forms" (embodied in small separate color planes against a white ground) for which they had both striven in 1917, or his intention to "tie the forms together again."[57] This change was related to the discussion about the figure/ground problem in which the De Stijl painters were involved in 1917 and 1918. Their common aim was to reconcile the painted image with the flatness of the canvas, and therefore they avoided depth. Besides Mondrian, Huszár had come to the conclusion that separate color planes on a white ground did not, visually, stand on one level. Huszár had solved this problem by interweaving color and ground. Van der Leck disapproved of the resulting overlapping of colors, in which he saw depth.[58] Apparently, Mondrian was somewhat more open to Huszár's argument. After his experiment with *Compositie met kleurvlakjes* he began to fit color planes and shades of gray and white into a regular pattern of lines running through an entire painting, thus bringing color and ground onto the same level. No experiments by van der Leck illustrating a need to link separate color planes more closely to their surroundings are known; obviously, his priority was the openness of the painted image.

The discussion of the use of oblique lines is closely related to the figure/ground problem: Hadn't oblique lines in painting traditionally been linked to perspective and thus to depth? As mentioned, Mondrian and van der Leck differed on this question from the beginning; however, each respected the other's viewpoint. In the spring of 1918, a vehement discussion on this subject broke out between van der Leck and van Doesburg. The occasion was van der Leck's request for an article on Peter Alma for *De stijl*. Alma, an old acquaintance of Mondrian, had also become a friend and disciple of van der Leck. Van Doesburg responded that Alma's work "could not be justified as plastic art"; the representation remained too recognizable, and therefore it added a "psychic accent" to the (incorrectly handled) destructive means of visualization. The diagonal compositions of Alma's paintings caused the "space to fall, as it were, out of the plane"; moreover, because of that they were ambiguous in combination with architecture.[59] Van der Leck apparently understood van Doesburg's criticism reasonably well, but nevertheless he saw in Alma's work a start in the right direction—he thought that Alma had freed himself from "the baroque"[60] (which term was considered a curse in the inner circles of De Stijl).

Van Doesburg published an extensive article on Alma's 1918 painting *De zaag en de goudviskom* [*The saw and the goldfish bowl*] in the June 1918 issue of *De stijl*.[61] It was not exceptional in itself that attention was paid to an outsider in *De stijl;* for didactic reasons, the journal often published negative examples. However, the article on Alma had a somewhat wry flavor, not only because it concerned a work by a good friend of Mondrian and van der Leck but also because van der Leck might well interpret the criticism as implicitly directed at him. After some appreciative remarks, van Doesburg attacked *De zaag en de goudviskom* with the same arguments he had used in his letter to van der Leck; he went even farther, calling "this oblique destruction essentially baroque" and dismissing the theory "that in the abstract creation . . . nature should be represented at the same time as well (nature and spirit united)" as a "dangerous mistake." One need only recall van der Leck's 1918 works to imagine his mixed feelings about this article.

The correspondence between van der Leck and van Doesburg concerning Peter Alma took place in March and April of 1918; the article appeared in the June issue of *De stijl.* In the meantime a rather vulgar quarrel arose, more or less independent of any doing of van der Leck's, about a commission for the color design for Robert van 't Hoff's houseboat. At first this commission was promised to van Doesburg. When Huszár heard about it, however, he seems to have told van 't Hoff that van der Leck was a more suitable man for the job because of his experience with interiors over the years. Van Doesburg was very angry about this, and he seems to have suspected van der Leck (who really had no part in the controversy).

Under these circumstances, it is certainly understandable that van der Leck's esteem for van Doesburg flagged, and that his enthusiasm for *De stijl* was dampened. Perhaps there were other grudges. In 1956, van der Leck revealed that he had been convinced at the time of its founding that *De stijl* was to be a "painters' journal."[62] In the literature it is often assumed that van der Leck withdrew as soon as he perceived that there were architects among the contributors.[63] However, a slightly more subtle view should be taken; otherwise it proves difficult to explain why he published an article in the fourth issue (February 1918) when the first three had contained several articles by architects. It is possible that van der Leck's decision to dissociate himself from *De stijl* was prompted by the publisher's attempt to institute a separate editor for architecture, which would have diminished the painters' input.

Van der Leck's artistic differences of opinion about the application of overlaps (with Huszár), oblique lines (with van Doesburg), and separate forms (with Mondrian) were undoubtedly more important. It is not surprising, therefore, that in 1918 van der Leck, nurturing these doubts and objections, did not want to expose himself publicly as a contributor to *De stijl.* When he was invited around March 1918 to participate in a De Stijl exhibition being planned for October, he declined. In the meantime, he exhibited his works separately from the group at the Prins gallery in Laren and at Gerbrands in Utrecht.[64] This must have caused bad feelings among the other De Stijl artists. Van der Leck's unexplained refusal to sign the De Stijl manifesto in the summer of 1918 was not well received by the others, either.

Van der Leck after his De Stijl period

Thus, van der Leck's alienation from De Stijl came about very gradually during 1918. There were no big outbursts, but there definitely were differences of opinion about artistic ideas, and personal animosity. Van der Leck was rather rigid and unwilling to compromise. However, his parting with De Stijl had a less sudden and drastic effect on his paintings than is sometimes stated. In the literature, *De ruiter*[65] is usually cited as proof that he immediately cut himself off from his former associates. Indeed, a figure on horseback can be recognized instantly in this painting, and this almost demonstrative return to figuration is sometimes interpreted as a manifesto of van der Leck's secession from De Stijl and an indicator of his new direction. However, his next works were not exclusively figurative. Until 1921, he alternated recognizable paintings, obviously based on real subjects, with drastically abstracted or perhaps completely abstract compositions.

In the first few years after his parting with De Stijl, van der Leck completed remarkably few paintings. One reason for this may have been that he was occupied with the building of his house in Blaricum, into which he moved in 1919. In addition, he was active in monumental art. He succeeded Huszár as color consultant for an industrial display stand being built by Klaarhamer for Bruynzeel, and he let himself be persuaded by Mrs. Kröller-Müller to collaborate once again with Berlage—this time on the Jachtslot [hunting lodge] Hubertus at Otterlo.[66] As of old, van der Leck was maneuvered into a subservient position—his contribution to the interior was overshadowed by Berlage's brick and tile ornaments.

In his new home at Blaricum, van der Leck could have his own way. This resulted in a design for the south wall of his studio that was a continuation of his 1918 "design-interior"; a central diamond was projected onto a white ground and flanked by three stripes. The positions of the door and the window of the studio (now the living room) of the Blaricum house were designated on the white ground with thin lines that were just barely visible. Strangely, this design is known only as an oil painting on canvas, usually called *Compositie 1919.*[67] This shows once again the extent to which van der Leck went in integrating his uncommissioned art and his monumental art.

A second *Compositite 1919* has also been preserved (figure 168), but it is not quite certain whether van der Leck created this work in direct connection with his living environment. In view of the relatively large color planes, it is conceivable that the painting was meant as a design for a rug—compare the size of the color planes in the rug of the *Design-interior.*

168

168 Van der Leck, *Compositie 1919*. Oil on canvas, 32 × 40 cm. Private collection.

169 Van der Leck, *Compositie '18–'20*. Oil on canvas, 101 × 100 cm. Stedelijk Museum, Amsterdam.

170 X-ray photograph of *Compositie '18–'20*.

169

170

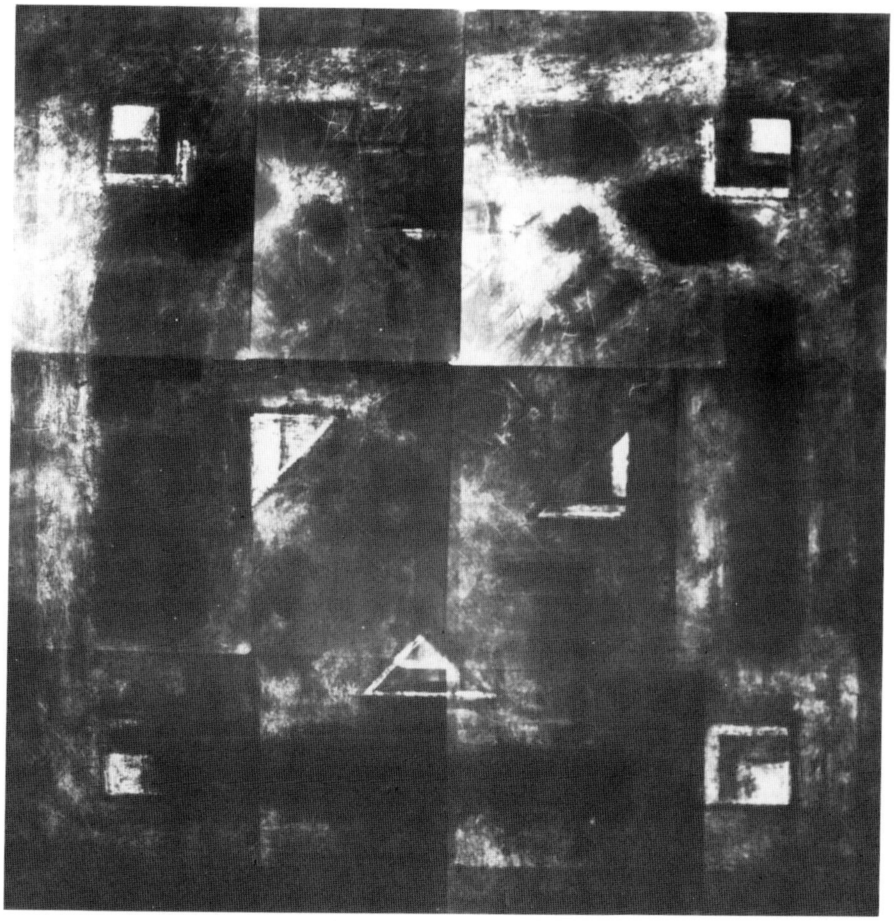

Only a portrait entitled *Jenny* and *Compositie '18–'20* were finished in the following year. The title of the latter indicates that van der Leck had been working on it for a long time. The layers of paint found in some places suggest that elements were painted over. Particularly along the diagonals and between the small squares in the corners, the paint is thickly impasted. Apart from the blue squares in the upper part and the red ones in the bottom part, only four small triangles rotating around the center of the composition are left; the bottom one is blue, the two middle ones are black, and the upper one is yellow.

No design sketches of *Compositie '18–'20* have been preserved, but it originally resembled *Compositie 1918, no. 5* (figure 164). Some new coats of paint appear in exactly those places where *Compositie 1918, no. 5* has small color planes. For instance, in *Compositie '18–'20* the bars that originally connected the four bordering squares, and two triangular forms under the upper squares, have been painted over with white. The supposition that *Compositie '18–'20* is a radical decomposition of *Compositie 1918, no. 5* is strengthened by the fact that each has a square format (rare in van der Leck's work) and, particularly, by the color arrangements in the two pieces. The forms have been changed considerably, but the colors of the various planes of the later composition are in about the same places in the earlier work. From bottom to top this makes for the following similarities: The forms in the bottom corners are red in both cases, the blue triangle appears to be a compressed version of the six rectangles, the two black triangles in the center have been derived from the three original black forms, the yellow triangle can be traced with some difficulty to four yellow rectangles, and in both cases blue color planes serve as closure in the upper corners. Any remaining doubt about the connection between these two paintings is removed by an x-ray photograph of *Compositie '18–'20* (figure 170). The white forms on the x-ray are the color planes as they are visible in the painting. The white ground of the painting comes across as light gray in the x-ray, while the dark gray and black discolorations indicate color planes that van der Leck painted over with lead white. Most of these planes appear to be similar to those in *Compositie 1918, no. 5*.

What prompted van der Leck to first copy the original composition for the most part and then alter it in such a way remains an enigma. Since the representation of reality was already reduced to a minimum in the 1918 composition, it cannot be claimed that in the 1918–1920 composition van der Leck still wanted to represent a natural starting point. Nevertheless, it must be concluded that *Compositie '18–'20* essentially goes back to the farm motif, via *Compositie 1918, no. 5* This conclusion also has repercussions for the unnumbered compositions from the years 1918–1921 (figures 156 and 160), whose strict symmetry contributes to the impression they they are nonfigurative. A symmetrical arrangement apparently does not always preclude decomposition from a naturalistic theme, but in these cases such a theme apparently served only to trigger a process of abstraction which resulted in a composition with a predominantly formal structure.

Van der Leck's gradual return to reality, which had already started in 1918, continued with *Jenny* in 1920. After painting one more "abstract" composition in 1921, van der Leck—until just before his death in 1958—went on, virtually without exception, to paint in a style in which he started from visual reality, which he then translated into geometric forms. In the meantime, his subjects had changed in character. From 1918 on, domestic scenes—families, still lifes, vases with flowers, motifs from nature, and pets—overshadowed the weightier themes. Only the monumental work was still abstract.

This return to recognizable motifs must have been a great relief to Bremmer and to Hélène Kröller-Müller. There are several indications that they were never really able to appreciate van der Leck's work from his De Stijl period. Bremmer never paid any attention to those paintings in *Beeldende kunst,* and in his other publications he always dismissed this phase with a few words. He seems to have been happy that van der Leck had repented. The following quote, from 1946, is a good example: "Now follow two years in which he arrives at complete abstraction, without any representation, and where the visual artist, in my opinion, has been almost completely repressed."[68]

In letters to van der Leck dated December 11, 1916, and January 4, 1917, Hélène Kröller-Müller expressed the hope that in time she would learn to appreciate his far-reaching abstraction. This never came about, however. His work from the De Stijl period is underrepresented in her collection. Moreover, a comparison of different catalogs shows that some works from the years 1916–1918 were once in the collection but were removed from it in the course of time. Even when the collection (which had been in the care of a foundation since 1928) was moved in 1938 to its present home at the Hoge Veluwe, near Otterlo, Mrs. Kröller-Müller refused to take several of van der Leck's paintings from his De Stijl phase along; they ended up with relatives or on the market.[69]

Notes

1
W. C. Feltkamp, *B. A. van der Leck, leven en werken* (Leiden, n.d. [1956]); R. W. D. Oxenaar, *Bart van der Leck tot 1920, een primitief van de nieuwe tijd* (The Hague, 1976). Oxenaar's book contains an extensive bibliography, which includes the articles H. P. Bremmer devoted to van der Leck in his periodical *Beeldende kunst* between 1913 and 1931. In his article "The birth of De Stijl II, Bart van der Leck" (*Artforum* 11, 1973, pp. 36–43), Oxenaar gave an abstract of the ideas he would later elaborate in the above-mentioned book. Translations of this article into Dutch, German, and French appear in *Bart van der Leck, 1876–1958* (exhibition catalog, Otterlo and Amsterdam, 1976), *Mondrian und De Stijl* (exhibition catalog, Galerie Gmurzynska, Cologne, 1979), and *Bart van der Leck, 1876–1958* (exhibition catalog, Institut Néerlandais, Paris, 1980), respectively; these catalogs also contain a wealth of illustrations.

In some respects, Oxenaar's picture of van der Leck's work is open to correction and amplification—especially regarding the years 1918–1920.

2
Biographical data are taken from Oxenaar's *Bart van der Leck tot 1920* (passim).

3
For information on these two schools and their curricula during this period, see A. Martis. "Het ontstaan van het kunstnijverheidsonderwijs in Nederland en de geschiedenis van de Quellinusschool in Amsterdam (1879–1924)," *Nederlands kunsthistorisch jaarboek* 30 (1979), pp. 79–171, and M. Trappeniers, "Antoon Derkinderen als hoogleraar-directeur van de Rijksacademie van Beeldende Kunsten in Amsterdam," in *Antoon Derkinderen, 1859–1925* (exhibition catalog, Noordbrabants Museum, 's-Hertogenbosch, 1980), pp. 52–53.

4
These data are taken from annotations by Mrs. van der Leck; see Oxenaar, *Bart van der Leck tot 1920,* p. 24, n. 77.

5
In his "Open brief als vervolg op verhandeling 1956," written in 1957, van der Leck said that this was to be seen as a first impetus to his use of color from 1916 on. This letter is reproduced on pages 186–188 of Oxenaar's *Bart van der Leck tot 1920.*

6
This cabinet is mentioned in a postcard from van der Leck to Klaarhamer dated March 12, 1904. It is in a private collection.

7
The former is the original title of the painting now known as *De aanbidding van de wijzen;* see *Werken door B. van der Leck* (exhibition catalog, "Voor de Kunst," Utrecht, 1919), no. 10; it is reproduced in *Van Gogh tot Cobra, Nederlandse schilderkunst 1880–1950* (exhibition catalog, Utrecht, 1980), figure 30. On the latter painting, see no. 9 in the 1919 catalog. The whereabouts of this painting are uncertain, but a communication from Mrs. J. A. Klaarhamer suggests that it is still extant. There must also have been a painting entitled *Man with a crown of thorns;* it is mentioned in note 3 on page 186 of A. B. Loosjes-Terpstra's *Moderne kunst in Nederland, 1900–1914* (Utrecht, 1959). In a personal communication, P. Luykx has remarked that Klaarhamer modeled for it.

8
Tekeningen uit de 19de en 20ste eeuw (catalog, Rijksmuseum Kröller-Müller, Otterlo, 1968), p. 181, no. 23. The drawing is reproduced on page 8 of Feltkamp's book (note 1 above).

9
Feltkamp, *Van der Leck* (note 1), pp. 20–21; Oxenaar, *Bart van der Leck tot 1920,* p. 42.

10
The first evaluation of the socio-political aspects of van der Leck's work is contained in Paul Bonaventura's M.A. thesis, *Bart van der Leck, a reflection of the new age* (Courtauld Institute of Art, University of London, 1984).

11
Remarkable in *Naar het vliegveld* (figure 141) is the depiction of an automobile, a motorcycle, and a bicycle. These modern means of transportation were not often represented in works of art of the period.

12
See Oxenaar, *Bart van der Leck tot 1920,* p. 45, note 188.

13
This note is in the Bremmer archive, which is now in the municipal archive of The Hague. The letters van der Leck wrote to Bremmer are also there. On the relationship between Bremmer and Vilmos Huszár see the chapter on Huszár in this volume and also S. Ex and E. Hoek, *Vilmos Huszár, schilder en ontwerper 1884–1960* (Utrecht, 1985), pp. 16–21.

14
H. P. Bremmer, "Arabieren," *Beeldende kunst* 7, no. 2 (1919), p. 19.

15
On the one hand, Bremmer meant by monumentality a generalization of reality, without the interplay of individual emotions. On the other hand, he occasionally used the word as the common denominator of painting and architecture. In some cases Bremmer referred explicitly to the effect a painting would have if executed as a mural; see "Buiten met de fiets," *Beeldende kunst* 6, no. 9 (1919), p. 103, and "De ordonnans," ibid. 7, no. 9 (1919), p. 17.

16
Bremmer, "De ordonnans" (note 15), p. 16.

17
See *Schilderijen van het Rijksmuseum Kröller-Müller* (catalog, Otterlo, 1970), no. 411. The still life is reproduced on page 41 of Feltkamp's book (note 1 above).

18
This letter is partially quoted on page 76 of Oxenaar's book (note 1 above).

19
One exception is *De kat* (1914). However, van der Leck made this painting at Bremmer's request, because the patron's son was fond of cats, and so the choice of subject was not the artist's own.

20
H. P. Bremmer, "De hondekar," *Beeldende kunst* 5, no. 5 (1918), p. 51; van der Leck, letter to Bremmer, March 23, 1918.

21
Van der Leck referred to the "insipid and somewhat allegorical images" in a letter to Bremmer dated February 13, 1914. On Derkinderen, see *Antoon Derkinderen, 1859–1925* (exhibition catalog, Noordbrabants Museum, 's-Hertogenbosch, 1980), pp. 52–53.

22
Letter from van der Leck to Bremmer, February 13, 1914.

23
Brieven van kunstenaars aan H. P. Bremmer, van commentaar voorzien door A. M. Bremmer-Beekhuis (manuscript, 1937–1941; in Bremmer archive, Gemeente Archief, The Hague), p. 246.

24
Werken van Bart van der Leck (exhibition catalog, Kunsthandel W. Walrecht, The Hague, 1913).

25
C. Veth, "Werken van Van der Leck bij Walrecht, Den Haag," *Elseviers geïllustreerd maandschrift* 23 (1913), pp. 319–320.

26
Schilderijen van het Rijksmuseum Kröller-Müller (catalog, Otterlo, 1970), nos. 405, 408–410, 413, 414.

27
The Kröller-Müller collection contains eight designs for this poster; see *Tekeningen uit de 19de en 20ste eeuw* (catalog, Rijksmuseum Kröller-Müller, Otterlo, 1968), p. 188, no. 47. Three of these drawings are reproduced in *Bart van der Leck, 1876–1958* (exhibition catalog, Institut Néerlandais, Paris, 1980); see nos. 34–36. The poster itself is reproduced on page 15 of the latter catalog.

28
This letter was not dated. In note 344 on page 100 of *Bart van der Leck tot 1920,* Oxenaar dates it to early February 1916.

29
It can be assumed that van der Leck was familiar with this play, which criticized the poor social conditions of fishermen. In a letter written in the summer of 1907, he invited Klaarhamer to see the play in Amsterdam.

30
B. van der Leck, "Toelichting van de nieuwe vorm van schilderen" (stencil, 1956), reproduced in *Museumjournaal* 2, no. 9/10 (1957), pp. 148–149.

31
See J. M. Joosten, "Documentatie over Mondriaan (4), tweede deel," *Museumjournaal* 18 (1973), p. 219.

32
Van der Leck's influence on Mondrian is discussed in the chapter on Mondrian in this volume. On page 29 of his article "Mondriaan-architectuur" (*Wonen/TABK* 4/5, 1982), Carel Blotkamp attributes much of Mondrian's thinking about the application of painting in interiors to van der Leck. Mondrian's influence on van der Leck is particularly perceptible in the drastic abstraction and in the fact that during the next few years van der Leck called all his works "compositions," as did Mondrian.

33
This poster (the commission for which was obtained through Mrs. Kröller-Müller) was never realized. An odd set of circumstances surrounds the design. After van der Leck had sent the definitive version (see *Tekeningen uit de 19de en 20ste eeuw,* p. 190) to The Hague, he apparently decided that some changes were necessary. To avoid having the design dispatched to and fro, on August 12, 1916, he sent a retouched photo to Bremmer, asking him to transfer the alterations to the original design. However, Bremmer did not do this, because the design had in the meantime been rejected by the clients. The retouched photo is illustrated on page 53 of C. Blok's *Piet Mondriaan, een catalogus van zijn werk in Nederlands openbaar bezit* (Amsterdam, 1974).

34
See, for example, *Bart van der Leck, 1876–1958* (exhibition catalog, Institut Néerlandais, Paris, 1980), pp. 18–19; *Bart van der Leck 1876–1958* (exhibition catalog, Otterlo and Amsterdam, 1976), material preceding figure S42/43; Oxenaar, *Bart van der Leck tot 1920,* pp. 228–229. The catalog *De stijl, 1917–1931: Visions of utopia* (Walker Art Center, Minneapolis, 1982) contains on page 74 a series of illustrations of sketches (nos. 39–41); no. 40 is reproduced in mirror image.

35
Cat. verzameling van mevrouw H. Kröller-Müller (The Hague, 1917), p. 35.

36
Cat. verzameling van mevrouw H. Kröller-Müller, deel 1: Verzameling op 1 januari 1921 (The Hague, 1928), p. 70, no. 377.

37
Cat. verzameling van mevrouw H. Kröller-Müller, deel 2: Aanvullingen na 1921 (The Hague, 1928), p. 149.

38
This does not imply that the connection between painting and architecture was henceforth less important to van der Leck; see the discussion of this later in the chapter.

39
These sketches are illustrated, in color, on pages 18 and 19 of the Paris catalog (see note 34 above).

40
On pages 10–15 of his *Triptieken in Stijl* (Amsterdam, 1984), Carel Blotkamp deals with the triptychs made by De Stijl artists—particulary the *Mijntriptiek* and its possible sources of interpretation. Bonaventura (see note 10 above) refers to remarkable composition outlines in van der Leck's work, which in his opinion may be related to the triptych form.

41
Apparently, Mrs. Kröller-Müller and Bremmer (the second party of her "us" and "we") did not know that Mondrian was still abstracting from specific motifs in nature. Mondrian's intentions had certainly come across. He wanted to free himself from the accidental appearances of nature, and to evoke a general image of reality by means of horizontals and verticals in equilibrium. Therefore, he did not resent it when Bremmer ascribed to his 1915 painting *Compositie X* a "Christmas mood" when the motif was actually a seascape.

42
From copy of undated letter, dated to October 1916 by Oxenaar (dissertation, p. 111, note 383).

43
Both letters are reproduced on page 191 of Ex and Hoek's *Vilmos Huszár, schilder en ontwerper 1884–1960* (Utrecht, 1985).

44
T. van Doesburg, "Bij de bijlagen. I. B. van der Leck. Schilderij 1917," *De stijl* 1, no. 1 (1917), p. 11.

45
According to a letter to van Doesburg (dated July 7, 1917), Mondrian did not agree. He had told van der Leck that the representation was still too recognizable; for instance, one could still the donkeys. Van der Leck agreed but "still thought that it should be like that for this thing."

46
Van der Leck's drawing, *Voorontwerp interieur, opdracht van mevr. Kröller '16–'17; meubels Berlage,* is in the collection of the Rijksmuseum Kröller-Müller; see *Tekeningen uit de 19de en 20ste eeuw,* p. 190, no. 55. The drawing is illustrated on page 24 of the Paris catalog (see note 34 above).

47
Van Doesburg, too, referred to this possibility. It appears that van der Leck had declined an invitation to participate in the Section d'Or exhibition; in response, van Doesburg wrote on May 21, 1920: "As long as there is no modern architecture that needs, and enables us to achieve, the consequences of our aims, this kind of exhibition will prove as necessary for manifesting the new attitude as *working on separate pieces of canvas by way of exercise.*" (emphasis added)

48
Oxenaar, on pages 135–136 of *Bart van der Leck tot 1920* (note 1 above), clearly distinguished the works of 1916 and 1917 from those of 1918. H. P. Bremmer ["De ruiter," *Beeldende kunst* 7, no. 2 (1919), p. 19] and Feltkamp [*Leven en werken* (note 1 above), p. 58] group all the "compositions" of 1916–1918 together, erroneously labeling all of them completely abstract.

49
It is unlikely, however, that van der Leck ever saw van Doesburg's windows. Perhaps the topic of symmetry and rotation came up during one of van Doesburg's rare visits to Laren. Van der Leck might have seen reproductions of van Doesburg's windows *Dans I, Compositie II,* and *Compositie III* in J. J. P. Oud's article in the *Bouwkundig weekblad* of August 1918.

50
See *Werken door B. van der Leck* (exhibition catalog, Voor de Kunst, Utrecht, 1919), nos. 60–64. Only two of the five works mentioned in the text seem to have been preserved: *Naar 'Noortje'* (mentioned in a number of catalogs) is in a private collection, and *Naar 'Man te paard'* undoubtedly is the painting how known as *De ruiter*—a color lithograph with this motif was featured on the poster that van der Leck designed for the exhibition. No data on the other three works or reproductions of them are known, but the catalog suggets that they were painted in the same manner as *Naar 'Noortje'* and *Naar 'Man te paard.'*

51
See the sketchbook page reproduced on page 228 of Oxenaar's book (note 1).

52
Compositie 1918, no. 4 is in the collection of the Rijksmuseum Kröller-Müller; see *Schilderijen van het Rijksmuseum Kröller-Müller* (catalog; Otterlo, 1970), p. 177, no. 429. It is illustrated in the Paris catalog (note 34 above) as no. 54 on page 49.

53
It is generally assumed—though no sources are quoted—that this design was meant for the house named D'Leewrik [The Lark] in Laren; see, for example, page 137 of Oxenaar's book. There are reasons to doubt this. D'Leewrik was designed and built in 1914–15 by K. P. C. de Bazel on the commission of J. de Leeuw. Apart from the unlikelihood that a renovation would have been commissioned after only three years, it is questionable whether de Leeuw and van der Leck were on good terms in 1918 (communication from Petra Dupuits). Moreover, the many designs and architectural drawings of D'Leewrik at the Nederlands Documentatiecentrum voor de Bouwkunst, in Amsterdam, do not show any room whose floor plan and arrangement of doors and windows is comparable to the *Design-Interior.*

54
Attribution to 1916–17 seems implausible because the sketch shows (stretched) diamond shapes, which van der Leck did not begin to use until 1918. Rotating the gouache a quarter-turn to the left (as in figure 167) brings out some resemblances to *Compositie 1918, no. 2* (figure 159).

55
Anonymous, "Van der Leck, tentoonstelling Utrecht," *Nieuwe Rotterdamsche courant,* January 21, 1919 (evening edition).

56
See *Werken door B. van der Leck* (exhibition catalog, Voor de Kunst, Utrecht, 1919), p. 2.

57
Mondrian had already accomplished this to some extent in his *Compositie met kleurvlakjes* at the end of 1917; he had divided the ground into different tones of gray. Even in 1957, van der Leck still stated that Mondrian did this in order to take the wind out of the sails of those critics who recognized van der Leck's influence on him. He saw in Mondrian's step an essential lack of understanding of the openness of forms. (See "Open brief," note 5 above.)

58
In a letter dated September 25, 1917, Huszár tried to convince van der Leck that he was right: "What you say about placing in back/putting in front, by which means the equivalence of the parts is perturbed (because the planes overlap) is exactly the plastic principle I aim at." [Translator's note: Huszár's Dutch is ungrammatical here, and thus unclear.]

59
Letter from van Doesburg to van der Leck, April 3, 1918.

60.
Letter from van der Leck to van Doesburg, April 8, 1918.

61
T. van Doesburg, "Aanteekeningen bij Bijlage XII. De zaag en de goudvischkom van P. Alma," *De stijl* 1, no. 8 (1918), pp. 91–94.

62
See van der Leck's "Open brief" (note 5 above).

63
Michel Seuphor stated on page 138 of his *Piet Mondrian, life and work* (New York, 1956) that van der Leck told him that he had parted company with De Stijl because of the collaboration of architects. This version of what supposedly happened was taken up by Nancy Troy in her book *The De Stijl environment* (Cambridge, Mass., 1983); see page 16.

64
These two exhibitions were mentioned in van Doesburg's letter to van der Leck of April 3, 1918. It is not known whether they were one-man shows.

65
De ruiter was featured on the poster for van der Leck's first exhibition after his adventure with De Stijl, held in 1919 at "Voor de Kunst" in Utrecht. This poster is visible above Rietveld's sideboard in figure 252 of the present volume.

66
This was Berlage's last project for the family.

67
This painting is neither signed nor dated. The exhibition catalog *Overzicht van het levenswerk van Bart van der Leck* (Stedelijk Museum, Amsterdam, 1949) mentions under the number 54 a *Compositie R,* which is said to have originated in 1917. This composition does not occur anywhere else in the literature; however, its dimensions are those of the work now known as *Compositie 1919,* and the R suggests a connection to the red diamond (in Dutch, rode ruit) in the painting. In my opinion this painting should indeed be dated 1919; the relation to the studio and the very systematic composition make attribution to 1917 improbable.

68
See H. P. Bremmer, "B. van der Leck: 70 jaar," *De groene Amsterdammer,* November 23, 1946. Bremmer's view appears to have had an influence on the first full-fledged monograph on van der Leck, published by Bremmer's disciple W. C. Feltkamp: *B. A. van der Leck, leven en werken* (Leiden, n.d. [1956]). Feltkamp dismissed the period between *De storm* and *Compositie '18–'20* in a few noncommittal sentences, although he did mention that van der Leck himself considered the latter his most important work of this kind.

69
Communication from a descendant of Mrs. Kröller-Müller, who wishes to remain anonymous.

171 Jan Wils (right) and H. P. Berlage, ca. 1925.

Jan Wils

Sjarel Ex and Els Hoek

Jan Wils played only a modest part in the periodical *De stijl.* He wrote two rather contemplative articles about modern architecture, published some designs and some photographs of realized works, and signed the manifesto of November 1918. Soon afterward, a disagreement with Theo van Doesburg resulted in the end of Wils's contributions to the journal. However, he did not turn away from the ideas and ideals of De Stijl. Through Vilmos Huszár he maintained some contact with the others who were involved in it, and he continued the same line in his work.

The designs Wils created between 1919 and 1922 culminated his development toward a modern style of building, which had begun in 1916. Like Robert van 't Hoff and (to a lesser extent) J. J. P. Oud, Wils was inspired by Frank Lloyd Wright's architecture. Of the three charter members of De Stijl who were architects, Wils followed Wright's example for the longest time.

In the formative years of De Stijl, Wils collaborated intensively with van Doesburg and Huszár but had little contact with the others. As far as can be ascertained, he did not even know Mondrian or van der Leck personally. There is evidence from letters that he did know Oud, and that a certain rivalry existed between the two. (To keep the peace, van Doesburg assured Oud repeatedly that he was the only true De Stijl architect.) This rivalry may have been one of the reasons why Wils took refuge in the journals *Levende kunst* and *Wendingen.*[2] However, Wils's designs and executed projects from 1919 on are evidence that he continued to honor the principles of De Stijl. More than van 't Hoff and Oud, Wils put the ideal of monumental collaboration with a painter into practice. In the early 1920s, Wils realized, in collaborations with Huszár and with Piet Zwart, projects that belong among the most important of De Stijl's accomplishments in monumental art.

1912–1919

Wils's contribution to De Stijl coincided with the beginning of his career as an autonomous architect. Born on February 22, 1891, he had studied architecture at the Delft Institute of Technology, rounded off his studies with a trip through Germany, and done practical work in several architectural firms. In 1912 he had worked voluntarily for a short while with the public works department in his native city of Alkmaar.[3] After that he worked with the firm of the architect Johan Mutters in The Hague. Around 1912–13 Wils built a number of rustic houses and vacation homes in Alkmaar and in Bergen aan Zee.

From 1914 to 1916, Wils worked as a draftsman in H. P. Berlage's office in The Hague. Like many other young Dutch architects, he admired the rationality in Berlage's work. Wils's own designs—not only those from this early period, but also the later ones—show Berlage's influence in several respects. Berlage must have considered Wils very talented; it is said that he sent Wils away in 1916 because he had nothing more to teach him.[4]

In addition to his importance as a teacher, Berlage stimulated Wils's interest in the work of Frank Lloyd Wright. After returning from a visit to the United States in 1911, Berlage lectured about his trip and published a book entitled *Amerikaansche reisherinneringen* [*American travel reminiscences*]. He paid a surprising amount of attention to Wright, and soon several Dutch architectural journals published well-illustrated articles on the American architect. Wright's greatest merit was said to be the fact that he had torn himself away from historical forms of building. For instance, the journal *Architectura* quoted Berlage as follows: "Frank Lloyd Wright has an 'aversion to tradition, detests all imitation of style, all formality and convention, and traditional attachment to one type or another,' and . . . [has] achieved the image of his own character, the character of his people, his country, of the situations with which he was confronted in his art."[5] These articles also focused on the richly illustrated book *Frank Lloyd Wright ausgeführte bauten* [*realized buildings*], published in 1910 by Wasmuth in Berlin, which played a crucial role in the establishment of Wright's reputation in Europe. Wils undoubtedly knew that book, but after he went to work in Berlage's office in 1914 his interest in and knowledge of Wright increased.

In 1916 Wils established himself as an autonomous architect in Voorburg, near The Hague. On October 15 of that year he became a member of the Architecture and Arts and Crafts division of the Haagsche Kunstkring [Hague Art Circle].[6] Around that same time he must have met Theo van Doesburg. It is difficult to trace how the contact was established, in part because no correspondence is known to be extant. It is possible that Wils met Vilmos Huszár at the Haagsche Kunstkring, and that Huszár introduced him to van Doesburg. However, it is more likely that van Doesburg took the initiative. As his letters to Oud show, van Doesburg was looking desperately for a commission on which he could collaborate with an architect. In November 1916 Oud gave him the names of a number of architects whom he had met at Berlage's. Wils was, presumably, among those listed. Shortly thereafter, Wils and van Doesburg must have met.[7]

During the course of 1917, van Doesburg and Wils entered into a collaboration much like the one van Doesburg had started with Oud a short while earlier. (See the chapter on van Doesburg in this volume.) Wils was commissioned to design a house for the De

172 **Wils, Sketch of dwelling at Alkmaar, December 1916. Nederlands Documentatiecentrum voor de Bouwkunst, Amsterdam.**

Lange family on Wilhelminalaan in Alkmaar, and van Doesburg was called in to design the colors for the interior and the exterior and to create three stained-glass windows for the stairwell.

The design sketch for the Villa De Lange (figure 172) is, in its concept, its composition, and its coloring, much like Wright's drawings. Wils used only the upper half of the paper. The frontal view of the facade is flanked by two large trees, colored in reddish brown so as to contrast strongly with the light blue sky. Here Wils followed precisely Wright's watercolor of the Unity Church, which was reproduced in color in the Wasmuth book. He even copied details, such as the red flowers in the planters.[8] Given this close imitation, one might expect a revolutionary piece of architecture; however, the Villa De Lange is, on the whole, fairly traditional. Neither the floor plans nor the high brick elevations are very different from those of the average Dutch house of the time. Still, certain details show that Wils was mindful of Wright's work. For instance, the shift in the facade may be considered as a timid attempt to show the arrangement of the interior space on the outside of the house, and the use of windowboxes and planters is an adaptation of Wright's ideas.

The De Lange house (which still stands) was executed a little differently from the design. The pilasters enclosing the windows of the protruding section of the facade reach only as high as the second floor in the design, but in the actual house they reach nearly to the eaves. They are ornamented with reliefs by Willem C. Brouwer, a potter and sculptor who also created two fireplaces in the interior. Moreover, the house was widened near the entrance in order to add extra windows upstairs and down.

Van Doesburg's contribution to the interior of the De Lange house was extensive. He determined the colors for the woodwork and for the fabric wall coverings. In a letter to Antony Kok, dated September 9, 1917, he described his plans for "the colored house" as follows. "Hall: yellow with purple wall covering. Bordered with black, wainscoting bright green. Dining room: wainscoting black, panels gray, freed by means of white. Herein the doors of the sideboard dark-deep-blue, freed by means of bright yellow. Moulding around them green, freed by means of white. Outermost border black. Parlor: predominantly purple; the moulding of the upper wainscoting, running through the purple: green. All planes and panels freed by means of white. Living room adjacent to parlor: everything the opposite of the parlor: predominantly green, moulding purple, everything freed by white. The study is the most magnificent: the bookcase green, black, and white. The wall covering is billiard cloth! Everything freed by means of white. The mantelpiece of green stone with red tiles on the sides. In the middle a glass mosaic designed by me. The doors: black panels freed by means of white. Green wood on the doors. I have also applied red by way of experiment in the daughter's bedroom. Vermilion wainscoting, white wall covering. Washstand: white, red, green, and blue. Everything freed. The ceilings violet, gray, white, etc. Everywhere I have thought of the need of the room's occupant. Thus for instance a girl's room: bright yellow, purple, and green. A guest room for children: yellow and blue. . . . The attic corridor and staircase yellow, black, and white. I have solved the cellars, including the wine racks and the fruit containers. The result is that I have not slept a wink for two nights. I have to think continually of the whole entity. I wonder whether everything proceeds logically coloristically, etc. . . ." Van Doesburg also designed the above-mentioned window and a sculpted banister post.

Van Doesburg's intervention in the exterior of the Villa de Lange was fairly modest. He wanted to destructurize the architecture, as he wrote to Kok in the same letter: "I am applying a black strip around the whole house, which I interrupt by red planes, causing the house to be torn from its stability." Judging from photographs, this idea must have fallen through. Only the woodwork (the fascia and the window frames) was painted in contrasting colors (probably black and white), and this actually accentuated the structure of the facade.

The tool shed in the garden (visible in figure 173) was more extraordinary in its architecture and its color design than the house. The walls were constructed of brick up to about one-third of the height; on top of this were wide horizontal boards, which van Doesburg painted black and separated with white lines. The roof was flat. Just under the fascia was a series of small windows. The door was treated in the same way as that of the house, with dark panels "freed" by white frames and sills.

Wils must have been pleased by van Doesburg's color solution for the De Lange house, and by the collaboration. At least, it is known that he enlisted van Doesburg's assistance in a subsequent project: the renovation of the café-restaurant De Dubbele Sleutel in Woerden.

In 1918 and 1919 Wils published several articles in *De stijl* and in *Levende kunst;* moreover, he lectured before the Haagsche Kunstkring and other audiences.[9] His writings and lectures give a clear picture of the aims he tried to realize in De Dubbele Sleutel. For Wils, architecture was in the first place a composition of spaces, a plastic interaction between rooms: "Every room has been studied in itself in detail, not as a projection, but as a voluminous body." The volume relations were not only to be experienced in the interior but also to be perceived on the exterior. Therefore, designing a building meant "the arrangement of masses; those masses are the different organs of the house." "Architecture," Wils continued, "is not a planar art but a spatial art; that is to say, in the ground plan the masses may be imagined in the plane, but they must be expressed in space as individual masses in a logical mutual relationship in a rhythmic alternation of high and low, light and dark."[10] In De Dubbele Sleutel (figure 174) these principles were carried through rather extensively. Wils had to start from an existing ground plan, but in the elevations he could work according to his own insight. The building was indeed a clear and orderly arrangement of masses. The entirety had a pyramidal shape, with the three-story central part surrounded by some lower parts. The separate blocks were connected at the second-floor level by smooth horizontal concrete strips, between which the windows were situated. The wide chimney, extending high over the roof, worked as a vertical counterbalance. This grouping of masses can be traced back to Wright, but Wils may also have seen an example of a similar structural architecture closer to home, in the village Huis ter Heide, where Robert van 't Hoff had built the Villa Henny.[11] The concrete strips and the positioning and partitioning of the windows indicate that Wils had this house in mind when he designed De Dubbele Sleutel.

It is worthwhile to look more closely at the different types of windows used in De Dubbele Sleutel. Downstairs the restaurant had four very wide windows. Such large, uninterrupted glass surfaces had become possible only recently, with the development of strong plate glass. Thus, the windows of De Dubbele Sleutel were a sort of calling card for the modern architect Jan Wils wanted to be.[12] They were flanked by tall, narrow windows, which could be opened for ventilation. The windows of the second floor were a little higher than their width and had asymmetrical mullions. Wils positioned them in groups between horizontal concrete strips. On the third floor, the central part again had a series of horizontal windows positioned just below the fascia, so that the roof almost seemed to float.

Varied forms of windows, imaginatively positioned, also appeared in Wils's later designs. This is further evidence of the influence of Wright, who had stated in his 1908 theoretical essay "In the cause of architecture" that the necessary openings in buildings, such as windows and doors, were not obstacles that should be spirited away for the sake of design; rather, they could be used to clarify a building's structural unity. Wright linked three, four, or more windows together into a series, creating the effect of a horizontal beam in the wall plane. His window frames were usually recessed into the wall plane, so that a contrast was created between the surfaces of the facade and the glass. Wils quoted

173

174

173 **Rear view of De Lange house, showing tool shed at left. From J. H. W. Lelyman, *Het stadswoonhuis in Nederland gedurende de laatste 25 jaren* (The Hague, 1920), p. 46.**

174 **De Dubbele Sleutel, Woerden, 1918. Photograph in collection of Nederlands Documentatiecentrum voor de Bouwkunst, Amsterdam.**

Wright's ideas about windows and doors several times in his lectures and articles. "The openings should originate logically from the house's structure, they are the natural ornamentation of the building," he wrote in 1918.[13]

De Dubbele Sleutel was a striking building, and it garnered a lot of attention. Robert van 't Hoff reviewed it in the March 1919 issue of *De stijl,* and the authoritative architecture critic Huib Hoste devoted a whole column to it in *De telegraaf* of May 6. "More than once," wrote Hoste, "I was asked why I did not write about the work of the young architect Jan Wils. . . . I wanted to wait, because I suspected that the architect was at a turning point; I thought I saw in his buildings an indication that he soon would achieve something more in his architecture than he had been able to do up to now . . . and I decided to wait until the town house, and the hotel De Dubbele Sleutels, in Woerden, were finished. . . ."

Both Hoste and van 't Hoff reviewed De Dubbele Sleutel as an example of modern architecture. They were very appreciative of the composition of the building volumes, the unifying effect of the concrete strip, the large horizontal windows, and the vertical effect of the chimney. Yet there were remnants of "the old," which they saw as detrimental to the entity. Hoste mentioned the traditional roofing: "The building is covered by slightly sloping roofs with red tiles, which are in my opinion much too hollow; the ridge tiles and particularly their endpieces are definitely offensive." Van 't Hoff criticized the materials—not only the roof tiles but also the bricks: "If constructed in modern materials, such as reinforced concrete, the masses could have had a purer effect in themselves, as well as in relation to each other, which would have enhanced the monumental planar-plastic character even more. Now the latter is broken up too much by the brick walls and the tile covering. . . . Given the materials used—they were partly the cause of the sloping roof—this house is a satisfactory solution as a transitional work toward a completely modern architecture."

In their reviews, both van 't Hoff and Hoste dwelt all but exclusively on the architecture. Van Doesburg's color design was listed, but it received scant discussion—probably because the painting had not yet been completed. It is remarkable that their reaction to the collaboration between a painter and an architect was rather lukewarm. Hoste was the more enthusiastic of the two. Evidently, he knew that van Doesburg had intended to destructurize what the architect had constructed. (Here Hoste used the jargon that Bart van der Leck had introduced in *De stijl.*) Hoste also mentioned the colors of the mullions and the window frames: Veronese green and orange, combined with black and white.[14]

About the tap room of De Dubbele Sleutel, Hoste wrote: "After the painting is finished, that room certainly will be very cozy; I hear that the ceilings as well as the walls will be very colorful; the upper part of the walls, which has the effect of a frieze, must get the same color as the ceilings; this frieze continues very regularly over the top of the inner doors and over the low outside windows, but it has a dead end against the taller bay windows and the wall on Voorstraat." A photograph of this room, although made after the café had been in use for years, gives an impression of the original interior (figure 175). The front of the bar consisted of a number of rectangular color planes, separated by black slats. Dark slats were also applied along the walls and the ceiling. The "frieze" mentioned in Hoste's review is clearly visible.

The Wils archive in the Nederlands Documentatiecentrum voor de Bouwkunst, and some private collections, contain furniture designs by Wils and van Doesburg. The forms and colors suggest that this furniture was meant for De Dubbele Sleutel. According to the inscription, the study of the buffet (not the large bar in the tap room, but rather a tall cabinet) shown here as figure 176 is a *Destructieve compositie.* Van Doesburg broke through the completely symmetrical structure of this piece of furniture by applying colors (blue, green, and orange). The result shows an apparently asymmetrical construction of color planes.

Probably the original plan was for Wils to design the rest of the furniture for De Dubbele Sleutel as well. His archive contains some photographs and a drawing that may be related to the project. The drawing (figure 177) is a design for a chair, colored in red, green, and black. The construction and the distribution of colors are very original. The back is composed of a closed wooden plane, constructed from slats of different widths and a square panel. The panel is bright red; the slats are green and black. A similar distribution of planes and colors occurs in the base of the chair. There the construction has been kept open, however; the alternating narrow and wide legs are connected at mid-height by a slat. All four sides of the base look alike. (One of the photographs in the Wils archive shows an abacus hanging near the billiards table in the tap room, and this abacus shows the same alternation of rectangular elements. This similarity suggests that the chair was also meant for the tap room.) Van Doesburg may have decided on the colors for this chair; however, his name does not appear on the drawing, as it does on the drawing of the buffet.

In the mid 1970s De Dubbele Sleutel, Wils's most important work from the early years of De Stijl, was demolished. Another building from the same time has been preserved, though: a church in Nieuw-Lekkerland (a village near Rotterdam) designed in 1916

175

176

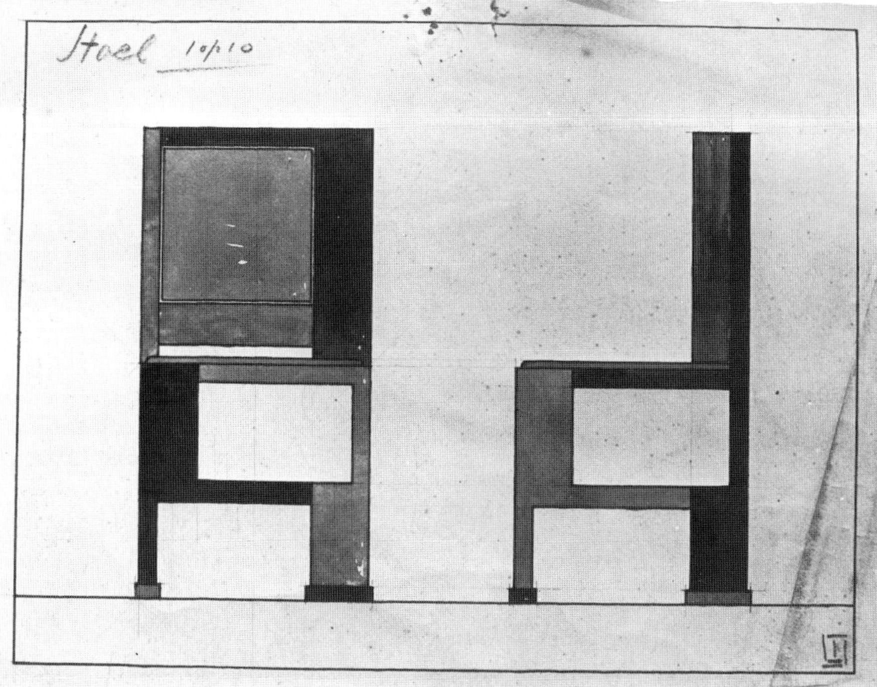

177

and built in 1918–19. This building has a traditional shape, but it does display some modern traits, particularly in the construction of the tower. Different levels are built into the brick facades, and the vertical character is further interrupted by horizontally protruding concrete slabs. An old photograph shows that the marquee at the main entrance was painted in an unusual manner that recalls the marquee and the fascia of the Alkmaar villa; an elongated light plane is surrounded by a dark border. Another photograph suggests that the horizontal concrete strip over the entrance of the tower was "destructurized" with color.[15] It is not clear whether van Doesburg was involved with this project or whether the church only bears the marks of his influence on Wils.

175 **Tap room of De Dubbele Sleutel, 1918–19. Photograph in collection of Nederlands Documentatiecentrum voor de Bouwkunst, Amsterdam.**

176 **Wils (form) and van Doesburg (color), Destructieve compositie III, tekening V, buffet, 1918. 23 × 39 cm. Private collection.**

177 **Wils, design for a chair, ca. 1918. Ca. 18 × 24 cm. Nederlands Documentatiecentrum voor de Bouwkunst, Amsterdam.**

The town houses in Alkmaar

The two town houses at Nassau Square in Alkmaar that Wils designed shortly after De Dubbele Sleutel have been virtually ignored. The drawings for these houses were ready in November 1918, and construction was started in the next year. These houses still stand, their exteriors almost unaltered. Although they were completed after the period during which Wils contributed to *De stijl,* they are good examples of his work as a De Stijl architect. See figures 178 and 179.[16]

Like De Dubbele Sleutel, the town houses express the division of the floor plan in the elevation through the arrangement of block-shaped building volumes. (Van 't Hoff called this "mass architecture."[17]) In this case Wils put small blocks in front and larger ones in the back. For the first time he did not use a sloping roof; here the flat roofs of the smallest blocks serve as terraces. The wide, high chimneys add a strong vertical accent. Along the borders of the terraces and over the window frames he applied wide concrete strips with a coarse, gravelly structure. With their flat roofs and their concrete strips, these town houses were a step beyond De Dubbele Sleutel. They fell short of the De Stijl ideal only in their lack of smoothly finished walls.

The interior designs of the Alkmaar town houses are unmistakably Jan Wils's, although they have undergone many changes over the years. The most interesting thing about these interiors is that they are entirely different from one another, although on the outside the two houses appear as a single complex. The house on the corner is considerably larger than the row house. The corner house is built around a beautiful stairwell, which is literally and figuratively its center. All doors on the ground floor and on both upper levels open onto this high space, which receives light from above. The double-quarterturn staircase consists of perpendicular parts, flanked by banisters with slats. Wils's attention to detail is

178

179

178 Wils, design sketch for town houses in Alkmaar, 1918. Dienst Bouw- en Woningtoezicht, Alkmaar.

179 Wils, town houses in Alkmaar, 1919. Photograph in collection of Dienst Bouw- en Woningtoezicht, Alkmaar.

180 J. Wils (form) and V. Huszár (color), design for spatial color composition, 1920–21. Dimensions and whereabouts unknown; photograph in Huszár's estate.

immediately perceptible in the large living rooms, in which there are magnificent fireplaces lined with square black tiles.

As with De Dubbele Sleutel and the Villa De Lange, Wils called in a De Stijl painter to help with the color determination of the Alkmaar house. This time it was not Theo van Doesburg but Vilmos Huszár. Figure 180 shows a "spatial color composition" probably intended for the hall of the smaller house. Huszár dated this photograph 1920; a second print (now in the Stedelijk Museum in Amsterdam) bears the date 1921, also in Huszár's handwriting. It is possible that he started working on the design in 1920 and finished it in 1921; in any case the collaboration was not planned from the beginning. It is uncertain whether this design was ever realized. No photographs of a realization are known, and no traces of any such painting can be found in either of the houses.

Over the years, the various inhabitants of the Alkmaar houses have removed the original paint and repainted the surfaces according to their own tastes. The only use of color that corresponds to the original scheme is the black on the stair banister of one of the houses. The interiors must have been very colorful in the beginning. The present inhabitants told us that there was a lot of gray and violet, particularly near the stairs. In the smaller house, moss-green paneling, edged by a black frame, remains on the upper level, and remnants on the doors to the garden show that those doors were once blue and violet. In the larger house, there are traces of orange paint on the walls of the top landing. It is possible that Huszár was responsible for these colors, but that cannot be ascertained; Wils had already collaborated several times with van Doesburg, and he also may have handled the color solutions for these interiors by himself.

180

Designs, 1917–1919

Wils's progressiveness is more evident from his designs of the years 1917–1919 than from his realized buildings. In 1917 Wils took part in a competition for the design of a pavilion for the public park of the city of Groningen. His archive contains two designs for this competition, a conventional one and a more daring version; it is possible that he submitted both. The pavilion was to be situated in a cultivated rural setting, without existing floor plans, surrounding buildings, or other restrictions. Therefore, these designs are good indications of Wils's thinking at the time. In the more daring design (shown here as figure 181), the influence of Wright's spacious country houses is clear, and the turrets are strongly reminiscent of the ornamentation on Wright's Midway Gardens in Chicago. Yet Wils's design should not be regarded as a direct quotation. It certainly shows individualism, particularly in the staggering of the windows.

181

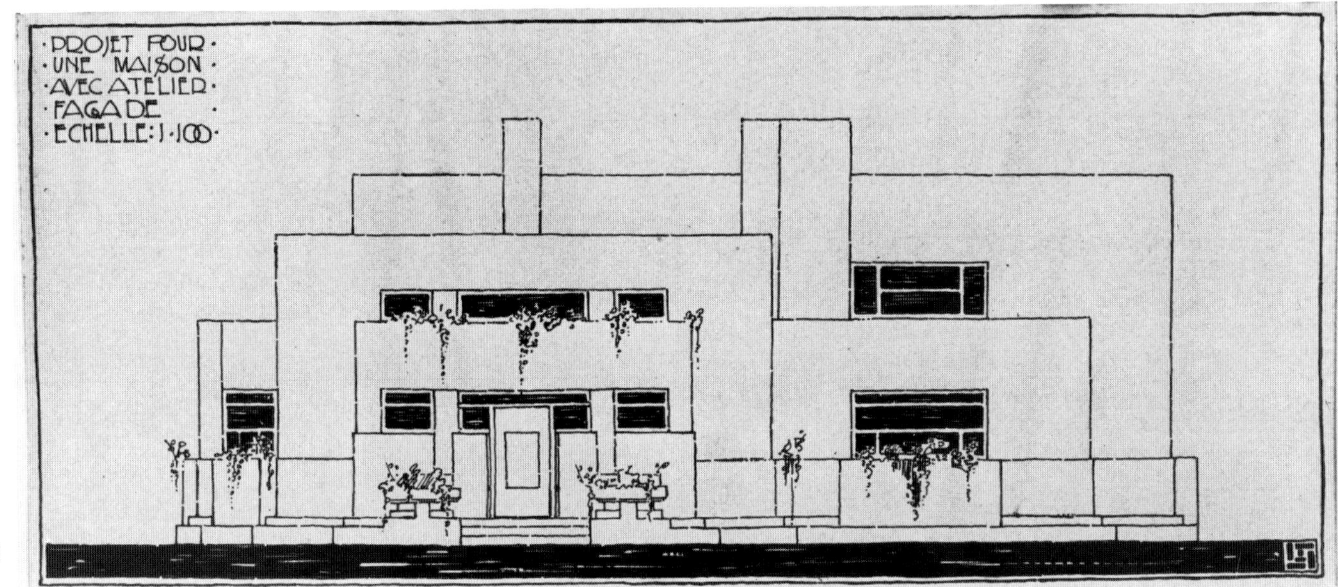

182

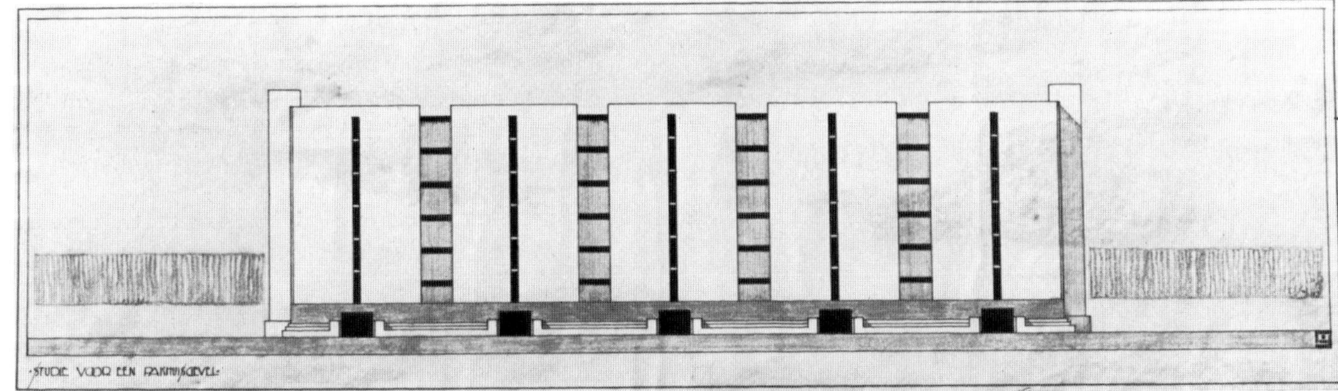

183

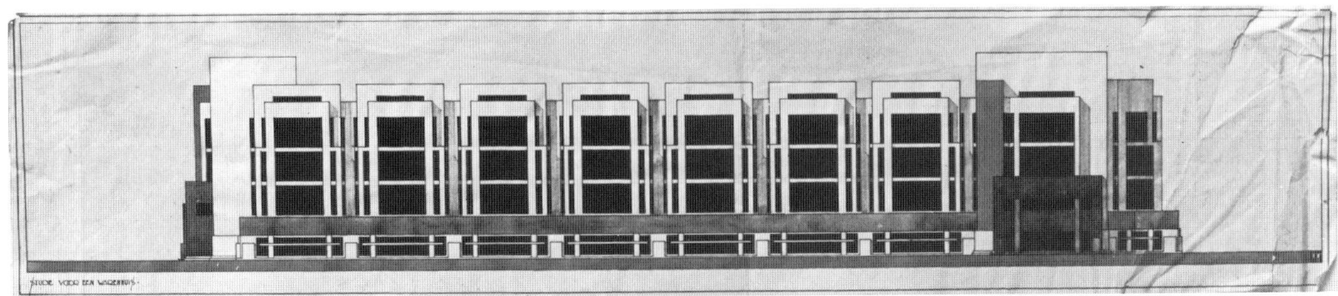

184

181 Wils, design of rear facade for pavilion in public park in Groningen, 1917. Nederlands Documentatiecentrum voor de Bouwkunst, Amsterdam.

182 Wils, design for house with studio, ca. 1920. Nederlands Documentatiecentrum voor de Bouwkunst, Amsterdam.

183 Wils, study for facade of warehouse, ca. 1919. Nederlands Documentatiecentrum voor de Bouwkunst, Amsterdam.

184 Wils, study for department store, ca. 1919. Nederlands Documentatiecentrum voor de Bouwkunst, Amsterdam.

Around 1919 Wils designed two studio-dwellings. One of these designs, dated January 1919, is fairly conventional. It has a symmetrical ground plan based on that of Wright's studio-dwelling for Richard Bock.[18] The pyramidal elevation, also symmetrical, is closed off by a sloping roof. The other design (figure 182), which probably dates from later in the same year or from the beginning of 1920, presents a much more varied picture. Just as in De Dubbele Sleutel and the two Alkmaar townhouses, the asymmetrical ground floor is strongly evident in the elevation; it is a well-balanced composition of separate block-shaped masses. Again, high chimneys provide the necessary vertical counterweight against a wide, predominantly horizontal facade.

Other designs by Wils from the same period are to be found in an important article by H. de Fries in the German architectural journal *Wasmuths monatshefte für baukunst.* This article is entitled "Zu den arbeiten des architecten Jan Wils, Holland" ["On the works of the architect Jan Wils, Holland"]. Besides Wils's rather traditional workers' dwellings in Woerden and his designs for the housing block "Daal en Berg" at Papaverhof in The Hague, this article includes illustrations of two unrealized projects. The first, said to be a design for a villa in Voorburg, shows two cubelike masses connected by an oblong rectangular room (perhaps a studio). The wall of the connecting room is interrupted by alternating horizontally and vertically elongated windows, and a crenellated border is created by the shifting of the horizontal windows. The horizontal profile of the villa is enhanced by overhanging roofs on both sides, and (as in the design for the pavilion in Groningen) antennalike turrets provide vertical accents. The second design illustrated is one for a concrete warehouse (figure 183). It shows a series of five buildings, each six stories high, connected by open passageways. The series is closed off on either end by a narrow entryway extending above the roof, but more units can be added at the rear. The floor plan of each building is square, crossed by perpendicular passages. There was probably to be a service elevator in the center, forming a connection between the floors. The original design drawing has been preserved and is now in the Wils archive. The design is usually dated 1923 in the literature, because of the businesslike and austere appearance of the building. However, it was published in *Wasmuths monatshefte für baukunst* of 1920–21.

The Wils archive contains yet another drawing of a series of building elements (figure 184). The similarity of this design to the one just discussed suggests that they originated around the same time. This complex consists of eight block-shaped buildings, the first and the eighth of which have Wils's typical cubical elevation.

Whereas the warehouse (figure 183) had only narrow windows, arranged in vertical strips, the facades in this design are almost entirely of glass. The legend on the drawing describes this as a design for a department store.

These examples demonstrate that Wils's development cannot be reconstructed just by juxtaposing executed and unrealized projects without differentiation. His works cannot be dated solely on the basis of more or less modernistic traits. Traditional forms connected with the functions of the buildings (house, café, church, etc.) constrained the executed buildings more strongly than they did the designs. In general, the designs appear more revolutionary. That is undertandable, in that the designs were free of the considerations of practical building. The "drawing-table buildings" were situated freely in space and were not impeded by other buildings or by technical or financial restrictions.

Parting with De Stijl

The Dubbele Sleutel project, on which Wils collaborated closely with van Doesburg, was the culmination and the end of Wils's relations with *De stijl.* In November 1918 he signed the manifesto, but in the beginning of 1919 his ties with the periodical were severed.[19]

Various reasons have been put forward for Wils's sudden resignation. Oud, in his 1958 booklet *Mein weg in "De Stijl,"* suggested that Wils had been only moderately interested in De Stijl's principles. However, Wils's post-1919 work did not show estrangement from these principles; on the contrary, it developed logically from his work of the years 1917–1919. Therefore, Oud's explanation does not seem very plausible. In 1967 Wils said in an interview for the periodical *Cobouw* that the immediate occasion for his leaving had been a disagreement with van Doesburg.[20] This sounds familiar; collaboration with van Doesburg nearly always generated problems. We know from letters that in December 1918 van Doesburg was still highly pleased with Wils, who, he thought, showed the proper hostility toward the "stinking baroque practices of the Amsterdam School" and was tending "in the right direction." However, a month later van Doesburg threatened to have a writ served on Wils for money owed him. When Wils contributed two articles to *De stijl*'s competitor, *Levende kunst* (a review of an exhibition in Haarlem[21] and an article on Wright), his fate was sealed. Huszár, too, found out that van Doesburg considered publication in *Levende kunst* a flagrant sign of disloyalty to *De stijl.* Van Doesburg wrote to Oud on May 20, 1919, that Wils and Huszár were completely "out," and in a letter written in November he stated the grounds: financial matters and publication in *Levende kunst.*

Politics, too, may have figured in the estrangement between Wils and van Doesburg. Around the time he stopped contributing to *De stijl,* Wils developed an interest in the efforts of Chris Beekman to reestablish written correspondence between Dutch and Russian artists. For a while, Wils was convinced that revolution would not be long in coming to the Netherlands. This evoked a derisive reaction in van Doesburg, who wrote to Oud on July 12, 1920, that Wils took the same line as those "re-ra revolutionaries (Beekman, van 't Hoff, van der Leck, et al.) who obstructed the new."

After their falling out, Wils and van Doesburg ran into each other several times. Van Doesburg's comments to Oud after he saw Wils at a Haagsche Kunstkring lecture in March 1920 offer some insight into the varied reasons for Wils's disgrace in his eyes: "How is it possible for Christ's sake—writ—manifesto—Levende Kunst—plagiarism—threatening letters. All this goes through my head with the speed of a boulevard taxi."

Papaverhof

Wils's contributions to *De stijl* ended in early 1919; however, as already noted, this did not entail a change in his ideas about modern architecture. Therefore, a discussion of the housing block Daal en Berg [Vale and Mount] at Papaverhof in The Hague—one of Wils's best works—is certainly appropriate. Although this project dates from the years 1919–1922, when Wils was no longer a contributor, it was cited in *De stijl* as an example of good architecture, and van Doesburg gave it favorable mention in lectures in the early 1920s.

In 1919, Wils was commissioned by the Coöperative Woningbouwvereniging Tuinstadswijk "Daal en Berg" [Cooperative Housing Association of the Garden District "Daal en Berg"] to design sixty or seventy single-family dwellings. The commission was expanded in consultation with the municipal authorities so that Wils was also asked to design buildings housing sixty apartments; these buildings, which were to have something of the houses' open character, were to serve as a transition between the one-family houses and the surrounding area.[22]

The Cooperative Housing Association had been created through the initiative of middle-class residents of The Hague who had felt the need for a neighborhood of their own. The houses were to "provide well-earned rest after . . . daily tasks" and to "charm the inhabitants by their character and furnishings."[23] There was no mention, however, of the manner in which these desires were to be fulfilled. The only guidance Wils received in this matter was, in his own words, to "privide these houses with much greenery and flowers."[24] It was noted in the minutes of the association that "the Architect has been able to formulate a variegated entity, which, the Board trusts, will have a pleasing effect on the local cityscape."[25]

Wils developed a plan in which 68 houses were arranged around a park of about 70 × 100 meters. The asymmetry of the plot made the connection of the dwellings at its corners rather complicated. On the other hand, the long sides of the plot show a simple but ingenious positioning. The houses are situated back to back, two by two, with partly overlapping rear facades. Thus, the living rooms of one pair of houses look out on the park, those of the next pair on the surrounding street. The kitchens do exactly the opposite. Seen as a whole, the linking of the houses presents a greatly varied picture of protruding and receding masses (figure 185). The apartments in the zone of transition to the surrounding buildings have three stories and screen the housing block on two sides.

Daal en Berg is often and justly compared to Frank Lloyd Wright's design for housing for the employees of the Larkin Company in Buffalo, New York. That design also shows a row of houses in which parts periodically recess. The front doors, however, are all on the same side; thus, the recesses have nothing to do with the back-to-back positioning of the houses.

The execution of the Daal en Berg project presented some difficulties, particularly in the use of materials. Originally the houses were to be constructed of cinder concrete, but halfway into the construction this was changed to brick. The board of the housing association explained this to its members in a letter: "As you know, we have not been fortunate with our construction. After obtaining good results with the foundations and cellars, we were forbidden to continue the construction in cinder concrete beyond the first floor, contrary to the vision of our Architect. . . ." The exterior walls of the one-family dwellings were finished smoothly in cement. The apartments had been conceived in brick.[26]

Because of the unusual shape of the plot, there were thirteen different types of houses; however, the arrangements and the sizes did not differ very much. The houses were roomy by the standards of the time. On the ground floor they had a large living room and a kitchen that could double as a dining room. The hall also served as storage space. The upstairs was divided into three bedrooms and a bathroom. Wils attempted to make the living at Papaverhof as comfortable as possible by means of extra attention to details. He saw to it that the back of the living room got enough light by putting small windows in the wall over the large bay windows. He provided an opening in the wall between the kitchen and the living

185 Wils, two-family houses at Daal en Berg, Papaverhof, The Hague, 1920. Photograph in artist's estate.

room through which food and dishes could be passed—a novelty in those days.

The apartments, too, were furnished with various conveniences. The mailboxes and the gas meters were grouped together at the main entrance of each block. Dumbwaiters were installed, chutes in the kitchens led to a central garbage tank, intercoms connected each apartment to the main entrance, and the front door could be opened automatically.[27]

Wils, in his usual way, paid attention to the aesthetic details of the houses as well as to convenience. The aforementioned opening between the living room and the kitchen was fitted into a built-in buffet. The glass in the doors that flanked this buffet had a beautiful asymmetrical latticework, and the composition of one door was mirrored in the other one. The banister was composed of vertical and horizontal slats. The application of stained glass in the upper rooms shows that, even after his De Stijl period, Wils had not lost his interest in a coalescence of different fields of art.

Collaborations with Zwart and Huszár

The projects Wils undertook in collaboration with van Doesburg, and his subsequent autonomous designs, give evidence that he was very positively inclined toward the use of color in architecture. In this respect he differed from the other architects of the early De Stijl period, J. J. P. Oud and Robert van 't Hoff. In several architectural drawings (meant not as presentations but purely as working drawings), he applied color himself. For instance, in the drawing of the facade of a house on Papaverhof (figure 186) he colored the frames of windows and doors yellow and blue. Here Wils followed the alternating system applied by van Doesburg to the buffet of De Dubbele Sleutel, making a symmetrical entity asymmetrical by means of a color division. In this color solution, Wils did not restrict himself to the woodwork; he colored the whole facade green. In his designs for a concrete warehouse and a department store, Wils applied the complementary colors of the primaries: purple, green, and orange. However, the extreme color applications of such design drawings were usually not realized in Wils's executed buildings.

Further evidence of Wils's enduring interest in color within the daily environment is provided by his collaborations with Piet Zwart and Vilmos Huszár between 1919 and 1922. Zwart came to work with Wils as a draftsman in 1919. He was a recent convert from the ornamentation of the Wiener Werkstätte and the Amsterdam School. In retrospect, he described his confrontation with De Stijl's language of form and color as "the shock of recognition."[28] For Wils, Zwart made beautiful color perspective drawings of the housing block at Papaverhof. He made a similar drawing of the Haagse Dansinstituut Gaillard-Jorissen, and several floor plans of corridors and rooms of the same institute on which the sometimes intricate color schemes are worked out in detail. He also drew a view of the hall of the Tehuis voor Ongehuwde Vrouwen (Home for Unmarried Women) and designed stained-glass windows for it and the Dansinstituut.

No illustrations of Wils's and Huszár's first collaborative works—interior designs for a dining room and a drawing room—are known to be extant, but one such interior was shown at an exhibition of La Section d'Or that traveled around the Netherlands in the summer of 1920. The reviews only mentioned the colors: purple and orange.[29] The second collaboration of Wils and Huszár was the spatial color composition shown above as figure 180. In the third collaboration (which has been documented extensively), Wils and Huszár, respectively, designed the shape and the color scheme of the studio of the photographer Henri Berssenbrugge, whom they had met through the Haagsche Kunstkring. Wils probably renovated the facade on the Zeestraat slightly, and he designed a sign. The most important task, however, was the design of the studio itself. This studio had to be suitable for Berssenbrugge's special lighting effects. Wils built a high oblong space in which the walls and the ceiling had windows of different sizes with dark drapes to control the direction of the incoming light. Wils's furniture—two chairs, two small tables, and a high chair for children—was constructed of black-stained oak. Wils added two built-in settees to increase the seating without disrupting the effect of Huszár's spatial color composition. With this studio, finished in June 1921, Wils and Huszár proved that collaboration between a painter and an architect could be successful.

Van Doesburg devoted much attention to this project in his lecture "Der Wille zum Stil" ["The Will toward Style], which he gave in several cities in Germany in 1921 and which was published in *De stijl* in March 1922. His recent attempt at collaboration with Oud on the Spangen housing had been a failure. Oud had withdrawn from De Stijl, and its architectural ranks were thus in need of reinforcement. Van Doesburg distanced himself from Oud's work in the journal *De bouwwereld,* but he listed Wils along with van 't Hoff and Rietveld as "pioneer" of modern architecture.[30] Wils, however, did not rejoin the ranks of contributors to *De stijl,* as Huszár did. Van Doesburg contacted him directly only once, to invite him to take part in an exhibition in Düsseldorf. Wils replied that he would not be able to assemble photographs suitable for the exhibition in time. A few of Wils's designs for Daal en Berg were shown at De Stijl's 1923 architectural exhibition in Paris,

186 Wils, design for houses at Daal en Berg. Nederlands Documentatiecentrum voor de Bouwkunst, Amsterdam. Wils applied colors to the portion of the drawing labeled "gevel [facade] II·III."

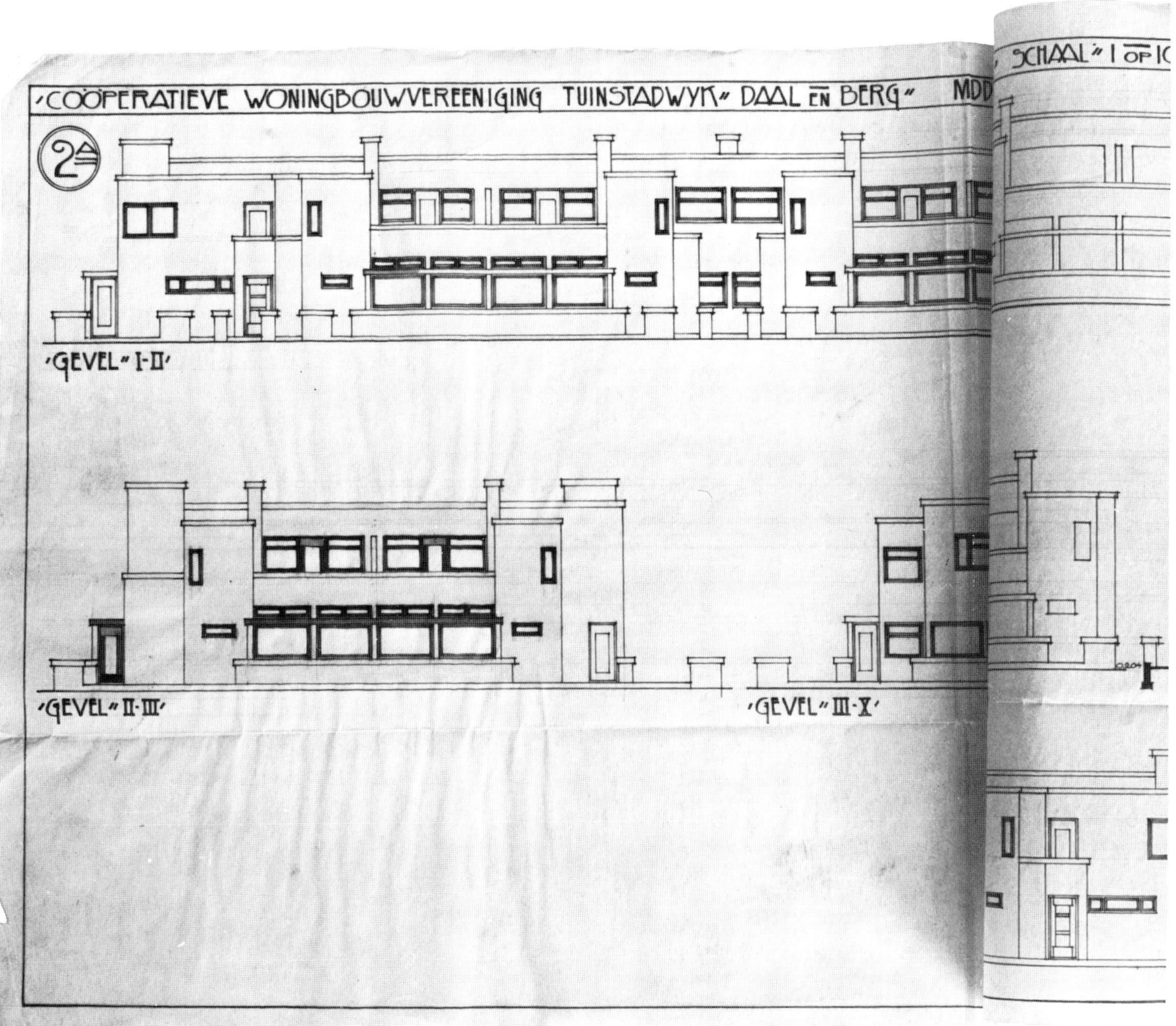

187 Presentation of garden bench, Huis ten Bosch, The Hague, ca. 1931. Photograph in Wils's estate. (Wils is the leftmost of the men with their backs turned to the camera.)

but there was no question any more of a real involvement in the periodical.

Wils appears not to have collaborated so intensively with any painter after 1922. In that year his firm had to retrench drastically because there had been a mistake in the cost calculations for Daal en Berg. A number of his collaborators—among them Piet Zwart—were laid off.[31] Some of Wils's architectural designs from the subsequent years are known, but he did not get another opportunity to realize a building until 1924. However, a few of the handsome furniture designs he created in this period for the factory Eik en Linde [Oak and Linden], in Alkmaar, were executed. In the mid 1920s Wils was working on several projects in The Hague, together with Dr. J. Kalf and the architect F. L. J. Lourijssen. The real breakthrough in his career was the commission for the Olympic Stadium in Amsterdam, which was finished in 1928. That established his reputation. His fame resulted in a few commissions by the Royal Court, the nicest product of which is a garden bench he created around 1931 for Queen Wilhelmina (figure 187).

Notes

1
J. Wils, "De nieuwe bouwkunst," *De stijl* 1, no. 3 (1918), pp. 31–33; J. Wils, "Symmetrie en kultuur," ibid. 1, no. 12 (1918), pp. 137–140. See also the following: sketch of small house with hollow concrete walls, *De stijl* 1, no. 8 (1918), p. 96; R. van 't Hoff, "Het hotel-café-restaurant 'De Dubbele Sleutel' (eerste gedelltelijke verbouwing) te Woerden, bijlage 10, architect Jan Wils," ibid. 2, no. 5 (1919), pp. 58–60; illustration of Daal en Berg project, ibid. 12 (1922), pp. 315–316.

2
Wendingen [*Turns*] was the journal of De Stijl's opposite number, the Amsterdam School.

3
For biographical data on Wils see E. Godoli, *Jan Wils, Frank Lloyd Wright e De Stijl* (Florence, 1980), pp. 88–94.

4
Communication from Mrs. G. Wils-van der Veen.

5
Anonymous, "Moderne bouwkunst in Amerika," *Architectura* 20 (1912), p. 106.

6
For further information see R. Eggink and P. Fuhring, "Tweede afdeling: Architektuur en kunstnijverheid," in *Haagsche Kunstkring, werk verzameld* (The Hague, 1977), p. 61.

7
Wils's participation in an exhibition of the Leiden art club De Sphinx in January 1917 was, presumably, a direct result of this encounter.

8
This similarity was previously pointed out by Auke van der Woud in his article "Variaties op een thema," in *Americana, Nederlandse architectuur 1880–1930* (exhibition catalog, Rijksmuseum Kröller-Müller, Otterlo, 1975).

9
See J. Wils, "Tentoonstelling van kunstnijverbeid en volkskunst te Rotterdam," *Levende kunst,* 1918, pp. 113–119; J. Wils, "De nieuwe bouwkunst. Bij het werk van Frank Lloyd Wright," ibid., 1918, pp. 208–219. The Nederlands Documentatiecentrum voor de Bouwkunst has some notebooks containing texts of lectures.

10
J. Wils, "Frank Lloyd Wright," *Elseviers geillustreerd maandschrift* 31, no. 61 (1921), p. 222.

11
The construction of the Villa Henny was begun in 1915. Huis ter Heide is near Utrecht.

12
In a review, Co Brandes called large plate-glass windows "indispensable for a modern restaurant." See C. Brandes, "Enige gedachten over de komende architectuur in verband met het werk van Jan Wils," *Levende kunst,* 1918, p. 139.

13
Wils, "De nieuwe bouwkunst" (note 9 above), p. 213.

14
Photographs of the exterior show that van Doesburg accentuated the asymmetrical partitioning of the windows by alternating light and dark colors. A photo clearly showing the painting of the mullions is reproduced on page 36 of Godoli's *Jan Wils, Frank Lloyd Wright e De Stijl.*

15
Good photographs of the church are reproduced on pages 4–5 of *Jan Wils* [a publication in the series Meister der Baukunst] (Geneva, 1930).

16
Access to the photographic material was allowed by P. Verhoeven of the Dienst Bouw- en Woningtoezicht in Alkmaar.

17
Van 't Hoff, "Het hotel-Café-restaurant 'De Dubbele Sleutel'" (note 1 above), p. 59.

18
Van der Woud, "Variaties op een thema" (note 8 above), p. 31.

19
Two years later, he again became connected with *De stijl*—tenuously—as a result of his collaboration with Huszár on the studio of the photographer Henri Berssenbrugge.

20
F. van Dongen, "Jan Wils en de Stijlgroep," *Cobouw,* June 16, 1967, pp. 27–28.

21
The Tentoonstelling voor Aesthetisch Uitgevoerde Gebruiksvoorwerpen [Exhibition of Aesthetically Executed Useful Objects].

22
J. Wils, "Woninggroep 'Daal en Berg,' 's-Gravenhage," *Bouwkundig weekblad* 43, no. 46 (1922), p. 458.

23
L. Knug, "Herenhuizen als heren van standing. Haags Papaverhof frappant werkstuk van architect Jan Wils," *Eigen huis,* June 1980, pp. 36–37.

24
Wils, "Woninggroep 'Daal en Berg'" (note 22 above), p. 458.

25
Knug, "Herenhuizen" (note 23 above), p. 38.

26
Wils, "Woninggroep 'Daal en Berg,'" p. 463.

27
Ibid., p. 462.

28.
Zwart's memoirs, in his estate (Wassenaar). Zwart was sometimes mentioned in *De stijl* as a collaborator; however, he never contributed to the periodical.

29
"La Section d'Or in de Haagsche Kunstkring," *Provinciale Overijsselsche en Zwolsche courant,* July 27, 1920: "It seems to me that room no. 29 had a beautiful solution, in which the lower part was predominantly black, purple, and gray, with a single spot of orange, while in the upper part the colors were lighter."

30
T. van Doesburg, "De architect J. J. P. Oud: 'voorganger' der 'kubisten' in de bouwkunst?" *De bouwwereld,* July 26, 1922.

31
Communication from Mrs. N. Zwart-Cleyndert, Wassenaar.

Robert van 't Hoff

Eveline Vermeulen

"And I remember a young man named van 't Hoff, who was filled with high purpose when I met him here seven or eight years ago, whom I expect to find has done some good things. . . ." Thus wrote Frank Lloyd Wright to H. P. Berlage on November 30, 1922.[1] Robert van 't Hoff had indeed done "some good things" by that time. He is mentioned in nearly every survey of modern architecture, not only as a contributor to *De stijl* but also as one of the first European architects to build in the manner of Wright. Van 't Hoff's fame is due mainly to two villas: the Villa Verloop (1914–1915) and the "Concrete Villa" (1915–1919). The Concrete Villa is well known as an early application of concrete-skeleton construction. When van 't Hoff is mentioned in reference works, it is often stated that these two projects were his first and his last.

The image of van 't Hoff as a promising architect who turned his back on a brilliant career is not incorrect, but it needs to be refined.

Van 't Hoff's encounter with Wright occurred in 1914, during a sojourn in the United States. Van 't Hoff had been educated as an architect in England, and he had already executed his first autonomous designs. However, in comparison with the buildings he designed after his trip to the United States, his early works seem picturesque. Wright's form language was clearly an important stimulant to van 't Hoff's quest for a more abstract architecture. Furthermore, van 't Hoff was interested in advanced industrial techniques in the rationalization of the construction process, which he expected to give rise to better working conditions.

Carrying this artistic and ideological baggage, van 't Hoff came into contact with Theo van Doesburg and De Stijl in 1917. The possibilities of belonging to a movement and collaborating with artists from different disciplines must have appealed to him. He probably expected to find in De Stijl not only an aesthetic but also an ideological framework. His belief in such a concerted effort and his dedication to promoting "the movement" are evident from the fact that he made a sizable financial contribution in order to guarantee the continued publication of the periodical *De stijl.* He also recruited subscribers. Moreover, he published a number of articles in *De stijl* during 1918 and 1919; in these he did not come across as an outspoken theoretician, but he did show enthusiasm for the cause.

The consequences of the First World War—the spiritual and moral collapse, the lowered standard of living, and the housing shortage—strengthened van 't Hoff's conviction that radical changes should be made in society, and he developed from a social utopian into a communist. He was convinced that there was a relationship between the artistic avant-garde and proletarian revolution. Neither De Stijl nor the Communist Party could fulfill his high expectations, however; when it came down to hard facts, De Stijl served the arts exclusively, and the Communist party did not bring the revolution much closer. Not one to remain marginal, to compromise, or to make concessions, van 't Hoff declared himself an "ex-architect" and henceforth remained aloof from the dilemma.

Youth, education, and early works

Robbert van 't Hoff, son of Jeanette Titsingh and Herminus van 't Hoff, was born in Rotterdam on November 5, 1887. Robert, as he was called, grew up in a well-to-do milieu. His parents were artistically inclined and moved in artistic circles. His mother was particularly interested in the visual arts and was acquainted with painters, among them Willem Witsen. His father, a chemist-bacteriologist, had become acquainted with the physician-author Frederik van Eeden during his student years in Amsterdam,[3] and after 1898 young Robert accompanied his parents on visits to van Eeden's social-utopian commune, Walden, which was located near Bussum on the Cruysbergen estate.

In 1904 the van 't Hoff family moved to Bilthoven, where in 1905 Robert assisted in the building of a house for one of his aunts. (It was on this occasion that he met the contractor Pastunink, whose name will come up later.) Robert felt drawn to construction and decided to become an architect. In 1906, having finished his secondary education, he enrolled in the School of Art in Birmingham, England, on the advice of an architect named Hanrath who was a friend of the family.

During his studies in Birmingham, van 't Hoff worked as an assistant in the architectural firms of Buckland and Gresswell. He also visited sites where houses were being built, in order to study them and make notes. He did the same during his short stays in Rotterdam, where his family had returned in 1908. He made drawings and took measurements of several villas and farmhouses (for example, the Port-Landt homestead in Rhoon). His interest in the craft of building, evident in these activities, emerged later in his most advanced designs.

In 1911 and the next several years, van 't Hoff took advanced courses at the Architectural Association in London. It was during that period that his own designs were first executed—first a house for his parents, then a model farmhouse, and then a studio-dwelling.

On August 1, 1911, H. J. van 't Hoff applied for a building permit for a villa in Huis ter Heide. The architectural drawing mentions the name of the architect: "Robt. van 't Hoff, Chelsea, London."

188 **Van 't Hoff, Løvdalla, Huis ter Heide, 1911–12.**

189 **Detail of staircase, Løvdalla.**

He planned to direct the construction from England. During the design phase, van 't Hoff had the contractor Pastunink come over from the Netherlands. Together with this man of practical experience, whose judgment he valued highly, van 't Hoff studied the methods of building used in the environs of London. Consequently, he used motifs that occurred in English villas around the turn of the century: a spacious hall surrounded by the living rooms, tall chimneys, and high gabled roofs.

The original design had a rectangular floor plan. With the exception of a square addition in the back, this plan was elaborated symmetrically. The entrance, situated in the front center, opened into a large hall flanked by the living rooms. Directly opposite the entrance was a staircase leading to the second floor. About a month and a half after the building-permit application, a request was filed for an enlargement of the house. It was in this form that the design was eventually realized. The two projecting rooms that were added enclosed a kind of entrance court. The front remained symmetrical, but it was enlivened by the addition. The added rooms, which extend from the front, have saddle roofs that flare out at the lower edge; the three parallel saddle roofs of the original plan rise above them. The house is built of brick, with the front ornamented with horizontal clapboards and mullioned windows.

Løvdalla, as the house is named, has a rustic character and displays craftsmanlike attention to detail. For instance, the downspouts are entirely enclosed in wood and finished with scalloped wooden rims, and the ingenious locks and hinges show careful execution. The interior, too, is well detailed and meticulously finished. The fireplaces are decorated handsomely with tile and copper, and the staircase that leads to the attic is remarkably open (figure 189).

Van 't Hoff's second design of 1911 was that for the model farmhouse De Zaaier [The Sower] in Lunteren, commissioned by a certain Pieter Duijs. This design, too, was conceived in London. The architectural drawing mentions van 't Hoff's address in the artists' quarter of Chelsea: 297 King's Road. The second date on the drawing, 1913, is probably the year of delivery. The execution was again in the hands of Pastunink. In this design, English influences are less evident than in Løvdalla. Only the wide chimneys give an English impression; however, such chimneys also were found in the Netherlands. The source of inspiration for the De Zaaier may have been the Dutch farmhouses of the hall-house type that occur in the Gooi region and along the IJsselmeer (the former Zuider Zee)—the low side facades and the irregular lower line of the thatched roof point in that direction.

188

189

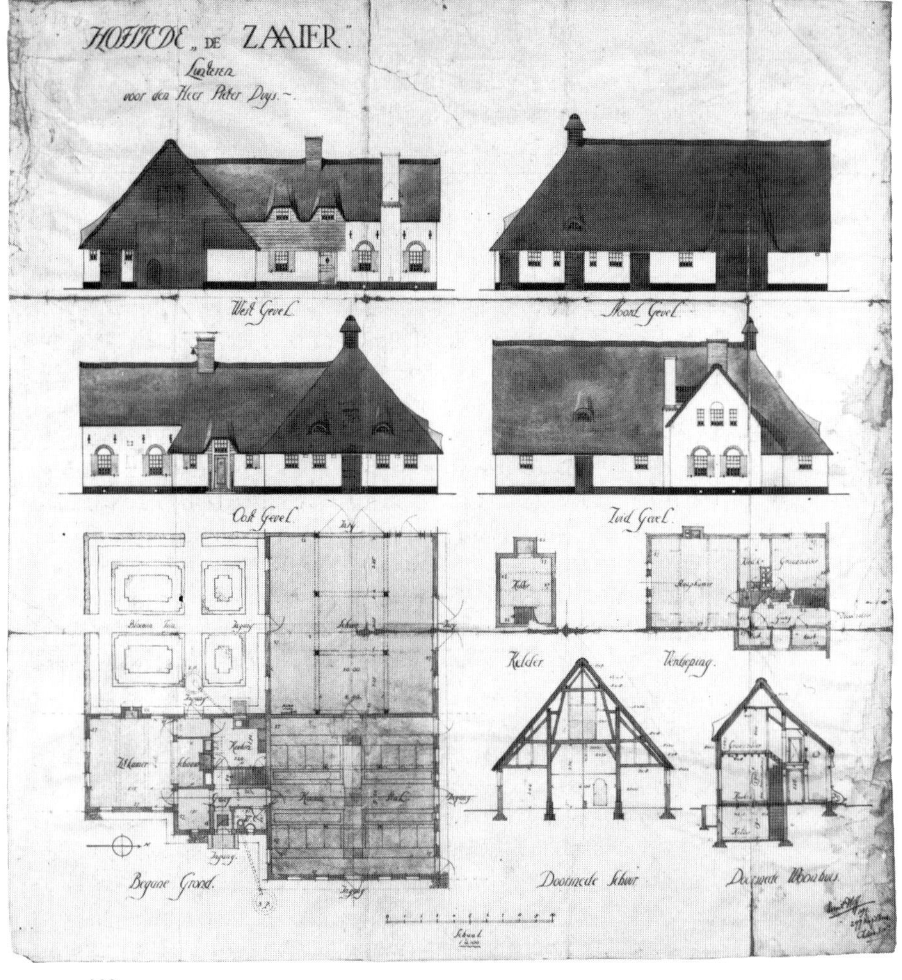

190

The facades of De Zaaier are not flat, but have projecting and recessed sections. The surface, like that of Løvdalla, has a variety of decorative materials. Part of the facade of the stable is covered with horizontal clapboards, which contrast with the vertical ones of the doors. The front door, recessed in the plastered wall, is surrounded by a brick border. A dark, fairly high plinth runs around the entire farmhouse, unifying the various parts and emphasizing the horizontal element. The floor plan is a simple grouping of four squares, including the garden. As in Løvdalla, the fireplaces are central to the living rooms.

In external appearance as well as in use of materials, both Løvdalla and De Zaaier followed the usual architectural forms for such houses. They were in harmony with their rural surroundings and well suited to their purposes. The facades were varied, the floor plans were simple, and the details were executed with care and in a manner appropriate to the materials used. These are houses with character, much to the credit of a beginning architect.

The third house designed by van 't Hoff in his English period was commissioned by the British painter Augustus John, who described in his memoirs how he met van 't Hoff. One day in early 1913, John stood in the doorway of a Chelsea pub and inquired loudly whether there was, perchance, an architect on the premises. Van 't Hoff was at the bar having a drink, and in a few hours the artist and the architect came to an agreement.[4] In May 1913 the design for the studio-dwelling on Mallord Street was finished and construction could begin.

Unlike Løvdalla and De Zaaier, the John house was to be built in urban surroundings, between existing buildings. Van 't Hoff solved the problem of the limited site by designing an elongated building with a narrow street front. Two sets of turning stairs led to the front door, which was located on an elevated terrace and flanked by large mullioned windows. Dark-colored downspouts contrasted decoratively with the facade.

From the street the John house appeared to be an ordinary row house. However, the design drawings reveal its dual functions, and the roof design suggests the distinction between the living quarters and the studio. The studio, which was on a lower level than the living quarters, could be reached from those quarters by a connecting door or from the outside by way of an alley and a wrought-iron staircase. The gate and the window near the stairs, visible in figure 192, were remarkably decorative—the use of open geometric forms is reminiscent of motifs from the Glasgow School. (Van 't Hoff later wrote that while studying in Birmingham he had attended lectures by architects who were working after the manner of Charles Rennie Mackintosh.[5]) Even such a detail as

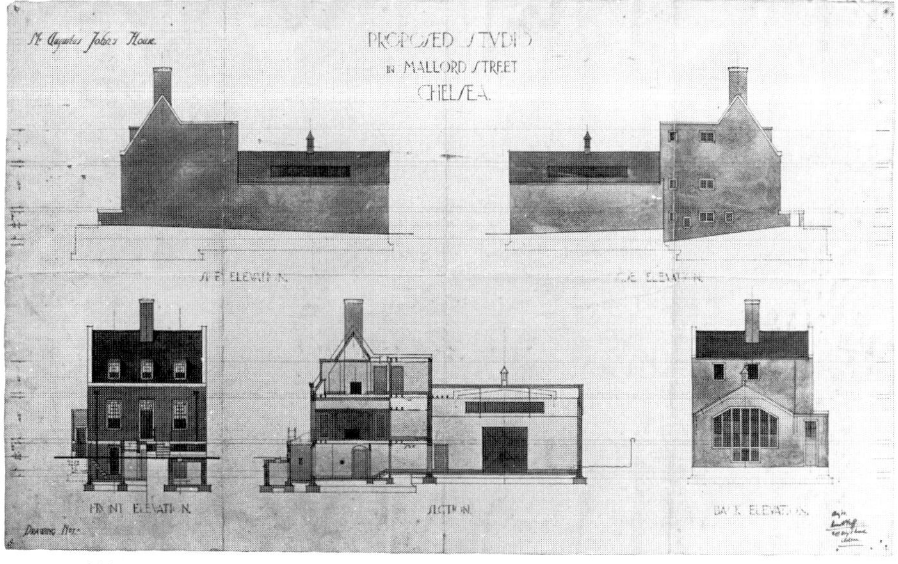

191

190 Van 't Hoff, design for Hofstede De Zaaier [Homestead "The Sower"], Lunteren, 1911–1913. Nederlands Documentatiecentrum voor de Bouwkunst, Amsterdam.

191 Van 't Hoff, design for studio-dwelling of Augustus John, London, 1913–14. Nederlands Documentatiecentrum voor de Bouwkunst, Amsterdam.

192 Detail of John house, showing stairs to studio.

192

the mail slot was decoratively stylized. The ceiling of the studio followed the lines of the large window in the rear facade.

The house was finished in the spring of 1914, after some delays in the construction. Augustus John was apparently very pleased with it; on June 24 he wrote to his American friend John Quinn (whom he had kept informed of the progress) that the studio looked "fine." "It is certainly rather Dutch," he continued, "but it has a solidity and tautness unmatched in London. . . ."[6]

New impulses

During his time in London (from 1911 to 1914), van 't Hoff gradually made connections with various artistic and social movements. At the beginning of the century, the artistic climate in England had been strongly influenced by Whistler and the Impressionists. However, in the years following 1910 a series of sensational exhibitions gave the English public an opportunity to get acquainted with the most recent European developments in the visual arts. The critic Roger Fry organized two important exhibitions entitled "Post-Impressionism," in which paintings by Matisse, Picasso, and other young Parisian artists were shown along with works by Cézanne, Gauguin, and van Gogh. From 1912 on one could also see in London works by the Italian futurists Balla, Boccioni, and Severini.

Some English artists were very impressed by these new art forms and ideas. For instance, in the spring of 1914 the Art Rebel Centre was founded on the initiative of Wyndham Lewis. Although this club was short-lived, Lewis continued his activist practices. In July 1914 he published the first issue of a periodical named *Blast, review of the great English vortex.* The "vorticists" who congregated around *Blast* took a stand against all tradition, after the example of the futurists. They glorified the machine as the true expression of dynamic modern life, and they incorporated cubist and futurist influences in their work.

Van 't Hoff visited a number of the aforementioned exhibitions together with the painter David Bomberg, whom he had met in Chelsea.[7] It may have been through Bomberg that van 't Hoff came into contact with some products of the Omega Workshops, a studio (established by Roger Fry) in which artists made tables, rugs, screens, and even whole interiors on commission. Some Omega products were decorated with completely abstract images. Apart from his uncommissioned works (among which were some nearly abstract paintings), Bomberg is known to have executed commissions for the Omega Workshops around 1913. The Omega Workshops had an ideological goal of serving as a "vital communal centre for the avant-garde, where they all could meet, exchange views and earn a guaranteed thirty shillings a week to subsidize their own experimental work." Few of the articles that came out of the Omega Workshops can be attributed to specific artists. Little value was placed on the artist's identity; it was considered more important that the objects properly serve their aesthetic and practical purposes in the home. The principles of anonymity, close collaboration between designer and craftsman, and harmonious unity of design are in the line of the English Arts and Crafts tradition. Fry's emphasis on the vocational side of production also points in the direction of Arts and Crafts. The integration of art and surroundings and the close collaboration must have appealed to van 't Hoff.

Van 't Hoff's ideas about architecture also developed further during his years in London. W. R. Lethaby had a certain influence on this development. According to notes made by van 't Hoff later in life, he came into possession of a copy of Lethaby's book *Architecture, an introduction to the history of the art of building* in 1913. He may also have attended Lethaby's lectures to the London Architectural Association. Lethaby advocated architecture without ostentation, "without affectation"; in his designs he put usefulness first. His interest was directed toward clear and simple methods of construction in which form and function were closely connected. In 1918, van 't Hoff quoted the following statement of Lethaby's in *De stijl*: "Plastic art had gone through a process of mental evolution far higher than the futile pleasure of decoration. Proportion, properly, is the resultant of fitness. To talk of proportion without attempting to realise what is meant, is mere confusion."[9] In spite of his theories on unornamented, purely proportioned architecture with an emphasis on function, Lethaby remained sympathetic to certain Arts and Crafts principles. For instance, he never favored mechanical production; he valued honest, vocational craftsmanship. Other ideas that were common to the Arts and Crafts movement and Lethaby's thinking were an interest in all areas of creativity and a recognition of the social responsibilities of the artist-architect.

Van 't Hoff's attraction to Lethaby's theories suggests that he held similar artistic and social opinions. In this respect it is significant that van 't Hoff later noted as an important biographical detail that in 1913 he had read H. P. G. Quack's book *De Socialisten, personen en stelsels* [*The Socialists, persons and systems*], a well-known work in which Quack unfolded his ideas about the family and society. Van 't Hoff's interest in experimental forms of society must have been stimulated by this work, particularly by the chapters devoted to William Thompson's utopianism.

Thus, the period 1911–1914 was important to van 't Hoff's development in several respects. He came into contact with English avant-garde artists, became familiar with the most recent developments in the visual arts, received ideological inspiration from Quack's social-utopian ideas, and was initiated into the principles of Arts and Crafts.

For his architectural development, however, his confrontation with Frank Lloyd Wright's work was of decisive importance. This occurred in the same period. In 1913 van 't Hoff's father sent him a German book devoted to Wright.[10] C. R. Ashbee's introduction to this volume was principally based on Wright's 1908 article "In the cause of architecture," in which Wright renounced the old forms of architecture and emphasized the new building techniques. A characteristic statement by Wright, quoted by Ashbee in the introduction, reads: "The machine is the normal tool of our civilization; give it work that it can do well; nothing is of greater importance. To do this will be to formulate new industrial ideals, sadly needed. Only when we strive for this ideal will architecture be able to retain its leading position among the arts."[11]

In June 1914 van 't Hoff traveled to the United States in order to study Wright's architecture at first hand, missing the costume ball August John gave to celebrate his new studio-house. He visited Wright's home and the Unity Church in Oak Park, Midway Gardens in Chicago, and the Larkin Building in Buffalo. The idiosyncratic architecture, with its open structure and its monumental character, made a deep impression on van 't Hoff. He found the floor plans well thought out, and he had not encountered the predominant horizontality or the staggered walls, with their plastic effect and their well-balanced proportions, in such pure form in Europe.

Van 't Hoff met Wright, and seems to have discussed with him the possibility of their working together on a project.[12] But, although van 't Hoff admired Wright's buildings tremendously, he was not very impressed by his personality. It seems that their attitudes toward the architectural profession differed quite a bit; thus, it remains an open question whether a collaboration between them would ever have gotten off the ground.

When van 't Hoff left American shores at the end of July 1914, he took with him an extensive collection of illustrated documentation about Wright's architecture. His knowledge of the buildings and the documentary material proved to have a great influence on his own work and on the ideas about architecture that were developed some years later by him and by others within De Stijl.

193 Villa Verloop, Huis ter Heide, 1914–15, as illustrated in *De stijl* 2, no. 9 (1919), appendix XVII.

The Villa Verloop

Immediately after his return from the United States, van 't Hoff must have started work on a design for a summer home in Huis ter Heide. The client, J. N. Verloop, applied for a building permit for the villa on October 26, 1914. In addition to van 't Hoff, the architectural drawing lists a second architect: Ru Mauve, a son of the well-known painter Anton Mauve. Mauve's role was probably to oversee the construction while van 't Hoff was still living in London. On January 13, 1915, van 't Hoff returned to the Netherlands and settled in Huis ter Heide.

The typically Wrightian characteristics of the Villa Verloop suggest that the design was entirely van 't Hoff's. Actually a small bungalow, it had slate hipped roofs. The low, staggered facades were finished in white stucco. Underneath the austere windows were gray bands, and a fairly high gray plinth ran around the whole house. The living room faced south and opened onto a terrace. The cruciform floor plan and the predominant horizontality (emphasized by the low, slightly overhanging roof) are strongly reminiscent of the forms used by Frank Lloyd Wright, particularly in his Prairie Houses. The same is true of the large planters at the front door, under the windows, and along the terrace.

Wright had said the following about the role of plants in his architecture: "[The] use of natural foliage and flowers for decoration is carried to quite an extent in all the designs and, although the buildings are complete without this efflorescence, they may be said to blossom with the season." (This remark seems incompatible with the one quoted above—from the same article[13]—in which Wright extols a machine aesthetic.)

It was Wright's aim to create an organic entity of a building and its surroundings, of architecture and nature. The Villa Verloop's harmony with its rural surroundings was not entirely inspired by Wright, however; it was also closely connected with van 't Hoff's earlier rustic designs, Løvdalla and De Zaaier. This harmony was less appreciated a few years later, when *De stijl* advocated an austere, anti-nature architecture. In the January 1919 issue, Theo van Doesburg wrote: "The summer home is in some aspects still reminiscent of the earlier, more rustic notion about architecture, although the entire concept (see floor plans) is no longer directly related to it. Only the partitioned windows and the slanting roof—which still strikes us as a separate element, not being organically a part of the house—are rudiments of an obsolete architectural viewpoint, linked to non-modern materials. The dominant horizontal aspect also makes the total impression less harmonious than the house in appendix 3 by the same architect, in which the modern form-definition strikes us as much more consistent."

The Concrete Villa

By "the house in appendix 3" van Doesburg meant the so-called Concrete Villa in Huis ter Heide, designed by van 't Hoff a little less than a year after the Villa Verloop. The client was A. B. Henny, a businessman from Amsterdam, and the building permit was granted in November 1915. The concept of this house was idealistic, and the division of the jobs and the technical execution were experimental. The commission for the building was given *en régie*[14]—that is, no fixed price was agreed upon before the construction was begun, and therefore the contractor was left a certain margin. Such a commission is rather unusual in the construction of private houses; there must have existed a bond of confidence between the client, the architect, and the contractor (Pastunink). Van 't Hoff was not only responsible for the design; he also was usually present at the construction site, standing side by side with the construction workers to live up to his old ideal of collaboration "without masters or servants."

The Concrete Villa was also experimental in its method of construction, particularly because of its concrete frame.[15] The use of concrete made possible the simplification of the building process and offered great aesthetic freedom. Overhangs and unsupported balconies, which were otherwise difficult to construct, could be realized more easily. Through his inventive use of the new technical possibilities, van 't Hoff arrived at an architectonic conception in which light, air, and space could be emphasized.

Though the Villa Verloop and the Concrete Villa had similar motifs, such as projecting and receding walls, planters, and gray plinths, the overall impressions they created were quite different. In the Concrete Villa, closed rows of windows were replaced by large glass surfaces without mullions, and a slanting roof by a flat one. The closed wall planes next to the windows—the so-called piers—formed a vertical counterbalance to the predominant horizontality. Because of its balanced relationships between horizontals and verticals and between closed and open volumes, and its austere finish of white planes with gray bands, the house stands out from its setting—instead of blending with nature, it manifests itself as an autonomous product of man. This autonomy is expressed in the clear geometric arrangement of the parts. The facades show a varied appearance of projecting and receding wall planes. The south facade, in particular, has a stepped profile, in which the concrete frame of the pond, the planter, the overhang of the terrace, the rim of the balcony, and the overhang of the roof form a rhythmic sequence of steps. With an eye on the developments in aviation, van 't Hoff designed the roof as a fifth facade.[16]

Although the Concrete Villa had a varied look, its floor plan was based on a simple geometric form, as was usually the case in van 't Hoff's designs. In this case it was a rectangle approximating a square. On the first floor the rooms were arranged symmetrically around the shorter axis; on the second floor they were arranged around the longitudinal axis. The orientation of the house was taken into account in the location of the different rooms. The service and work rooms were on the north side. On the south an enormous living room extended over the full width of 15 meters. The ceilings of this room were lowered at the sides; thus, a division in three parts was effected, while the spatial effect remained intact. The living room received light from three sides; reflected light from the pond in front of the terrace was guided into the interior via the overhang of the conservatory. Meticulous care was expended on the design of the interior, as the stairwell (figure 197) shows.

In the center of the house, against the interior wall of the living room, was a large open fireplace. This was, in fact, superfluous, for the house had central heating. The radiators were ingeniously hidden in shafts in the walls, which also contained the pipes and the drains. Though hidden from sight, these fixtures were easily accessible for maintenance and repair. Such details demonstrate van 't Hoff's concern for the practical matters of building and living as well as for aesthetics.

The construction of the Concrete Villa was protracted over several years. The construction had not started until 1916 because of the war (Pastunink was mobilized and had to leave the execution to his half-brother Strübbe). Henny withdrew in early 1917, and the villa had to be sold unfinished. The final construction took another two years because materials were expensive and scarce during the war.

When the Concrete Villa was finished, little was left of the original idealistic concept. However, that did not affect the appreciation van 't Hoff received in *De stijl* and in other publications. The extensive review devoted to the villa by the Belgian architect Huib Hoste in *De telegraaf* of March 19, 1919, is particularly informative. Hoste expressed admiration for the aesthetic qualities of the house, and he devoted particular attention to the technical and social aspects of the construction: "How does the architect realize his social viewpoints in the construction? He designs in such a way that the skilled laborer can easily discover the 'how' and 'why'; all parts develop logically from one another; for instance, a constant window width is used as much as possible; the length of the room then amounts to an integral number of window widths. The dimensions for the height originate in the same way; for instance, an

194

194 The Concrete Villa under construction. Nederlands Documentatiecentrum voor de Bouwkunst.

195 The Concrete Villa. Photograph in collection of Petra ten Doesschate-Chu, South Orange, New Jersey.

196 Aerial view of Concrete Villa. At the left, the three roofs of Løvdalla can be seen. Photograph in collection of Petra ten Doesschate-Chu, South Orange, New Jersey.

195

196

197 Detail of stairwell in Concrete Villa.

outside plinth is equivalent to the height of one or two steps. . . . For many a reader it will be a revelation to learn from these writings how architecture can really be understood as something that bears the mark of our time in all respects, not only after the conclusion of the work but already during the construction; seen in this way, architecture is one of the buildings stones of the future." This suggests that Hoste was well informed about van 't Hoff's ideas and ideals concerning "alternative" living circumstances and forms of society. Through collaboration, standardization, and rationalization in the labor process, van 't Hoff hoped to create an architecture suitable to the new society. For the time being, however, his experiments were confined to the building of country houses and villas.

Contact with De Stijl

When Huib Hoste wrote the aforementioned newspaper article, shortly after the completion of the Concrete Villa, he had known about its existence for some time. He had met van 't Hoff in the spring of 1917. There are several accounts of the encounter. According to van 't Hoff, Hoste had passed Huis ter Heide on a bicycle ride. When he saw the remarkable villa under construction, Hoste entered the construction site and asked the first construction worker he met whether he could speak to the architect. "You are talking to him" was Robert van 't Hoff's answer. Subsequently the two architects entered into a lively discussion about the villa and its basic principles. It is said that Hoste introduced van 't Hoff to Theo van Doesburg after this encounter.[17]

However, Hoste said in his autobiographical article "Evolutie naar de moderne architectuur"[18] that he met van Doesburg, Vilmos Huszár, J. J. P. Oud, and Jan Wils through van 't Hoff. This seems somewhat more plausible. No direct contact between Hoste and *De stijl* in 1917 can be pinpointed, although Hoste did support the periodical in his architectural column in *De telegraaf.* Hoste was one of the few critics to react positively to the publication of *De stijl.* On November 17, 1917, he wrote about the first issue: "It is in part devoted to the new movement in painting, which seeks a visual effect through abstract forms. The decision of the editorial board to devote a substantial portion of the new periodical to architecture shows good judgment; indeed the effect of architecture is solely dependent on abstract means, forms not to be found in nature but devised in certain proportions and mutual relationships by the visual ingenuity of the artist."

Thus, it remains somewhat uncertain how the acquaintance between van 't Hoff and van Doesburg originated. Even the time when it occurred is uncertain, because of a lack of extant correspondence and other data. The spring of 1917 seems somewhat improbable; as far as is known, van 't Hoff was not involved in the preparations for the publication of *De stijl.* His name did not occur in the correspondence of *De stijl* contributors until late 1917. In a letter of December 4, 1917, to van Doesburg, Vilmos Huszár made the following remark: "Van 't Hoff visited me unexpectedly last Sunday. He is also working for *De stijl.*" One could conclude from this sentence that van 't Hoff and Huszár knew each other at the time of this letter, but that van 't Hoff's involvement with *De stijl* was rather recent. Piet Mondrian wrote to van Doesburg on January 30, 1918: "Your acquaintance with van 't Hoff pleased me. Yes, there still are really modern people." These few bits of information support the likelihood that van 't Hoff and van Doesburg first met in the fall of 1917. Perhaps the publication of the first issue of *De stijl* was the occasion.

Van 't Hoff's attraction to *De stijl* and to its contributors is understandable. In the introduction to the first issue, van Doesburg had stated certain fundamentals with which van 't Hoff undoubtedly identified: the suppression of individuality in favor of collectivity, collaboration between artists from different disciplines, the principled stance of the artist vis-à-vis society, and the (vaguely outlined) expectations of a better future. In the same issue, Oud had written that these principles should be realized in the housing block, which he considered the characteristic expression of modern aesthetics.[19]

Another likely reason that van 't Hoff felt at ease with De Stijl was that the architects involved in it—Oud and, particularly, Wils—admired Wright greatly. It appears that on one of his first visits to Oud in Leiden, van 't Hoff brought along a number of foreign publications and a large amount of documentary material on Wright. In the literature it is assumed that this was Oud's first exposure to Wright.[20] In fact, Oud had become acquainted with Wright's work years earlier, through H. P. Berlage. However, it is true that the view of Wright put forth in Oud's *De stijl* articles differs from that set forth in Berlage's early publications. In "Kunst en machine" ["Art and machine"], published in the third issue, Oud cited Wright's buildings as examples of architecture realized by means of the machine. This emphasis on the machine aesthetic was not based on Berlage's views; Berlage considered Wright a romantic architect. Rather, it is a very specific interpretation that Oud may have arrived at through his conversations with van 't Hoff. In 1918 and 1919, Oud's designs began rather suddenly to show motifs strongly reminiscent of Wright. (This is particularly true of the designs shown in figures 124, 126, and 127 of the present volume.) Van 't Hoff probably was the intermediary in Wright's temporary influence on Oud.

Van 't Hoff wrote five articles for *De stijl* in 1918 and 1919. The first three were installments in the series "Architectuur en haar ontwikkeling" ["Architecture and its development"], the intent of which was not to give a historical survey of architecture but to discuss its relation to society. When van 't Hoff discussed architecture of the past, he did so only to clarify his own views. In van 't Hoff's opinion, architecture's most important task was to create the forms for a future society. Only when architecture abandoned its pretense of being art would objective universal design be possible. It needed to be technically perfected according to the requirements of the modern age, and it needed to go through an evolution similar to that of, for instance, bridge construction. The form language that would then emerge would be a logical, pure, and understandable one. This logic would have to be present not only in the final product, but in the process of creation (which, in its turn, could be simplified by rationalization and standardization).

Van 't Hoff took a rather absolute stance. He did not care much for half-hearted solutions and compromises, as is evidenced by his remark about modern buildings in traditional surroundings: "Every architectonic entity in an existing city is quite impossible. We never can achieve unity here unless all the buildings are radically demolished. . . ."[21]

In the second and third articles of the series, van 't Hoff paid much attention to his inspiring force, Frank Lloyd Wright. He expressed admiration for Wright's ability to suggest the three-dimensionality of a building in the floor plans. As an example he mentioned a principle which he had already applied himself in his Concrete Villa: "By repositioning the floor plans—construction in concrete in particular makes this possible—by moving all lines or just the intersecting ones, new vertical as well as horizontal boundaries are created." He praised the Unity Church for its consistent use of materials (concrete), its logical design, and its anti-nature tendency, and for the fact that the design was not limited to the building; it involved the totality of the environment, extending to the sidewalks. (Van 't Hoff had applied this principle to his Concrete Villa, as figure 196 shows.) But van 't Hoff's admiration did not mean that he accepted all Wright's methods. He criticized the Larkin Building on the grounds that, although the design was good, the realization was rather ambivalent because the concrete construction was hidden by brickwork. He condemned decorative effects and ornaments, which occupied Wright to a considerable extent (particularly at the time).

Van 't Hoff's next two articles were more commentaries than contemplative essays. One was devoted to the café-restaurant De Dubbele Sleutel, built by Jan Wils.[22] Van 't Hoff listed the building's successful and not-so-successful aspects and stated that it was not a free architectonic creation but a partial renovation. He was not very enthusiastic about the results, but he noted that within the given limits De Dubbele Sleutel was "a satisfactory solution as a transition to an absolutely modern architecture."

Van 't Hoff was able to summon much more enthusiasm in his last article, because he was writing about an architecture without concessions: that of the Italian futurist Antonio Sant' Elia.[23] He included an illustration from Sant' Elia's series Città Nuova, which contained designs for electric power plants, railway stations, and multilevel transportation channels for a future city. This illustration, "Case a gradinate" ["Stepped housing"], showed an enormous housing block with receding stories. Van 't Hoff was disappointed that there were no floor plans or directions for construction available, and found it difficult to judge the building from one sketch in perspective, but he appreciated the intention that was apparent. He quoted approvingly Sant' Elia's statement that "while the artists of antiquity derived inspiration from nature's elements, we . . . have to find our inspiration, in material as well as spiritual respects, in the elements of this completely new mechanical world, which we have created; architecture should be its most glorious expression, the most complete synthesis, the most forceful artistic integrity."[24] (The supplementary article about Sant' Elia that van 't Hoff announced was never published in *De stijl*, probably because of the estrangement between van 't Hoff and van Doesburg that will be discussed below.)

Van 't Hoff's work from his De Stijl years

Besides articles, van 't Hoff also published designs in *De stijl*. The first was not an architectural design but rather an item related to applied art: the so-called banister post shown here as figure 198. This design, which dates from late 1917 or early 1918, was ex-

198

ecuted with the help of the Bruynzeel Company. A 2.5-cm cube was the starting point of the design. Van 't Hoff later described the principle he had applied: "By means of a gradual vertical diminishing of the number of cubes used in the horizontal base, 25 cubes square (5 × 5), it finally ends with one single cube." Van 't Hoff often used geometric figures (mostly rectangles) as the starting points of his architectural designs; in this study he was able to apply his mathematical generation of forms without being limited by the restrictions imposed in architecture.

When van Doesburg reviewed van 't Hoff's banister post in the April 1918 issue of *De stijl,* he called it an example of "spatial-plastic interior architecture." According to van Doesburg, there was one requirement that was equally valid for a building and a sculpture: the creation of an "omnidirectional well-balanced proportion of volumes and spaces." A banister post, he wrote, has a predominant vertical position that cannot be counterbalanced by a horizontal counterpart." (Van Doesburg himself was able to counteract his objection against a predominantly vertical position in his 1918 design for a monument for the city of Leeuwarden. Judging from the extant photographs, it was strongly reminiscent of van 't Hoff's banister post, which probably had originated earlier.)

Also in late 1917 or early 1918, van 't Hoff designed a houseboat. When he married Lady P. C. A. W. Hooft, on July 15, 1918, the boat must have been nearly, or even completely, finished. The young couple spent the summer on the Loosdrecht lakes. As of November 14 they were registered as residents of the town of Breukelen. Their address was "woonschip [houseboat] De Stijl."[25] Moored among converted barges, fishing boats, and cutters, the houseboat, with its austere lines, must have made quite an impression.

That van 't Hoff chose to build such a modest pied-à-terre for himself and his wife is not as surprising as it would appear at first glance. In view of the troubles with the Concrete Villa (the withdrawal of the client and the sale of the unfinished house) and the worsened situation in the building industry because of the war, a houseboat seemed a plausible alternative to a house. Because a boat could be moved, no existing buildings had to be taken into consideration; in that respect, the houseboat offered a choice opportunity for van 't Hoff to test some of his theoretical fundamentals in practice. His correspondence with van Doesburg demonstrates how seriously he took the construction of the boat; for example, in a letter dated May 9, 1918, he wrote emphatically about using the boat as an example in order to "further the new direction".

The houseboat De Stijl does not exist any more, but some photographs and the floor plan give a good impression of how it looked. It was rectangular, with a length of 16 meters and a beam of 3 meters. There were partially covered terraces at both ends. Each window had several panes, at least one of which could be opened. All the windows were of the same overall height; their various widths were 3 meters, 2 meters, 1 meter, and half a meter. Behind the row of three windows was a large living room, behind the two windows a bedroom. The small study and the kitchen had one window each. The doors between the rooms were aligned with one another, only slightly off-center; when all these doors were opened, it must have created a pleasant spatial effect. (Van 't Hoff had already applied this principle in the Villa Verloop and in the Concrete Villa.) The French doors to the terraces were centered in the end walls.

Van 't Hoff invented various ingenious solutions to the problems posed by limited space. For example, a sleep sofa was built into a sideboardlike unit. Dimensions were standardized in the interior; for example, it appears in figure 200 that the end cabinets of the sideboard-sofa had the same width as the wall panels. This standardization allowed fixtures to be mounted quickly and efficiently. The boat shows the meticulous craftsmanship and the attention to detail that also characterized van 't Hoff's earlier designs.

Apart from the built-in furniture, there were also separate pieces. The small white chair visible in figure 200 recalls Gerrit

199

198 Van 't Hoff, Trappaal, ruimte-plastische binnenarchitectuur [Banister post, spatial-plastic interior architecture]. Dimensions and whereabouts unknown. As illustrated in *De stijl* 1, no. 6 (1918), appendix XI.

199 Van 't Hoff's houseboat De Stijl, moored at Loosdrecht-Breukelen in 1918. Photograph in collection of Nederlands Documentatiecentrum voor de Bouwkunst, Amsterdam.

200 The living room of the houseboat De Stijl. Photograph in collection of Nederlands Documentatiecentrum voor de Bouwkunst, Amsterdam.

200

Rietveld's chairs, but it was actually designed by van 't Hoff, who had met Rietveld after the latter had copied Wright's furniture for the Villa Verloop. Van 't Hoff undoubtedly knew Rietveld's furniture designs. Yet van 't Hoff's chair was not a copy of one of Rietveld's; rather, it embodied van 't Hoff's own construction concepts. The slats of the back were connected to the elongated hind legs by means of half-lap joints, and were beveled for greater leaning comfort. The double underframe, with its crossed rungs, gave the chair sturdiness but was graceful nonetheless.[26]

Either during the design phase or shortly after the construction of the boat began, the plan arose to call in a painter to determine the color scheme. This appears to have been van 't Hoff's first venture into such a connection between painting and architecture. It is evident from the correspondence that several artists had their way in the choice of the painter. Theo van Doesburg claimed to be the right man for the job, but Vilmos Huszár advised van 't Hoff to grant the commission to Bart van der Leck, who had more experience in this kind of work (having demonstrated his ability in his occasional collaborations with Berlage) and who had written for *De stijl* some very fundamental articles on the coexistence of painting and architecture. Van 't Hoff was sympathetic to Huszár's arguments, and he incurred van Doesburg's anger when he informed him of his preference for van der Leck.

On May 9, 1918, van 't Hoff wrote to van Doesburg: "You know very well that [van der Leck] . . . has thought more about painting in relation to architecture than either of us." What happened thereafter is not known. Neither in the correspondence nor in any of the designs are there any indications that van der Leck or van Doesburg worked on the boat, but the photographs suggest that the boat was given some sort of color application. Differences in color can be seen in the woodwork of the sideboard cabinets and in the upholstery, though not in the walls and the floors. The exterior was divided into different planes and appears to have had striking color accents. The hull, the walls, and the flat roof were kept "separate" from one another; no plane of volume encompassed another. This accentuated rather than destructurized the architectural forms. Destructurizing was the De Stijl painters' ideal of color application in architecture, but it is probable that van 't Hoff, like Oud, was more inclined toward the view that color should enhance the architectural form. That is apparent from a single remark in one of his articles in *De stijl*: "Painting will apply itself to a pure color solution for the planes originating from the plastic forms."[27]

The "houseboat affair" resulted in quite a bit of tension among the contributors to *De stijl*,[28] but it did not lead immediately to a split between van 't Hoff and van Doesburg. In fact, later in 1918 van 't Hoff obtained a commission for van Doesburg for a color solution for the interior of the de Ligt house in Lage Vuursche. Van 't Hoff may have met the pacifist former minister Bart de Ligt through political activities. When de Ligt asked van 't Hoff to renovate and redecorate the house at Lage Vuursche, van 't Hoff advised him to visit the as yet unfinished vacation house De Vonk at Noordwijkerhout. De Ligt was so charmed by van Doesburg's work there that he asked him to "find a color solution" for his house as well. In a letter to Oud dated October 22, 1918, van Doesburg reported that "because of the vacation home he sent a small commission my way." Van Doesburg made designs, but those were probably not executed, or only partially executed, because of de Ligt's sudden move to Katwijk. A close collaboration between van Doesburg and van 't Hoff never developed.

Neither does the houseboat affair appear to have impaired van 't Hoff's good relations with van der Leck. The literature mentions that van 't Hoff designed a studio for van der Leck in 1918. No trace is left of this design, and so it is not certain whether there were problems in the execution or whether the plan never progressed beyond the design phase. A collaboration between van 't Hoff and van der Leck could have been interesting; van der Leck was, at the time, the most radical of the De Stijl painters in his ideas about the integration of painting and architecture.

Middle-class housing and mass construction

In 1918–19 van 't Hoff worked on designs for middle-class housing and mass construction. He appears to have been far more involved in the architectural developments that occurred in the Netherlands during those years than has previously been supposed.

Some Dutch architects had been speculating on the role of "ferro-concrete" in a "new trend in architecture" since the turn of the century. The first all-concrete house in the Netherlands, built in 1911 in Santpoort, was an experiment in lower-class housing. This house, designed by Herman Hana and H. P. Berlage, was built by pouring concrete into a frame at the site. However, that so-called Edison process proved cumbersome and was not suitable for large-scale use. Mass construction in concrete became possible only after 1920, when the technique of assembling prefabricated slabs at the construction site was developed; however, architects had been at work on designs for concrete buildings for years.

The socio-economic circumstances were no less important than the technique. The economic crisis of 1913 and the First World War had caused stagnation in the building of private housing. Although the country was not officially involved in the hostilities, importing raw materials from the colonies became very difficult. Construction costs rose to unprecedented heights, and the uncertainties in international politics caused entrepreneurs to refrain from taking high risks in investments. The construction of private housing bottomed out in 1918 and did not pick up again until 1920, when the mortgage interest rates were lowered as a stimulating measure.

The crisis did not strike public housing as hard, because of subsidized construction costs and other government measures. But here, too, the consequences of rising costs were felt, and an enormous housing shortage resulted. In 1917, under pressure from the leftist parties, an act was passed restricting the rents of inexpensive housing. A year later, newly built housing was brought under this act as well. Meanwhile, plans were made to build semi-permanent emergency housing to take the brunt of the shortage. The idea was to build this housing with a government subsidy amounting to 90 percent and a supplementary municipal subsidy of 10 percent. In 1918 the construction of middle-class housing, which had become attractive as a result of these subsidies, picked up greatly. There was extensive experimentation with new materials, inexpensive construction methods, standardization, and prefabrication.[29]

Van 't Hoff's designs from 1918 and 1919 should be considered within this context. In those years van 't Hoff worked for a time in Utrecht in the firm of the architect P. J. C. Klaarhamer.[30] Klaarhamer was not directly involved with De Stijl, but he maintained close relations with a number of artists who were. Gerrit Rietveld had taken a course taught by Klaarhamer in his youth and had executed some of his furniture designs. Van der Leck, a boyhood friend of Klaarhamer, collaborated with him on several projects, including the Bruynzeel Company's display stand for the Annual Industrial Fair of 1919.

Van 't Hoff, who had met Klaarhamer through van der Leck, is thought to have collaborated with him on designs for mass construction. Yet there appear to be no traces of designs for middle-class housing or apartment buildings in the van 't Hoff collection of the Nederlands Documentatiecentrum voor de Bouwkunst. The fact that the center's Klaarhamer collection has not been opened to the public in its entirety makes it difficult to get a complete view of Klaarhamer's work. Furthermore, there are still great uncertainties about dates and attributions. Nonetheless, there are in the Klaarhamer archive a number of designs that can be attributed to van 't Hoff with a reasonable degree of certainty.[31] One of these is the design for a townhouse shown here as figure 201. At first glance, this design has a rather traditional look. However, the sketches shown in figure 202 suggest that the shape was arrived at only after a number of compromises. For instance, in the left sketch the house is flat-roofed, but in the right one it has a sloping roof. Perhaps that was the client's wish. It could also be explained by the fact that the house had to be built in brick; van 't Hoff was of the opinion that a sloping roof was not suitable for a concrete house.

Also in the Klaarhamer archive is the design for a four-family house shown in figure 203. The monumental character of this house, the receding middle section, and the horizontal bands evoke associations with Wright's Larkin building (figure 204), and the idiosyncratic interpretation of Wright's architecture suggests van 't Hoff as the designer.[32] However, there is some question as to the attribution of this drawing. Van 't Hoff had a good, flowing style and could represent a building in correct perspective with only a few strokes. But this particular drawing is rather faulty in technique and in the details of construction. For instance, it is not clear how the steps at the front door are meant to be arranged or how they were conceived spatially. The volume treatment of the right wing betrays a second inaccuracy: The edge of the roof to the right of the central section runs into the blind wall behind it. Therefore, this drawing does not seem to have come from the hand of van 't Hoff. Among the Klaarhamer papers is a second, more precise drawing of the project, an elevation with floor plans (figure 205). This shows some characteristics that are entirely in van 't Hoff's line—for instance, the alternation of windows and closed wall surfaces in the front and side facades.[33] The floor plan, too, shows motifs characteristic of van 't Hoff. The dining room and the music room were conceived as a single entity. (Compare the living room of the Concrete Villa.) This large room was probably intended for communal use by all the residents. There are, however, separate sitting rooms and bedrooms for each family. The attic has extra bedrooms and storage space. Other motifs typical of van 't Hoff (such as built-in closets and central chimneys) are lacking here, but this design is only partially detailed. If van 't Hoff did indeed draw the elevation and the floor plans, the course of events may have gone as follows. On the basis of this design, Klaarhamer or someone working for him made the sketch shown as figure 203 for the purpose of presenting the project. This seems all the more plausible because the sketch suggests how the building was to fit into the existing surroundings. The exact extent of the collaboration on this design between Klaarhamer and van 't Hoff cannot be determined, but it seems clear that some interaction took place and that the result bears van 't Hoff's stamp.

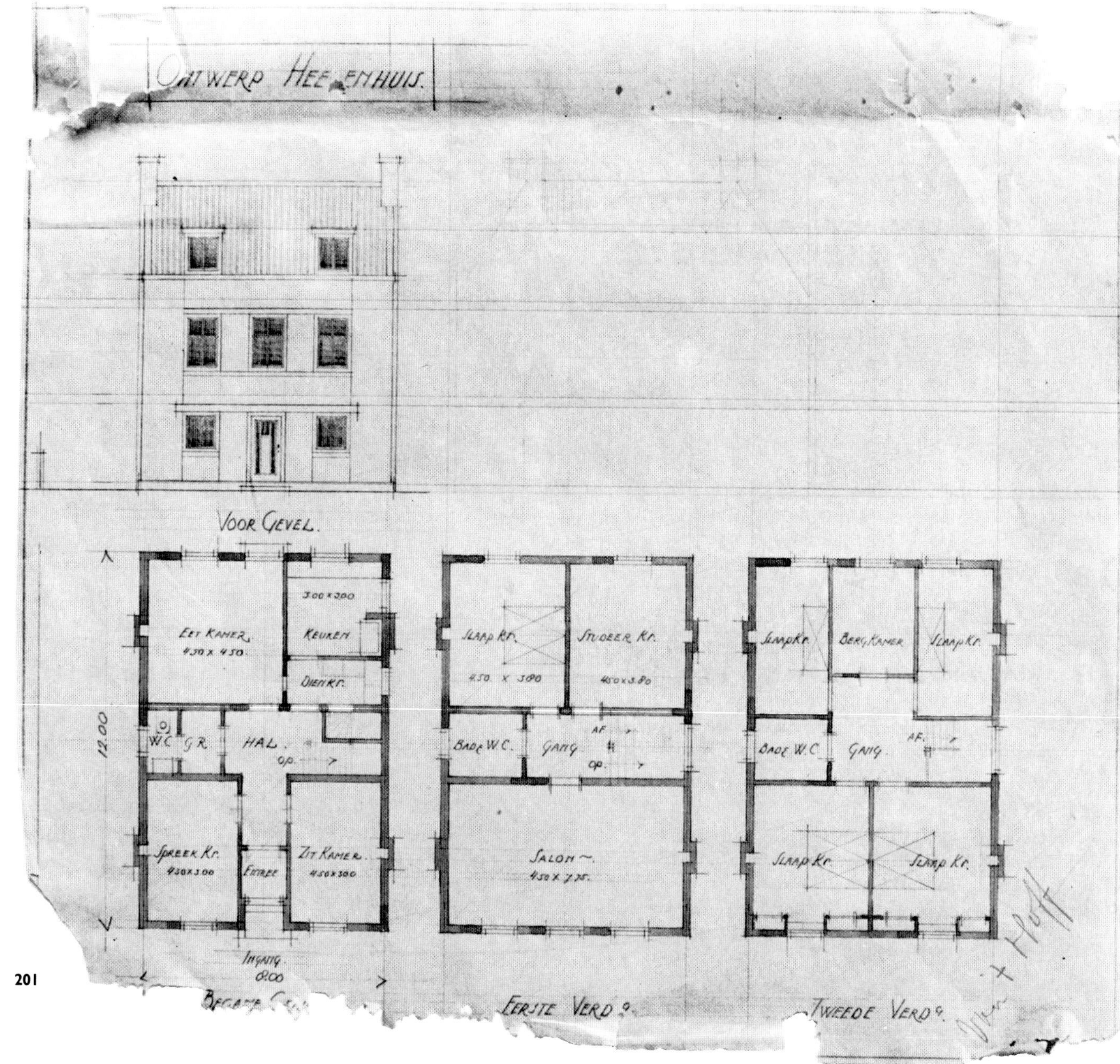
VOOR GEVEL.
EET KAMER 4.50 x 4.50.
3.00 x 3.00
KEUKEN
DIEN KR.
W.C.
G.R.
HAL
OP.
SPREEK KR. 4.50 x 3.00
ENTREE
ZIT KAMER 4.50 x 3.00
INGANG
12.00
SLAAP KR. 4.50 x 3.80
STUDEER KR. 4.50 x 3.80
BADE W.C.
GANG
AF
OP.
SALON 4.50 x 7.75
SLAAP KR.
BERG KAMER
SLAAP KR.
BADE W.C.
GANG
AF.
SLAAP KR.
SLAAP KR.
EERSTE VERD?
TWEEDE VERD?

201

202

201 Van 't Hoff, design for a town house. Nederlands Documentatiecentrum voor de Bouwkunst, Amsterdam.

202 Van 't Hoff, sketch of a townhouse, 1918–19. Nederlands Documentatiecentrum voor de Bouwkunst, Amsterdam.

203 Perspective drawing of a four-family house, 1918–19. Nederlands Documentatiecentrum voor de Bouwkunst, Amsterdam.

204 Frank Lloyd Wright, Larkin Building, Buffalo, N.Y., 1904. As illustrated on page 109 of C. R. Ashbee's *Frank Lloyd Wright,* volume 8 of the series Architektur des XX jahrhunderts (Berlin: Wasmuth, 1911).

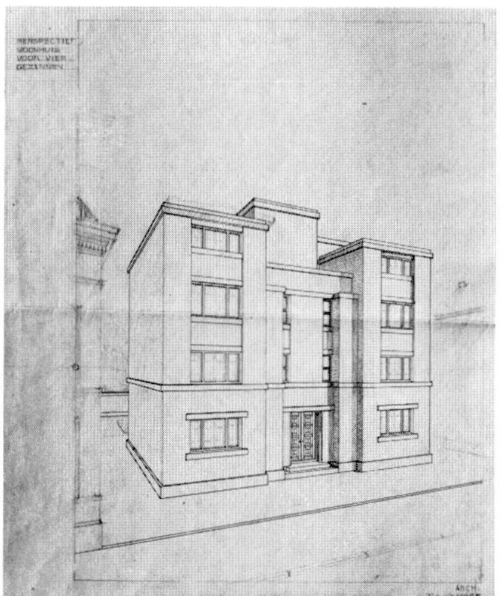

203

204

205

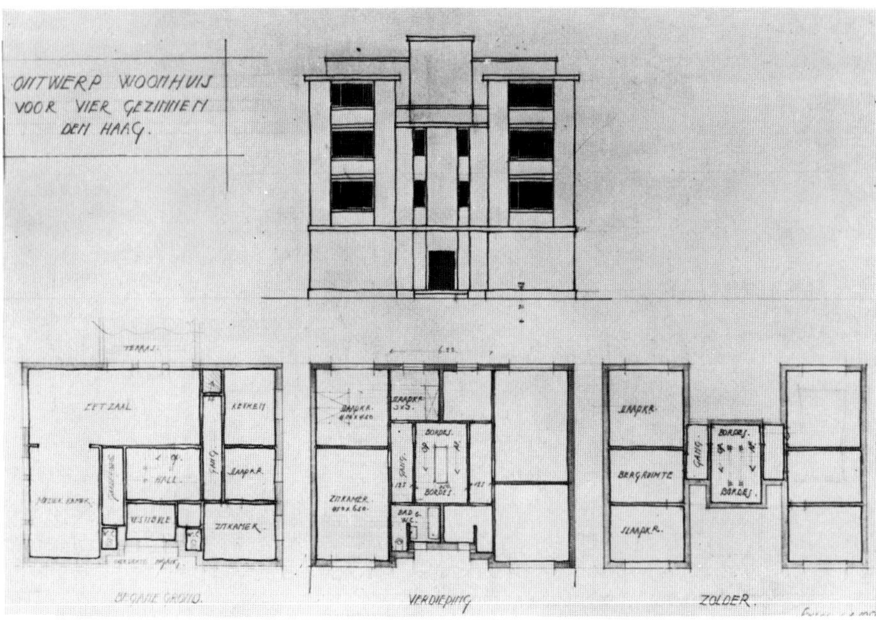

206

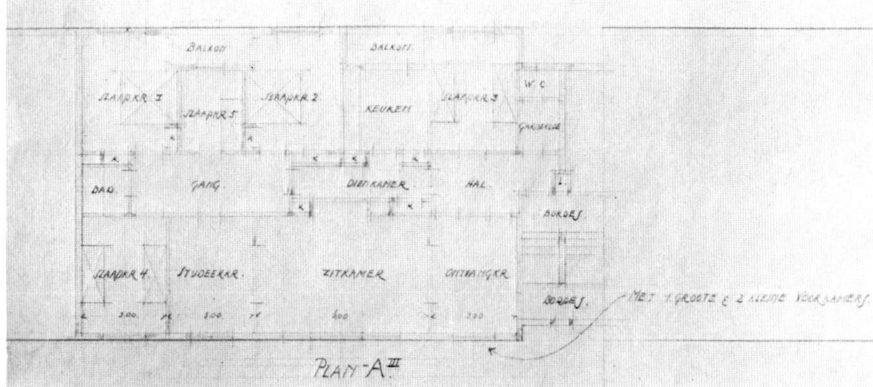

205 Van 't Hoff, design for a four-family house, The Hague, 1918–19. Nederlands Documentatiecentrum voor de Bouwkunst, Amsterdam.

206 Van 't Hoff, "Apartments plan A I, II, and III" (detail), 1918–19. Nederlands Documentatiecentrum voor de Bouwkunst, Amsterdam.

The third and last design that will be discussed here is one for a concrete apartment building. Van 't Hoff's input into this collaboration with Klaarhamer remains unclear, but three floor plans are probably from his hand. The differences among the three apartments are minimal; the subdivision of the space is for the most part identical, except for the front rooms. These are arranged as follows: one large and two small front rooms, three rooms of equal size, or two large living rooms (figure 206). There are various characteristics that may point to van 't Hoff as the designer. The rooms are not conceived as strictly closed spaces; their large openings result in a strong spatial effect. A relation between interior and exterior space is effected by means of large balconies. This design was probably never executed, because the construction material had to be concrete. In point of fact, concrete was not used in mass housing until much later.

Thus, in the years when he was involved with De Stijl, van 't Hoff did create designs, but he had little opportunity to realize them.

Political engagement

The fact that van 't Hoff was so active in designing mass construction can also be explained in terms of his ideological background. As mentioned in the beginning of this chapter, he was socially engaged from his youth. Most of the avante-garde architects and artists had a certain notion of the need for a renewal of society, but most did not link this to membership in a political party. Van 't Hoff did, however. Stimulated by the Russian revolution, he became more radical during the course of 1918–19. Following the political implications of his social utopianism, he joined the Communist Party. In a letter to Chris Beekman, a fellow artist and a fellow communist, he expressed his convictions clearly: "I myself am a communist, member of the communist party and have asked Wijnkoop [chairman of the Dutch Communist Party] to assist us in getting the first manifesto to Russia! He will try, and this proves to us that the tie you wrote about already exists. Anyone who reads the Russian manifesto in the latest issue of *De stijl* can have no doubts about the attitude of our movement toward the new communism. I often talked to van Doesburg about coming out decisively. . . . I myself am convinced that we will get a Soviet government, albeit that the transition will take a toll of some of our lives. I am trying to anticipate and to be ready for the implementation after the revolution, by designing mass-production buildings—no more private villas. Therefore, I am advocating an association of all avowed communist artists whose work is truly communist."[34]

The "first manifesto" mentioned in the above quotation was the De Stijl manifesto, printed in the first issue (November 1918) of the second volume of the periodical. The opening lines read: "There is an old and a new consciousness of time. The old is connected with the individual. The new is connected with the universal. The struggle of the individual against the universal is revealing itself in the World War as well as in the art of the present day." The publication of this manifesto in four languages was meant to give *De stijl* international status and to seek connections with foreign avant-garde artists. However, the manifesto was subject to differing interpretations. While others saw in it a mainly artistic stance, van 't Hoff obviously interpreted it as a polemic in favor of the "world struggle."

In the April 1919 issue of *De stijl* there appeared an article[35] by the Soviet Commissariat for Public Information that advocated a complete reorganization of art and art policies, including an abrogation of the differences among the various fields of art, the promotion of public art education, the assignment of equal status to craft and industrial products, and the legal protection of art. Tatlin, Kandinsky, Malevich, Rodchenko, and others were named in connection with this program.[36]

To remain informed about post-revolutionary developments in Russia, some Dutch artists planned an exchange program. In connection with this, van 't Hoff and Beekman sent drawings and photographs of their work to Russia. However, responses (particularly from Malevich, to whom they had sent the material) were slow in coming.

There was a great demand in the Netherlands for information on developments in Russia, but the mails were greatly impaired by restrictions. In the autumn of 1919, a number of Dutch artists petitioned their legislature to restore free postal interchange.[37] Besides van 't Hoff, the *De stijl* contributors who signed the petition were van Doesburg, Huszár,[38] Kok, Rietveld, and Wils. Van Doesburg was asked to use his influence as editor of *De stijl* to drum up international support for the effort. He had copies of the petition in various languages, but he neglected to send them out. Van 't Hoff and Beekman were furious when they discovered this negligence.

In the first half of 1919 van Doesburg and van 't Hoff had been on good terms, despite the houseboat affair. Van 't Hoff was even lending financial support to *De stijl*, and van Doesburg was able to write to Antony Kok on March 15 that "van 't Hoff does all he can." Soon, however, there were more conflicts. Van 't Hoff reproached Van Doesburg for taking part in exhibitions on his own after he had agreed to exhibit work only as a member of the De Stijl movement. Even worse in van 't Hoff's eyes was van Doesburg's failure to circulate the petition; he took this to be a direct anti-revolutionary act. On October 10 van 't Hoff wrote to Kok that collaboration "between van Doesburg as [editor] of *De stijl* and [van 't Hoff]" was "no longer possible," and eight days later he added the opinion that "Does, by returning the addresses . . . [had] taken a stance counter to the common interest." This van 't Hoff would "never be able to forget, not till eternity." "In Russia," he wrote, "they execute such people. They are our greatest enemies."

On November 4, a number of radical artists and "brain-workers" formed the Bond van Revolutionair Socialistische Intellectueelen, with Bart de Ligt as leader. This organization was not involved directly with the petition for free postal interchange, but it supported the initiative. Among its members were Peter Alma, Hildo Krop, John Raedecker, and (for a short time) Theo van Doesburg. Though his name does not appear on early membership lists, van 't Hoff seems to have been a member as well. Van 't Hoff had already expressed the need for an association of communist artists to Beekman. After renouncing De Stijl, he had even more reason to look for a new association in whose bosom the revolutionary idea could be nurtured. However, the Bond van Revolutionair Socialistische Intellectueelen wilted within a few years.

But van 't Hoff maintained some of his revolutionary élan and his anger at van Doesburg. This is shown by his criticism of an Amsterdam arts-and-crafts fair in the December 3, 1919, issue of *De tribune:* "In none of the works can there be perceived an ideological thought, a unified concept of art in relation to society, or a sense of cooperation between artists and executors. None of the artifacts manifests that it has been created in a time of developing world revolution." One of the objects in this exhibition was a garden urn by van Doesburg; though van 't Hoff was considerate enough to leave the designer's name out of the review, he condemned the urn as "an attempt to be quasi-modern" and stated that it was much too expensive for the common man.

Two small houses in Laren

After his break with De Stijl and the scant success of his political actions, van 't Hoff withdrew from the artistic life. He had met very few like-minded people among the artists, and he was probably especially disappointed by the failure of his expectation of a proletarian revolution brought about by artists, in general, and abstract artists, in particular.

In 1920 van 't Hoff sold his houseboat and built two simple "workers' houses" in Laren, one for his parents and one for him-

207

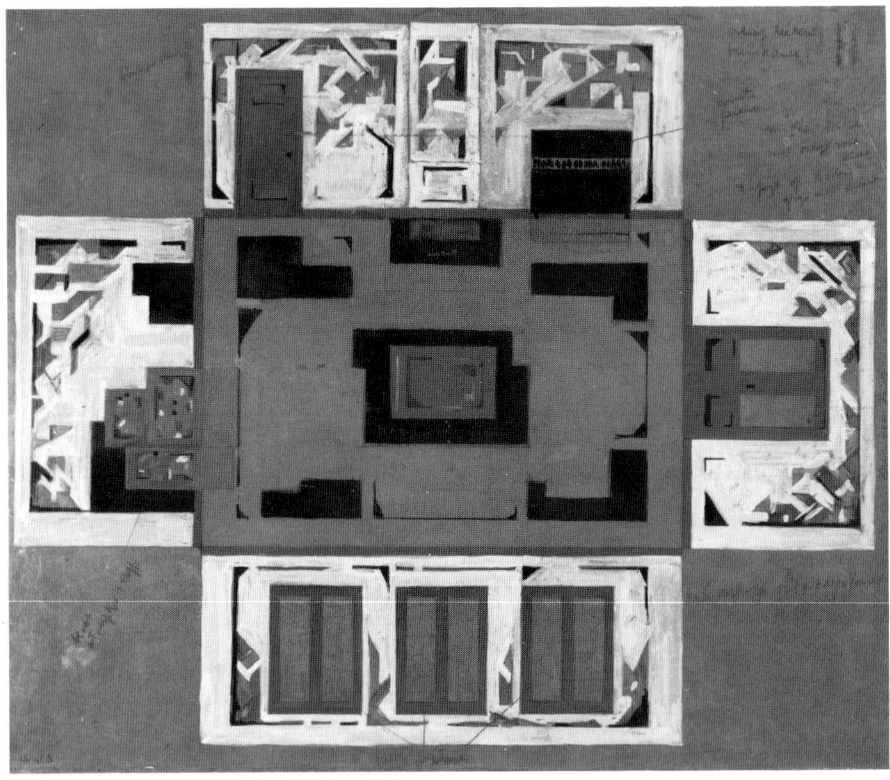

208

207 **The house of Dr. H. J. van 't Hoff, in Laren, built in 1920. This photograph shows the house after a renovation not carried out by Robert van 't Hoff; nevertheless, it does give an impression of how the house originally looked.**

208 **Chris Beekman, Ontwerpteekening tuinkamer [Design drawing of living room], 1920 (?). Centraal Museum, Utrecht.**

209 **Van 't Hoff, cabinets in standard sizes, 1920 (?). Whereabouts unknown. As illustrated in *De stijl* 7, no. 79–84 (1927), pp. 25–26.**

self. Once he had written that "architecture should be interpreted as the attempt to freely and courageously make the human environment harmonious, which means to convert the world of things into a direct projection of the spiritual world,"[39] but these houses are a far cry from that ideal. Van 't Hoff never considered them part of his artistic output; he thought of them as ordinary houses, devoid of aesthetic pretense.

The application for the building permit for the house of Dr. H. J. van 't Hoff was dated January 23, 1920. The permit stated that the work was to be executed "by the architect himself." The floor plan was sober, and there was no attempt to achieve ingenious spatial effects. Van 't Hoff's attention to detail was apparent in the woodwork. The facades were finished in white stucco, with a dark plinth around the house. The construction was of brick. The saddle roof was covered with gray tiles. Shutters, a rain barrel, and a fascia finished with perpendicularly positioned bricks completed the "picturesque" image.

The second house, in which Robert van 't Hoff was to live himself,[40] was built somewhat later. The permit was granted on October 15, 1920. This time the work was executed by a certain J. van de Wolk from Baarn. This unassuming house went still farther in the use of traditional materials from the "picturesque" epoch; it even had a thatched roof.

There is an interior design by Chris Beekman that bears the inscriptions "design drawing for room looking onto the garden" and "design of a room for R. van 't Hoff/architect." This design (shown here as figure 208) is not dated, but it was probably made in 1920. The way in which architectonic details such as the windows, the inner door, and the chimney are marked suggests that this design was meant for an existing space. It seems perfectly matched to the living room in the floor plan of the first of the Laren houses. The windows on the garden side, the door to the outside (to the left in the interior design), and the inner door (top left) conform to those of the floor plan. Only the location of the chimney does not tally; in the design it is situated on top in the center, while in the floor plan (and in the realized house) its place is to the left against the inner wall. Could Beekman's drawing have corresponded to a first design by van 't Hoff, which was then changed? Whatever the case, Beekman's interior design was modern and remarkable. The rug is shown in gray with black rectangles. In the center a rectangular red table stands on a black area. The transition between the floor surface and the walls is marked by a gray plinth. The walls, with their accents in the upper corners, are extraordinarily lively. The manner of decoration is different from the familiar work of van Doesburg and Huszár. It is not constructive or destructive to the architecture; it is more an adornment.

Beekman's interior includes, at the left, three cabinets designed by van 't Hoff. Without Beekman's addition of color, they are simple wooden boxes, designed according to a system of fixed dimensions. Van 't Hoff's cabinets were shown in their plain state in the tenth-anniversary issue of *De stijl* (figure 209). In a letter to van Doesburg (reproduced in *De stijl*), van 't Hoff wrote: "At your request I am sending you a variety of my work created during the first years of the 'De Stijl' movement and never reproduced; after this work I have not created anything more. . . ." A correction in the next issue dated the cabinets 1917–18; this, however, does not tally with van 't Hoff's statement that these were his last works. Actually, the cabinets must have been, like Beekman's interior, designed in 1920.

A 1920 letter from Rietveld to Oud provides further evidence: "I executed a cabinet for van 't Hoff which I think is very good, and beds, also very good. I'd like to see how Beekman treats the interior for van 't Hoff."[41] Though van 't Hoff had distanced himself from De Stijl, and had renounced abstract architecture, he apparently could not resist privately collaborating with Beekman on this abstract interior. In the same letter that was reproduced in the tenth-anniversay issue of *De stijl,* van 't Hoff explained why he was no longer interested in building: The time was not yet ripe for his ideals, and life "essentially consists of self-righteousness." He wanted to try independently to achieve true communism on a small scale, without property and without overproduction. This letter was sent from England, to which van 't Hoff had returned in 1922, and was signed "Robert Van. ('t Hoff)., ex-architect."

209

1
Paul Hefting, "Correspondentie met Amerika," in *Americana* (exhibition catalog, Rijksmuseum Kröller-Müller, Otterlo, 1975), p. 97.

2
"Brief van Rob. van 't Hoff," *De stijl* 7, no. 79–84 (1927), p. 24.

3
Data derived from biographical notes by van 't Hoff, intended as supplement to the biography in *Robert van 't Hoff* (exhibition catalog, Stedelijk Van Abbemuseum, Eindhoven, 1967). The annotations are in the archive of the Van Abbemuseum.

4
Michael Holroyd, *Augustus John, a biography* (Harmondsworth, 1976), p. 511.

5
Letter to J. Leering, January 7, 1969.

6
Holroyd, *Augustus John* (note 4 above), p. 513.

7
Letter from van 't Hoff to J. Leering, August 7, 1964. Around 1913 and 1914, Bomberg's work showed strong similarities to that of the vorticists, although he was not among the signers of their manifestoes. It is said that van 't Hoff was in London in 1919 and tried to persuade Bomberg to associate with De Stijl; see Richard Cork, *Vorticism and abstract art in the first machine age* (London, 1976), volume 2, p. 516.

8
Cork, *Vorticism* (note 7 above), volume 1, p. 86.

9
R. van 't Hoff, "Architectuur en haar ontwikkeling," *De stijl* 1, no. 5 (1918), p. 57.

10
C. R. Ashbee, *Frank Lloyd Wright,* volume 8 of Architektur des XX jahrhunderts (Berlin, 1911).

11
The German text reads as follows: "Die Maschine ist das Werkzeug das unserer Kulturperiode eigentümlich ist, und es ist eine wichtige Aufgabe, für diese Maschine Arbeit zu schaffen, die sie bewältigen kann. Das Anpassen an die Möglichkeiten der Maschine ist der Inhalt des modernen industriellen Ideals, das wir aufbauen müssen, wenn die Baukunst ihre führende Stellung in der Kunst nicht verlieren soll." In the English rendition given in the text of the present volume, the first two sentences are quoted from Wright's original article; the last sentence is translated from Dutch.

12
Actually, van 't Hoff was asked to build a private museum for the above-mentioned John Quinn. Van 't Hoff probably got this commission on the recommendation of Augustus John. Quinn and van 't Hoff looked on Long Island for a suitable site for the museum, which was to house an exquisite collection of works by Gauguin, Brancusi, Duchamp-Villon, Derain, Gaudier-Brzeska, Matisse, and Picasso. It appears that a design was drafted; however, the ambitious plan did not get beyond that stage. In the meantime, the First World War broke out, and the execution was tabled.

13
Frank Lloyd Wright, "In the cause of architecture," *Architectural Record* 23 (1908), pp. 155–221.

14
Verbal communication, J. Leering, January 11, 1982.

15
As a result of a lack of know-how on the part of the Hollandsche Beton Mij., the first frame collapsed (verbal communication, N. Tummers, January 19, 1982).

16
R. van 't Hoff, "Architectuur en haar ontwikkeling (vervolg)," *De stijl* 2, no. 5 (1919), pp. 54–55.

17
J. Leering, "Rob van 't Hoff de ex-architect," *Wonen/TABK* 11 (1979), p. 2.

18
Huib Hoste, "Evolutie naar de moderne architectuur," *Streven* 10, no. 7–12 (1957), p. 1064.

19
J. J. P. Oud, "Het monumentale stadsbeeld," *De stijl* 1, no. 1 (1917), pp. 10–11.

20
Reyner Banham, *Theory and Design in the First Machine Age* (London, 1960), p. 154.

21
R. van 't Hoff, "Architectuur en haar ontwikkeling," *De stijl* 1, no. 5 (1918), pp. 57–59; 2, no. 4 (1919), pp. 40–42; 2, no. 5 (1919), pp. 54–55.

22
R. van 't Hoff, "Het hotel-café-restaurant 'De Dubbele Sleutel' (eerste gedeeltelijke verbouwing) te Woerden," *De stijl* 2, no. 5 (1919), pp. 58–60.

23
R. van 't Hoff, "Aanteekeningen bij bijlage XX," *De stijl* 2, no. 10 (1919), pp. 114–116. As was mentioned above in the text, van 't Hoff had become acquainted with futurism before the war, in London. He had met Marinetti, but he had not known of the work of Sant' Elia (who had died young). He was probably introduced to it by Theo van Doesburg, who read the foreign journals and who had been sent a considerable amount of material on futurism by Marinetti on April 22, 1919.

24
Quoted from a "messaggio" by Sant' Elia, published on the occasion of the exhibition Nuove Tendenze, Milan, 1914.

25
Data from the municipal register of Breukelen.

26
It cannot be ascertained precisely when the chair was designed and executed. In any case, the photograph in which it appears must have been taken after August 1919—two pages from *De stijl* pinned to the wall (one showing the Concrete Villa and one showing a diamond-shaped composition by Mondrian) are from the May and August 1919 issues, respectively. Van 't Hoff probably designed his chair in 1919, shortly after Rietveld created his high chairs.

27
Van 't Hoff, "Architectuur en haar ontwikkeling," *De stijl* 1, no. 5 (1918), pp. 57–59.

28
See the chapters on Huszár and van der Leck in this volume.

29
See M. Casciato et al., *Architektuur en volkshuisvesting* (Delft, 1980), and *Bouwen '20–'40, de Nederlandse bijdrage aan het Nieuwe Bouwen* (exhibition catalog, Stedelijk Van Abbemuseum, Eindhoven, 1971).

30
Van 't Hoff wrote the following to J. Leering on December 22, 1973: ". . . had not expected to hear anything more about Klaarhamer ever. Thought him a sensitive human being, and therefore sympathetic. Met him at van der Leck's, visited him afterward in Utrecht, and came to collaborate with him."

31
A number of designs in the Klaarhamer archive bear van 't Hoff's name but not his signature.

32
This drawing was attributed to van 't Hoff on page 86 of *Architektuur en volkshuisvesting* (note 29 above).

33
Because this is not an elaborated architectural drawing, one can only guess at certain details. It may be that the horizontal band drawn across the entire length of the facade, which delineates the ceiling-floor line, was to be continued over the entrance as well. The inscription "overdekte ingang" [covered entrance] on the floor plan is an indication that this may have been the case. Probably an overhang was planned, which for technical reasons could be best executed in concrete. Van 't Hoff preferred that material; in any case, this would seem to be one more reason for assuming that he wanted the house to be executed in concrete.

34
This letter is dated May 2, 1919. See Ger Harmsen, "Nederlandse en russische kunstenaars tijdens de revolutiejaren," *De nieuwe stem* 22, no. 6 (1976), p. 318.

35
"Algemeen kunstprogramma van het tegenwoordige Rusland," *De stijl* 2, no. 6 (1919), pp. 68–70. This article was copied from the March 1919 issue of the German art magazine *Das kunstblatt.*

36
Curiously, parts of this program were later echoed in Dutch newspapers and magazines. For example, in late 1919 *De nieuwe Amsterdammer* and *De tribune* published stories on the relationship between abstract art and proletarian revolution.

37
De tribune of November 24, 1919, reported that Peter Alma had sent the petition to the Tweede Kamer on November 10. Chris Beekman is sometimes mentioned in the literature as the force behind this initiative; see page 314 of Harmsen (note 34 above).

38
Huszár had reservations about the petition, as he informed Beekman in writing: It had been circulated among artists of diverse artistic and political convictions, including some naturalists and the traditionalist authors Herman Heijermans and Frans Coenen as well as more modern artists such as Jan Sluyters and Erich Wichman.

39
This quotation is from van 't Hoff's comments on an architectural design by Sant' Elia in "Aanteekeningen bij bijlage XX," *De stijl* 2, no. 10 (1919).

40
According to data in the Laren municipal register, Robert van 't Hoff lived in Laren from 1920 on. His address is not known, but he may have lived temporarily in the house built for his father, who is listed as a resident of Laren from 1921 on.

41
Letter from Rietveld to Oud, February 26, 1920.

210 Georges Vantongerloo, ca. 1935.

Georges Vantongerloo

Nicolette Gast

Georges Vantongerloo is usually considered as the sculptor of De Stijl. Yet he was just as much a painter (and, later, a designer of furniture and buildings). The paintings from his De Stijl years are as important a part of his output as his sculptures; however, in Theo van Doesburg's early publications, in the first De Stijl manifesto, and in the periodical *De stijl* he was presented as exclusively a sculptor.

Although Vantongerloo published regularly in the early volumes of *De stijl,* his position within the circle of contributors remained somewhat marginal. He knew hardly any of the others personally (van Doesburg was an exception), and he encountered distrust from some of them (e.g., Vilmos Huszár). He was defended by van Doesburg, who believed in his ideas and his work. This is understandable, because Vantongerloo's works from the early years of De Stijl until about 1920—especially the paintings—show a great dependence on van Doesburg's works.

After 1920, when he moved to Menton in the south of France, Vantongerloo did not publish in *De stijl* any longer. This was probably due to a change in his relationship with van Doesburg and Mondrian. What little of the correspondence between Vantongerloo and van Doesburg is extant suggests that their relationship deteriorated dramatically in 1927. In the tenth-anniversary issue of *De stijl,* van Doesburg had harsh words for Vantongerloo and for other early contributors who were then writing for the magazine *i 10.* This and other unpleasant experiences gave Vantongerloo a great aversion to everything connected with Theo van Doesburg, even after the latter's death. On August 16, 1931, he responded bitterly to a request to contribute to the final issue of *De stijl,* which J. J. P. Oud, Nelly van Doesburg, and Helena Milius were preparing as a commemoration of the late editor: "What is that Stijl but a puppet show deceiving people with publicity for Does? . . . What remains of Does? Subtract those 7 contributors and nothing remains of De Stijl + Does."

Vantongerloo never lost the feeling that he had been slighted. Later in life he did not want to have anything to do with exhibitions or publications dedicated to De Stijl. On the other hand, he tried in his own articles and in his documentation to present his role as more important than it had been. He also annotated his copies of other people's texts—for instance, in van Doesburg's 1919 booklet *Drie voordrachten over de nieuwe beeldende kunst* he wrote: "Theo van Doesburg has read Vantongerloo's Réflexions, but takes care not to say that. . . . He copies my sentences but does not mention my name."[1] In addition, in the catalog he made of his works from the early years of De Stijl, Vantongerloo antedated many of them. The catalog of the large Vantongerloo exhibition held in 1980 and 1981 at several American museums and in Brussels and Zurich was based entirely on the data found in his estate, which at present is with Max Bill in Zurich; it gives many insights into Vantongerloo's colored vision of his past with De Stijl.

The impression of Vantongerloo's early work evoked in this chapter deviates from that provided by other literature[2] in several respects. Where documentary material from the time was available, this chapter is based on it; the rest is based mainly on a consideration of Vantongerloo's work in relation to that of the other De Stijl artists. Although this leads to different conclusions about dates and influences, it does not take away anything from the extraordinary quality of Vantongerloo's work; his small sculptures, which together could easily be put in one suitcase, deserve a prominent place in twentieth-century sculpture.

Education and first works

Little is known about Vantongerloo's youth or the milieu in which he grew up. We only know the names of his parents, Leonard Vantongerloo and Marie Dams, and his date and place of birth, November 24, 1886, in Antwerp, Belgium.

In 1900, at the age of 13, he was enrolled as a student at the Academy of Fine Arts in Antwerp. For the first two years he pursued a rather general program; after that he chose to receive training in sculpture.[3] During his fourth and final year he took evening courses and worked during the day as an assistant in the studio of the sculptor Emile Jespers, the father of his fellow student Oscar Jespers.[4] Emile Jespers was much in demand as a portrait sculptor. In his studio Vantongerloo became acquainted with the realistic representation that portraiture required, while the traditional education he received at the academy was mainly directed toward the idealistic representation of the human body, after the examples of classical antiquity.

In 1904 Vantongerloo left the academy. He may have stayed in Jespers's studio as an assistant; this may be why no works of his own from this period are known. In 1906 he decided to continue his studies, this time at the Royal Academy of Fine Arts in Brussels. For three years he followed the program of that academy, which was thorough but very traditional, like his courses in Antwerp. In his last year he took part in two competitions organized by the academy, winning first prize in one and third in the other. In the same year, 1909, Vantongerloo entered the competition for the Prix de Rome. He did not get beyond the strict preliminary screening; however, this competition probably provided him with the chance to meet Rik Wouters, who some years later would have a considerable influence on his sculpture and his painting. In

1912 Vantongerloo reached the second round (the screening for admission), but he got no farther than that.

From 1909 until the outbreak of the First World War, Vantongerloo was busy building his career as a sculptor in Brussels. Not much work from this period is extant, but there are photographs that show traditional heads, modeled or hewn in marble. Vantongerloo rapidly established himself as a portrait sculptor; he was even commissioned to portray the Belgian royal family.[5] He exhibited at least twice in those years. At Charleroi, in January 1912, he sold (for 250 Belgian francs) the sculpture *Le rire* [*The laugh*].[6] Now known only from reproductions, *Le rire* was a clownish head with a grimacing expression. Although it was modeled, the surface was rather smooth. The hair resembled a smooth cap. In 1914 Vantongerloo exhibited a child's head and a portrait of his brother Frans (a painter) at the Salon Triennal de Belgique, in Brussels.[7] These two modeled pieces probably did not differ much from *Le rire* in their execution. The one extant example of Vantongerloo's work in marble from this period is the child's head shown here as figure 211. This small sculpture has a smooth finish and shows vestiges of Vantongerloo's classical training (particularly in the idealized, angelic expression).

Vantongerloo's known work from before 1914 shows no trace of any interest in the modern trends of the time, although several exhibitions of cubist and futurist art were held in Brussels in 1912 and 1913. A 1965 article quotes Vantongerloo as saying that he was introduced to futurism in the Netherlands during the First World War by the Belgian painter Jules Schmalzigaug.[8]

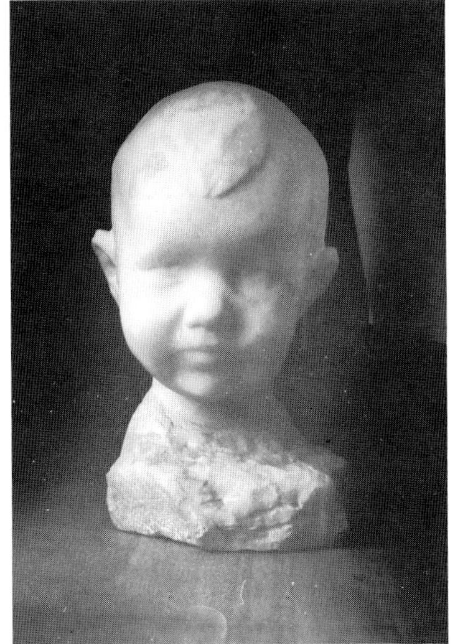

211 Vantongerloo, *Kinderkop* [*Child's head*], ca. 1910. Marble. Collection of L. Tas, Amsterdam.

Stay in the Netherlands

When Belgium was drawn into the war in the summer of 1914, Vantongerloo was mobilized. In the same year, he fled from the German occupation, and soon he settled in The Hague.[9] Exactly when he arrived in the Netherlands is uncertain; however, he cannot have taken any work with him from Belgium, and so he must have been in the Netherlands at least a few months when he participated in exhibitions there in February 1915.

It is not clear in which circles Vantongerloo moved in the Netherlands. He did not join any of the art associations in The Hague, such as Pulchri or the Haagsche Kunstkring. It seems plausible that he was mainly in contact with other Belgian refugee artists; he regularly participated in group exhibitions with Rik Wouters, the sculptors Oscar Jespers and Albert Termote, and the painters Valentijn van Uytvanck, Willem Paerels, Gust de Smet, and Frits van den Berghe.[10]

Vantongerloo still did not clearly demonstrate an interest in modern artistic trends. He did not join the Open Wegen [Open Roads] art circle, which was founded in 1916 or early 1917 by the above-mentioned de Smet and van den Berghe and the critic André de Ridder[11] and which had as one of its aims the promotion of a convergence of painting, sculpture, and architecture. The only indication that Vantongerloo may have had a growing interest in the new direction is his association with Jules Schmalzigaug,[12] who even before the war had been in close contact with the Italian futurists. From 1914 until his early death in May 1917, Schmalzigaug worked in the Netherlands, and Vantongerloo probably met him in 1915. Vestiges of futurist influence can be found in Vantongerloo's later abstract work and in his theories, although he still adhered to a more traditional method for a while after his exposure to this influence.

Vantongerloo had lost all his commissions when he had left Belgium, and one of his motives for taking part in many exhibitions in the Netherlands must have been to obtain new commissions, particularly for portraits. He was represented in at least three group exhibitions in The Hague in 1915, but soon he had produced enough works to fill an exhibition room. His first one-man show was held from March 15 to March 29, 1916, in the Pulchri Studio, in the Hague. (Pulchri allowed him to rent a room, although he was not a member.) In the second half of 1916 and in 1917 he took part in at least four group exhibitions (in Amsterdam, Arnhem, and The Hague), and then in October 1917 he had another one-man show, this time in the gallery of the Kunstkring Hollando-Belge, in the Hague.

Vantongerloo suddenly ceased exhibiting in late 1917. It is difficult to say whether this was due to the rigorous changes in his work or to other factors. Perhaps his marriage to Tine Kalis, on November 28, 1917, made him more financially independent[13]—no portraits made after that date are known.

The development of Vantongerloo's work between 1915 and 1917 can be traced fairly accurately through catalogs, reviews, and some photographs.[14] At the 1915 exhibitions, he showed almost nothing but portraits of adults and children. (Some reviews mention studies of a cow and a pregnant horse.) At his first one-man show, in March 1916, a new and rather worldly theme was in evidence: women getting dressed. In the reviews these works are often described as a *tranche de vie* [slice of life]. That expression can also be applied to *Hurkende Volendammer* [*Squatting man from Volendam*], Vantongerloo's most ambitious sculpture of these years. Probably made in late 1916, it was exhibited for the first time in December of that year, and subsequently at all Vantongerloo's exhibitions in 1917.

From the time of his first exhibition in the Netherlands, Vantongerloo's sculptures were described as impressionistic. The critic G. D. Gratama wrote extensively about this in a review on the occasion of the Pulchri exhibition.[15] He distinguishes academic and impressionist sculpture, and describes the first as "flawless, beautifully modeled [sculpture] . . . which smoothly and coldly represents the shapes as correctly as possible, which couples grace with pure proportion, [and] against which nothing can be said except that it is too academic, too lifeless." With Vantongerloo's sculpture, on the other hand, "life is precisely what it is all about. That must seethe and fizz under the high light in the hall. He observes a figure as an impressionist does, catching it in the act, which will momentarily transform into another act. This moment of transition, which Rodin so rightly calls the life-inspiring element in art, is what Vantongerloo wants to give us. He sacrifices all details of minor importance to this end. With a broad gesture he models the large shape in clay, in a sprightly manner he applies a characterizing brushstroke here and there, energetically he applies his thumb for a catching detail, kneads and grubs until he achieves the result that he wants."

Gratama's remark about academic sculpture recalls the fact that, while in Brussels, Vantongerloo had worked in the traditional style in which he had been trained. After moving to The Hague, however, Vantongerloo appears to have freed himself of this style in short order, owing largely to the influence of Rik Wouters. Wouters was well known as a painter and sculptor in the Netherlands (where he was interned during the war) as well as in his native Belgium. He often took part in Belgian group exhibitions, in addition to holding his own one-man shows. While still in Belgium he had been greatly influenced by Rodin and had adopted his impressionistic method, in which the human figure was not represented in a static position but was caught at a certain moment in the middle of a movement or an action. The most pronounced example of this method in Wouters's work is *Het zotte geweld* [*The foolish violence*], a sculpture of a furiously dancing woman made in 1912.[16] To record a moment is exactly what Vantongerloo was trying to do in his sculptures of women who appear to have been taken by surprise in the act of dressing. Another aspect of Wouters's impressionism was the variation in the surfaces of his sculptures. Not only were they not finished smoothly (by which means the attention of the viewer is directed to the shape and the volume); they were roughened on purpose, with deep furrows and

212 Vantongerloo's studio in The Hague, as illustrated in *De kroniek* 2, no. 3 (1916).

213 Vantongerloo's exhibition at the gallery of the Kunstkring Hollando-Belge, as illustrated in *De prins* of October 20, 1917. *Hurkende Volendammer* is in the foreground.

ridges which break the light. Vantongerloo adopted this technique, roughening the surfaces of his sculptures more and more. In *Hurkende Volendammer*—perhaps the apotheosis of this development—there is no longer any smoothness to the surface; everywhere there are scraped-out furrows and indentations made by patting the clay with a board or a hand. The deep hollows form sharp shadows (particularly in the trousers), while the protruding areas catch the light; thus the heavy mass of the sculpture is destructurized.

Sculptures modeled in clay are rather vulnerable. For this reason, they are usually cast in plaster and then, eventually, in bronze. The pieces Vantongerloo showed at his various exhibitions in the Netherlands were almost always plaster castings of the original clay sculptures. In Belgium he had used stone; however, now he had to produce a lot of pieces in a short time in order to give potential customers an impression of his work. Also, during the war plaster was easier to get than stone in the Netherlands, and much less expensive. But Vantongerloo's choice of this material was determined mainly by its suitability for the creation of impressionistic sculptures.

In The Hague, Vantongerloo also worked in other media. Reviews of exhibitions from 1915 mention etchings, and the Pulchri show of 1916 included etchings, pastels, and drawings. These works were discussed rather summarily in the reviews. The newspaper *De hofstad* of March 18, 1916, reported: "For the rest Vantongerloo exhibits pastels, the colors brightly and luminously juxtaposed, vernis-mous, and drawings which are now evoking a mood, then expressionist and naturalistic, and then again sculptural, like the one single torso broadly hewn in shadow and light." And Gratama, in the above-cited review in *Onze kunst,* wrote: "He . . . shows himself to be an artist who goes for light and movement in his drawings and etchings . . . much of the form is sacrificed to the light that dominates all other things, permeates everything, and bites into the contour."[17] These two quotes suggest that Vantongerloo did not restrict himself to one style in these works but rather experimented with different styles and techniques.

Vantongerloo's most important public exhibition in these years was the aforementioned one-man show in October 1917 at the gallery of the Kunstkring Hollando-Belge. A photograph of this exhibition (figure 213) appeared in the weekly magazine *De prins.* Practically every one of the sculptures visible in this photograph is known from a previous exhibition; apparently Vantongerloo created little in the way of sculpture in 1917. However, the paintings were new; they had not been shown earlier. Most of the

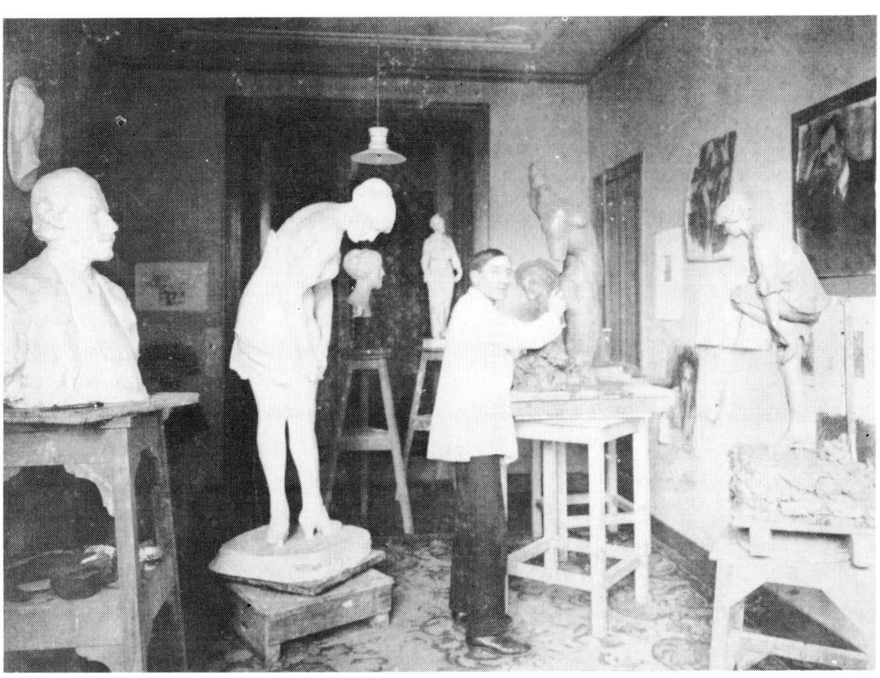

212

213

paintings that can be recognized in the photograph are, at present, signed and dated 1916, or even 1915. However, the photograph gives the impression that these paintings were neither signed nor dated at the time of the exhibition. For instance, at the far left of the photograph part of the painting *Zittende man* is visible, minus the date and signature it now bears (see figure 214). Presumably, Vantongerloo signed and (mis-) dated these paintings at a later time. The paintings themselves probably did not originate before 1917.

In a review in the *Algemeen handelsblad* of October 14, 1917, these paintings are called "not more than a draft." One can understand such a judgment when one looks closely at *Zittende man.* The paint is applied in short, dry brushstrokes, like a coarse version of pointillism. The canvas can be seen through the paint everywhere, and it is completely bare between the strokes. Details such as the nose, the mouth, and the eyes are lacking, and the figure is barely discernible from its surroundings. All solid forms seem to be leached by the effect of the bright sunlight.

It is said that Rik Wouters had a great influence on Vantongerloo's paintings.[18] There is indeed a similarity in the use of bright colors; however, Vantongerloo's method of painting differed strongly from Wouters's.

Vantongerloo's comprehensive one-man exhibition was held in the same month—October 1917—in which the first issue of *De stijl* was published, but there is no evidence that he was involved with the periodical at that time. He first published in it in July 1918. His work and his ideas must have undergone a great change in the intervening months.

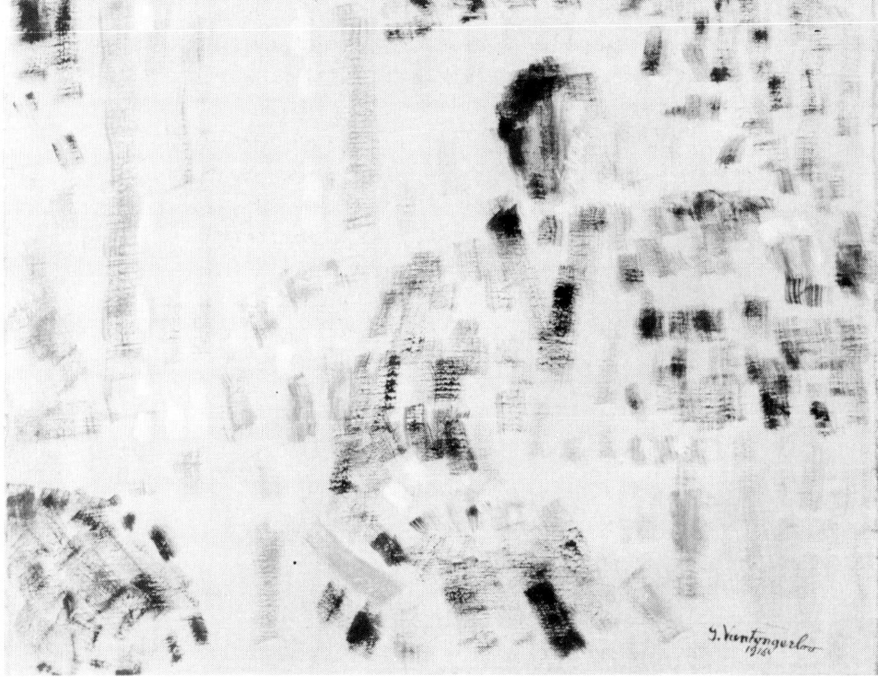

214 Vantongerloo, *Zittende man* [*Sitting man*], 1917. Oil on canvas, 50 × 68 cm. Private collection.

Acquaintance with De Stijl

When Theo van Doesburg, Vilmos Huszár, Antony Kok, Piet Mondrian, J. J. P. Oud, and Bart van der Leck were founding *De stijl* in the spring of 1917, probably none of them knew the Belgian sculptor who would associate with them a year later. The works Vantongerloo created and exhibited in 1917 can hardly have been an incentive for inviting him as a contributor. His sculpture followed too much the tradition of Rodin and Wouters, and his paintings that of impressionism and luminism.

Exactly how Vantongerloo became acquainted with De Stijl is uncertain. Perhaps his estate contains documents that could shed some light on this.[19] The sources to which I have had access contain no written evidence of contacts with the members of De Stijl before the publication of Vantongerloo's first article in the periodical, in July 1918. He met most of them much later, some of them never. In a letter to Oud dated August 16, 1931, he said that he had never met van der Leck, Kok, or van 't Hoff, and in a letter dated July 31, 1931, he wrote that he had met Mondrian in 1920, Oud in 1925, and Huszár in 1927. Only Jan Wils and Theo van Doesburg are not mentioned in the two letters from 1931. It has been suggested that Vantongerloo knew Wils before 1917,[20] but there is not the slightest proof of this. That leaves van Doesburg as the most likely contact person.

The answer to the question why Vantongerloo joined De Stijl is equally hypothetical. Perhaps he was immediately attracted by the new periodical, in which he could find articles related to his interest in futurism and other new trends.[21] It is also possible that van Doesburg took the initiative. During the winter of 1917–18, his writings in the weekly *Eenheid* evidenced a strong interest in sculpture. Michelangelo's sculptures were the starting point of Van Doesburg's lengthy considerations,[22] but what he was trying to get across was how sculpture had to change in order to become more universal. In view of this interest, it is plausible that van Doesburg wanted to get a sculptor involved in De Stijl.

But there must have been something in Vantongerloo, in particular, that appealed to van Doesburg. In the literature about Vantongerloo it is sometimes said, without elaboration, that van Doesburg saw some of Vantongerloo's nearly abstract sculptures—the *Constructies in de bol* [*Constructions in a sphere*], shown below as figures 223–225—and became enthusiastic about them.[23] It is questionable, however, whether those sculptures existed yet in 1917 or early 1918. The first time one of them was illustrated was in 1919, and they were not exhibited until late 1920.[24] It is more likely that the first works by Vantongerloo that van Doesburg saw were transitional between Vantongerloo's luminist works and his geometric-abstract works.

It is also uncertain whether Vantongerloo's first articles for *De stijl* were written before or after his first meeting with van Doesburg. Thus, many aspects of his joining De Stijl remain in the dark; however, it appears likely that van Doesburg granted him space in the periodical because of his work and ideas as well as because he was a sculptor.

After the publication of the first of the "Réflexions" (as Vantongerloo called his articles), van Doesburg asked Mondrian and Kok for their opinions of it. In September 1918 Mondrian replied: "That piece by Vantongerloo I have not yet read: when I see round lines, that doesn't appeal to me. But it seems to me to be very well suited for *De stijl* because it contains the new element, and it grows, or can grow, through that." It is understandable that Mondrian objected to the round lines in the four drawings that accompanied the text, though it is odd that he gave this as a reason for his not reading the article. But apparently Mondrian had blind faith in van Doesburg—if he had put the article in *De stijl,* then surely it contained "the new." Kok was much more negative. In a reply to his criticism, van Doesburg defended Vantongerloo (although rather cautiously): "I do not quite agree with your opinion about Vantongerloo's article in *Stijl* 9. Metaphysically speaking it is perhaps relative but seen from a plastic point of view it is in my opinion very clear. Particularly filling space, vide + volume = espace [emptiness + volume = space]."[25] Later in the same letter, van Doesburg asserted that Archipenko, who was much in esteem within the ranks of De Stijl, would certainly agree with Vantongerloo's article.

Even after his subsequent articles in *De stijl,* Vantongerloo was not accepted by all the other contributors. In the autumn of 1918, Huszár was strongly opposed to Vantongerloo's signing the manifesto. After the publication of the manifesto, Huszár wrote letters to Mondrian and van Doesburg in which he threatened to resign as a contributor because Vantongerloo, whose work he considered bad, had been allowed to sign.[26] But Huszár's letter only had the effect of making van Doesburg doubt his sincerity, as is evident from a letter to Kok dated December 3, 1918. In the same letter, van Doesburg wrote: "I have also perceived in his [Huszár's] Vth essay a dig at Vantongerloo." Although van Doesburg himself was not above digs, he called Huszár's absurd. The dig he was referring to must have been in the following lines of Huszár's article "Aesthetische beschouwing V": "Thus Brancusi has brought the round shapes to plasticity in a rhythmic movement; the renaissance artists did this by representation of the *natural body movements*; the moderns differ from them in that they mainly visualize aesthetic movements in an *abstract* way. This differs essentially from the construction of geometric forms in a natural subject."[27] (The last sentence of this quotation must have referred to Vantongerloo's small sculptures, such as those shown in figures 223 and 224, in which the human figure was still recognizable but had been constructed from spheres, triangles, and rectangles.) Mondrian, too, stood up for Vantongerloo; he wrote to van Doesburg: "I myself am of the opinion that one can agree with the concepts without necessarily carrying them to extremes oneself; this happens . . . to some extent in architecture."[28] In spite of Huszár's opposition, van Doesburg regarded Vantongerloo as a full-fledged partner, as is clear from a letter to Oud in which he said: "As to the other contributors, I also gave [Wils] and Vantongerloo . . . a certificate of their status as collaborators."[29]

"Réflexions"

The articles Vantongerloo published in *De stijl* between September 1918 and October 1920, all entitled "Réflexions,"[30] form an entity in which he tries to formulate the aim of the arts and the task of the artist, using a comparison between art and nature. He interprets nature as consisting of not only discernible elements but also the unseen. In his opinion, comparison between art and nature is possible because they are both based on the same phenomena: time and space. Time and space entail a perpetual motion; space expands without limits, in a manner comparable to wave motion in physics, and time has neither beginning nor end. The point is the unit of time and space. Everything originates from there. The task of the artist is to make the unseen in nature visible. Nature has laws of unity, harmony, and equilibrium, which the artist must equally observe in his re-creation. Futurists and cubists had failed in this respect.

It is clear from the "Réflexions" that the concept of space held a particular fascination for Vantongerloo. He designed a sort of formula according to which volume + void = space. In sculptural terms, one might say that he tried to visualize space by combining the volume with the "nothingness" around it. This can be compared to the problem the De Stijl painters brought up in their work: how the forms and the background of a painting could be put on one level.

Van Doesburg explored similar ideas in his article on Michelangelo,[31] which he wrote in the spring of 1918 and published in *Eenheid* in August. In that article van Doesburg dealt extensively with the concept of space, which he considered to be of great importance to sculpture. In Michelangelo he saw a slow development from merely frontal and flat sculptures to statues that made use of the space around them. Of Michelangelo's *David,* van Doesburg wrote: "Although this sculpture still has a frontal effect, the dominating *sculptural accent* that strikes us is the need to transfer the proportions of the front and the sides to the back. Here M.A. senses for the first time the need (*sculptural intuition*) to give an *aesthetic* expression to the *atmosphere*, to open space, in order to create a more universal aspect. Characteristic phenomena are (at all times): a) ascension from massive terrestrial enclosure, b) tranferance of the proportions of volumes (for example from the front to the side and the back, so that a well-balanced relation of volumes is created)."

Thus, both van Doesburg and Vantongerloo were of the opinion that the space around a sculpture—the void, as Vantongerloo called it—had an important function. Whether van Doesburg adopted this notion from Vantongerloo cannot be ascertained, because neither the precise date of their meeting nor the date on which van Doesburg wrote his article is known. However, van Doesburg's emphasis on Vantongerloo's definition of space ("vide + volume = espace") in his letter to Kok of September 22, 1918, suggests that he may well have been inspired by it.

The series "Réflexions" clearly shows the influence of M. H. J. Schoenmaekers's books *Het nieuwe wereldebeeld* [*The new image of the world*] and *Beeldende wiskunde* [*Plastic mathematics*],[32] whether Vantongerloo came to read these books on the recommendation of van Doesburg (who read them himself in the spring of 1918) or whether he had read them previously. It is very noticeable that, in his writings, Vantongerloo relied on his long experience as a sculptor until he had to deal with abstract concepts, at which point he became very dependent on Schoenmaekers. In *Het nieuwe wereldbeeld* Schoenmaekers had written that the method of positive mysticism leads to an understanding of nature by means of which its inner construction becomes visible. This is exactly what Vantongerloo considered to be the task of the artist: to make nature's unseen elements visible. An even more obvious instance of derivation is Vantongerloo's view that nature is composed of opposites.[33] Schoenmaekers considered time and space as absolute (infinite) opposites which, when they couple into a "plastic middlepoint," create living organisms. This plastic middlepoint is identical with Vantongerloo's point which originates when time and space coincide. The rays originating from this point evoke new opposites. Thus nature is, according to the principle of evolution, in perpetual motion.

Vantongerloo did not adopt Schoenmaekers's symbols, as Mondrian did, but he did copy his pseudo-scientific terminology and manner of reasoning. Vantongerloo also said, very explicitly, that science should be called in as a means of visualizing the unseen. In one of his last "Réflexions," published in the January and February 1920 issues of *De stijl,* he retreated somewhat, having been reproached on the grounds that his artistic viewpoint was scientific. He hastened to declare that this was not the case, but that art and science were based on the same laws. In this part of the "Réflexions" (obviously written in self-defense), he differentiated *"science déterminée"* from *"science infuse,"* interpreting the former as science that can be learned and can be taught in curricula and the latter as the innate science, for which one has to have the right intuition. Vantongerloo claimed that he himself used *science infuse.*

Painting and sculpture: the first half of 1918

The first sign that Vantongerloo's work had undergone a great change can be seen in the four drawings (figure 215) that accom-

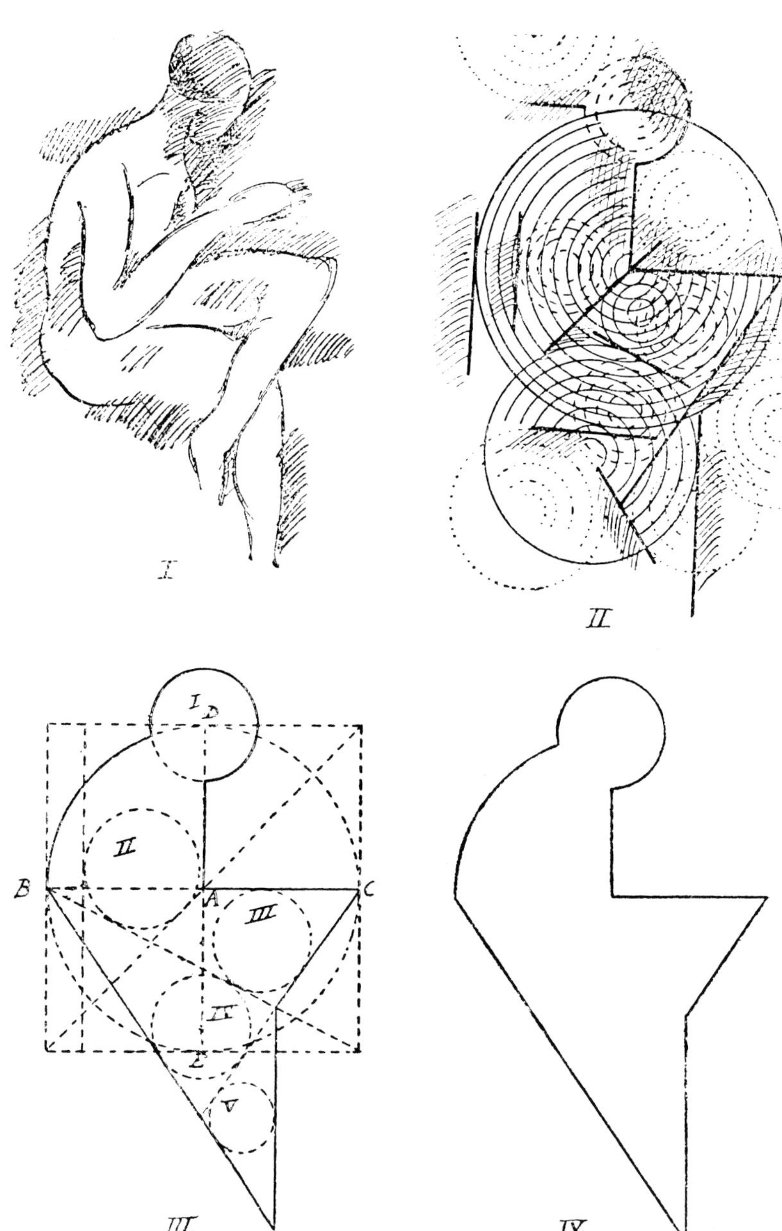

215 Vantongerloo, four analyses of *Zittend naakt* [*Sitting nude*], 1918, as illustrated in *De stijl* 1, no. 9 (1918), p. 99.

panied the debut of the "Réflexions" in the July 1918 issue of *De stijl*. Drawing I is realistic and is related to Vantongerloo's old work; the other three show some similarities to the first (so a relation exists with the old work) but have an abstract, geometric character. In drawing II several groups of concentric circles are superimposed on the form of the original nude, which is denoted by a few straight line segments. The traditional hatching that indicates shadows has been retained, so that figuration and abstraction are mingled. Drawing III has a strongly constructive character. The hatching is gone, along with the concentric circles. Only the outer circles remain, and these are incorporated into a system of squares and triangles with auxiliary lines. The nude is practically unrecognizable. In drawing IV, segments of the circles and parts of the triangles and the squares are connected into one closed form.

It is clear that Vantongerloo used the realistic drawing only as a starting point for an abstract construction. The circle played an important part in this. As mentioned above, Vantongerloo assumed that everything (including the unseen) was in perpetual motion. He represented this motion by concentric circles starting from certain points. In the article he said that the closed circles in drawing II were the vibrations caused by the volumes, that the circles formed by the small hatch marks were the vibrations caused by "negative" volumes, and that the circles consisting of dots indicated the vibrations of the surrounding void.

Vantongerloo made at least ten different analyses of the sitting-nude motif on paper, using pen and ink, watercolor, and gouache,[34] and two oil paintings with the same theme.[35] The more definitive versions in gouache and oil are strongly reminiscent of Theo van Doesburg's work from 1916 and 1917. The similarities between Vantongerloo's *Studie* (figure 217) and van Doesburg's *Stilleven III* are so striking—particularly when the latter is rotated 180 degrees (as in figure 216)—that they can hardly be coincidental. Each artist used a grid of squares, which is still visible, as the basis for a composition of overlapping triangles and circles. The overlappings are emphasized by variations in the colors of the forms, as if they were transparent. There are some differences in the use of color, but it seems clear that Vantongerloo was familiar with van Doesburg's still lifes.

Vantongerloo dated the series of drawings and paintings discussed above, and other geometric abstract works, retroactively to 1917. However, since he exhibited only figurative sculptures and paintings until late in that year, that dating is not plausible. The earliest possible date seems to be winter 1917 or spring 1918. Around the same time, he approached the theme of a sitting nude in a different way, starting not with preliminary drawings but with

216

217

216 Theo van Doesburg, *Stilleven III* [*Still life III*], 1916. Oil on canvas, 82 × 67.5 cm. Rotated 180 degrees in comparison with figure 9. Private collection.

217 Vantongerloo, *Studie,* 1918. Oil on canvas, 50 × 50 cm. Private collection.

218 Vantongerloo, *Naakt met rode kousen* [*Nude with red stockings*], ca. 1917. Oil on canvas, 100 × 75 cm. Collection of L. Tas, Amsterdam.

a painting: *Naakt met rode kousen* [*Nude with red stockings*]. In this painting (shown in figure 218), as in his pointillist paintings of 1917, the paint was applied thinly, though in long strokes rather than in loose touches. The contours and the shadows are indicated only sketchily. But in the red stockings (which contrast sharply against the pale body) the paint is thicker. The paint was applied much more heavily in the background as well, so that the colors of the three cushions (red, yellow, and blue) produce a strong effect. The rest of the background is predominantly green.

Vantongerloo is known to have made fifteen analyses of *Naakt met rode kousen* (figure 220). The last of these was *Studie no. 2* (figure 219), an apparently abstract painting that was the culmination of the other fourteen analyses. These studies do not show an entirely regular and logical development; Vantongerloo appears to have divided his attention between the nude figure and the composition of the background. The definitive version, *Studie no. 2,* differs from the aforementioned *Studie* and *Studie no. 1* in its complete lack of round forms. The canvas is filled with closed color planes defined by straight lines. In this, Vantongerloo came closer to the work of other De Stijl artists from 1917 and 1918 than when he still used circles. Like the others, he wrestled with the problem of bringing the forms and ground to one level so that an entirely two-dimensional composition would result. He had not yet mastered that at the time of these studies; the large angular shape of the figure was still somewhat detached from the background.

Another important respect in which Vantongerloo's paintings resemble those of the other De Stijl painters is his use of special frames. In *Studie no. 2,* he put two narrow, hook-shaped black slats on top of the regular frame of white slats, and in subsequent paintings he sometimes used such frames without any difference in color. Vantongerloo's frames are plastic variants of the frame made by Huszár for *Stillevencompositie (Hamer en zaag),* which was reproduced in color in the January 1918 issue of *De stijl.*

218

As with his paintings, Vantongerloo antedated his early geometrical abstract sculptures to 1917. That date does not seem correct, for the reasons mentioned above; 1918 is more plausible. It is hard to ascertain the sequence of the sculptures because of the lack of reliable data; however, a hypothetical sequence can be ventured on the basis of their visual characteristics.

The small sculpture *Compositie uitgaande van het ovaal* [*Composition starting from an oval*] is a likely candidate for the first in the sequence. Contrary to what the title suggests, this work is not entirely abstract. It is a stylized version of the 1916 sculpture

219

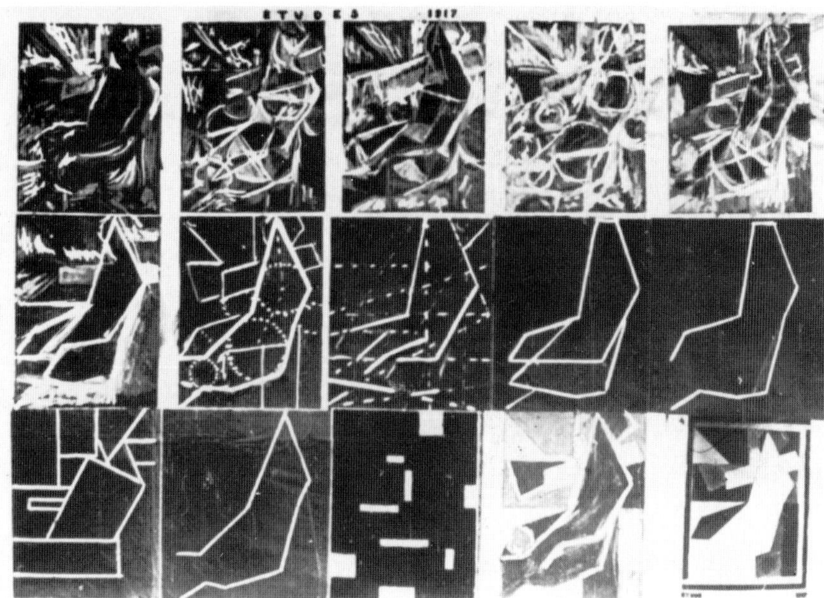

220

representing a woman attaching a stocking to her corset, with all details eliminated and with the head, the torso, and the legs reduced to flattened volumes. There is no geometrization in the strict sense.

Vantongerloo analyzed many of his sculptures in drawings, in order to explain their structure. He did this for *Compositie uitgaande van het ovaal.* His analysis (figure 221) reveals that the title of the work is derived from the fact that the stylized figure is enclosed in an oval, in which circles, triangle, and auxiliary lines are drawn. Apparently the oval was an important geometric form to Vantongerloo. He says in one of his "Réflexions" that it is the form that contains the most opposites, that these opposites come together in a point from whence new opposites can originate, and that the oval is the embodiment of the evolution principle and of perpetual motion.[36] Vantongerloo must have adopted these ideas from Schoenmaekers, who called the oval the most fundamental form of organic life.[37]

Vantongerloo also analyzed the works of other artists. For instance, the September 1918 issue of *De stijl* contains his analysis of Archipenko's *Gondolier* (figure 222), in which the oval occurs as the most definitive form. Not only do Vantongerloo's analyses of his *Compositie uitgaande van het ovaal* and Archipenko's *Gondolier* show many similarities; the two works themselves resemble each other in the stylizing of the figures. That Vantongerloo (like van Doesburg) admired Archipenko greatly can be gathered from the text that accompanies his analysis of *Gondolier.*

The *Compositie uitgaande van het ovaal* can be considered a transitional work, because of the rather clumsy combination of figuration and abstraction. It probably was made in the winter of 1917–18. During the following spring or summer, Vantongerloo created four sculptures entitled *Constructie in de bol* [*Construction in a sphere*]. These, too, are very small, ranging in diameter from only 6 centimeters to about 30 centimeters. Some exist in various versions, executed in plaster, bronze, or wood painted monochromatically in blue or yellow. In three of the four sculptures, a sphere is literally the center. Each of the four fits precisely within a sphere. In all four the human figure can be recognized, although with much difficulty. Clearly Vantongerloo was no longer very interested in the characterization of figures; he now used them only as starting points.

The first *Constructie in de bol* (figure 223) is a geometric variant of the *Hurkende Volendammer,* composed of a sphere and triangular and rectangular forms. A construction drawing of this sculpture (figure 224) shows how thoroughly thought out and accurately

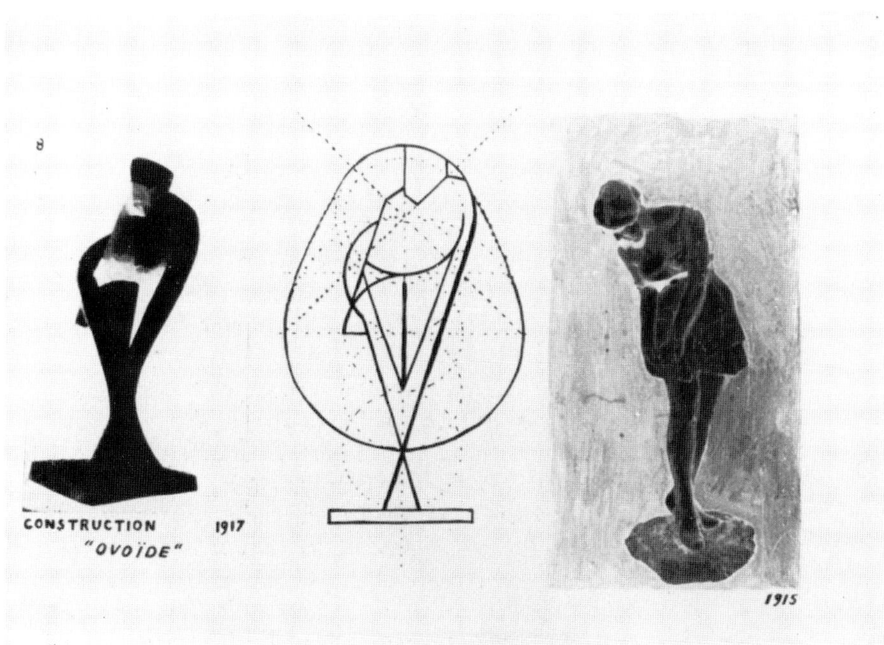

221

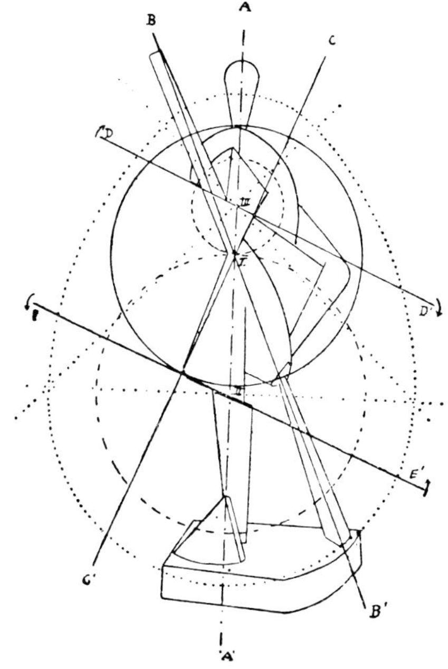

222

223

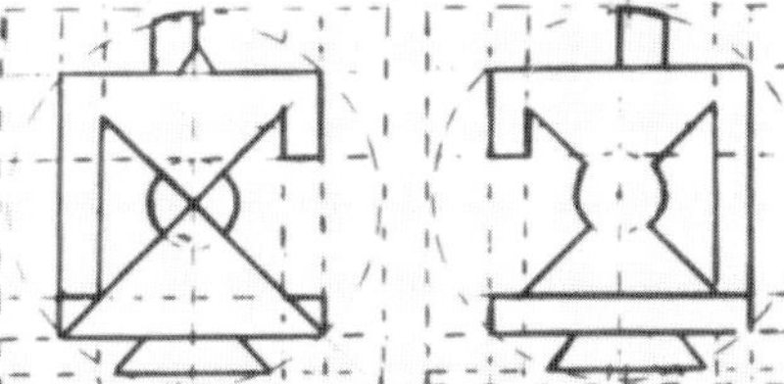
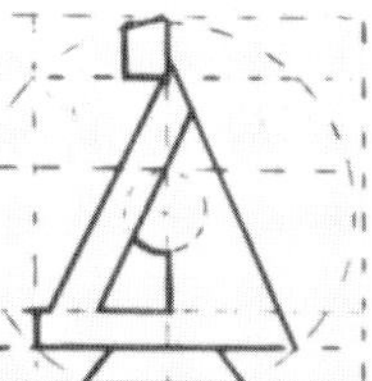
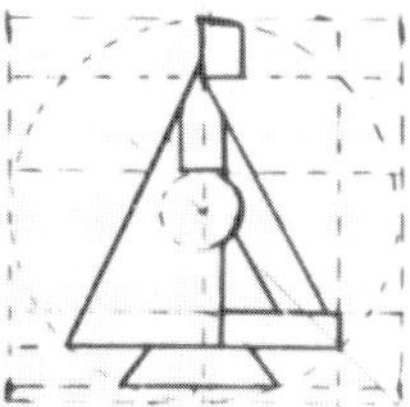

224

219 Vantongerloo, *Studie no. 2, 1918.* Oil, 45 × 34 cm. Whereabouts unknown; photograph in private collection.

220 Vantongerloo, fifteen analyses of *Naakt met rode kousen,* 1918. Technique, dimensions, and whereabouts unknown. As shown in the filmstrip *G. Vantongerloo, evolution (1910–1936) vers l'art abstrait* (Paris: Fixus Films). See note 45.

221 Vantongerloo, *Compositie uitgaande van het ovaal* [*Composition starting from an oval*], 1917–18. Cement, 19 × 7 × 7 cm. Private collection. With construction drawing and starting point, as shown in the filmstrip *G. Vantongerloo, evolution (1910–1936) vers l'art abstrait.*

222 Vantongerloo, analysis of Archipenko's *Gondolier,* 1918. Dimensions and whereabouts unnown. As illustrated in *De stijl* 1, no. 11 (1918).

223 Vantongerloo, *Constructie in de bol* [*Construction in a sphere*], 1918. Painted wood, 17 × 17 × 17 cm. On loan to Gemeentemuseum, The Hague, from private collection.

224 Construction drawing for *Constructie in de bol,* as shown in the filmstrip *G. Vantongerloo, evolution (1910–1936) vers l'art abstrait.*

225

designed it is. The arms and shoulders are a square inscribed in a circle, and the head is tilted in order to fit within the sphere.

The second *Constructie in de bol* (figure 225) makes a less closed-in and awkward impression. It seems to be an opened-up version of the first. Again the nucleus is a sphere. A human figure with arms, legs, and a head is still vaguely recognizable but it is not clear whether this *Constructie* was based on an earlier, figurative work.

The third *Constructie in de bol* (figure 226) is not made up of geometric forms, except for the sphere in the center. At first glance this piece seems to have little in common with the first two; however, close scrutiny reveals that despite external differences it is closely related to the second piece. It is as if Vantongerloo made a specimen of the second piece in clay and rotated it rapidly around both axes, probably in a effort to represent the perpetual motion of evolution. The way in which the effect of motion is visualized here is strongly reminiscent of the sculpture *Unique forms of continuity in space* by the futurist Boccioni (figure 227), which Vantongerloo may have seen illustrated in a Boccioni catalog that van Doesburg had.[38]

The fourth *Constructie in de bol*[39] shows little similarity to the other three. It does not have a sphere at the center; it seems to be cut out of a board, which makes for a rather flat effect; and it is much more difficult to see that the piece fits exactly into a sphere.[40]

Vantongerloo's small sculptures from early 1918 are much less dependent on the examples of van Doesburg and others than his studies and paintings from the same period. One is occasionally reminded of Archipenko and Boccioni, but the first two pieces entitled *Constructie in de bol* are quite original and seem quite unconnected with the works of other contemporary sculptors. Vantongerloo established himself firmly as a De Stijl artist in 1918, but as a sculptor he occupied a rather special place. The painters could discuss stylistic problems and solutions with one another, and this resulted in strong similarities among their works, but Vantongerloo was rather isolated. This was to change somewhat in the course of 1918.

The "real" De Stijl work

It was probably not until the second half of 1918 that Vantongerloo created a small sculpture and a painting that show strong connections to the works of the other De Stijl artists.[41] The sculpture (figure 228) has the same title as one of the works discussed above: *Compositie uitgaande van het ovaal.* However, it differs greatly from the piece illustrated in figure 221—especially in terms of formal language. It consists of rectangular, rather flat blocks of various dimensions, which are glued together. With much imagination one can recognize a standing human figure. Vantongerloo's restricting himself to rectangular volumes in this piece is comparable to the De Stijl painters' restricting themselves to rectangular color planes.

This was the first sculpture to which Vantongerloo applied primary colors. In 1917 and 1918 there were many discussions among the De Stijl painters about the use of color. Bart van der Leck had been using unmixed primary colors ever since the beginning of 1916. Mondrian was theoretically in favor of this, but in practice he found it difficult. Van Doesburg favored the use of primary colors, but he did not always use them in his work. Vantongerloo must have heard about this discussion from van Doesburg, and this may have led to the extraordinary use of color on this *Compositie.* Rather than always using a single color on each side of a block, he sometimes let a color continue over the rim onto part of another side, thus destroying rather than accentuating the form.

The painting of sculptures was rather common in the beginning of this century. Often color was only used for decoration, but some sculptors tried to use it to achieve certain optical effects. For example, the different colors of Archipenko's *Carrousel Pierrot* (1913) cancel out the plasticity, so that the round head seems to fall apart in segments.[42] In the piece shown in figure 228, Vantongerloo used colors in a comparable manner—not only on the sculpture itself, but also on the pedestal, the blocklike character of which he mitigated by applying black and white alternately, much as with the frames he made in this period for his paintings.

Two Vantongerloo paintings entitled *Compositie* (one of which is shown here as figure 229) are closely connected to the above-mentioned sculpture and can therefore be dated to about the same time: autumn or winter 1918. Vantongerloo used unmixed primary colors in these paintings, and—equally unusual—he applied separate rectangular color planes on a white ground, as if he had plucked the elements of the sculpture apart and scattered them over the canvas. Here, as before, Vantongerloo seems to have drawn his influence from van Doesburg. The *Compositie* shown here resembles van Doesburg's *Compositie XI* in the use of colors and his *Compositie VIII* in the eccentric placement of the forms. Van Doesburg's *Compositie VIII* was an abstract decomposition of a cow motif. There are no preliminary studies for Van-

226

227

228

225 Vantongerloo, *Constructie in de bol* [*Construction in a sphere*], 1918. Painted wood, 17 × 17 × 17 cm. Private collection.

226 Vantongerloo, *Constructie in de bol* [*Construction in a sphere*], 1918. Bronze, 17 × 17 × 17 cm. Private collection.

227 U. Boccioni, *Unique forms of continuity in space,* 1913. Bronze, 111.2 × 88.5 × 40 cm. Museum of Modern Art, New York.

228 Vantongerloo, *Compositie uitgaande van het ovaal* [*Composition starting from an oval*], 1918. Painted wood, 16.5 × 6.5 × 6.5 cm. Private collection.

229

229 **Vantongerloo, *Compositie,* 1918. Oil on canvas, 33 × 53 cm. Musée National d'Art Moderne, Centre Pompidou, Paris.**

230 **Vantongerloo, *Constructie der volumenverhoudingen [Construction of volume relations]*, 1918. Stone, 18 × 12 × 12 cm. Whereabouts unknown. As shown, with construction drawing and starting point, in the filmstrip *G. Vantongerloo, evolution (1910–1936) vers l'art abstrait.***

231 **Vantongerloo, *Constructie der volumenverhoudingen [Construction of volume relations]*, 1919. Stone, 22.5 × 13.5 × 13.5 cm. Tate Gallery, London. With design diagram, as shown in the filmstrip *G. Vantongerloo, evolution (1910–1936) vers l'art abstrait.***

tongerloo's *Compositie* to enlighten us about a figurative starting point, but such starting points can be found for all his other works until 1921.

When the war ended, Vantongerloo decided to return to Brussels. Exactly when he did so is uncertain, but the first article in his booklet *l'Art et son avenir* bears the dateline "Brussels, February 1919." Although he left the Netherlands, he remained involved with De Stijl. His "Réflexions" appeared regularly in the periodical until 1920.

In 1961, looking back on his days in Brussels, Vantongerloo wrote: "And then, 1918. The end of the war. Back to Brussels. The Ministry of Fine Arts invited me to exhibit in the Salon. I am telling you all this because it was connected with my urge to understand space, which I gradually extended to a study of the universe. I had, therefore, no reason to go back to my previous life. I wanted to go on with my research, for which there was, of course, no room in the Salons de Beaux-Arts."[43]

The works Vantongerloo created in Brussels were related to those that were being reproduced in *De stijl.* However, the two sculptures shown in figures 230 and 231, which were probably made in the first half of 1919, were different in character from the sculptures he had made in the Netherlands. Each of the sculptures discussed so far had a fairly definite front. But neither of these Brussels pieces has a front; all the sides are equivalent, which results in a strong spatial effect. In the photographs, these two constructions give a monumental impression. This is due, in part, to their blocklike character and to the fact that they were hewn from stone. In reality, however, they were (like many of Vantongerloo's sculptures) very small. At first sight they appear to be completely abstract; van Doesburg seems to have gotten the same impression: "As sculptural art in itself, which has no other basis than a purely aesthetic aim, these two free sculptures . . . seem to us a very successful result, as the sculptor concentrated solely on the determination of volume relationships in *three-dimensional equilibrium.*"[44] Yet in actuality Vantongerloo was still working with the human figure. The piece shown in figure 230 was based on his earlier *Hurkende Volendammer,* and the other one on his more recent studies of a human figure sitting half-turned in a chair, with one arm supporting the chin and the other on the armrest.[45]

These two "constructions of volume relations" display much more clearly than the previous sculptures the principles van Doesburg had put forth in his article on Michelangelo, particularly the transference of the volume proportions from the front to the sides and the back. Vantongerloo may have learned practical matters as

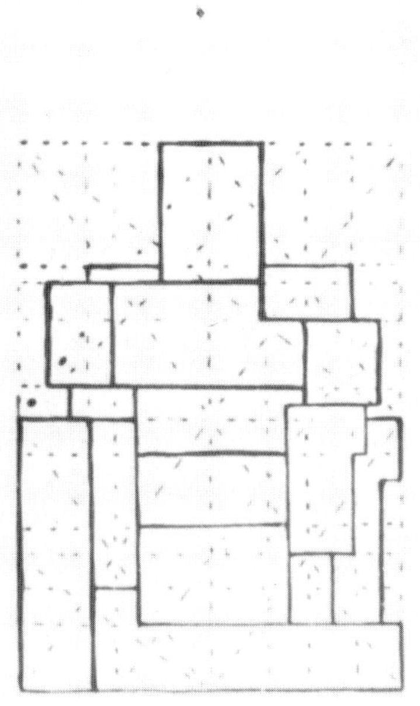

230

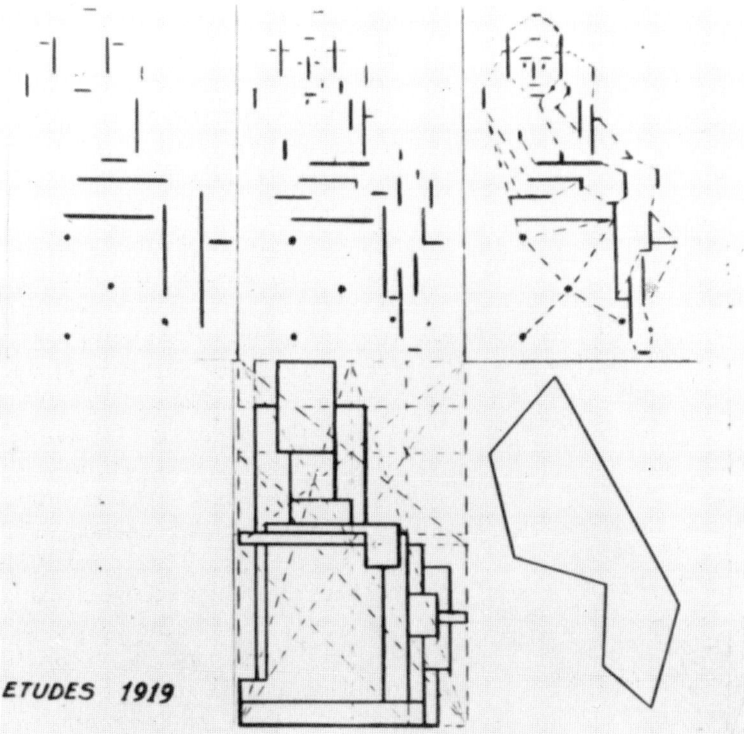

231

well as theoretical ones from van Doesburg—his method of enhancing the spatial effect seems to have been inspired by van Doesburg's *Monument voor Leeuwarden.*[46] Another source of influence may have been van 't Hoff's *Trappaal* [*Banister post*], which Vantongerloo must have seen illustrated in *De stijl.* Vantongerloo appears to have assimilated the influences of van Doesburg and van 't Hoff in his own way. His sculptures were composed much more ingeniously than theirs; whereas the monument and the banister post have rather simple vertical compositions, in the "constructions of volume relations" there is an alternation of vertically and horizontally positioned rectangles, which interlock and protrude from the block shape.

Also in 1919, Vantongerloo used the sitting figure that had served as the point of departure for the second sculpture as the starting point for a painting (figure 232), which he gave the usual title of *Studie.* This is evident from figure 233, an extant photograph of a board full of sketches. The sketches at upper right show the development toward the final abstract painting. As he had done before, Vantongerloo was trying to bring the figure and the ground onto one level; he divided the background by using horizontal and vertical lines, and he reduced the figure to a conglomerate of rectangular forms. In the final painting, lines divide the entire plane into rectangles of various sizes, with the result that the depth effect is, for the most part, suppressed. The figure is no longer recognizable, but the positions and the dimensions of the rectangles are still predominantly determined by it. (That was also the case in the two sculptures discussed above, to which the *Studie* bears many resemblances—notably in the "head," the descending "shoulder line," and the horizontal "arm.")

Vantongerloo filled in the rectangles of the *Studie* with light yellow, light blue, and a salmonish pink. In 1918 he had occasionally used the primary colors in their full intensities, but here he toned them down with white. He may have seen this done in van Doesburg's or (more likely) Mondrian's work.[47]

In a subsequent painting, *Studie no. III* (figure 234), Vantongerloo began to deviate from this path. Eight preliminary studies for this painting make up the bottom row in figure 233. The sketch above the fifth from the left is the image from which the preliminary studies were derived; it is another sitting figure in an interior, this time leaning on a table. The last two of the sketches delineate the definitive composition of *Studie no. III.* This painting resembles the *Studie* discussed above in the use of lines to divide the plane into unequal rectangles, and again the division is partly determined by the original image; however, the colors are very different. Vantongerloo no longer used only the three primary colors, nor did

232

232 Vantongerloo, *Studie,* 1919. Casein, 33 × 40 cm. Private collection.

233 Photograph of board containing design sketches and analyses by Vantongerloo, as illustrated on page 72 of M. Seuphor's *l'Art abstrait* (Paris, 1950).

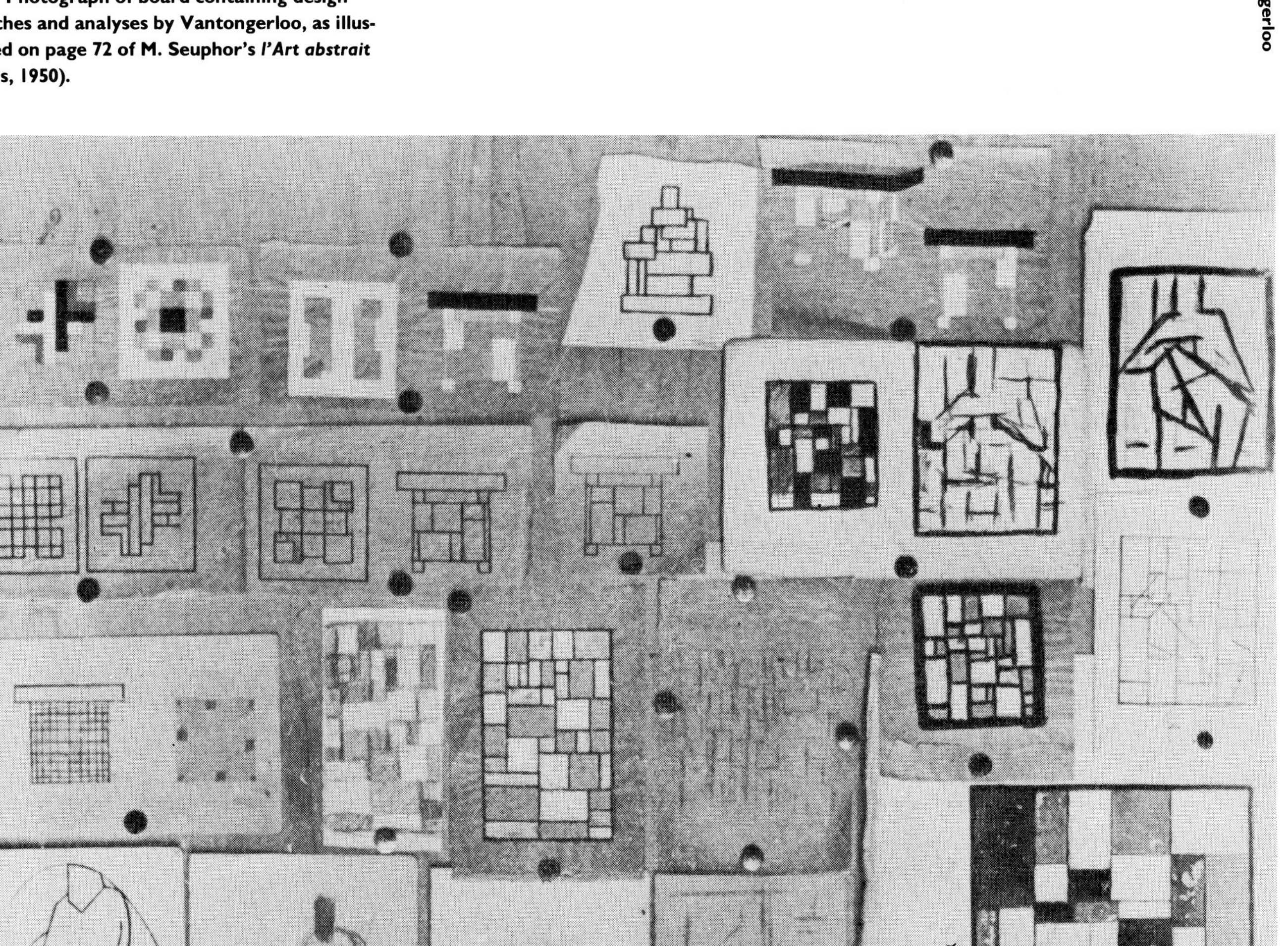

233

234

he attune the colors to one another by adding white; rather, he used all seven colors of the spectrum, and he strongly emphasized the color contrast.[48] The preliminary studies (especially the third from the left) also demonstrate that in some cases Vantongerloo tried to abolish the difference between figure and ground by overlapping bars and rectangles, rather than through his usual method of reducing both figure and ground to juxtaposed rectangles. This overlapping resulted in an effect that suggests weaving—much as in Huszár's 1917 *Compositie stilleven (hamer en zaag)*, which was illustrated in the January 1918 issue of *De stijl*. However, by the time Vantongerloo tried it, Huszár had abandoned it. In any case, Vantongerloo tried it only in the preliminary studies; in the painting he juxtaposed color planes within the "usual" grid.

Thus, in 1919 and 1920 Vantongerloo depended on the examples of other artists far more in the field of painting than in the field of sculpture. He rather easily adopted a specific use of color or form, experimented with it, and abandoned it. His use of the colors of the spectrum in *Studie no. III,* however, was his own idea, and therefore that painting marks an important change in his work.

Encounter with Mondrian

Van Doesburg had mentioned Vantongerloo several times in his letters to Mondrian, and on August 21, 1919, Mondrian wrote to van Doesburg that he was interested in what he had heard and that Vantongerloo should visit him in Paris. In another letter, dated January 6, 1920, Mondrian wrote: "Nice that van Tongerloo associates with us. What I wrote about sculpture he demonstrates in the reproduction!" This was a reference to Vantongerloo's two "constructions of volume relations," which were illustrated in the December 1919 issue of *De stijl*—the same issue in which Mondrian had published an installment of his trialogue "Natuurlijke en abstracte realiteit"[49] in which the abstract-realist painter known as Z. says the following about the formal garden in which the imaginary trialogue takes place: "With this garden we pass from the field of painting to that of *sculpture*. Sculpture has to deal with the third dimension in a different way than painting: The painter has his three colors, plus black and white; the sculptor has only black and white. The sculptor has to find the straight in three dimensions. Thus he creates volume, although he can reduce *the round element, the property of form* to the prismatic, and there again can abolish form 'as something separate' by means of contrast and interruption. Therefore it seems to me that the Neo-Plastic sculptor needs to follow the direction toward compositions made up of prisms." When the naturalistic painter X. asks whether sculpture doesn't then become architecture, Z. answers: "Not at all. Architecture remains construction-of-space and is also subject to practical requirements. Sculpture is freer." X. says: "Then this garden in your opinion is closer to pure sculpture than a 'statue'?" Z. replies: "Exactly. According to me 'the statue' has to be *completely abolished* in sculpture." This, apparently, is what Mondrian saw realized in Vantongerloo's work.

After living in Brussels for about a year, Vantongerloo decided to move to Menton, in the south of France. On his way there, in April 1920, he visited Mondrian. A few days later, Mondrian described his first impressions to van Doesburg: "On Saturday the Tongerloos were here. . . . to tell you the truth, they haven't quite lived up to my expectations. He is somewhat like Huszár. And she is not at all French, but nice anyway. He has a circumstantial way of explaining, but I believe that he is indeed very clever in technical matters. I did not know that he is also a painter. I find his use of purple and the 7 colors a bit premature: perhaps later that can be done. In theory, it can be defended, it even seems to be better."[50]

Vantongerloo's unusual use of color was the main subject of the correspondence that ensued between him and Mondrian. At first, Mondrian was not inclined to reject the use of the seven spectral colors. Perhaps he did not quite understand Vantongerloo's method; he wrote to van Doesburg on June 12, 1920, that he would ask what Vantongerloo meant by "the new color harmony." Some months later, Vantongerloo sent Mondrian his article "Unité,"[51] in which color was discussed extensively.

The central idea of "Unité" was that man strives after the coalescence of spirit and matter, but that these concepts had always been misunderstood by artists who had represented only material reality. The unity between spirit and matter could be manifested visually by a well-balanced proportion among the visual elements—in painting, among the colors. Up to this point, Vantongerloo's arguments were in agreement with the ideas of Mon-

234 Vantongerloo, *Studie no. III*, 1920. Casein, 22.5 × 30 cm. Private collection.

235 Vantongerloo, *Studie*, 1920. Oil, 52 × 61.5 cm. Private collection.

235

drian and other De Stijl artists. But it became a different matter when Vantongerloo started to discuss the character of the colors and the determination of the relative weights of color planes. As already mentioned, Vantongerloo thought that everything was in vibration. The color spectrum was, he thought, a pure manifestation of these vibrations, as were the seven fundamental musical notes. He devised a system by which a painter could, after a great deal of calculation, find the correct ratio of the colors and determine exactly how much of the surface of a painting a particular color should take up in relation to the other colors used.

When Mondrian read "Unité," he became certain that Vantongerloo was wrong. His letter to van Doesburg dated September 5, 1920, was not so much a dismissal of the use of the seven colors as a criticism of Vantongerloo's systematic implementation: "Now he, with his Belgian intellect, sets up an auxiliary system which is, in my opinion, based on nature. He has not the faintest idea of the difference between in the way of nature and in the way of the arts. I now see how well I discriminated between the unconscious and the conscious: he is computing everything with his ordinary consciousness. . . . I had only expected something of him as a sculptor, and to tell me technical things about color. . . . It is too bad that he is part of De Stijl. . . . He behaves like an ordinary Theosophist.

The remarkable painting by Vantongerloo shown here as figure 235 is usually dated 1918, but in fact it can only have originated in 1920, when Vantongerloo was deeply involved in the development of his color theory. This *Studie* is composed of six horizontal bars, divided by thin lines into a number of blocks. These blocks have slightly different dimensions, resulting in a somewhat irregular checkerboard. The *Studie* appears to be related to Mondrian's so-called checkerboard compositions of 1919, one or both of which Vantongerloo may have seen in Paris. However, there are also great differences. Obviously, Vantongerloo was not interested in the uniform division of the plane per se; he used it only in order to research the effect of colors within such a pattern. In his *Studie,* thick black lines separate areas containing two, four, six, or ten colors—the colors of the spectrum, but also mixtures. It is hard to imagine that this painting, like the previous ones, is a decomposition of a realistic image. It reminds one most of a kind of sample chart by means of which the mixing of colors and the interaction between colors could be demonstrated. Perhaps Vantongerloo used his "schijruif" in mixing the colors. Mondrian reported to van Doesburg on June 12, 1920, that Vantongerloo thought Ostwald's color method wrong and preferred his own method "with the schijruif." It is not clear what this schijruif was, but it may have been a kind of disk that could be rotated around its axis to produce an optical mixing of colors.[52]

Furniture and interior designs

While living in Brussels in 1919, Vantongerloo began to design furniture—perhaps on the inspiration of photographs he saw reproduced in *De stijl.* His first piece was the low table that is visible in figure 236. (See also figure 233, upper left.) On April 20, 1921, Mondrian, responding to the photograph Vantongerloo had sent him earlier that month, wrote back that he thought this table somewhat "heavy-monumental." That it certainly is. The top, which is painted gray on its upper surface and black on its sides, was very thick. It did not rest on legs, but on a kind of socle composed of blocks of various dimensions, which according to the reports were painted in the primary colors.[53] Unlike Gerrit Rietveld's furniture, which was very open and of a light construction, Vantongerloo's table was a massive entity, nearly a sculpture. It recalls the "constructions of volume relations" shown in figures 230 and 231.

After moving to the South of France, in 1920, Vantongerloo increased his activities in the field of interior decoration. On May 15 he sent van Doesburg an enthusiastic letter about his encounter with Mondrian and his new apartment in Menton. About the interior of this apartment he wrote: "Here we have a neat French apartment, and have decorated it entirely in the new Style [de nieuwe Stijl]. I think it would be to your liking." Clearly Vantongerloo had come to the conclusion, following the other De Stijl artists, that Neo-Plasticism should be realised not only in the free visual arts, but also in the living environment, so that a synthesis of architecture, painting, and sculpture would be brought about.

Two photographs made during Theo and Nelly van Doesburg's visit in April 1921 give an impression of the manner in which Vantongerloo had decorated his apartment (figures 236 and 237). In figure 236, the tea table is placed like a showpiece. Above it hangs a variant of the *Studie* discussed above (figure 235). At the left in the photo is a rectangular dark frame around a white plane, perhaps a blinded window. Figure 237 shows several sculptures and paintings which have been discussed in this article. On the table is one of the "constructions in a sphere" (figure 225), and on a

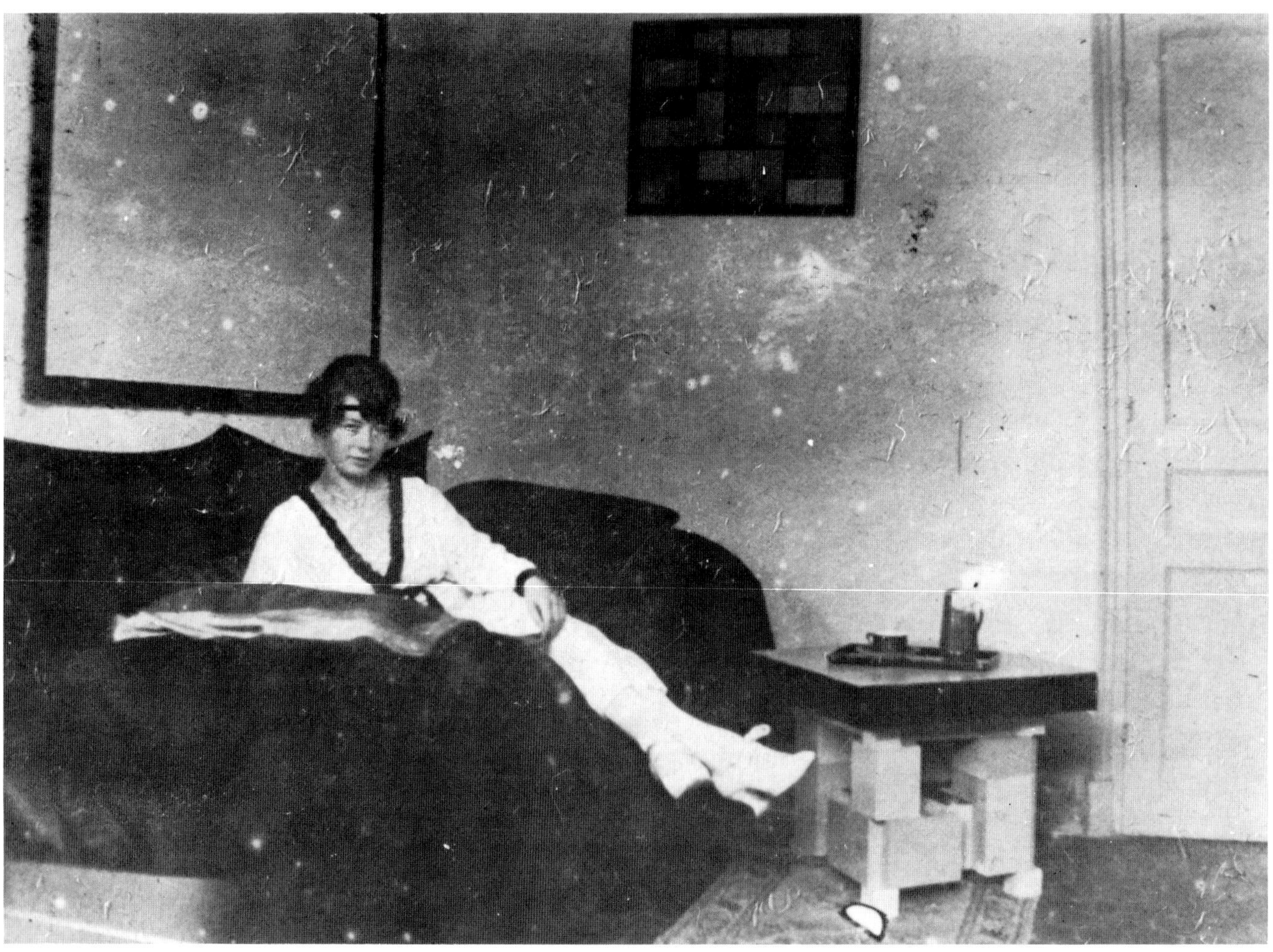

236

236 Tine Vantongerloo in the interior of the apartment in Menton. Photograph taken during visit of Theo and Nelly van Doesburg, April 1921.

237 Interior of the apartment in Menton, April 1921. Left to right: Theo van Doesburg, Nelly van Doesburg, Tine Vantongerloo.

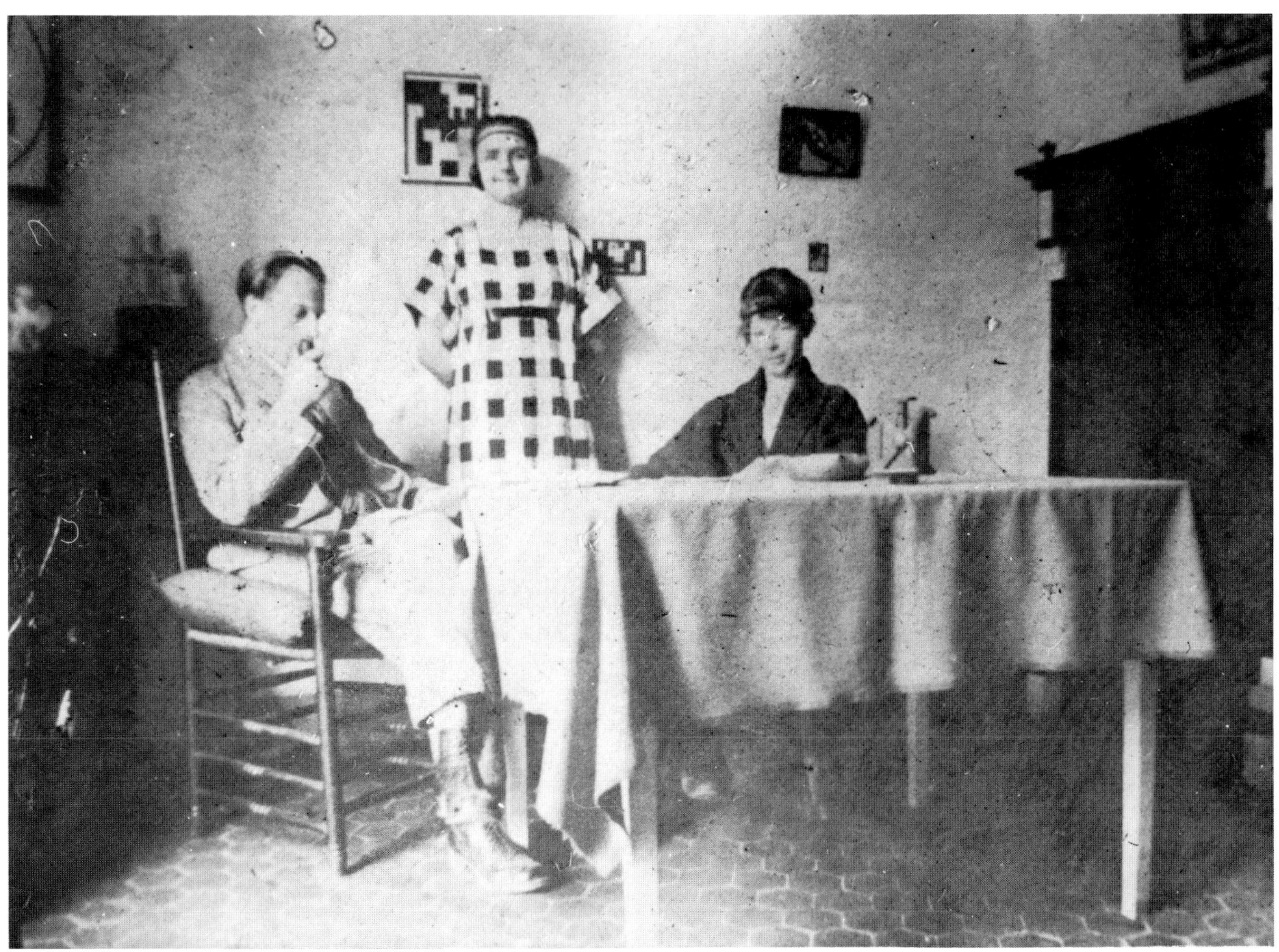

237

cabinet to the left is another one (figure 226). In the left corner is a "construction of volume relations." At the right is an old cabinet that Vantongerloo appears to have tried to transform into a piece of "De Stijl furniture" by painting a few planes in its upper part and replacing its legs with blocks of various colors. In comparison with the radical treatments of walls and furniture Huszár and van Doesburg had realized, Vantongerloo's interior seems halfhearted. The photographs show a mishmash of old-fashioned items (the table with the tablecloth, the cabinet), abstract paintings, and very extraordinary objects (the tea table). There was no synthesis between architecture and visual arts, only an attempt to adapt some loose details in the interior to the standards formulated in *De stijl*.

For a time, Vantongerloo achieved good results only in separate pieces of practical furniture. A desk and a chair designed in 1921 are fairly simple in construction, in contrast with the tea table.[54] The chair consists of four closed planes: the seat, the back, and the armrests (which continue almost to the floor). The four blocks at the base are painted gray, white, and black; the endgrains are a different color. The desk, too, has a closed character. A thick top rests on a block-shaped pedestal, in which a rectangular space is left open. The desk is painted in the same colors and in the same manner as the chair.[54] The massive character of the chair and the desk is mitigated somewhat by the use of color; nevertheless, these pieces are a far cry from (for example) Rietveld's spatial constructions.

Compositions based on geometric figures

At the same time that Vantongerloo started to grow apart from the other De Stijl artists because of his idiosyncratic use of color, important changes occurred in his use of form—that is, in his manner of abstraction and composition. Up to this point, he had always started from preliminary studies which he had made of common subjects, mostly sitting figures. By means of the process of decomposition, which he had learned from Theo van Doesburg in particular, he arrived at well-balanced compositions of rectangles. His decisions about the dimensions of those forms were based on his visual starting points; at first they were not founded on systems of measure. A head became an all but square form, an arm an elongated horizontal or vertical one. This approach changed at the beginning of Vantongerloo's Menton period. Having recently developed a system for the use of the seven spectral colors, he now looked for a system of forms.

Analysis of existing works of art was an important aid in this endeavor. In 1918 Vantongerloo had already tried to demonstrate the geometric basis of a sculpture by Archipenko (figure 222); in 1920 and 1921 he directed his attention to paintings by Flemish primitive masters. The results of his research are reflected in some articles which were collected in 1924 in *l'Art et son avenir* [*Art and its future*]. The article "l'Art ancien et l'art nouveau," written in March 1921, included two analyses of Roger van der Weyden's *Pietà*. It is clear what fascinated Vantongerloo about this altarpiece. In his first analysis (figure 238) he left the image intact and only drew a grid and a diagonal over it in order to clarify the composition, but his second analysis (figure 239) very much resembles the method of abstraction he had once used in paintings such as *Studie no. 2* (figure 220)—the representation is reduced to angular forms in different colors. Such analyses are not uncommon; there has been much speculation (more or less justified) on the hidden geometry in the work of old masters. However, it is unusual for an artist to create a work based on the supposed geometric arrangement in another artist's work, as Vantongerloo did here. Vantongerloo later used these two analyses as the basis for his *Compositie indigo-violet* (*zevende mineur*) [*Composition indigo-violet (minor seventh)*]. In that painting (figure 240) there was no longer any abstraction like that in Vantongerloo's decompositions of figure studies. The painting does not represent the figures of the *Pietà* in abstraction; it only represents the geometric composition of the image, and the grid and the diagonal of the first analysis play an important role in this. *Compositie indigo-violet* is divided into juxtaposed color planes, for which Vantongerloo claimed to have examined all the variations in the indigo-violet range of color. The areas of the various color planes were determined with mathematical exactness. In order to produce the desired equilibrium, the colors had to be equivalent in tonal value as well as in quantity. Vantongerloo had already pointed out, in his article "Unité," that the seven colors of the spectrum were comparable to the seven fundamental notes in music, and that in both cases one could determine extent and proportions. His parenthetical addition of "minor seventh" to the title *Composition indigo-violet* makes it plausible that he equated that range of color with that particular musical interval. Apparently, he found both to be in harmony with the melancholy mood of the *Pietà*.

Compositie indigo-violet, which can be seen hanging on the wall in figure 239, probably originated in the spring of 1921, about the same time as the article in which the *Pietà* was analyzed. In that same year, Vantongerloo examined other paintings by van der Weyden. He concluded that the composition of the triptych *De zeven sacramenten* [*The seven sacraments*] was based on an equilateral triangle, and in 1921 he used such triangular compositions several times himself, first in the painting *Compositie uitgaande van*

238

239

238 Vantongerloo, analysis of Roger van der Weyden's *Pietà*, 1921. Technique, dimensions, and whereabouts unknown. As illustrated in Vantongerloo's *l'Art et son avenir* (Antwerp, 1924).

239 Vantongerloo, analysis of Roger van der Weyden's *Pietà*, 1921. Technique, dimensions, and whereabouts unknown. As illustrated in Vantongerloo's *l'Art et son avenir* (Antwerp, 1924).

240 Vantongerloo, *Compositie indigo-violet (zevende mineur)* [*Composition indigo-violet (minor seventh)*], 1921. Oil on canvas, 13.5 × 8.65 cm. Private collection.

240

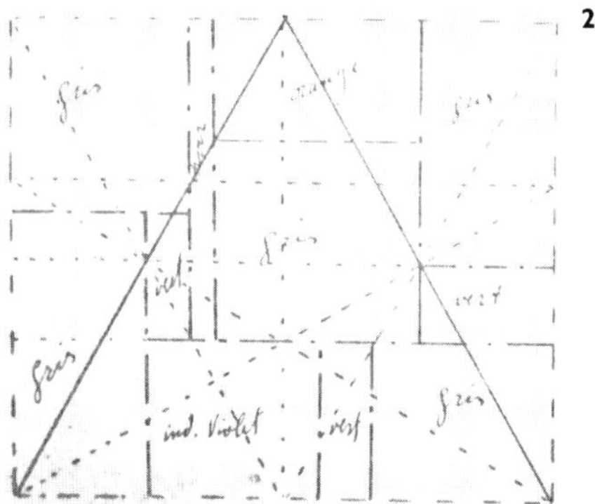

241 **Vantongerloo, design sketch for *Compositie uitgaande van de gelijkzijdige driehoek* [*Composition starting from an equilateral triangle*], 1921. Enclosed with letter from Vantongerloo to Jean Gorin, April 3, 1927.**

242 **Vantongerloo, *Triptiek* [*Triptych*], 1921. Wood and oil on panel, 13 × 13 cm (closed). On loan to Gemeentemuseum, The Hague, from private collection. (Color plate on page xx.)**

de gelijkzijdige driehoek [*Composition starting from an equilateral triangle*].[55] In that painting, it is at first difficult to perceive a triangle at all. On a gray-white ground, one sees a number of thin horizontal and vertical lines, which never continue from one side of the canvas to the other but rather stop where they meet another line (in a manner recalling, to an extent, Mondrian's compositions from the same time). These lines form eleven rectangles, one of which (a narrow one) is black, one ochre-yellow, one purple, and three green. However, the design sketch (figure 241) shows that Vantongerloo did start from an equilateral triangle (though not so much from the form of the triangle as from the regularities inherent in it). In general, the intersections of the dotted lines in the sketch form the vertices of the rectangles in the painting. Here, for the first time, Vantongerloo departed not from a realistic image but from a geometric form and its mathematical qualities. His research of van der Weyden's compositions—whether he interpreted them correctly or not—certainly played a role in this new approach.

The small triptych shown in figure 242, an important work, is closely related to the one just discussed. Vantongerloo made at least two copies, which differ in color. Both are tiny—13 × 13 centimeters when closed and 13 × 26 centimeters when open. When closed, the panels look exactly like *Compositie uitgaande van de gelijkzijdige driehoek*.[56] When opened, they reveal a relief executed in natural mahogany, with horizontally and vertically positioned block shapes lying on top of and underneath one another. The side panels are painted in the same manner as the outside of the triptych. It is probable that this work was based on Roger van der Weyden's triptych *Kruisafname* [*Deposition from the Cross*].[57] At the outside of the panels Vantongerloo only used ochre-yellow, green, and purple; on the inside he used red and blue also. He did not use all seven colors of the spectrum; perhaps he had heeded Mondrian's criticism (quoted above). An undated letter from Mondrian to van Doesburg, written in 1920, contains this remark: "In reaction to my firm disapproval I now get a mealy-mouthed letter saying that [Vantongerloo] did not always use all seven colors in one work—this is again a contradiction, for he says that there is no harmony without all of the seven." After 1921, Vantongerloo never used all seven colors in a painting.

The small triptych has a special place among Vantongerloo's works. When closed it is a painting; when opened it is a combination of painting and sculpture. It was probably meant to be hung on a wall; the middle part is quite flat, and it has much less of a spatial effect than Vantongerloo's sculptures. Vantongerloo may have considered it a synthesis between sculpture and painting. It may have been inspired by his studies of van der Weyden's triptychs, or of other fifteenth-century altarpieces that show a similar combination.

No works made by Vantongerloo in 1922 or 1923 are known. He was probably engrossed in his studies of mathematics and music during those years. He had already shown signs of an interest in music by comparing the colors to the notes and by referring to music in the titles of some of his works. His interest in geometry went back even farther. At first, he had seen geometry as only an aid in arriving at an abstract sculpture or painting after starting from a realistic theme. However, in 1921, through his studies of van der Weyden's works, he found a way to arrive at abstraction without starting from reality. He became fascinated with geometric diagrams, particularly because of the regularities inherent in them, and he immersed himself in books on arithmetic, non-Euclidean geometry, and related subjects.[58] As is often evident from their titles, his works from 1924 and later years were based on mathematical formulas.

During this period of self-instruction (1922 and 1923), Vantongerloo withdrew from De Stijl,[59] probably because of his difference of opinion with Mondrian and van Doesburg over colors. Unlike some of the other artists, he did not have a falling-out with Theo van Doesburg; he simply went his own way, having perceived that his studies of mathematics and music and his use of geometric systems had caused him to move away artistically from the others. J. J. P. Oud probably summed up the situation correctly when he wrote to Vantongerloo on August 31, 1931: "I was glad that you normally, soundly, did your own thing, without being disturbed by 'intrigues' and so on."[60]

242

1
Georges Vantongerloo 1886–1965 (exhibition catalog, Koninklijke Musea voor Schone Kunsten van België, Brussels, 1981), p. 210.

2
Two important catalogs are *Georges Vantongerloo* (Marlborough Fine Art Ltd., London, 1962) and *Georges Vantongerloo 1886–1965* (note 1 above). The following are some of the important articles: C. von Wiegand, "Georges Vantongerloo, a pioneer of abstract sculpture," *Arts* 34, no. 10 (1960), pp. 40–45; U. Appollonio, "E morto Georges Vantongerloo," *Casabella* 30, no. 301 (1966), pp. 52–59; E. Bergen, "Georges Vantongerloo," *Bulletin Musées Royaux des Beaux Arts de Belgique* 4 (1966), pp. 271–299; M. Staber, "Georges Vantongerloo," *Werk* 6 (1967), pp. 353–357; V. Anker, "Vantongerloo," *Art international* 24, no. 5–6 (1981), pp. 158–193; G. Baines, "Georges Vantongerloo, de invloed van het werk van Wouters en het ontstaan van de eerste abstracte beelden," *Wonen/TABK* 9 (1981), pp. 6–15; A. T. Jankowski, "Georges Vantongerloo 1886–1965," *Du* 4 (1981), pp. 64–66.

3
Information on Vantongerloo's education and his application for the Prix de Rome was provided by G. Persoons of the Nationaal Hoger Instituut en Koninklijke Academie voor Schone Kunsten and by F. Vanhemelryk of the Koninklijke Academie voor Schone Kunsten, Brussels.

4
Written communication from J. Boyens, Groesbeek. On Emile and Oscar Jespers, see J. Boyens, *Oscar Jespers, zijn beeldhouwwerk met een overzicht van de tekeningen* (Antwerp, 1982).

5
C. von Wiegand, "Georges Vantongerloo, a pioneer of abstract sculpture" (note 2 above).

6
Written communications from G. Baines, based on material in Vantongerloo's estate.

7
D. E. Gordon, *Modern art exhibitions 1900–1916* (Munich, 1974), p. 835.

8
M. Bilcke, "Georges Vantongerloo is eenzaam begraven," *De standaard,* October 19, 1965.

9
However, he was not registered as a citizen of The Hague until October 22, 1917, according to a communication from the municipal archive.

10
The Belgian government, through its embassy in The Hague, had established a service committee for refugees, whose activities included the organization of these exhibitions. The purpose was to make the sculptors and painters among the refugees known to the Dutch public, which would then support them by purchasing their works.

11
The founding and the aims of Open Wegen are mentioned in *Architectura* of December 29, 1917. The architect Huib Hoste was also a member.

12
On Schmalzigaug, see P. Mertens, "Kennismaking met een Antwerps futurist: Jules Schmalzigaug," *Bulletin Koninklijke Musea voor Schone Kunsten van België* 1/2 (1971) App. 121–137.

13
Communication from the municipal archive of The Hague. Woutrina Adriana Kalis was born in Sliedrecht on August 20, 1897.

14
See *Belgische kunst* (exhibition catalog, Gallery Kleykamp, The Hague, 1915) and the following reviews: anonymous, *Algemeen handelsblad,* February 3, 1915; anonymous, *Nieuwe Rotterdamsche courant,* February 12, 1915; anonymous, *De nieuwe courant,* February 2, 1915. Another exhibition entitled "Belgische kunst" was held at the Gallery d'Audretsch, in The Hague, in February 1915; no catalog is known; see review by A. Heyting in *Eenheid* of February 27, 1915. In addition, see *Exposition d'oeuvres d'artistes Belges* (catalog, Gallery d'Audretsch, The Hague, 1915) and the following review: anonymous, *l'Echo Belge,* October 2, 1915. An "Exposition des dernières oeuvres de Georges Vantongerloo, sculpteur" was held at the Pulchri Studio, in The Hague, on March 15–29, 1916, and reviewed by D. B. in *De hofstad* of March 18, by an anonymous critic in the *Nieuwe Rotterdamsche courant* of March 17, by another anonymous critic in *De kroniek* 2, no. 3 (1916), p. 173, by G. D. Gratama in *Onze kunst* 15, no. 30 (1916), p. 24, and by Plasschaert (March 21, 1916; newspaper unknown; clipping in Rijksbureau voor Kunsthistorische Documentatie, The Hague). See, in addition, *Exposition d'oeuvres Belges, peinture, dessin, sculpture* (catalog, Pulchi Studio, The Hague, 1916) and the following review: anonymous, *De hofstad,* June 24, 1916. See also *Tentoonstelling van Belgische kunst* (exhibition catalog, Stedelijk Museum, Amsterdam, 1916–17); *Tentoonstelling van Belgische moderne kunst* (exhibition catalog, Artibus Sacrum gallery, Korenbeurs, Arnhem, 1917). A "Tentoonstelling Georges Vantongerloo" was held by the Kunstkring Hollando-Belge in The Hague in October 1917 and reviewed anonymously in *De prins* of October 20 and in the *Algemeen handelsblad* of October 14. Finally, see *Exposition d'art moderne Belge* (catalog, Panorama Mesdag, The Hague, 1917).

15
G. D. Gratama, "Tentoonstelling Georges Vantongerloo in Pulchri Studio," *Onze kunst* 15, no. 30 (1916), p. 24.

16
This is illustrated on page 79 of A. Franzke's *Skulpturen und objekte von malern des 20. jahrhunderts* (Cologne, 1982).

17
Gratama, "Tentoonstelling Georges Vantongerloo" (note 15 above), p. 24.

18
Baines, "Georges Vantongerloo" (note 2 above), p. 8.

19
Vantongerloo's estate, now in the possession of Max Bill, in Zurich, is unfortunately not open for research at present.

20
H. Wescher, "Entretien avec Nelly van Doesburg," *Cimaise* 17, no. 99 (1971), pp. 36–41. Jan Wils is probably confused here with H. Wils, a Belgian etcher who lived in Rotterdam during the First World War and who participated, along with Vantongerloo, in the Moderne Belgische Kunst exhibition at Panorama Mesdag, in The Hague, in 1917.

21
For instance, a series of articles by Gino Severini entitled "La peinture d'avant garde" began in the second issue of *De stijl,* and the work of the sculptor Archipenko (whom Vantongerloo admired greatly) was featured in the first volume.

22
Michelangelo was discussed in a series entitled "Grootmeesters der beeldende kunst" that appeared in the February 2, May 29, August 22, and September 26, 1918, issues of *Eenheid.*

23
Wescher, "Entretien avec Nelly van Doesburg" (note 20 above).

24
The earliest illustration is on page 98 of Theo van Doesburg's *Drie voordrachten over de nieuwe beeldende kunst* (Amsterdam, 1919). The first showing was at the Exposition Internationale d'Art Moderne in Geneva (December 23, 1920, through January 25, 1921).

25
Van Doesburg to Kok, September 22, 1918.

26
This is evidenced by a letter from van Doesburg to Kok dated December 3, 1918, and by a letter from Mondrian to van Doesburg dated December 10, 1918.

27
V. Huszár, "Aesthetische beschouwing V," *De stijl* 1, no. 12 (1918), pp. 147–150. This quote is from pp. 149–150.

28
Mondrian to van Doesburg, December 10, 1918.

29
Van Doesburg to Oud, September 10, 1918.

30
G. Vantongerloo, "Réflexions," *De stijl* 1, no. 9 (1918), pp. 97–102; 2, no. 2 (1918), pp. 21–22; 2, no. 3 (1919), pp. 35–36; 2, no. 5 (1919), pp. 55–57; 2, no. 7 (1919), pp. 77–79; 2, no. 8 (1919), pp. 89–91; 3, no. 2 (1920), pp. 19–21; 3, no. 3 (1920), pp. 31–32; 3, no. 4 (1920), pp. 21–24.

31
T. van Doesburg, "Grootmeesters der beeldende kunst," *Eenheid,* August 22, 1918.

32
M. H. J. Schoenmaekers, *Het nieuwe wereldbeeld* (Bussum, 1915); M. H. J. Schoenmaekers, *Beeldende wiskunde* (Bussum, 1916).

33
In his articles in French he used the word *complementaire,* which expressed his meaning even better.

34
The ten analyses are illustrated in an auction catalog (Sotheby, London, April 1, 1981).

35
Two extant oils, known as *Studie* and *Studie no. 1,* are illustrated on page 40 of *Georges Vantongerloo 1886–1965* (note 1 above).

36
De stijl 2, no. 7 (1919), pp. 77–79.

37
Schoenmaekers, *Het nieuwe wereldbeeld* (note 32 above), p. 128.

38
This catalog is mentioned in a list of books belonging to *De stijl*'s library that was published on page 71 of *De stijl* 2, no. 6 (1919).

39
Georges Vantongerloo 1886–1965 (note 1 above), p. 40.

40
I have placed this construction at the end of the series because it is only loosely related to the others. However, one could argue that it should be placed at the beginning; it gives a rather heavy and clumsy impression in comparison with the other three sculptures in the series.

41
It is possible that only then did he become better acquainted with their work, or that this is at least true with respect to van Doesburg. He could have seen works by Mondrian only at a single exhibition in 1918 or reproduced in *De stijl,* and he could have seen works by the others only in *De stijl.* As mentioned above, van Doesburg was the only member of the group that he knew personally.

42
For an illustration, see A. E. Elsen, *Origins of modern sculpture: Pioneers and premises* (Oxford, 1974), p. 105.

43
G. Vantongerloo, "An intimate biography," in *Georges Vantongerloo* (exhibition catalog, Marlborough Fine Art Ltd., London, 1962).

44
T. van Doesburg, "Aanteekeningen bij bijlage II," *De stijl* 3, no. 2 (1919), p. 23.

45
This identification is possible because of the filmstrip *Georges Vantongerloo, evolution (1910–1936) vers l'art abstrait* (Paris: Fixus Films), a photographic copy of which is in the Rijksbureau voor Kunsthistorische Documentatie, in The Hague.

46
For an illustration, see E. van Straaten, *Theo van Doesburg 1883–1931, een documentaire op basis van materiaal uit de Schenking Van Moorsel* (The Hague, 1983), p. 81.

47
In March 1918, well before Vantongerloo departed for Brussels, Mondrian exhibited some paintings in which he had divided the plane with dark gray lines into rectangles of irregular size and filled them in with gray and various pastel colors. One of these was *Compositie met kleurvlakken en grijze lijnen* (figure 48 in this volume). Mondrian's paintings were on view from March 16 to April 7, 1918, in the exhibition of the Hollandsche Kunstenaarskring at the Stedelijk Museum in Amsterdam. A similar painting was reproduced in *De stijl.*

48
On his first visit to Mondrian, in April 1920, Vantongerloo told him that he used the seven colors. Vantongerloo probably had painted *Studie no. III* shortly before that visit.

49
P. Mondrian, "Natuurlijke en abstracte realiteit," *De stijl* 3, no. 2 (1919), p. 17.

50
Letter from Mondrian to van Doesburg, April 19, 1920.

51
"Unité" was published in Vantongerloo's book *l'Art et son avenir* (Antwerp, 1924). It was written in 1920.

52
Bergen ["Georges Vantongerloo" (note 2 above)] mentions that, on a visit to Vantongerloo, he was shown such a disk.

53
According to G. Baines (personal communication), the bottom part was painted in the primary colors. However, the photograph gives the impression that, when it was taken, the bottom part was painted in pastel colors.

54
The chair and the desk are illustrated on page 49 of *Georges Vantongerloo 1886–1965* (note 1 above).

55
This painting is illustrated on page 50 of *Georges Vantongerloo 1886–1965* (note 1 above).

56
It is not clear how the triptych should be positioned. The nailhole suggests the position shown in figure 242; however, when the side panels are closed in this position the "composition starting from an equilateral triangle" emerges as having been rotated 180 degrees.

57
Baines, "Georges Vantongerloo" (note 2), p. 15.

58
According to a communication from G. Baines, the following books (among others) belong to Vantongerloo's estate: J. Duffailly, *Aritmétique* (Paris, n.d.); H. Commissaire, *Algèbre et trigonométrie* (n.d.); G. Francolin, *Physique* (Paris, 1886).

59
He had not contributed a new article to *De stijl* since early 1920. In the 1927 commemorative issue he is listed as a contributor for the years 1918, 1919, 1920, and 1922; however, his 1922 contributions (such as "Plastiek," *De stijl* 5, no. 12, pp. 203–204) were fragments from previous articles.

60
Vantongerloo's relations with van Doesburg did deteriorate in 1927, owing to the controversy over publication in the journal *i10.*

243 Gerrit Rietveld with two of his children, ca. 1918. Photograph in collection of E. Eskes-Rietveld, Amsterdam.

Gerrit Rietveld

From the very beginning of his involvement with De Stijl, Gerrit Rietveld stood out from his colleagues in two particular ways: He published very little, and he avoided quarrels and intrigues.

Early in his career as a furniture designer and an architect, he did not deem it necessary to explain or justify his work in articles, books, or lectures. His only publications in his early De Stijl years were two short articles in which he described his furniture and its construction.[1] Not much was written about him, either. His correspondence with Theo van Doesburg and J. J. P. Oud is the greatest source of information about his ideas and his methods. The source material is rather summary, but the work itself is very informative.[2]

Rietveld never fell out with van Doesburg or any of the others. He did not take part in the evolving polemics, nor did he malign those who thought differently. He stayed on as a contributor to *De stijl* right to the end.

Today, Rietveld is thought of as one of the De Stijl architects, or even as the quintessential De Stijl architect. However, this image developed over the course of time, and it is due mainly to the so-called Schröder house (constructed in 1924). In 1919, when he became involved with *De stijl,* Rietveld had not achieved anything as an architect. He developed into an architect gradually, through the experience he gained designing furniture and interiors and renovating facades. In contrast, J. J. P. Oud and Jan Wils ventured into the design of furniture and interiors only after obtaining thorough training as architects. (Another point of contrast is that, unlike Rietveld, they had even their earliest designs executed by others.)

Rietveld was the furniture specialist; his was the only furniture to be reproduced and discussed in *De stijl* during the first five years of the periodical's existence. He created this furniture primarily for himself. He realized that it would not be widely accepted at first, but he firmly believed that "the new" would gradually overcome. On January 23, 1920, he wrote to Oud: ". . . let us not say that we are working in order to satisfy the people, because the people have no need for it. Generally they do not go beyond the wish of just possessing something special. I know people thoroughly in this respect." This was not a sour remark, but a conclusion based on experience.

Those who were interested in Rietveld's furniture were not "common people," but a physician (ten Doesschate), an engineer (Schelling), an architect (Elling), and a clergyman (de Ligt). In a letter to Oud dated May 14, 1920, Rietveld elaborated on the fact that his furniture was fully appreciated by only a few: "You know as well as I that in any enterprise one experiences constraints from all sides, even if one imagines that one is responding to the general superficial demands. I am so used to this that my reply to the rash remarks, even from those who should have a broader view, is 'just you wait, you will come to see more in it, and I shall give some more as well, when I am good and ready.' . . . However, I should like to add this: I do not make my furniture for 'the people' in the sense that I let the people make demands and deliver judgments (the needs of others). But I am myself one of the people, and I am creating them according to my own needs. This is wrong insofar as I myself march to a different drummer (understand me well, not as a person, but as a furnituremaker)." This was written at a time when, as a result of the Russian revolution, there were many heated discussions in art circles about the relation between art and society. Rietveld's remarks show how soberly he viewed reality. He had little of the missionary zeal or the heaven-storming idealism that characterized some of the others.

Youth, training, and early works

Gerrit Rietveld was born on June 24, 1888, one of six children of the furnituremaker Johannes Cornelis Rietveld and his wife, Elisabeth van der Horst. From 1890 on, the family lived at 98 Poortstraat in Utrecht. Young Gerrit went to work in his father's workshop as soon as he finished elementary school.

According to the literature on Rietveld, his first furniture design dates from around 1900. This was for a table and some chairs for the gatekeeper's house at the Zuilen Castle. It is said that Rietveld designed a Louis XV interior for the Utrechtse Hypotheekbank [Utrecht Mortgage Bank] about six years later.[3] The attribution of these designs is not certain, but at least they give an idea of the sort of furniture that was produced in the Rietveld shop.

Gerrit Rietveld used the professional title *meubelmaker* [furnituremaker], as did his father. He was listed as such in the address books of Utrecht from 1907 on,[4] and he continued to use that title for some years after his contact with De Stijl. However, his interests transcended furnituremaking quite early in his career. Around 1906 he began to take evening lessons from the architect P. J. C. Klaarhamer. From 1904 to 1908 he was enrolled in evening "industrial art classes" offered by an institute known as "Het Utrechtsch Museum van Kunstnijverheid te Utrecht" ["The Utrecht Museum of Arts and Crafts at Utrecht"].[5] There were classes in drawing, painting, anatomy, theory of proportion, clay modeling, technical drawing, and theory of style and ornaments. Rietveld was rated as a very good student, and was awarded three prizes. While enrolled in these classes he was working for the Begeer jewelry firm,[6] and for years afterward—even during his De

244

Stijl period—he was occasionally commissioned by that firm to design plaquettes and medallions. Thus, furnituremaking was by no means his sole occupation.

In 1909, Rietveld got one of his first creative commissions. It was for the design of a tombstone commemorating E. Nijland, the late headmaster of the Nederlandse Hervormde Burgerschool [Dutch Reformed High School].[7] This commission came to Rietveld through Carel Begeer, of the jewelry firm, who had been a good friend of Nijland.

Rietveld also painted, and from 1911[8] on he was listed as a member of a "painting and drawing association" known as Kunstliefde [Love of Art].[9] Rietveld showed his paintings publicly only once, at the exhibition of "works created by members of the painting and drawing association Kunstliefde" held from April 21 to May 5, 1912. The catalog of this exhibition lists only three works by Rietveld: *Portret van J. van Noordenne* (an oil), *O haupt voll blut und wunden,* and *Portret van Mevr. Koelman.*[10] However, the Kunstliefde archives contain a form that shows that he had submitted a fourth: *Portret van wijlen Anth. Begeer* (figure 245). That painting may have been exhibited, although it was not listed in the catalog. Anthonie Begeer was a member of Kunstliefde until his death on May 7, 1910, and it was probably his son Carel Begeer who commissioned the posthumous portrait (which Rietveld painted after a black-and-white photograph). It is not a bad work, and it is certainly better than dilettantish; perhaps, at the time, Rietveld had ambitions as a painter. His expertise in woodworking is evident in the frame, which is festooned with carved roses and inscribed with the subject's dates of birth and death.

Rietveld probably kept abreast of developments in arts and crafts, furniture, and interior design both in the Netherlands and elsewhere. At Klaarhamer's studio and in the library of Kunstliefde he had access to such journals as *The studio, Art et décoration, Dekorative kunst, Deutsche kunst und dekoration, Kunst und kunsthandwerk,* and *Kunst für alle.* Looking at his furniture, one cannot escape the impression that he knew the products of the Vienna Secession, the Wiener Werkstätte, and the Glasgow School, and that he also knew about Frank Lloyd Wright's work. Foreign influences are most noticeable in the works Rietveld produced after 1917.

It is a pity that so few of Rietveld's pre-1917 works are known. Those that have been preserved follow lines that had been established by Klaarhamer and by H. P. Berlage. (See, for example, figure 246, which shows a cabinet that Rietveld built in 1911 for his own home.) Rietveld must have designed more furniture in those years, but because he worked for his father it was done anonymously.

245

244 Rietveld, tombstone of E. Nijland, Utrecht, 1909.

245 Rietveld, *Portret van wijlen Anth. Begeer* [*Portrait of the late Anth. Begeer*], ca. 1910. Oil on canvas, 90 × 59 cm. Collection of S. A. C. Begeer, Voorschoten.

246 **Rietveld, cabinet, 1911. Collection of E. Eskes-Rietveld, Amsterdam.**

In 1917 Rietveld and his family moved to 93 Adriaan van Ostadelaan in Utrecht, where at the age of 29 he opened his own furniture workshop.[11] Now he had the opportunity to create furniture to suit his own taste.

Rietveld and *De stijl*

It is impossible to ascertain the date of Rietveld's first contact with *De stijl,* or exactly when he became a contributor to the periodical, or to what extent the designation "contributor" was applicable to him during the periodical's early years. But he was certainly not one of *De stijl*'s founders, and he was not a signer of the first manifesto (which appeared in the November 1918 issue). His name first appeared in the July 1919 issue.

The earliest extant letter from Rietveld to Theo van Doesburg is dated October 7, 1919.[12] Referring to an article by van Doesburg about one of Rietveld's chairs, Rietveld wrote: "I thank you for your letter and the forwarding of *De stijl* containing the reproduction. My special thanks also for the annotation—this appreciation is very encouraging to me. It is most joyful to note that, while I was always on my own, there are others who felt and thought the same." Apparently Rietveld had not been reading *De stijl* for long (perhaps not at all); it seems that he had just become aware of the existence of those "others." Moreover, the impersonal salutation ("Dear Sir") and the formal tone of the letter suggest that Rietveld and van Doesburg hardly knew each other. A month later, in a letter to Oud dated November 8, van Doesburg wrote: "Wednesday Rietveld was here. . . . He is a nice fellow. Fresh and simple." This seems to suggest that he had just met Rietveld for the first time. However, the first communication between Rietveld and van Doesburg—probably indirect—must have taken place before July 1919, for some work by Rietveld was reproduced in that month's *De stijl.* It is not known who brought about the contact. It may have been Bart van der Leck, whom Rietveld had known (albeit superficially) since 1905.[13] Rietveld must have known van Doesburg, by name at least. Other possibilities are the Utrecht artists Erich Wichman and Janus de Winter, with whom van Doesburg had been in contact since 1915, and the art-loving oculist G. ten Doesschate. Then again, van Doesburg gave a number of lectures in Utrecht. Another possibility is that Rietveld had met some of the contributors to *De stijl,* or had heard of them, through Klaarhamer or someone else. However, it is most probably Robert van 't Hoff who brought about the actual contact between Rietveld and van Doesburg. In 1914–15, van 't Hoff had built a house on a commission from J. N. Verloop in the village of Huis ter Heide, close by Utrecht. The house was inspired by the work of

Frank Lloyd Wright, and the client is said to have asked Rietveld to produce copies of some of Wright's furniture. If, as it is thought, van 't Hoff visited Rietveld after seeing the copies, he may have arranged Rietveld's first appearance in *De stijl*.[14]

Furniture, 1918–1920

The first piece of Rietveld furniture to be shown in *De stijl* (see note 14) was the baby chair shown here in figure 247. The three photographs—a front view, a side view, and a rear view—were accompanied by a short text written by Rietveld. It was rather unusual to show three views of a single chair, but Rietveld appears to have considered this essential; the emphasis on the chair's structure and construction was also evident in the text.

In comparison with the usual furniture of its time, Rietveld's baby chair was rather striking. The horizontal slats were not connected to the vertical posts by the traditional pin-and-hole method; instead, the slats ran alongside the posts and were connected to them by loose pins called *deuvels*. The structure of the chair was very clear, yet the method of construction was hidden from view. In some places, as at the upper part of the back, the posts and the slats continued farther than was strictly necessary. The only decoration was the use of colors—the leather was red and the wood was painted green. The boards and fillets were neither beveled nor thickened. Such sobriety of design was not common, although it was sometimes found in the furniture of the Glasgow School. Some of the details of the baby chair, such as the long, narrow board in the back, which gives the chair its emphatic vertical character, are reminiscent of Wright's chairs and (even more so) Charles Rennie Mackintosh's. The leather straps of the baby chair have the same visual effect as the slats in the back of Mackintosh's Ladderback Chair (figure 248). Thus, certain elements of the baby chair can be compared with domestic and foreign examples, but Rietveld's manner of having posts and slats cross without intersecting was unique. He addressed this detail in his article: "The wood connection used here is obvious because of its simplicity and the clarity of expression. . . . the greatest advantage is that one is very free in placing the rails; this gives the object a greater spatial expression, which liberates one from the constructive bound plane." This explanation indicates clearly what Rietveld had in mind with the baby chair: The lower part of a normal chair can be viewed as outlining a kind of box, with coplanar legs and rungs; however, if these elements cross without intersecting, they come out of the plane and penetrate the space around them.

The second of Rietveld's chairs to be reproduced in *De stijl* in 1919,[15] an as-yet-uncolored version of the famous Red-Blue Chair, was constructed in the same way as the baby chair. Here, even more consistently than in the baby chair, the posts and the slats passed one another by, so that their independence from one another was strongly emphasized. This chair resembles the skeleton of an ordinary armchair; the structure is completely visible. In the earliest chairs, the space below the armrests was still more or less closed off by side panels. Some of these were rectangular and some trapezoidal; with the latter the inclination followed the line of the seat. In later executions these side panels were omitted, and then it could truly be asserted that the chair was constructed of only the most elementary and essential parts.

Like the baby chair, this armchair (two early versions of which are shown in figure 252) shows signs of the possible influence of other designers. The protruding, inclined backrest seems revolutionary, yet rudiments of the design can be seen in several designs from the turn of the century. In many of H. P. Berlage's chairs from that time, the legs were disconnected from the seat and the backrest. (See, for example, figure 249.) Furthermore, the backrest was not a plane between continuations of the back legs but a separate element; thus, it could be placed in its oblique position without the need for bent-back posts. There is a Mackintosh chair from 1902 in which the autonomy of the inclined backrest is even more evident; perhaps Rietveld had seen the photograph of this chair that appeared in *Deutsche kunst und dekoration* in 1905.[16]

Frank Lloyd Wright, too, had worked with a comparable concept. Besides being similar in structure, his 1909 chair for the Robie House (figure 250) bears an immediate resemblance to Rietveld's armchair—particularly from the side. In each of these chairs the openness of the construction is striking, and in each the backrest is a simple, straight, obliquely mounted board without decoration or profile.[17] In Wright's chair the board rests on a fillet between the elongated back legs; in Rietveld's the mounting of the board is similar, but the back legs do not extend nearly as high and therefore the point of support for the backrest is much lower. In each of these chairs the back extends behind the seat down to a rung just slightly above the floor.

Another possible source of inspiration for Rietveld's armchair is a set of furniture designed by P. J. C. Klaarhamer[18] and executed (in 1915) in the workshop of J. C. Rietveld. The chairs of this set (figure 251) have undecorated, elongated posts and separate backrests that are more or less disconnected from the back legs.

Though it may have had predecessors, Rietveld's armchair achieved a much greater spatial effect than any of them. It also

247

247 Rietveld, baby chair, 1918. As illustrated in *De stijl* 2, no. 9 (1919), p. 102.

248 Charles Rennie Mackintosh, ladderback chair, 1902. As illustrated on page 59 of F. Alison's *Charles Rennie Mackintosh as a designer of chairs* (London, 1974).

249 H. P. Berlage, buttress chair, 1902. As illustrated on page 35 of *Stoelen* (Delft, 1980).

250 Frank Lloyd Wright, chair, 1909. As illustrated on page 36 of *Stoelen* (Delft, 1980).

251 P. J. C. Klaarhamer, chair, 1915. Centraal Museum, Utrecht.

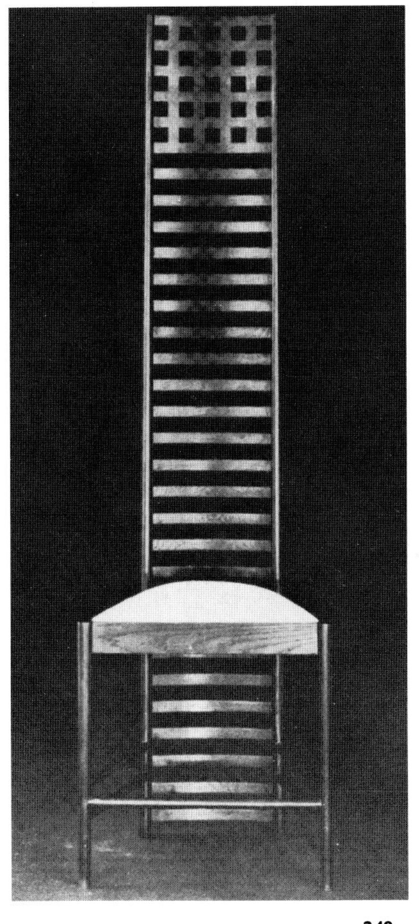
248

249

250

251

252 Rietveld, two armchairs for P. Elling, designed in 1918. Collection of Paul Smit, Utrecht.

differed in its construction. Whereas the other chairs illustrated here give the impression of having been made by hand (e.g., because of their profiling), Rietveld's chair clearly was designed with an eye toward mass production; all the wood was of standard sizes. There was not enough interest in the chair to justify mass production, but the possibility was there.

Rietveld's armchair (particularly the painted version) has, over the course of time, come to be seen as a manifesto. Therefore, its date has become important. Some date it as early as 1916 or 1917[19]—earlier than any of Rietveld's other autonomous furniture designs. But it is more likely to have been created in mid 1918, after the baby chair. Gerard van de Groenekan remembers that he was already working for Rietveld when the first of the armchairs was made.[20] As was mentioned above, the first publication about the chair appeared in *De stijl* of September 1919; however, no date was given. Subsequent publications (in 1921 and 1929) gave 1918 as the date of origin, and Rietveld never corrected this. In any case, the chair was designed a good while before Rietveld's first direct contact with De Stijl.

Rietveld's armchair appears to have had its first public showing at the "tentoonstelling van aesthetisch uitgevoerde gebruiksvoorwerpen" [exhibition of aesthetically executed useful objects], held in the Museum voor Kunstnijverheid in Haarlem from September 22 to October 22, 1919. Rietveld is not listed in the catalog, but a review of the exhibition in the 1920 *Nederlandsch ambachts- en nijverheidskunst jaarboek* mentions him, along with Theo van Doesburg and Jan Wils, as an exhibitor. That yearbook also mentions that some of Rietveld's works were sold, and that he received repeat orders.[21] Thus, there were a few people who appreciated this new style of furniture, although in the beginning most of them were Rietveld's personal friends.

There were some variations among the various examples of the Rietveld armchair. For example, the chair on the left in figure 252 has a shorter backrest, and the one on the right has side panels. The version pictured in *De stijl* had trapezoidal side panels. Other variants differed in form, color, kind of wood, and dimensions.

The two chairs shown in figure 252 were bought, along with a buffet, by Piet Elling, a beginning architect whom Rietveld had met in 1919.[22] These chairs were delivered with the wood stained. The buffet was constructed like a traditional sideboard, with two cabinets in the middle, two drawers at each end, and a shelf above the top surface. The openness of the construction, however, was not at all traditional. The different parts of the buffet were separated by fillets and by open space. Rietveld emphasized the spatiality and the looseness of the entity by painting the doorknobs and the endgrains of the fillets white, so that they contrasted sharply against the dark-stained surfaces.[23] Notwithstanding the functional differences between a chair and a buffet, Rietveld tried to achieve a similar visual effect in both cases. His aim was to create pieces of furniture that, rather than stand in space as obstacles, would be transparent and would let the space continue. Rietveld expressed this aim in a letter to van Doesburg, dated February 28, 1920, in which he talked about his recent visit to the home of Bart de Ligt in Katwijk. (Van Doesburg had painted a room in this house, and this room was to be furnished by Rietveld.) Rietveld wrote: "Mrs. de L. has shown the room to me and my wife—Actually I found it a miserable hole, and the doors in particular are bad. The size I liked, and you completely succeeded in showing [the space] at once (by means of color). This is very important to me, more than all other achievements, and although I cannot imagine everything in detail—this instantaneous perception of space has stayed clearly in my mind and strikes me as pleasant. Actually we have never achieved this quite so deliberately. I would have liked to see whether my furniture—in which I always try not to enclose space—really would let the space here continue. . . ."

The furniture Rietveld created for de Ligt—an armchair with rectangular side panels and an ordinary chair and table—was as open in construction as the chair and the buffet for Elling. In the photo of the de Ligt interior that appeared in the November 1920 issue of *De stijl* (figure 30 in the present volume), the furniture is white with dark endgrains; the small dark planes harmonize well with the large color planes that van Doesburg painted on the walls and the ceiling.

Around June of 1920, some furniture by Rietveld was exhibited in an interior (designed by van Doesburg) of a model unit in a housing block (built by Oud) in the Spangen quarter of Rotterdam. The furniture in the model unit consisted of two straight-back chairs (one with arms), a table, a buffet, an armchair, and a mirror (figure 254).[24] This seems to have been the most extensive presentation of Rietveld's early De Stijl work.

On May 4, 1920, Rietveld wrote a letter to Oud about the Spangen furniture. "This morning," he said, "I dispatched [the] buffet and a chair in advance; I do have the feeling, though, that they are not a boon to humanity—Look closely at them and tell me your impression. . . . And then please answer me very soon whether it would not be better to consider such things as studies, which at most could influence one's regular work a little. I actually see it that way. Anyway, have a good look for yourself. Above all, do not let it be forced on anyone." These and other statements support the conclusion that Rietveld saw his furniture pieces

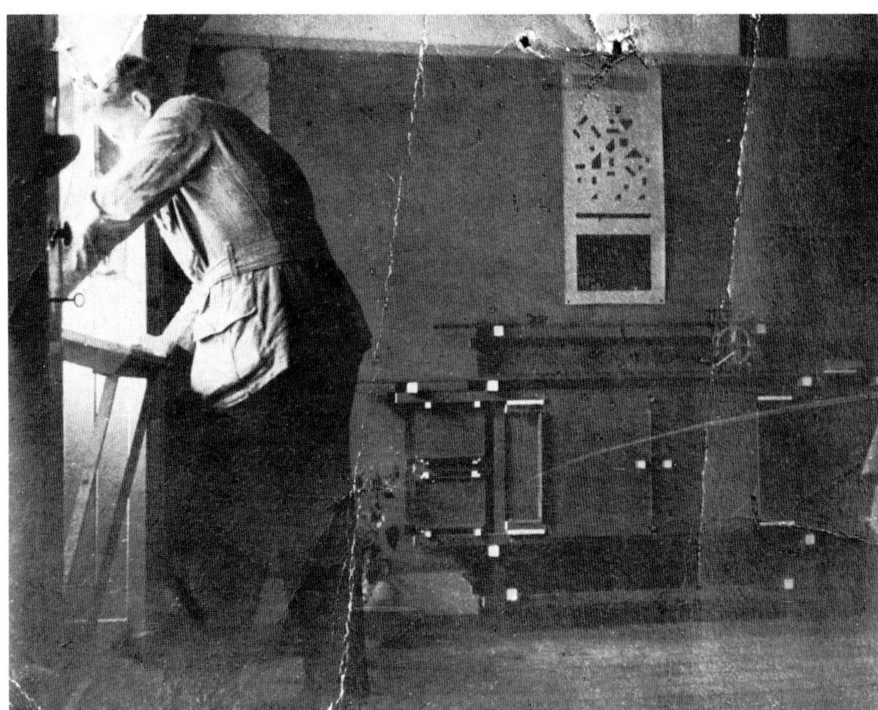

253

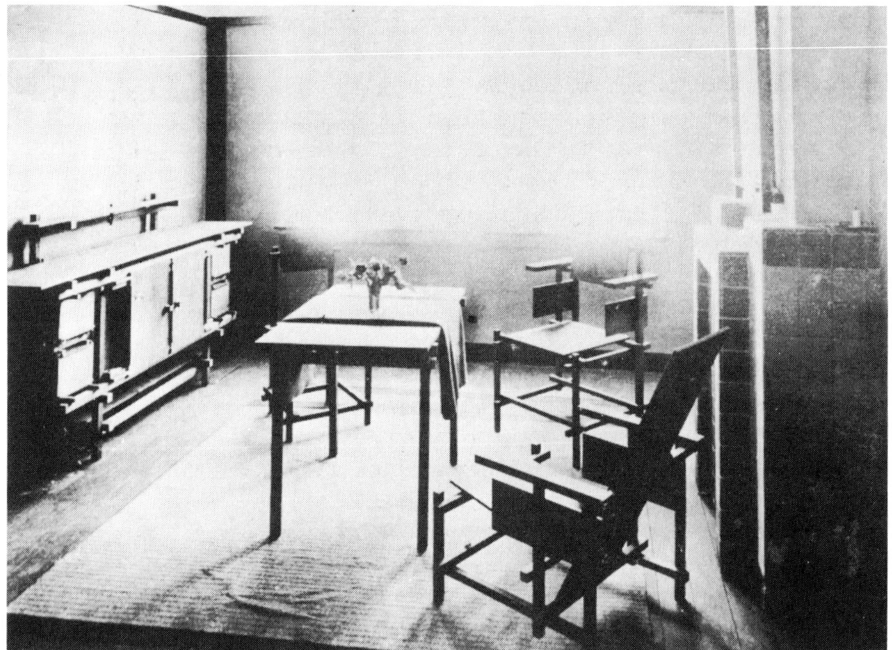

254

253 Photograph of room in home of Piet Elling, early 1920s. Photo in collection of Paul Smit, Utrecht.

254 Rietveld, set of furniture for model apartment, Spangen, Rotterdam, 1920.

255 Rietveld, facade of store of Goud- en Zilversmidscompagnie, Amsterdam, 1921. As illustrated in *De stijl* 5, no. 2 (1922), next to p. 24.

primarily as trial models which he absolutely did not want to have held up as paragons of good and modern taste. As was mentioned above, he made them mainly for himself and for a few people in his immediate circle.

Renovations of interiors and facades, 1921–22

Rietveld continued to design furniture, but from 1921 on he received commissions in the field of architecture as well. He had been interested in architecture for years. The earliest commissions were only for minor renovations. For example, he was asked in 1921 to do over a study in the Schröder residence at 135 Biltstraat in Utrecht. Rietveld had known Mr. and Mrs. Schröder for some years, and he had visited their home a few times to do some work in his capacity as a furnituremaker. He probably knew them socially through the art associations Kunstliefde and Voor de Kunst.[25]

When Mrs. Schröder wanted her study renovated, she asked Rietveld for a design, which was executed after some changes. This interior was not preserved, the literature does not convey Rietveld's interventions clearly,[26] and the photographs of the interior do not reveal much; however, it is known that Rietveld, according to Mrs. Schröder's wish, visually lowered the space by covering the upper part of the tall windows and by adding horizontal accents to the walls. The photographs do not show any furniture of the kind that Rietveld had created for Bart de Ligt and for the Spangen apartment; he probably had to make do with the furniture Mrs. Schröder already possessed. In any case, the client was very satisfied with the result.

The year 1921 also saw the execution of Rietveld's first exterior design[27]: the renovation of the store of the Goud- en Zilversmidscompagnie [Gold- and Silversmiths' Company] on Kalverstraat in Amsterdam.[28] Rietveld made drastic changes in both the exterior and the interior, but apparently the results did not quite satisfy him. After the renovation was completed he sent photographs to van Doesburg with a laconic commentary: "Here are a few pictures of the jewelry store on Kalverstraat in Amsterdam. A commission with contradictions. One has to do something."[29] In another letter to van Doesburg (dated March 28, 1922) he wrote: "The design for the jewelry store is completely mine (this in answer to your question), in the interior as well as on the exterior. The colors are: black, white;—rugs purple. It should really only be a large etui, or rather a showcase with etuis." Rietveld also sent photographs of the renovated store to Oud. He wrote in the accompanying letter: "I enclose some pictures of the jewelry store in Amsterdam which I fitted up—a somewhat inconsistent commis-

255

256

256 Rietveld, interior of store of Goud- en Zilversmidscompagnie, Amsterdam, 1921. As illustrated in *De stijl* 5, no. 2 (1922), next to p. 25.

257 Rietveld, consulting room of Dr. A. M. Hartog, Maarssen, 1922. As illustrated in *De stijl* 6, no. 3–4 (1923), appendix.

sion in our view. Here I have not worked on details, I have only demonstrated that it is possible to transform a long, narrow room into a quiet interior by arranging things."[30] The "inconsistency" Rietveld spoke of was probably the need to take the existing architecture into account. In the interior, particularly, the unfavorable architectural forms could only be disguised by means of color and furnishings.

Rietveld divided the walls of the long, narrow shop into color planes in such a way that their length was broken up. He did this very precisely, without making planes overlap or continue across corners or over the borders of the ceiling. The incoming daylight was rather scant, because the display window was screened off from the shop by a backdrop. Clusters of unshaded light bulbs hung, at different levels, from square plates. Rietveld made the shop front into a handsome asymmetrical stack of rectangular glass volumes.

After the renovations of Mrs. Schröder's study and the jewelry store, Rietveld got more commissions of this kind. Unfortunately, not one of his early interiors has been preserved; photographs are the only visual evidence of how they looked.

One important interior-design commission was the refurbishing of a physician's consulting room, executed in 1922.[31] The client, Dr. A. M. Hartog, of Maarssen, was, like Rietveld, a member of Voor de Kunst; they may have met through that association. It is also possible that they knew each other through the painter Willem van Leusden, whom Rietveld had known for some years and who lived in Maarssen.

Rietveld divided the walls and the ceiling of Hartog's consulting room into planes, much as in the shop interior described above. Again, the planes respected the architectural boundaries. Whereas the painters Theo van Doesburg and Vilmos Huszár used color and applied separate planes against a white or colored ground, Rietveld—with the exception of the large red circle on one of the walls of the consulting room—used only black, white, and shades of gray, and he kept the planes of the walls as intact as possible.

As figures 257 show, the ceiling of Dr. Hartog's office was divided into two interlocking L-shaped planes, one dark (probably black) and the other white. From a square black plate fixed to the white plane there hung a remarkable light fixture that held four tubular incandescent lamps—two horizontally and two vertically—in a cubelike configuration.[32]

All the furniture in Dr. Hartog's consulting room was either designed or adapted by Rietveld, with the exception of the instrument chest that stood by the door. The desk[33] in the middle of the room is an exception to Rietveld's other known work. The thick

257

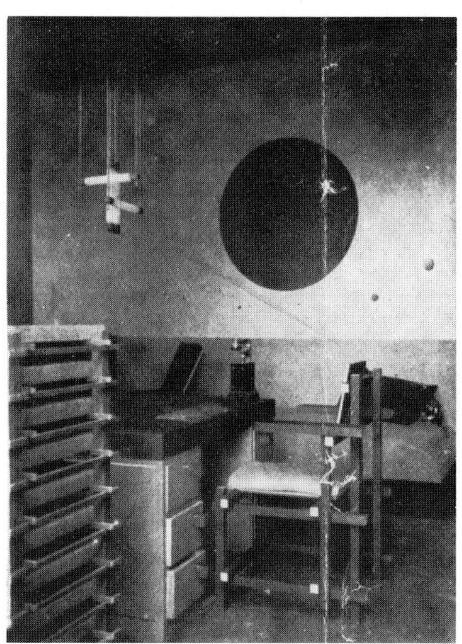

table top, its massiveness emphasized by its darkness, sits right on top of two yellow blocks of drawers. This desk shows none of the transparency that characterizes Rietveld's other furniture. However, that characteristic is evident in the chest of drawers that stands next to it; the long drawer handles running between connecting horizontal and vertical slats show Rietveld's usual method of construction. The photos suggest that the chest was painted in contrasting colors. The two high-back chairs are later versions of the chairs Rietveld had made for Bart de Ligt (figure 30) and for the model apartment at Spangen (figure 254), with the side panels omitted. The frame of the doctor's chair is dark with white endgrains; the frame of the other chair is white with dark endgrains.

Rietveld must have been pleased with this interior. Under fairly favorable conditions, he had brought about a good coalescence of architecture and furniture. Except for the desk, the furniture seems to have fulfilled his ideal of open structure and unimpaired space. Rietveld was probably referring to this interior when he wrote to Oud on November 10, 1922: "One of these days I will send you a photograph . . . of a renovated room from which I have learned a lot."

Use of color

During the first decades of this century, painted furniture was not common in the Netherlands. Chairs, tables, and cabinets were usually left in wood tones; shades and contrasts were obtained through the use of different kinds of wood and through staining. Rietveld's painted furniture must have been quite a sensation in Dutch arts and crafts circles.

Preserved pieces and photos reproduced in publications suggest that until about 1922 all Rietveld's furniture was probably either stained brown or black or painted white. In any case, it can be gathered from the available sources that the furniture was not painted in primary colors. Sometimes, as mentioned above, the endgrains of posts and slats were given colors that contrasted with the other surfaces.

Rietveld did apply bright colors to children's furniture and toys, however. The baby chair of 1918 (figure 247), with its red leather straps connected to a green frame by light green pins, is the earliest known example. In 1919, Rietveld made a red, yellow, and blue cradle for his son Jan. He wrote the following to Oud on August 19: "We got another little one . . . recently, so while working on your child's bed we felt a need for a small, light cradle that we would be able to take with us everywhere. I had the boy plane some slats, and I finished the whole thing in one evening, so that my wife found it the next morning. It is colored in red and yellow, and lined with a blue piece of fabric. It looks festive." (We may conclude that Rietveld's use of primary colors was not based on the same metaphysical principles as Mondrian's.) In 1921 Rietveld exhibited a sled at the Tentoonstelling van Kunstnijverheid [Exhibition of Arts and Crafts] in the Buitensociëteit [Community Center] in Zwolle. According to a review, this sled consisted of "rectangular and square planes in red, blue, or black," and "where the wooden spindles [had] been cut, the cut surfaces [had] been painted white."[34] Except for these children's items, Rietveld was quite restrained in his use of colors.

In 1922, with the refurbishing of Dr. Hartog's consultation room, Rietveld began to use colors in combination with white, black, and gray. From that time on, his use of primary colors in combination with the noncolors increased, and it was no longer limited to children's furniture and toys. Perhaps his contacts with van Doesburg and Huszár figured in this development; they, too, were using the primary colors more consistently (particularly in their architecture) around 1923.

The changes Rietveld made in the facade of the shop of the Goud- en Zilversmidscompagnie in 1923 evidenced his increasing use of the primary colors. The rabbets of one display case now became red, and those of another case blue; the rabbets of the window behind these cases, which had been black and white, were repainted in yellow. The plastered walls and the other woodwork were painted white and gray.

Rietveld also made some toys in 1923, including the wheelbarrow shown in figure 258. Brown dates this 1920, but it was first mentioned in a letter dated October 5, 1923, in which Rietveld told J. J. P. Oud that he was sending him the toy for his son Hans's fourth birthday.[35] (In this letter Rietveld did not use the word for "wheelbarrow"; instead, he sketched it.) The wheelbarrow was painted in red, yellow, blue, black, and white. The red wheel recalls the circle in Dr. Hartog's office. Around the same time, Rietveld made (possibly for his own children) a baby buggy.[36] This is usually dated 1918; however, the use of colors suggests 1923 as the actual date. Like the wheelbarrow, the baby buggy was painted red, yellow, blue, black, and white, and again red was used for circular forms (the large rear wheels).

Rietveld used the same colors in the furniture he created in 1923, including the small end table shown in figure 259. The circular base of this table was red, the two interlocked vertical boards were black and white, and the top (a square in which the base could just have been inscribed) was gray. A yellow slat on the

258

259

258 **Rietveld, toy wheelbarrow, 1923. As illustrated in *Mondrian und De Stijl* (exhibition catalog, Gallery Gmurzynska, Cologne, 1979), p. 199.**

259 **Rietveld, end table, 1923. Examples in several collections.**

underside of the top strengthened the construction. The line where the white board was notched into the top was delineated on the top in blue, in accordance with Rietveld's principle of accentuating the independence of the different parts of a piece of furniture. This independence—already defined in the construction of the table, and emphasized by the colors—was always the basis of Rietveld's color applications.

The Red-Blue Chair—the colored version of the chair discussed above—also fits into this line of the development of Rietveld's use of color, and thus it should be dated later than it has been. In the literature, the Red-Blue Chair is invariably presented as the first of Rietveld's works to be painted in primary colors; it is said that the chair was painted in red, blue, yellow, and black[37] soon after its creation. It is much more likely, however, that the colors were not applied until a few years later. The first published photo of the (as yet uncolored) chair appeared in *De stijl* of September 1919. When the chair was depicted in the 1921 yearbook of the VANK,[38] the accompanying text read: "Armchair of light beechwood, designed and executed by G. Rietveld, 93 Adriaan van Ostadelaan, Utrecht, 1918." The photograph was the same one that had appeared in *De stijl;* in 1923 it appeared again in the periodical *Merz.*[39] None of these publications mentioned vivid colors, which at that time would certainly have been worth mentioning.

Furthermore, if there had been Red-Blue Chairs in 1920, they would certainly have been shown in the model unit at Spangen; yet there is no evidence of such a chair in any photograph, letter, or description pertaining to that display. And such a chair would have gone well in Piet Elling's home (see figure 253), yet it has been ascertained that Elling's chairs, like his buffet, were stained in dark colors. All this argues in favor of a later date for the red-and-blue version of the chair.

The effect of color on the chair was remarkable. First, it gave a much more "modern" impression. The stained version of the chair still evoked some associations with traditional furniture, but not so the painted version. Second, and much more important, the color had a pronounced destructurizing effect. It accentuated the independence of the backrest and the seat, and it made the yellow endgrains seem to disconnect themselves from the black fillets. The chair appeared to be devoid of all solidity; it had become an abstract spatial color composition.

Forms

At the same time that Rietveld was occupying himself with colors, he was also achieving interesting results through the use of forms. Particularly interesting are his applications of asymmetry. All the architects involved in De Stijl took a more or less explicit stand with respect to symmetry and asymmetry in architecture. In a 1918 article on this subject in *De stijl,* Jan Wils called asymmetry preeminently modern, in contrast with the symmetric monumentality that was predominant in traditional architecture.[40] J. J. P. Oud agreed in principle. However, most of the buildings designed by the De Stijl architects were predominantly symmetrical in design.

Rietveld immediately distinguished himself from the others with one of his earliest architectural designs: the renovation of the facade of the store of the Goud- en Zilversmidscompagnie (1921). Whether Rietveld was free to determine the form of this facade, or whether he was restricted by constructional and practical requirements (such as the fixed position of the door) or had to take his client's wishes into account, is uncertain; thus, it cannot be ascertained whether the asymmetric composition of the facade reflects Rietveld's conscious choice. Nonetheless, as can be seen in figure 255, Rietveld treated the facade in such a way that it was no longer a flat plane; now it was a spatial stacking of rectangular glass volumes of different dimensions, with a fluid transition from the exterior to the interior. Immediately on the street, and receding somewhat in relation to the wall plane of the second floor, was a large box-shaped glass case in which the jewelry was displayed. In back of it, at the left in the photograph, stood a vertical glass construction bearing the logo of the company. Perpendicular to that box was an oblong window with the name of the company in letters designed by Rietveld; beneath this window was the entrance.

In its openness and its clear structure, this storefront was Rietveld's alone, although its plastic, blocklike composition recalls Vantongerloo's sculptures and Oud's design for a factory in Purmerend.[41] Even the materials contributed to the unrestricted spatial effect. The ample glass allowed light to penetrate the showcases from different angles; the only substantial element was the narrow framework of the display windows.

The facade of the Goud- en Zilversmidscompagnie was very unusual for its time, but it was highly appreciated. It was praised in the *Bouwkundig weekblad,*[42] and, when a model was exhibited at the De Stijl exhibition at the Galerie de l'Effort Moderne in 1923, van Doesburg referred to it in a letter to Antony Kok as "excellent."[43]

Asymmetry is quite the exception in furniture. Much more so than in architecture, the symmetry of a chair (for example) is due to a certain logic. In 1923, Rietveld created his first asymmetrical chair, usually referred to as the Berlin Chair. This chair, shown in

260

261

figure 260, was designed for an interior that is said to have been a collaboration between Rietveld and Vilmos Huszár (figure 261). On November 24, 1923, Huszár sent Oud a postcard (figure 100 above) on which two photographs of the maquette for this interior were reproduced. The text that is visible in the upper photo reads "spatial color composition for an exhibition executed in Berlin, Oct. 1923 color by V. Huszár form by G. Rietveld." The exhibition referred to was probably the Juryfreie Kunstschau [Nonjuried Art Exhibition] held in Berlin in the autumn of 1923.[44] It is not clear how the word *executed* is to be interpreted. The most obvious way would be to assume that the interior was realized in full scale; however, no exhibition catalog, no reviews, and no letters or other documents are available to support that interpretation, and the fact that all existing pictures represent the maquette suggests that the exhibit consisted only of it and some miniature furniture. It is not even certain exactly what each of the two men contributed to the design. According to the inscription on the maquette, the "form" was due to Rietveld; however, it is not clear whether his contribution was limited to the design of the furniture or whether it extended to the spatial design of the maquette. If the maquette was constructed in Berlin in October 1923, it must have been done by Huszár; he was there at the time and Rietveld was not. However, it is possible that Huszár made the maquette after a design by Rietveld. The chair and the table[45] were definitely Rietveld's designs.

Some specimens of the Berlin Chair were made. Besides the one shown in figure 260, a mirror-image version was made, so that the two chairs together would form a symmetrical composition. One of the armrests of the Berlin Chair was so wide that it formed a kind of table top; the other one was so high and narrow that a person sitting on the seat could hardly lean on it. The different parts were painted black and various shades of gray.

Aside from its asymmetry, which made it unique among Rietveld's chair designs, the Berlin Chair had some other aspects that were new within Rietveld's stylistic development. As in the table shown in figure 259 (which dates from the same year), the structural emphasis did not fall on linear elements, as it had in his earlier furniture; rather, the chair was constructed almost entirely of planes. It looks more like an open sculpture on which one might chance to sit than a chair.

Figure 262 shows an asymmetrical cabinet that Rietveld made for his own use, probably also in 1923. It is closely related to the furniture in the Berlin maquette. The storage part hangs, as it were, between two boards and a thin leg, just as the seat of the Berlin Chair is suspended from three points. The thin leg is the

262

260 Rietveld, Berlin Chair, 1923. Examples in several collections.

261 G. Rietveld and V. Huszár, maquette of interior, 1923. Photograph in private collection. (Color plate on page xvii.)

262 Rietveld, cabinet, ca. 1923. Collection of Bertus Mulder, Utrecht.

only linear element. The sides, the front, and the back, which consist of planes slid over and alongside one another, are painted in white, black, and grayish tones.

The various asymmetrical pieces of furniture discussed above were all designed within a period of about two years. After 1924, Rietveld laid these experiments to rest.

As Rietveld developed from a furnituremaker into an architect (a development that can be traced reasonably well in the pages of *De stijl*), he maintained a certain distance from the other contributors to the journal. While Oud, Wils, and van 't Hoff repeatedly collaborated with the De Stijl painters, Rietveld kept aloof, except in the case of the Berlin maquette. Sometimes he touched on the subject in letters to van Doesburg. In 1920 he wrote that he was looking forward to "a sizable work in good collaboration."[46] In 1922 he wrote to van Doesburg (on the occasion of a commission): "I would have loved to collaborate with a painter—you can't get people to do so." But in practice he nearly always did everything himself, even on projects well suited to collaboration. Except in his capacity as a furnituremaker, virtually his only involvement in the work of the other contributors to *De stijl* was as a modelmaker.[47]

During the years 1919–1923, Rietveld had less contact with the De Stijl artists than with artists from Utrecht and the surrounding area, such as the architect Piet Elling, the sculptor Johan Uiterwaal, and (in particular) the painter Willem van Leusden.[48] Van Leusden was never officially declared a contributor to *De stijl;* however, he was involved with it for some time, and some of his works were reproduced in it. This contact was brought about by Rietveld and was mostly maintained through him.

Willem van Leusden was born in Utrecht two years before Rietveld. From 1911 on, both he and Rietveld were members of Kunstliefde. They had probably met through that association, but from about 1920 on they saw each other more regularly, and they began to collaborate. A letter from Rietveld to Oud dated November 10, 1922, cites an example of this collaboration: "a cabinet created by me and painted by van Leusden—a painter in Maarssen."

Van Leusden's earliest paintings were impressionistic, but around 1915 his style changed to a moderate cubism. By 1920 he had begun to make compositions with flat geometric forms; these show the influence of van der Leck and van Doesburg. Probably because of Rietveld, he became interested in architecture and began to produce architectural models. None of his designs were realized, but his maquettes were displayed in exhibitions and illustrated in periodicals in the 1920s. (Van Leusden later claimed that he had not actually intended to have his designs realized: ". . . their practical execution was too much of a problem for me. It was only the spatiality that fascinated me.")

At the above-mentioned De Stijl exhibition in Paris in 1923, Rietveld was represented by only one design but van Leusden showed three: a tramway shelter (1922), a garage with a store (1922?), and a public urinal (1922).[49] These designs are very interesting in relation to Rietveld's first steps in the field of architecture. The tramway shelter (figure 263)—a stack of glass volumes of unequal size and height—shows the influence of Rietveld's 1921 shop facade. The colored photos of this maquette reproduced in *l'Architecture vivante* in 1925 show the rabbets and some of the planes painted in primary colors and in white, gray, and black.[50] Whether the 1922 version was painted in the same manner is not certain, because other illustrations in the same issue of *l'Architecture vivante* differed from their original versions.[51] But if van Leusden's maquette was indeed painted in primary colors, it may have influenced Rietveld's decision to apply those colors to his shop facade in 1923.

Van Leusden's most extraordinary design is the one for the public urinal (figure 264), also dated 1922. It has an open character; the volumes are reduced to horizontal and vertical planes, which seem to lean on one another. The only solid part is a vertical oblong block. This design can be seen as a precursor of Rietveld's Schröder house.

Van Leusden's activities as an amateur architect at the periphery of De Stijl remain something of a puzzle. Because the dates of his works are not known with certainty, it is difficult to tell who influenced whom. Perhaps it is better to speak of interaction than of influence here. This interaction continued until 1925; for instance, there are striking similarities between Rietveld's Schröder house and van Leusden's design for a teahouse.[52]

Conclusion

Gerrit Rietveld gradually became more prominent in De Stijl circles, despite the consternation aroused in Theo van Doesburg by the fact that, in the summer of 1923, he was invited to take part in a Bauhaus exhibition. On August 10, van Doesburg wrote to Rietveld that he had spotted Rietveld's name in the program of the Bauhauswoche [Bauhaus Week]. "One of these days," he wrote, "there will appear a double issue of *De stijl* with reproductions of your work in it! At the same time you exhibit with the opposition. . . . I am very sad because of this kick from you, from whom I least expected it."[53] Contrary to what is usually said in the litera-

263

263 W. van Leusden, tramway shelter, 1922. As illustrated in *l'Architecture vivante* 5 (autumn 1925), p. 19.

264 W. van Leusden, maquette of public urinal, 1922. Collection d'Art, Amsterdam.

264

ture, Rietveld probably did not actually participate in the exhibition, which was held in Weimar from August 15 through August 19. Walter Gropius, in response to J. J. P. Oud's proposal that he exhibit works by Rietveld (along with van Anrooy, van Loghem, and van 't Hoff), had written: "The toy by Rietveld interests me very much; [it] does not come into consideration for the exhibition because from nonmembers of the Bauhaus we exhibit only architecture."[54] At the time, the only accomplishment of Rietveld's that might have fulfilled Gropius's condition was the renovation in Amsterdam. Oud wrote to Rietveld on June 12 asking him, on the behalf of Gropius, to submit "some work (photographs, drawings, maquettes) for the Bauhaus exhibition," but apparently Rietveld did not follow this up. On September 5, after the Bauhaus exhibition had closed, Rietveld wrote to Oud: "I could not possibly send any work to Weimar—I have quite a job to get a lot of things done, so that I can submit a sizable bill for a change; at the moment things are not easy. I must give the impression of being terribly lax." Thus, van Doesburg's disenchanted reaction was based on a misunderstanding.

In the ensuing years, Rietveld's contacts with van Doesburg were invariably friendly. *De stijl* published new works by Rietveld quite regularly, and in those works the accent came to fall on architecture. After his fascinating experiments with asymmetrical compositions, open structures, and primary colors, he achieved in 1924 a synthesis of his artistic views and his abilities in the dwelling which he designed for (and in close collaboration with) Mrs. Schröder. Over the course of time, the Schröder house came to be seen as the paragon of De Stijl architecture.

In Rietveld's work it was, in a certain sense, a terminal point. In the following years, Rietveld tended toward international functionalism. He did not renounce his De Stijl past, but did adopt a critical attitude with respect to superficial imitations of De Stijl architecture. In a letter to the critic A. M. Hammacher, dated June 15, 1925, he wrote: "I . . . find it more difficult now that people are beginning to ask for work in our school of thought than when it was generally resisted and made impossible. Toil also has its merits. Now they are flinging color planes and cubes about too rashly for my taste."[55]

1
G. Rietveld, "Aantekening bij kinderstoel (bijlage no. XVIII)," *De stijl* 2, no. 9 (1919), p. 102, and some lines quoted in T. van Doesburg's "Aantekening bij een leunstoel van Rietveld" (*De stijl* 2, no. 11, 1919, n.p.).

2
The most important literature on Rietveld consists of the following: T. M. Brown, *The work of G. Rietveld architect* (Utrecht, 1958); *G. Rietveld architect* (exhibition catalog, Stedelijk Museum, Amsterdam, 1971–72); D. Baroni, *I mobili di Gerrit Thomas Rietveld* (Milan, 1977): *Uit de verzameling van het Stedelijk, G. Rietveld 1888–1964 Meubels* (catalog, Amsterdam, 1981); F. Bless, *Rietveld 1888–1964* (Amsterdam, 1982); M. Küper, *Rietveld als meubelmaker, wonen met experimenten 1900–1924* (exhibition catalog, Centraal Museum, Utrecht, 1983).

3
Brown, *The work of G. Rietveld architect* (note 2 above), p. 15.

4
These address books are in the municipal archives of Utrecht.

5
The as yet uncataloged archive of this institute is in the Centraal Museum, in Utrecht.

6
It is mentioned in the reports that Rietveld worked for "Balfoort, Begeer." A Mr. Balfoort was the manager of the manufacturing division of the Begeer firm.

7
This tombstone was pointed out to me by the late Mrs. B. H. Nijland, daughter of E. Nijland.

8
In 1911, Rietveld married Vrouwgien Hadders.

9
The archive of Kunstliefde is in the municipal archives of Utrecht.

10
The portraits, probably painted on commission, were not for sale; *O haupt voll blut und wunden* was priced at 40 guilders. The whereabouts of these works today are not known.

11
Gerard van de Groenekan became Rietveld's apprentice in 1918; he later worked on the furniture that made Rietveld famous.

12
The earliest extant letter from Rietveld to Oud is dated August 13, 1919. He must have had correspondence with both van Doesburg and Oud before the two letters mentioned.

13
In 1905, van der Leck was sharing a studio (at 19 Heerenstraat, Utrecht) with Klaarhamer; it was there that Rietveld was taking lessons at the time.

14
Rietveld, "Aantekening bij kinderstoel" (note 1 above), illustration beside text on page 102.

15
Van Doesburg, "Aantekening bij een leunstoel van Rietveld" (note 1 above), illustration after text on page 132. Originally, the chair was executed in beechwood. From 1927 on, the boards of the back and the seat were made of plywood in order to prevent cracking.

16
Deutsche kunst und dekoration 6 (1905), pp. 348–349. The chair is also illustrated on page 56 of F. Alison's *Charles Rennie Mackintosh as a designer of chairs* (London, 1974).

17
Neither of these chairs had an upholstered backrest. Wright later added upholstery to the seat of his chair.

18
We still know little about this architect from Utrecht. There is hardly any literature on his work or his relations with Rietveld and other De Stijl artists (van der Leck, Huszár, van 't Hoff). His furniture, and the designs preserved in the Nederlands Documentatiecentrum voor de Bouwkunst (in Amsterdam), suggest that he was influenced around the turn of the century by Art Nouveau, or at least by its sober Berlage variant. His furniture from around that time is ornamented with stylized nature motifs. Later these motifs were omitted, and his designs became gradually simpler.

Following Berlage's example, Klaarhamer tried to avoid the imitation of historic styles, which was then being practiced widely in the Netherlands, by creating a new style in the field of arts and crafts as well as in architecture. Both he and Berlage favored logical, visible construction, "honesty" in the use of materials, and sparse decoration. Features that are now sometimes called typical of Rietveld appear in Berlage's and Klaarhamer's furniture as well; an example is the extension of horizontal and vertical components beyond what is necessary for the construction.

Information on the relations between Klaarhamer and the contributors to *De stijl* can be found in the following sources: P. Luykx, *Utopia* 1, no. 3, p. 3; A. van der Woud, "Variaties op een thema," in *Americana* (exhibition catalog, Rijksmuseum Kröller-Müller, Otterlo, 1975), pp. 33–34; R. W. D. Oxenaar, *Bart van der Leck tot 1920, een primitief van de nieuwe tijd* (The Hague, 1976), passim. On Klaarhamer's furniture, see B. van der Leck, "Klaarhamers meubelen," *Onze kunst* 3, part 2 (1904), pp. 73–78.

19
Bless, *Rietveld 1888–1964* (note 2 above), pp. 25–26.

20
This was evident from a conversation with van de Groenekan. He said that he had gone to work for Rietveld in the winter of 1917–18, and that the first specimen of the chair was made a few months later, in the summer of 1918.

21
Nederlandsche ambachts- en nijverheidskunst, jaarboek (Rotterdam, 1920), pp. 72, 74.

22
I was told about the contact between Rietveld and Elling by the late Mrs. B. H. Nijland.

23
As can be seen in figure 253, the buffet harmonized well with the poster featuring Bart van der Leck's lithograph (after his painting *De ruiter*) that was hung on the wall above it.

24
In a letter to Oud dated February 26, 1920, Rietveld talked about "perhaps a baby chair and a crib . . . a few beds and a linen cabinet." "Perhaps," he continued, "drawings could supplement the pieces still lacking." The mirror mentioned in the text, which is visible in figure 254, is not mentioned in the correspondence but could well have been designed by Rietveld.

25
Mr. F. A. C. Schröder (a lawyer) was registered as a member of Kunstliefde from 1913 until 1916, and both he and his wife appear on the annual membership lists of Voor de Kunst for 1918 and subsequent years. (The archive of Voor de Kunst is housed in the municipal archives of Utrecht.)

26
The most informative description of the interior is that on page 22 of Bertus Mulder's article in *Rietveld Schröder huis 1925–1975* (Utrecht, 1975).

27
On pages 24 and 25 of *The work of G. Rietveld* (note 2 above), Brown mentions the 1919 renovation of the facade of the Begeer jewelry store. However, it is not

very clear what Rietveld contributed to that project. (A report of the Utrecht Building Commission mentions that in 1921 the Utrecht chapter of the Association Architectura et Amicitia awarded a bronze medal to "the designer of the shop premises of Mr. Cornelis Begeer, 27 Ouderkhof," but the name of the designer is not given.) It is possible that Rietveld designed the mural figures and the lettering on the facade, but in terms of style these do not fit in very well with his known work from that time. Rietveld's name does not appear on the application for the building permit, which Begeer filed in 1919; however, it does appear on the application filed for an extension of the same premises in 1936 (municipal archives, Utrecht), and that may be why his name was associated with the 1919 renovation.

28
This commission was arranged by Cornelis Begeer. See page 21 of *Rietveld Schröder huis* (note 26 above).

29
This is an undated letter. It was probably written in late 1921 or early 1922.

30
Undated; probably written in early 1922.

31
This interior has always been dated 1920. (See Brown, note 2 above, pp. 24–25; Baroni, note 2 above, p. 45.) However, a letter from Rietveld to Oud dated April 10, 1924, provides evidence that this interior was in fact renovated in 1922.

32
A later variant, made for the Schröder house, has only one vertical lamp; its expression of height, width, and depth is even purer.

33
This desk has been preserved and is now in the Gemeentemuseum in The Hague.

34
Elseviers geillustreerd maandschrift 31, 61, 5 (May 1921), p. 354.

35
The wheelbarrow Rietveld made for Hans Oud was probably the only one of its kind for some time. On May 5, 1925, Rietveld wrote to Oud: "Would you do me a favor and send me the measurements of the wheelbarrow, if possible with a small sketch. I would like to have a number of them made this season for the beach, but I am not sure about the measurements."

36
See page 51 of Baroni's *I mobili* (note 2 above) for an illustration of the baby buggy.

37
The fillets of the lower part of the chair were painted black, and their endgrains were painted yellow.

38
Nederlandsche ambachts- en nijverheidskunst, jaarboek (Rotterdam, 1921), pp. 12, 16.

39
Merz 4 (July 1923).

40
J. Wils, "Symmetrie en kultuur," *De stijl* 1, no. 12 (1918), pp. 137–140.

41
Oud's design (figure 127 of the present volume) was reproduced next to page 23 of *De stijl* 3, no. 2 (1919) and next to page 44 of *De stijl* 3, no. 5 (1920).

42
A. Boeken, "Eenige opmerkingen over de winkelverbouwing Kalverstraat 107 te Amsterdam," *Bouwkundig weekblad* 43, no. 49 (1922), pp. 476–478; A. Boeken, "De winkelpui Kalverstraat 107 te Amsterdam," ibid. 44, no. 45 (1923), p. 455.

43
Van Doesburg to Kok, October 18, 1923. This was the only work exhibited by Rietveld at the Paris show; but then, it was an architectural exhibition, and Rietveld had not yet done much in that field.

44
N. J. Troy, *The De Stijl environment* (Cambridge, Mass., 1983), p. 129.

45
It is uncertain whether this table was ever executed in full size.

46
This letter was not dated by Rietveld, but it was postmarked August 9, 1920.

47
On November 8, 1919, van Doesburg wrote to Oud: "On Wednesday Rietveld was here. He is waiting for the design drawings of the factory in order to carve the model in wood according to the most recently changed design." This must concern Oud's design for a factory in Purmerend, which appeared in *De stijl* of March 1920. (See note 41 above.) There are no indications that the model was ever built. However, in August 1923 Rietveld did build a maquette of the "Hotel Particulier," which Cornelis van Eesteren and Theo van Doesburg had designed for the De Stijl exhibition at the Galerie de l'Effort Moderne. Van Doesburg wrote in July 1923 to his friends Thijs and Evert Rinsema: ". . . Huszár and Rietveld are coming here to help me make the exhibition a success. We have to make large maquettes, because the French cannot make head or tail of architectural drawings." [This letter was published on page 180 of K. Schippers's *Holland Dada* (Amsterdam, 1974).] Apparently the idea was that Rietveld should go to Paris and build the maquettes there; however, van Doesburg sent him the drawings in August, and he probably built the maquettes in his workshop in Utrecht.

48
On van Leusden, see W. Enzinck, *Willem van Leusden* (Bussum, 1956); H. Redeker, *Willem van Leusden* (Utrecht, 1974); I. Spaander, "9 biografieën, Willem van Leusden," *Museumjournaal* 17, no. 6 (1972), pp. 289–290.

49
N. Troy, *De stijl's collaborative ideal: The colored abstract environment, 1916–1926* (dissertation, Yale University, 1979), p. 281.

50
l'Architecture vivante, autumn-winter 1925, p. 19.

51
For example, van Doesburg's interior design for the house of Bart de Ligt (figures 29 and 30 in the present volume).

52
For an illustration see C. Blotkamp, "Rietveld en De Stijl," in *Rietveld Schröder huis 1925–1975* (Utrecht, 1975), p. 15.

53
The whereabouts of this letter are not known. The text of the letter is given on page 154 of Brown's *Work of G. Rietveld* (note 2 above).

54
Gropius to Oud, May 31, 1923.

55
The letter is in the Rietveld archive of the Nederlands Documentatiecentrum voor de Bouwkunst, in Amsterdam.

Photographic credits

Centraal Museum, Utrecht: figure 208

Fondation Custodia, Paris: figures 31, 133

Gemeente-archief, The Hague: figure 43

Haags Gemeentemuseum, The Hague: figures 21, 25, 26, 41, 47, 52, 54, 74, 80, 82, 105, 107, 148

Kunsthistorisch Instituut, Utrecht: figures 111, 114, 123–125, 128 (G. T. Delemarre); figures 92, 252, 253, 262 (K. ter Wal)

Musée National d'Art Moderne, Centre Georges Pompidou, Paris: figure 229

Rijksbureau voor Kunsthistorische Documentatie, The Hague: figures 67, 68, 70, 149–151, 220, 223, 231

Rijksdienst Beeldende Kunst, The Hague: figures 2, 3, 5–8, 13, 14, 16, 17, 19, 26, 29, 58, 73, 78, 236, 237, 239

Rijksdienst voor de Monumentenzorg, Zeist: figures 188, 207

Rijksmuseum Kröller-Müller, Otterlo: figures 39, 40, 42, 45, 49, 60, 102, 143–147

Staatsgalerie, Stuttgart: figure 165

Stedelijk Museum, Amsterdam: figures 103, 170, 247, 255–257, 259, 260

Stedelijk Van Abbemuseum, Eindhoven: figures 5, 22–25, 166, 190, 191

Arthur Cohen, New York: figure 100

Editorial board of *Bouw:* figure 192

J. P. Smid, Gallery Monet, Amsterdam: figures 64, 65, 153, 157, 158, 160, 162, 163

Sjarel Ex, Amsterdam: figures 178, 179

Ko Karman, Amsterdam: figures 61, 79, 106

Alexander Moes, Amsterdam: figures 56, 57, 59, 62, 63, 66, 76, 77, 81, 84, 94–96, 108, 122, 130, 138, 139, 172, 174, 175, 177, 181–184, 186, 193, 194, 198–203, 205, 206, 208

E. van Ojen, The Hague: figure 161

Rob van der Staaij, Amsterdam: figures 211, 218

Arjan Steehouder, Amsterdam: figure 164

Page numbers in boldface indicate a monographic chapter on an artist. Numbers in italic generally indicate that the name occurs in a figure legend on that page; the name may also occur in the text.

The alphabetization of surnames with particles generally follows native practice; for example, Bart van der Leck is listed as Leck, B. van der.

Index